Selecting Employees Safely Under the Law

KENNETH J. McCULLOCH
Townley & Updike

Prentice-Hall, Inc., Englewood Cliffs, N.J. 07632

Library of Congress Cataloging in Publication Data

McCulloch, Kenneth J
   Selecting employees safely under the law.
   Bibliography: p.
   Includes index.
   1. Employee selection—Law and legislation—United States. I. Title.
KF3457.M3   344.73'01133   80-18242
ISBN 0-13-802959-8

Editorial/production supervision
   and interior design: Marian Hartstein
Cover design: RL Communications
Cover illustration: Justin Case
Manufacturing buyer: Gordon Osbourne

© 1981 by Prentice-Hall, Inc., Englewood Cliffs, N.J. 07632

All rights reserved. No part of this book
may be reproduced in any form or
by any means without permission in writing
from the publisher.

Printed in the United States of America

10 9 8 7 6 5 4 3 2 1

PRENTICE-HALL INTERNATIONAL, INC., *London*
PRENTICE-HALL OF AUSTRALIA PTY. LIMITED, *Sydney*
PRENTICE-HALL OF CANADA, LTD., *Toronto*
PRENTICE-HALL OF INDIA PRIVATE LIMITED, *New Delhi*
PRENTICE-HALL OF JAPAN, INC., *Tokyo*
PRENTICE-HALL OF SOUTHEAST ASIA PTE. LTD., *Singapore*
WHITEHALL BOOKS LIMITED, *Wellington, New Zealand*

Contents

PREFACE V

PART 1
OVERVIEW: THE RULES AND HOW THEY ARE INTERPRETED 1

INTRODUCTION 3

1 The Protected Groups and What Protects Them 7

2 The Uniform Guidelines 24

3 Techniques for Validation 33

PART 2
STANDARDS AND SYSTEMS FOR PREVENTING LIABILITY 43

4 Standards for Recruiting, Interviewing, and Hiring 45

5 Standards for Promotion, Transfer, and Assignment 99

6 Standards for Discipline, Discharge, and Reductions in Force 129

7 Standards for Terms and Conditions of Employment 151

PART 3
GUIDELINES FOR PROPERLY PREVENTING INDIVIDUAL CLAIMS AND DEFENDING AGAINST THEM 163

8 Individual Claims: Prevention and Defense 165

9 Handling the EEOC Charge and Investigation 176

10 The OFCCP Compliance Review or Complaint Investigation 243

PART 4
RECORDS THE EMPLOYER MUST KEEP 297

11 Documentation and Record-Keeping Systems 299

APPENDIX A
THE UNIFORM GUIDELINES ON EMPLOYEE SELECTION 315

APPENDIX B
SUMMARY OF TESTS, BY TEST NAME OR TREATMENT BY COURTS AND EEOC 353

INDEX 383

Preface

The personnel directors and labor counsels of American corporations are probably as hard-pressed today as any other corporate group, owing to equal employment opportunity issues. They are enormously sensitive to those issues, far more so than the government seems to believe. More change in the EEO area takes place through their actions than through those of all the government agencies combined.

This book is written for these corporate personnel directors and labor counsels. If it achieves its purpose, they will read it once cover to cover and thereafter use it as a reference source.

The book's format was selected to facilitate its purpose. The problems that arise at work are related to aspects of employment; thus, the information the personnel officer or labor counsel needs is, first, what the problem is, and second, the basis of the complaint. Here, this information is arranged in that order.

Chapter 4 deals with recruiting, interviewing, and hiring; Chapter 5, with promotion, transfer, and assignment; Chapter 6, with adverse action such as discipline, discharge, and reductions in force; and Chapter 7, with terms and conditions of employment. These four chapters together cover all subjects in the personnel function.

Additionally, within each chapter, the subjects are addressed on the basis of (1) age, (2) race and national origin, (3) sex, and (4) disabilities and handicaps. Thus, if the issue is whether an employer can establish a work rule prohibiting females from wearing slacks to work and can discharge them if they violate the rule, the relevant discussion would be in Chapter 6, "Standards for Discipline, Discharge, and Reductions in Forces" under the heading; "Sex Standards."

However, before this book is used as a reference volume, it should first be read in its entirety. This is because consideration of a particular issue may be aided by a relevant discussion of another subject. For instance, if the discussion in Chapter 6 on adverse action does not cover discharge of women for wearing slacks, it may be that Chapter 4, dealing with recruiting, interviewing, and hiring, will treat the matter under employer hiring standards.

Additionally, it may be that some standards are discussed on another basis. Thus, height and weight standards for employees may be at issue in the reader's particular case because of a claim raised by a female, but the law on such standards may have developed in cases where the issue was raised by Mexican-Americans, who are also adversely affected by the same standard.

To an extent, the need for the reader to be familiar with all the materials in the substantive chapters 4–7 may be reduced by use of the index. Every attempt was made to ensure that all subjects covered could easily be found by use of the comprehensive index. Thus, in using this book as a reference volume, the reader could look to the index, under "height standards" and find in the relevant discussion whether the issue had been raised by a female or a Mexican-American, and whether the subject had been raised in the context of hiring, promotion, discharge, or terms and conditions of employment.

As in any text that deals with a rapidly developing area of the law, there was concern that the material might become dated. This concern was alleviated by two other features of the book. First, there was no attempt to give all the cases on a subject, identifying those holding one way and those holding another. It was felt that such an approach would be confusing. Instead, when a statement is made that is supported by a case citation, the statement is a judgment of the author. It is his judgment that the law has been, or will become, firmly developed so that the principle stated is or will become firmly established. If, in addition to the case cited to support the proposition stated, there are other cases holding a contrary view and of considerable persuasiveness, then one of the cases holding the opposite view is cited.

A second technique for ensuring that the text does not become dated is the very manner in which statements are supported. Not only are there case citations in the text; there is an alphabetical index at the end of the text of all the cases cited, giving not only the official legal citation for those cases, but also the citations of those cases in the two main reporting services, published by the Bureau of National Affairs (FEP Cases) and Commerce Clearing House (EPD).

I have found that most employers subscribe to one or the other of these two publications, and that most people functioning in the EEO area know how to use these services. The reader who wants to assure himself that the proposition stated in the text is current and applicable to his jurisdiction can do so by using one of these services, especially the BNA. By finding the case noted in the text of this book in the BNA service, the reader will find "key numbers" in the case as reported there. Any case reported on the same subject will have the same key number. Consequently, by scanning the BNA reports that have been issued subsequent to the time the case was decided, the reader will be able to find any cases on the same subject that have been reported after the date of the case cited in this book.

Careful consideration was given to whether there should be any case citations at all, or, if there were, how extensive they should be. On the one hand, there is no doubt that case citations make the text less readable. On the other hand, I felt that the readers should know about the cases supporting a proposition so that they could have legal authority to rely on in putting forth positions to their fellow employees and to government investigators. A compromise was struck whereby just the case name is given in the text, with the appropriate citation in a footnote at the end of the chapter as well as in the Case Index.

The substantive areas, when necessary, are discussed in terms of the facts of a particular case. This was done only when it was felt that a statement of general principle might be misleading without some particular facts essential to the holding.

I have considered the fact that there are legal methods other than adverse-impact analysis that might be used to demonstrate discrimination. One of the most commonly utilized of these is disparate treatment. Thus, under the adverse-impact method, claimants attempt to prove that an apparently neutral selection device such as a high school diploma requirement is really a discriminating selection device because it is far more likely to screen out minorities than nonminorities. Under the disparate-treatment method, claimants attempt to prove that there were different standards for different groups—that is, that the employer required a high school diploma from black candidates for employment, but not from white candidates.

The book covers all possible methods claimants might use to prove discrimination. The methods of analysis described in the text are applicable regardless of the method used.

The statements made in this text cannot be considered legal advice or legal opinion. Such opinions can be rendered only by an attorney after he has considered all the facts in a particular situation.

Finally, it should be noted that two subjects are not covered in depth. These are religious discrimination and discrimination against persons protected by the Vietnam Era Readjustment Act of 1974. On the latter subject, there is simply no substantative case law. And the former has become of much less concern to employers since the Supreme Court decision in *Hardison* v. *Trans*

World Airlines, Inc., 432 U.S. 63 (1977). More important, for purposes of this book, religious discrimination hardly ever involves large groups of people. Thus, while it may be a complicated problem, it is not generally a potentially expensive one.

I must acknowledge my debt to five people who helped me greatly with this book: John Sabetta, Mary Faucher, Rory McEvoy, Sherri Venokur, and my secretary, Pat Grace. I would also like to give special thanks to the staff at Prentice-Hall, especially Marian Hartstein and Rita DeVries, who did such a fine job of editing and ensuring that my "lawyer's language" was made clear and understandable to nonlawyers.

This book is dedicated to Carmen and Kerry, who allowed me the time to write it.

Kenneth J. McCulloch

PART 1

OVERVIEW: THE RULES AND HOW THEY ARE INTERPRETED

Introduction

At the outset, it must be acknowledged that the equal employment opportunity issue has become the primary vehicle for an even more significant movement. The U.S. federal government is acting to enforce social and economic equalization, and the primary mechanism is the private employer.

A 1969 book by Lester Thurow,* funded in part by OEO and partially based on resources of the U.S. Department of Labor and Office of Federal Contract Compliance Programs, describes the government blueprint. The thesis of that book is that as long as any identifiable group is earning less than the median wage, that group is the victim of discrimination. Economic discrimination and the egregious types of discrimination have thus become synonymous.

Without acceptance of the fact that EEO laws are being used as tools for social change, one can never fully appreciate what is happening in the equal-opportunity law field, or, for that matter, in the fields of Social Security law and health care. When an employer "loses" an EEO case, the loss is sometimes comprehensible only with the understanding of this full picture.

The government's central focus in this approach is on testing and selection devices. Any method an employer utilizes to screen employees or applicants is a test. If the *achievement* on a given test of any group of minorities, females,

---

**Poverty and Discrimination* (Washington, D.C.: The Brookings Institution, 1969).

people in protected age categories, or disabled or handicapped people is not at least 80 percent as good as the best-achieving group, then there is *adverse impact*, and the employer will have the burden of validating that selection procedure. Validation under government guidelines is virtually impossible and under court decisions is very difficult.

Certain terms used in this book and a particular scenario are taken for granted. The terms are *protected group, adverse impact, business necessity,* and *bona fide occupational qualification* (BFOQ), and they are part of the scenario involving selection devices.

The term *protected group* is a variable. A member of such a group is usually a minority person, or a female, or a person over the age of 40, but it can be anyone. The groups for which EEO legislation was primarily intended, and the substance of that legislation, are described in detail in Chapter 1.

The scenario starts with a protected-group person claiming that he or she was denied some benefit in employment, that others similarly situated have been denied that benefit, and that the denial was discriminatory.

The benefit involved can be hiring, a promotion, a bonus, the opportunity to enter an apprenticeship program or training program, greater retirement benefits, or the like. The complainant's refrain is the same: "If I were white, or male, or under 40, or . . . you [the employer] would not have done this to me."

When the claim is made, neither the government investigators nor the courts are primarily concerned with whether that individual claimant was properly treated. Rather, they are concerned with determining whether the group of which he or she is a part is being properly treated. And they determine this by doing adverse-impact analyses. Adverse-impact analysis is a method of comparing how the group of which the claimant is a part has fared as against the best-achieving group. If the claim is discrimination in hiring, applicant-flow/ hiring ratios for the groups being compared will be analyzed. If it is a claim of discrimination in promotion, then people of that particular race, color, religion, national origin, or other characteristic who are available for promotion will be identified, and the rate at which they are promoted will be determined and compared to the promotion rate for the best-performing group. The same approach holds true for discharge or other adverse action, and also for comparing terms and conditions of employment. In this book, a section of each of Chapters 4, 5, 6, and 7 discusses establishment of systems for assessing and minimizing adverse impact in hiring, promotion, terminations, and terms and conditions of employment, respectively.

If it is determined that the selection device, or standard, has had an adverse impact, the employer has the burden of validating that selection standard— that is, proving that the standard is a valid predictor of job performance, or lack of performance. If the employer succeeds, it has demonstrated one type of business necessity.

Another type of business necessity might exist in situations where a selection device is not validated, but where the employer can clearly demonstrate that (1) there is a strong relationship between the selection standard and performance, and that (2) without this method of selection, the employer's training expenses and failure rate of persons trained would make operating costs prohibitive.

A standard is any selection device. It could be a requirement that a candidate have a high school diploma or a certain type of experience, or it could relate to height, weight, and so on. Chapters 4, 5, 6, and 7 of this book discuss standards that have been the subject of litigation, the reason they have been the subject of litigation, and the result of that litigation. Appendix B is a listing of 138 cases in which identified standards, mostly paper-and-pencil tests, have been at issue.

Validation for purposes of EEO law is the technical process whereby the employer defending the use of a selection device, or standard, demonstrates a very close relationship between performance against the standard and performance on the job. Types of validation are discussed in the federal government Uniform Guidelines on Employee Selection Procedures, which make up Appendix A. These Uniform Guidelines are the product of more than three years of negotiation and research by federal government enforcers, private and public employers, and public-interest groups. It is expected that, having been adopted by all the major federal enforcers, they will form the basis for government action in the EEO arena for the next decade. Since the Uniform Guidelines were issued relatively recently, a book on this subject is particularly appropriate now.

This book does not suggest that corporate personnel directors and corporate labor counsel should attempt to validate their own selection standards. Validation is a subject for experts, and even they have had very little success in validating any standard. Since validation is called for only when a standard is having an adverse impact, this book is concerned primarily with avoiding the necessity of having to validate. However, in Chapter 3, the various techniques for validation, and the requirements of each, are discussed.

In the legal scenario, if the employer cannot validate the standard and cannot successfully assert the business-necessity defense, another possibility is a BFOQ defense. This defense is extremely limited and relates almost always to sex-discrimination cases. BFOQ means that *no* person of a particular sex, age, religion, or national origin can adequately perform a particular job and, therefore, all persons of that sex or race may be kept from that job. One court, characterizing the limited availability of the BFOQ defense, said that there were only two jobs where it would be available—wet nurse and sperm donor. Although other courts have been more liberal in accepting this defense—as, for example, in cases involving clothing salespersons—all courts have rejected the concept that because *most* women cannot lift 50 pounds, *all* women may be precluded from jobs having such a requirement.

Assuming that the employer succeeds with any defense, be it validation, business necessity, or BFOQ, the government would have the employer meet still another burden—demonstrating that there is no alternative means of selection available that would be just as useful for business purposes but would have a lesser adverse impact. Most courts have thus far not required that the employer meet and satisfy this second burden in its defense.

Assuming that the employer fails in its defense of the standard, every person who was adversely affected by the employer's use of that standard has the opportunity to obtain relief. It is at this stage that these persons step forward and demonstrate that they sought some benefit and were denied it because of that standard. If the employer cannot show a legitimate nondiscriminatory reason (such as lack of job openings) that each of these persons would not have received that benefit even absent the discriminatory standard, then each person obtains full relief, including back pay, retroactive seniority, and so on.

In sum, the complainant is only a starting point. It is less important, in the larger context, whether he or she was treated fairly than whether the *standard* about which he or she is complaining is either (1) having no adverse impact, or (2) legally defensible.

In the absence of adverse impact, an employer is in a much more defensible position in rebutting discrimination claims. Thus, if the claimant does not attempt to prove he suffered from the adverse impact of a standard, or, having made the attempt, he failed in his proof, the employer's burden of proof at most is merely to *articulate* some legitimate, nondiscriminatory reason for the claimant's rejection. It is then up to the claimant, if he is to prevail, to prove that the reason given is a subterfuge and that the real reason is discrimination.

Chapter 1

The Protected Groups and What Protects Them

A minority female with a heart murmur who is over 40 and working in New York City for an employer who is a government contractor can precipitate legal or administrative action, or both, against that employer in twelve different forums because of alleged discrimination. Theoretically, she could lose in eleven forums, yet still receive relief from the employer in the twelfth.

She could accuse the employer of discrimination on the basis of race or sex under Title VII,[1] thereby precipitating "enforcement" either by EEOC or herself. In any event, she would precipitate an investigation by such a charge.

She could accuse the employer of discrimination on the basis of age, under the Age Discrimination in Employment Act of 1967,[2] and thereby precipitate court enforcement action by EEOC or herself. At a minimum, this would cause an attempted conciliation by EEOC.

She could file a lawsuit in federal court on the basis of race discrimination under the Civil Rights Act of 1866, 42 U.S.C. §1981.

She could file a claim of discrimination under the Equal Pay Act of 1963,[3] and thereby precipitate court enforcement action by either EEOC or herself. At a minimum, this charge would trigger an investigation.

She could file a claim of discrimination based upon her status as "handicapped"[4] and precipitate court enforcement action by the U.S. Department of Justice or herself[5] under the Rehabilitation Act of 1973. The same charge could also precipitate sanctions against the employer under the Rehabilitation Act of 1973, and the rules and regulations issued pursuant to that law.[6] Thus, this charge would trigger an investigation that could lead to an administrative hearing and, alternatively, a federal court proceeding[7]—as two possible forums.

By filing a charge of discrimination with OFCCP claiming race or sex discrimination in violation of Executive Order 11246,[8] she could precipitate sanctions against the employer because the employer is a government contractor. At a minimum, this charge would trigger an investigation, and it could precipitate an administrative hearing or a federal court action by the federal government[9]—again, two possible forums.

She could file a charge of discrimination on the basis of race, sex, disability, or age with the New York State Division of Human Rights and thereby precipitate an investigation.[10] She can either go to court directly herself, or await the administrative proceedings and then appeal an adverse determination to court. The New York statute offers her two distinct forums.[11]

She can file a charge of discrimination based on age, sex, race, or disability with the New York City Commission on Human Rights and thereby precipitate an investigation and an administrative determination, with court review.[12]

She can file a charge of discrimination based on age, sex, race, or disability under the Mayor's Executive Order, thereby precipitating sanctions against the employer because the employer is a city contractor. At a minimum, this charge would lead to another investigation.

If the woman were a disabled veteran, she could file a charge of discrimination with OFCCP on that basis, thereby precipitating possible sanctions against the employer because it is a government contractor and, possibly, court action initiated by either the Department of Justice or herself, or an administrative hearing.[13]

If the woman were covered by a collective-bargaining agreement, she could precipitate an arbitration if there were a nondiscrimination clause in the agreement, or a lawsuit, under the Labor-Management Relations Act, against the union and the employer.[14]

If the employer were a New York State defense contractor, a charge of discrimination on the basis of race could lead to investigation and criminal conviction of a misdemeanor.[15]

The various memoranda of understanding among the several government enforcement agencies almost always guarantee that a charge to one agency will trigger action by more than one. For example, by a memorandum of understanding, EEOC has agreed to notify OFCCP of any charges of discrimination filed with it.[16] By statute, EEOC must defer a charge of discrimination to the appropriate state or local government deferral agency.[17] Thus, a charge to EEOC triggers action by three different agencies. Similarly, by an unpublished memorandum of understanding, a charge to the New York City Commission on Human Rights triggers a referral by that agency to EEOC.

The Protected Groups and What Protects Them

Frequently, investigators or compliance officers will seek information that will enable them to find discrimination on one basis—for example, race—even though they originally began the investigation on another basis—for example, sex. (Information not relevant to the stated basis of the investigation generally does not have to be provided by the employer.)[18] Generally, the investigator or compliance agency will demand, and have the right to look at, information and documents relating not only to the particular individual who filed the charge but to other persons of similar race, age, sex, or physical status. Generally, investigators and compliance agents are more interested in determining whether or not the system operates fairly than in whether a particular person is treated fairly. If the system is determined to be operating fairly, it will be very difficult for an individual to prevail on his or her claim. Conversely, if not, there is a great likelihood that the individual will prevail.

All government enforcement agencies have adopted a posture of assessing the fairness of the system by ascertaining the extent to which different protected groups *achieve* under that system. This achievement could be in hiring, promotion, training, transfers, benefits, discharges, discipline, or any other aspect of the employment system. Although this assessment of fairness is the basic subject of this book, a preliminary description of the statutes, orders, and rules and regulations that identify protected groups is necessary.

TITLE VII

Title VII of the Civil Rights Act of 1964, as amended, prohibits discrimination on the basis of race, color, national origin, sex, or religion. It is enforced and administered by EEOC. It is the most significant vehicle for claims of discrimination because it has the broadest scope; because EEOC has assumed jurisdiction over enforcement of other civil-rights statutes in the federal area;[19] and because the most significant judgments and settlements in civil-rights employment discrimination cases have come in Title VII cases. It is also most significant because the law developed under Title VII relating to selection devices that have an adverse impact has formed the foundation for developments of the law under other civil-rights statutes, executive orders, and rules and regulations.[20]

Conversely, there is not a very well developed body of substantive law under Executive Order 11246; consequently, the Department of Labor, in enforcing that executive order, has looked to the developed body of law under Title VII. State enforcement agencies are funded in part by EEOC. A condition for their funding is that they maintain the standards expected by EEOC and consistent with Title VII.[21] In order to continue to receive funds, such state and local statutes must be enforced in a manner, and have a scope, consistent with Title VII.[22] By this funding mechanism, EEOC has established Title VII as the primary statute relating to employment discrimination on the basis of race, sex, color, religion, or national origin.

Coverage of Title VII extends to employers—including state and local governments, schools, colleges, and any other "employer"—unions, and employment agencies. The employers covered are those that have 15 or more employees for at least 20 calendar weeks in the year a charge is filed, or the year preceding the filing of a charge, and that are engaged in "an industry affecting commerce," a term very liberally interpreted. Labor organizations covered are those engaged in an industry affecting commerce, in which the employees participate, and that exist in whole or in part to deal with employers concerning grievances, labor disputes, wages, rates of pay, and so on. Employment agencies include any person or organization, and its agents, that regularly act, with or without compensation, to procure employees for an employer or work for employees.

Exempt from the coverage of Title VII are (1) religious institutions, with respect to the employment of persons of a specific religion in any of the institutions' activities; (2) aliens; (3) members of the Communist party; and (4) persons elected to public office or appointed to the personal staff of persons elected to public office. The statute does not protect noncitizens from discrimination based upon their lack of citizenship, although it would protect them from discrimination based upon their national origin. American Indians in certain circumstances can receive preferential treatment under Title VII.

The procedural mechanism of Title VII is totally charge-oriented; nothing can happen unless a charge is filed. A charge may be filed by one of the five presidentially appointed EEOC commissioners, by any aggrieved person, or by anyone acting on behalf of a person aggrieved. The charge must be filed within 180 days of the date of the act complained of, but that period may be extended to 300 days if there is a state or local fair-employment-practice law and agency prohibiting the type of discrimination complained of, and the person who files the charge has utilized the procedures of that agency. Also, where this is the case, by statute, EEOC cannot take jurisdiction of the charge of discrimination that is alleged to have taken place in that jurisdiction unless it has first deferred that charge to the state or local agency. EEOC must permit the agency to have exclusive jurisdiction of the charge for 60 days or until the agency terminates jurisdiction, whichever occurs earlier. At that point, EEOC assumes jurisdiction of the charge.

The Supreme Court has approved the EEOC procedure of acting as agent for a charging party who comes to one of its offices. EEOC will receive a charge from such a person and deliver it to the state on his or her behalf.

Within ten days after EEOC has assumed jurisdiction over a charge, it will notify the respondent that the charge has been filed and send a copy of the charge. EEOC will also send an accommodation copy of the charge to the headquarters office of a large company, if so requested.

The date when EEOC assumes jurisdiction of the charge is the date after the deferral and should be within 300 days after the act complained of occurred; however, some courts have found jurisdiction to exist even if the expiration of the deferral period is more than 300 days after the alleged discriminatory act.

In the early history of Title VII, there was a very liberal tendency to extend the time period for filing a charge by interpreting many alleged violations to be "continuing." However, the Supreme Court has indicated that the time period is to be literally construed and related to the act rather than its effects, and that EEOC will not be permitted to save charges by labelling violations "continuing."[23]

EEOC has varied its procedures in an attempt to cut down the backlog of charges that it has. It has reduced its backlog from approximately 125,000 charges outstanding just a few years ago to approximately 60,000 currently. Under the existing procedure, the first step is the no-fault settlement attempt, an invitation to the respondent to settle the case without an admission of guilt. It is the stage where the case is most likely to be settled or summarily dismissed, since relatively little time has passed from the date of the alleged violation to the date of the no-fault conference. However, there is no obligation under the law to engage in a no-fault settlement attempt.

If the charge is not resolved at this stage, the case will be placed in the backlog to await investigation, for a period that varies among district offices from six months to about two years. During this period, starting from the date the employer receives notice of the charge, the employer is under notice not to destroy any records relating to the charge.

Eventually, there will be an investigation that may or may not include an on-site visit by the investigator from EEOC. During the investigatory process, the respondent is invited to submit a position statement, and it is advisable to do so.

As a result of the investigation, a determination of "probable cause" or "no probable cause" will be issued by the district director of EEOC, who follows what are called "Commission's Decision Precedents" (CDPs), prior decisions of the commissioners. If there are no CDPs to rely upon, the district director is supposed to forward the case to Washington, to be decided by the commissioners themselves.

After the determination, there is an attempted conciliation. Failing conciliation, the case file will be reviewed for "litigation potential." In assessing litigation potential, EEOC considers the principle involved in the case, the number of people affected by the practice alleged, the amount of dollar remedy that can be achieved, procedural defects that might exist in the file, other outstanding charges against the same respondent or facility, and the egregiousness of the conduct complained of. Litigation recommendations are made in area litigation centers and passed upon by the general counsel of EEOC.

Assuming that the recommendation is against litigation, a right-to-sue notice will issue to the charging party, notifying the party that he or she may bring his or her own action in federal court within 90 days of receipt of the notice. This notice is a condition precedent to bringing an action under Title VII. However, there is no requirement that the charging party wait until the entire administrative process is completed. At any time during the process, but more than 180 days after EEOC has assumed jurisdiction of a charge, a charging party may request a right-to-sue notice and institute his or her own action in federal district court. Ordinarily, the request by a charging party for a right-to-sue notice will terminate further administrative processing of the charge filed with EEOC.

EXECUTIVE ORDER 11246

Executive Order 11246 prohibited discrimination on the basis of race, color, creed, or national origin by contractors doing business with the federal government. The original executive order became effective October 24, 1965, and was amended by Executive Order 11375, which changed the word "creed" to "religion" and proscribed sex discrimination in addition to the other prohibited bases of discrimination. This amendment became effective in 1968.

Executive Order 11246, as amended, delegated presidential authority for enforcement of the order to the secretary of labor. The secretary was empowered to cancel, terminate, or suspend contracts or condition their continuance upon a program of future compliance, to bar violators from future contracts, to recommend that enforcement action be commenced against violators by the Department of Justice or by EEOC, to investigate compliance, to exempt contractors from the requirements of the executive order, and to impose pre-award standards.

The secretary of labor created a new agency, the Office of Federal Contract Compliance Programs (OFCCP), to implement these powers and responsibilities. The director of the office reports to the assistant secretary of labor for employment standards. Since OFCCP originally did not have the funds or the mechanism to monitor contract compliance with the executive order, it delegated responsibility for ensuring compliance to some 19 "compliance review agencies." OFCCP retained the responsibility for issuing procedural and substantive regulations for the guidance of these agencies, but the agencies conducted the compliance reviews. One agency was assigned to monitor each government contractor, depending upon the standard industrial code (SIC) of the contractor. As of October 12, 1978, the function was taken away from these agencies and has reverted to the Department of Labor; compliance reviews are now conducted out of Department of Labor offices by department employees and personnel. It is anticipated that in a few years, this authority will be absorbed by EEOC.

Executive Order 11246 extends in scope to both federal procurement and federally assisted construction contracts. The degree of control the government will exercise depends upon the size of the contracts involved. The minimum standard for regulation is a contract of $10,000 or more. At that level, by entering into the contract, the employer agrees to advertise in a certain manner for prospective employees, to post certain notices advertising its status as an equal-opportunity employer, to advise employees of their right to contact EEOC or OFCCP if they believe discrimination is occurring, to open its business records to review by the agents enforcing the executive order, and to ensure that its facilities are not segregated on the basis of race, sex, color, religion, or national origin.

The next plateau in the enforcement system is the contractor who has a contract, subcontract or purchase order amounting to $50,000 or more. Such contractors must abide by all the regulations above, and in addition must also file EEO-1 reports and comply with the affirmative action program requirements.[24]

The affirmative action program concept is the heart of the entire Executive Order 11246 program. It requires an employer to group its jobs, conduct a utilization analysis, identify cases of underutilization, and project goals and timetables to correct the underutilization.

The third plateau for government contractors is a contract or subcontract for $1 million or more. In such instances, in addition to meeting all the requirements detailed in prior sections, the contractor or subcontractor must undergo an on-site pre-award compliance review. If the contractor is not in compliance, the award of the contract can be forfeited. The Department of Labor, through OFCCP, had adopted the position that it can deny up to two contracts, no matter how large the dollar value, without notice of any kind to the contractor, and without the latter's knowledge of the OFCCP determination.[25] The government has been enjoined on at least forty-one different occasions from employing this practice.[26] Nevertheless, it persists in the practice and does its strongest negotiating, including making demands for back pay, when the award of a multi-million-dollar contract is near at hand and must be either granted or forfeited. Because of the many defeats it has suffered on this issue of contract denial without a hearing, the OFCCP has pending a proposal that would permit an expedited hearing for a contractor that is about to forfeit a contract.

The fact that one facility of a corporate entity has government contracts does not necessarily mean that the entire corporation is covered and has to comply with the affirmative action program requirement. Standards for coverage were established in a decision B170536 of the controller general.[27] In that case, Armstrong Corporation had been granted a tile supply contract. Apache Floor Company complained that it should have received the contract, asserting that Armstrong had never established an affirmative action program for the Thomasville Furniture Co., in which it had a controlling interest. In upholding the award of the contract to Armstrong, the controller general construed the guidelines of the Department of Labor—which required each government contractor to "develop a written affirmative action compliance program for each of its establishments"— to mean that the guidelines covered only those establishments where there existed (1) common ownership; (2) common directors and/or officers; (3) de facto exercise of controls; (4) unity of personnel policies emanating from a common source; and (5) dependency of operations. That construction of the guidelines has been followed.

Unlike EEOC, the Department of Labor in enforcing Executive Order 11246 does not require the filing of a charge of discrimination before it can conduct an investigation. Consequently, the scope of such investigation is not dependent upon the scope of any originating charge.

The administrative process under Executive Order 11246 usually commences with the agents of the Department of Labor requesting that the contractor forward the affirmative action program for a particular facility for review. Thirty days are usually allowed for this. When the affirmative action program is received, a desk audit is conducted—that is, a check is made to determine whether all the required ingredients for the affirmative action plan are included. After that, there is usually an on-site investigation in which the compliance officer clears up questions relating to the affirmative action program and reviews personnel records. The officer might also talk to employees during this on-site visit, but the contractor has a right to have a representative present at such discussions.*

If deficiencies are found, the contractor is usually informed of them by the compliance officer at the end of the compliance review; an informal attempt is then made to resolve them. If this fails, a formal deficiency letter will probably issue from the compliance officer, setting the stage for formal conciliation efforts. If these fail, a 30-day show-cause letter usually issues from the compliance agency.

A show-cause letter is not a legal document, but it can have great significance. Administratively, it sets the stage for a final 30-day attempt to resolve deficiencies through conciliation. However, once the show-cause letter has been sent, a contractor is formally deemed not to be in compliance. For example, GSA regulations require that a contractor not in compliance not be informed of bid opportunities for which it might otherwise receive notice.[28] Additionally, it has been a practice of the government to put on Telex to various procurement agencies throughout the country notice of the non-awardable status of a contractor that has been sent a show-cause notice. Sometimes procurement agents, having received such notice by Telex, "pass over"** a contractor that would otherwise be awarded a contract, without checking any further. A show-cause

---

*This is discussed in more detail in Chapter 10.

**"Pass-over" is the technical term used by the government when it wants to deny a contract without affording the contractor a hearing. Since Executive Order 11246 requires a hearing before a debarment or suspension from future contracts, the government has created this term, and the "pass-over" procedure, to avoid the legal requirement of notice and hearing.

notice is also of significance because a contractor covered by Executive Order 11246 can jeopardize its contract if it sublets a part of it to a non-awardable contractor. For that reason, prime contractors may informally refuse to consider as a subcontractor an employer in receipt of a show-cause notice.

Assuming the deficiencies are not remedied during the show-cause period, a notice of hearing is supposed to be issued by the Department of Labor, thereby setting the stage for an administrative hearing procedure before an administrative-law judge. The period between failure of conciliation and issuance of the notice of administrative hearing can be years. And when the contractor does finally receive a notice of administrative hearing, the period from then to the time of the hearing can again be as long as three years, owing to the very heavy backlog on administrative hearings under Executive Order 11246.

In the interim, while the contractor is waiting for the notice of administrative hearing or the hearing itself, the government's position is that it can pass over—deny that contractor—any two contracts during the period. The government interprets this to mean it can permit relatively insignificant contracts to be awarded to the contractor but deny major multimillion-dollar contracts, or threaten to do so.

The Executive Order 11246 enforcement program is noteworthy for the further reason that the affirmative action program submitted by an employer can usually be obtained by any member of the public merely by filing a Freedom of Information Act request.

Little or no substantive law evolving from the administrative hearing process has been developed thus far under Executive Order 11246. The Department of Labor had routinely adopted the court decisions construing Title VII as the body of substantive law it sought to enforce; it abandoned that approach with the Supreme Court's decision in *International Brotherhood of Teamsters v. United States*,[29] and disavowed the applicability of *Teamsters* to the executive order program. Subsequent cases, including one decided by the US. Court of Appeals for the Fifth Circuit, have held that the strictures of *Teamsters* are binding on the Department of Labor under the executive order. The Department of Labor has declined, nonetheless, to change its position, formally or informally.

AGE DISCRIMINATION IN EMPLOYMENT ACT OF 1967

The Age Discrimination in Employment Act of 1967 (ADEA)[30] was significantly amended in 1978. The amendments, most of which became effective in 1979, affected both procedural and substantive provisions of the ADEA.

The ADEA protects employees and applicants for employment who are at least 40 but less than 70 years of age. It prohibits discrimination against persons within this age group by employers, labor organizations, employment agencies, the federal government and the states. Employers which are covered are those which engage "in an industry affecting commerce" and have 20 or more employees for 20 or more calendar weeks, either in the current or the preceding calendar year. Labor organizations are covered if they have 25 or more members. The prohibition extends to hiring, assignment, training, promotion, and terms and conditions of employment.

Authority for enforcement of the ADEA is vested with EEOC, having been transferred to that agency from the U.S. Department of Labor effective July 1, 1979. Enforcement is triggered by the filing of a charge of discrimination with EEOC. However, EEOC can undertake to review compliance even if there is no charge.

Prior to EEOC assuming jurisdiction over the ADEA, the Department of Labor had initiated its own investigation, filed its own charges, and filed its own lawsuits to enforce the ADEA. EEOC has indicated it will pursue this approach.

A charge under the ADEA must be filed within 180 days of the act complained of, except that if there is a state or local agency that prohibits the same type of discrimination, a charge may be filed within 300 days. Additionally, if there is to be a lawsuit, the legal action must be commenced within two years of the act which is the subject of the complaint, or within three years if the act is willful.

A provision was inserted in the amendments whereby the statute of limitations for filing a lawsuit will be tolled for up to one year while EEOC attempts conciliation. Previously, the government had faced a dilemma when it concluded it might wish to sue, because the statute of limitations (two years, or three, if the violation was willful) would start running against it while it attempted conciliation. The automatic tolling provision applies only in those situations where conciliation had not already commenced as of the effective date of the amendments.

The ADEA differs from Title VII in certain significant respects.

First, it provides for trial by jury. This is significant because the complainant is generally a person of long service and is able to gain the sympathy of the jury for this reason, if for no other.

Second, the ADEA provides for liquidated damages, in an amount equal to the lost wages, and in addition to the lost wages. Thus, there is a punitive aspect to an ADEA case.

Substantively, it had been difficult for a complainant to bring an ADEA case as a class action. Prior to the amendments to the ADEA, many courts had held that the only persons who might be in such a class would be those who had notified the Secretary of Labor, in timely fashion, that they intended to file suit. Since the amendments, there is no longer a requirement to give such a notice but only a requirement that a charge be filed. EEOC has already indicated that if an ADEA violation is found to have affected persons other than the complainant, then if it files an action it will seek remedy not only for the complainant but also for those similarly affected. EEOC will also try to establish that ADEA lawsuits, even if brought by individuals, can be prosecuted as class-type actions, even if the other persons in the class have not filed charges of discrimination themselves.

Prior to the 1978 amendments to the ADEA, the protected group status only extended to those who had not yet reached the age of 65. Even with the amendments, compulsory retirement at age 65 is still permissible for those who have been high-level executives, that is, if their nonforfeitable annual retirement benefit equals or exceeds $27,000, or for tenured faculty at the college level.

The amendments reversed the decision of the Supreme Court in *United Air Lines, Inc.* v. *McMann*.[31] By that decision, the Supreme Court ruled that an employer could require the retirement of an employee before the age of 65 pursuant to a bona fide retirement plan. In the *United Air Lines* case, since the retirement plan had been instituted prior to the effective date of the ADEA, the Supreme Court had held that it was bona fide. However, because of the amendment, an employer will not be able to force the involuntary retirement of an employee, before the age of 70, regardless of whether there is a bona fide retirement plan. The Department of Labor had indicated that it did not contemplate requiring employers to continue to make pension contributions for employees after they reach age 65, but this issue has not been judicially determined, and EEOC has not indicated what position it will adopt on this issue.

THE EQUAL PAY ACT OF 1963

The Equal Pay Act of 1963[32] is an amendment to the Fair Labor Standards Act of 1938. It provides that employers shall not discriminate between employees on the basis of sex by paying wages at a rate less for one sex than for the other for jobs that require equal skill, effort, and responsibility, and that are performed under similar working conditions, except if the payment is made pursuant to a seniority system, a merit system, or a system that measures earnings by quantity or quality of production. Another exception permits employers to pay a wage differential if it is based on a factor other than sex. For instance, it might be that if the employer has a higher profit margin and earns more money from the sale of men's clothes than women's clothes, it can pay male salesmen servicing the men's department more than women servicing the women's department.

Enforcement of this statute was originally within the jurisdiction of the Department of Labor but has become the responsibility of EEOC since July 1, 1979.

While it enforced the Equal Pay Act, the Department of Labor had issued regulations indicating what constitutes equal skill, effort, and responsibility and similar working conditions; however, EEOC has already indicated that it may not abide by the Department of Labor interpretations.

This statute has fallen into relative disuse since the proliferation of lawsuits under Title VII because a violation of the Equal Pay Act would also be a violation of Title VII, whereas not every violation of Title VII would also be a violation of the Equal Pay Act.

THE REHABILITATION ACT OF 1973

The Rehabilitation Act of 1973[33] covers government contractors or subcontractors or entities receiving federal grants. The threshold level for coverage is a contract or subcontract in excess of $2,500 entered into by any federal department or agency. Enforcement was delegated to the president by Congress, and the president delegated enforcement authority to the Departments of Labor and Health, Education and Welfare. The statute requires not only nondiscrimination, but also affirmative action on behalf of handicapped individuals.

A person is considered handicapped under the statute if that person has a physical or mental impairment that substantially limits one or more major life activities, or has a record of such an impairment, or is regarded by others as having such an impairment, even though in fact the person may not.

The Office of Federal Contract Compliance Programs (OFCCP) enforces the Rehabilitation Act. OFCCP construed alcoholism and drug abuse to be handicaps, contrary to the Congressional intention. Consequently, Congress amended the Rehabilitation Act to make it clear that current alcoholism or drug abuse rendering a person unfit does not constitute a handicap. The amendment, which became effective in 1978, provides that "for purposes of sections 503 and 504 as such sections relate to employment, such term [handicapped individual] does not include any individual whose current use of alcohol or drugs prevents such individual from performing the duties of the job in question or whose employment, by reason of such current alcohol or drug abuse, would constitute a direct threat to property or safety of others."

OFCCP considers a person to be handicapped even if his or her physical condition relates to the performance of only one job. In *OFCCP* v. *E. E. Black, Ltd.*,[34] the contractor argued that the complainant should not be considered handicapped unless the physical condition affects his ability to perform a substantial number of jobs. The issue was taken to administrative hearing, and the Administrative Law Judge ruled in favor of the contractor. However, since the decision of the Administrative Law Judge under the Rehabilitation Act is only advisory, it could be, and was rejected by the OFCCP. The contractor then appealed the issue to court, and it still has not been finally determined.

The regulations issued by the Department of Labor for administration of the Rehabilitation Act of 1973 provide for various levels of coverage. All contractors exceeding the $2,500 contract or subcontract limit are required to post notices that they have agreed with the government to take affirmative action to employ and advance in employment qualified handicapped employees and applicants for employment. Additionally, the contractor is required not to discriminate against people who are handicapped because of physical or mental impairments, to comply with the rules and regulations and orders of the secretary of labor issued pursuant to the Rehabilitation Act, and to abide by sanctions for noncompliance imposed in accordance with those rules and regulations.

At the level where the contract or subcontract exceeds $50,000, and for contractors having 50 or more employees, it is required that the contractor have, and make available to employees, an affirmative action program. Although this does not require the detail of the affirmative action program required under Executive Order 11246, it does require the contractor to indicate what reasonable accommodations it is making in employing and advancing in employment handicapped persons. The program must invite the applicants and employees who believe themselves covered by the Act, and who wish to benefit under the affirmative action program, to identify themselves.

Complaints by people who believe they are protected by the Rehabilitation Act may be filed with the Department of Labor, and are handled by OFCCP. If the contractor has an internal grievance procedure for the handling of such grievances, the Department of Labor must refer the charge to the contractor to see if it can be resolved without further resort to government action, but there is under consideration by the government a proposed procedural change that would make such referral optional, at the discretion of the Department of Labor. If there is no internal procedure, the government will not refer the complaint to the contractor.

The Rehabilitation Act is probably the most quickly developing area of employment discrimination law. This is because the definition of "handicap" has been expanding rapidly. Epilepsy, alcoholism, and even obesity are being considered handicaps. As yet, no court has definitively accepted or rejected the government's definition of "handicap," and no court has accepted OFCCP's position that contractors are required to make "reasonable accommodation" to physical and mental limitations of an employee or applicant. The Rehabilitation Act itself says nothing about the obligation to make reasonable accommodation. Additionally, the executive order conveying enforcement authority to the Department of Labor makes no mention of such a requirement.

Even though this area of employment discrimination law is relatively new, there have been some court cases, indicating that there is a private right of action permitted in federal court for persons claiming to be aggrieved by a violation of the act. Additionally, enforcement can come through action by the U.S. Department of Justice, which acts as attorney for the Department of Labor in enforcing the provisions of the Rehabilitation Act of 1973. Finally, an employer may suffer administrative sanctions, such as contract debarment, termination, or the withholding of progress payments. An administrative hearing procedure is provided for in the rules and regulations of the secretary of labor.

As a result, under the procedures established, an employer may be put in the position of defending against an alleged violation of the act in a private suit in federal court, in a suit by the U.S. Department of Justice in federal court, or in an administrative hearing.

THE VIETNAM ERA VETERANS READJUSTMENT ACT OF 1974

The Vietnam Era Veterans Readjustment Act of 1974[35] is another congressional enactment that relates only to government contractors. A contractor is covered if it has a contract or subcontract in the amount of $10,000 or more with the federal government. The act does not provide for an independent right to commence legal action in federal court for persons claiming to be aggrieved by violation of the act.

Persons covered by the act are disabled veterans and veterans of the Vietnam era. Disabled veterans are those with a compensable disability rated at 30 percent or more by the Veterans Administration, or whose discharge or release from active duty was for a disability incurred or aggravated in the line of duty. A veteran of the Vietnam-era is identified by the date of his discharge. The person must have been released from the service within the 48 months preceding the alleged discriminatory act. Additionally, the person must have served more than 180 days on active duty, some part of his active duty must have been between August 5, 1964 and May 7, 1975, and he must not have received a dishonorable discharge. Persons who are discharged from service for a service-connected disability also are covered by this act if they had served any active duty between the time periods indicated above.

Assuring compliance with the provisions of the Vietnam-era Veterans Readjustment Act is the responsibility of the Department of Labor. That agency may independently review compliance without a charge having been filed or may react to a complaint filed by some person claiming to be aggrieved. The act may be enforced by court actions or by administrative hearing and sanctions. Sanctions can include the withholding of progress payments, termination of government contracts, or debarment from government contracts in the future.

One of the most significant obligations imposed under the act's regulations is that contractors who are covered must agree that virtually all employment openings that exist be listed at an appropriate local office of the state employment service system. These listings must take place at least concurrently with, and preferably before, being made available to any other recruitment source. Additionally, the contractor had originally been required to file with the state employment service, at least quarterly, a report indicating the number of people hired during a reporting period, the number of nondisabled veterans hired, and the total number of disabled veterans hired. However, this requirement was invalidated by the Office of Management and Budget because OFCCP had failed to comply with the Federal Reports Act before issuing it.

As with Executive Order 11246, there are various levels of coverage. The contractor who has a $10,000 contract or grant must do all the things indicated above. The contractor with a contract of $50,000 or more and having 50 or more employees must do all of the things indicated above and, in addition, maintain an affirmative action program at each establishment. The burdens imposed by this requirement are quite significant. The contractor must provide a schedule for the review of all physical and mental job qualification requirements to ensure that to the extent that they tend to screen out qualified disabled veterans, they are job related and are consistent with business necessity and safe performance of the job. The contractor is also required to make reasonable accommodation to the physical and mental limitations of the disabled veteran unless the contractor can demonstrate that to make such an accommodation would impose an "undue hardship" on the business. There is as yet no case law, or even administrative interpretations, indicating what constitutes "undue hardship."

Finally, the contractor must pursue all those various requirements of the affirmative action program concept as embodied in Executive Order 11246, with the exception that the contractor does not have to establish job groups, perform a utilization analysis, identify areas of under utilization, and establish goals and timetables.

OTHER CIVIL-RIGHTS STATUTES RELATING TO EMPLOYMENT DISCRIMINATION

There are other federal civil-rights statutes that are of lesser significance to personnel administrators because they usually involve the direct filing of a lawsuit. Additionally, there are state and local statutes and agencies that have a very great significance for personnel administrators, but that are too diverse and numerous to be covered in this book. Publishers such as Prentice-Hall, the Bureau of National Affairs (BNA), and Commerce Clearing House, Inc. (CCH), cover these subjects. In the EEOC regulations[36], there is a listing of state and local deferral and notice agencies, but even this listing would not cover all the agencies active in this field. Even though these state and local laws are not discussed here, they are very important and should be considered in administering any personal policy, especially one that is corporatewide and has effects in various states. Some states, especially New York, Illinois, California, Wisconsin and Michigan, are very aggressive in expanding the sphere of "protected groups," both legislatively and by administrative interpretations.

FOOTNOTES

[1] 42 U.S.C. §§ 2000e *et seq.*

[2] 29 U.S.C. §§ 621 *et seq.* (now enforced by EEOC).

[3] 29 U.S.C. § 206(d) (now enforced by EEOC).

[4] 29 U.S.C. § 701.

[5] In *Carmi v. St. Louis Sewer District,* 20 FEP Cases 162 (E.D. Mo. 1979), the court recognized the individual's right of action, but ruled against the plaintiff on the merits. *Carmi* discusses the cases which have split on the issue of whether there is an independent right of action available to a private party under the Rehabilitation Act.

[6] 41 C.F.R. § 60-741.

[7] See *Davis v. Bucher,* 451 F. Supp. 791 (E.D. Pa. 1978).

[8] 3 C.F.R. § 339.

[9] See *United States v. New Orleans Public Service, Inc.,* 553 F.2d 459 (5th Cir. 1977), vacated and remanded, 436 U.S. 942 (1978).

[10] N.Y. Exec. Law §§ 290-301 (McKinney 1972); 3 Empl. Prac. Guide (CCH) §§ 26000 *et seq.*

[11] Under Section 291 of the New York State Human Rights Law, the opportunity to obtain employment without discrimination because of age, race, creed, color, national origin, sex, or marital status was recognized and declared to be a civil right. As such, it is enforceable by direct court action. Additionally, a complainant may follow the procedures outlined in Section 297, which leads to administrative action and possible court review.

[12] The New York City Commission on Human Rights and its powers are described in the Administrative Code of the City of New York, §§ B1-1.0 *et seq.* Commissions such as the New York City Commission are allowed to exist pursuant to the General Municipal Law, Article 12-D, §§ 239 *et seq.* That law, apparently, did not grant to cities full hearing and court enforcement powers. See General Municipal Law, § 239-R. However, in interpreting the law, the New York Court of Appeals has ruled that the New York City Commission on Human Rights does have jurisdiction to decide a controversy raised by a discrimination claim. See *Maloff v. City Commission on Human Rights,* 38 N.Y.2d 329, 342 N.E.2d 563, 379 N.Y.S.2d 788 (1975).

[13] The possibility of a court enforcement proceeding by the Department of Justice is indicated by 41 C.F.R. § 60-250.28(b). The possibility of an administrative hearing is indicated by 41 C.F.R. § 60-250-29 and 41 C.F.R. § 60-250.26(g) (3). The possibility of an independent right of action for an individual claiming to be aggrieved by a violation of the Vietnam Era Readjustment Act of 1974 is enhanced by the Supreme Court's decision in *University of California Board of Regents v. Bakke,* 438 U.S. 265 (1978), 17 EPD (CCH) ¶ 8402 (June 28, 1978).

[14] 29 U.S.C. §§ 141 *et seq.*

[15] See N.Y. Civ. Rights Law §§ 44, 44a (McKinney 1976); 3 Empl. Prac. Guide (CCH) ¶ 26,105.

[16] See 1 Empl. Prac. Guide (CCH) ¶ 3780.

[17] 42 U.S.C. § 2000e-5(c), which is § 706(c) of Title VII.

[18] See, e.g., *EEOC v. Hickey Mitchell Co.,* 372 F. Supp. 117 (E.D. Mo.

1973). The action was subsequently dismissed, on another basis, and the dismissal was affirmed, 507 F.2d 944 (8th Cir. 1974). This case was one in which EEOC sought to sue on two bases even though only one had been alleged in the initial complaint. A respondent that permits EEOC to investigate on both bases may waive the right to object if a suit is ultimately filed on both bases.

[19] The reorganization by President Carter became final 60 legislative days from February 23, 1978. Pursuant to that reorganization, (1) the enforcement functions of the U.S. Department of Labor under the Age Discrimination Act of 1967 were transferred to EEOC, effective July 1, 1979; (2) the enforcement functions of Labor under the Equal Pay Act of 1963 were transferred to EEOC, effective July 1, 1979; (3) the enforcement responsibilities of the Civil Service Commission, under Section 717 of Title VII, were transferred to EEOC, effective October 1, 1978; (4) the enforcement responsibilities of the Civil Service Commission with respect to the federal employment of handicapped persons pursuant to Section 501 of the Rehabilitation Act of 1973 were transferred to EEOC; (5) the function of the Equal Opportunity Employment Coordinating Council, established by the 1972 amendments to Title VII was transferred to EEOC and the Council disbanded, effective July 1, 1978; (6) pattern and practice authority of EEOC against state and local governments, previously transferred to EEOC by the 1972 amendments to Title VII, was transferred away from EEOC and back to the attorney general; (7) finally, the remaining contract compliance review agencies were abolished and their functions with respect to Executive Order 11246 were consolidated into Labor. This occurred on October 12, 1978.

[20] The most significant case regarding selection procedures has been *Griggs v. Duke Power Co.*, 401 U.S. 424 (1971), which was decided under Title VII.

[21] 29 C.F.R. §§1601.72 et seq.

[22] 29 C.F.R. §1601.72.

[23] See *United Airlines, Inc. v. Evans*, 431 U.S. 353 (1977).

[24] Revised Order 4, 41 C.F.R. §60-2.

[25] Pass-over without notice was suffered by Sundstrand Corporation. The company obtained an injunction in *Sundstrand Corp. v. Marshall*, 17 FEP Cases 432 (N.D. Ill. 1978).

[26] Address of Donald Elisburg, Esq., Assistant Secretary of Labor for Employment Standards as reported in 216 Daily Labor Report 1979 (November 6, 1979) A-5.

[27] Decision B170536, 50 Comp. Gen. 627 (1971).

[28] 41 C.F.R. §1-1.605.5 provides that "[b]ids and proposals shall not be solicited from suspended contractors." 41 C.F.R. §1-1.605-1(a) (iii) provides that bidders may be suspended because of "matters involving the EEO clause" in a government contract.

[29] 431 U.S. 324 (1977).

[30] 29 U.S.C. §§621 et seq.

[31] 434 U.S. 192 (1977).

[32] 29 U.S.C. §206(d).

[33] 29 U.S. §§701 et seq.

[34] 19 FEP Cases 1624.

[35] 38 U.S.C. Chapter 42, §2011.

[36] 29 C.F.R. §1601.74.

Chapter 2

The Uniform Guidelines

COVERAGE

The 1978 Uniform Guidelines on Employee Selection Procedures do *not* apply to the Age Discrimination in Employment Act of 1967 or to the Rehabilitation Act of 1973, but there will be a strong temptation for those enforcing these statutes to look to the Guidelines for direction in a very complicated area. The Uniform Guidelines do cover the other major federal equal employment opportunity statutes and orders—that is, Title VII, Executive Order 11246, the Equal Pay Act, federal fair-employment and revenue-sharing statutes, and statutes and regulations enforced by the Department of Justice and Civil Service Commission.

DEFINITIONS

Selection Procedure—"Test"

The concept of selection procedure, or test, has remained very broad, encompassing any standard used as the basis for any employment decision—except that recruiting is not covered. It was apparently omitted to permit affirmative action programs to operate unhindered in the area of recruitment. Nor do the Uniform

Guidelines cover the operation of seniority systems protected under Section 703(h) of Titles VII, except to the extent that tests are administered for determining qualifications for the job.

The exact words used in the Uniform Guidelines to describe selection procedure are as follows:

> Any measure, combination of measures, or procedure used as a basis for any employment decision. Selection procedures include the full range of assessment techniques from traditional paper and pencil tests, performance tests, training programs or probationary periods and physical, educational, and work experience requirements through informal or casual interviews and unscored application forms.[1]

Thus, if the user (this term includes employers, labor organizations, employment agencies, and testing organizations) considers some unsolicited résumés, then the standards that determine which résumés are considered and which are not is a test and covered by these guidelines; if there is an interview relied upon, a skill requirement, a license requirement, or an educational requirement or preference, it is a test. In sum, any concept or criterion used to affect any decision relating to any candidate, from the time the candidate, or his or her résumé, passes through the door of the employer, employment agency, union, or testing service, until the time the employee retires, could be considered a test. In fact, if benefits are given to retired employees and their surviving spouses, then the test concept could even continue until the time the employee dies.

Adverse Impact

The focal point of the Uniform Guidelines is the term *adverse impact*. The federal equal-opportunity effort seems thoroughly and forcefully directed toward eliminating adverse impact by making it almost impossible to legally continue with any selection device that has such an impact. Perhaps as a tradeoff, the term has been liberally defined in conformity with the traditional Office of Federal Contract Compliance Programs (OFCCP) definition, the Equal Employment Opportunity Commission (EEOC) definition having been abandoned.

Simply stated, as the term *adverse impact* has been defined in the Uniform Guidelines, there is no adverse impact if the worst-performing group is achieving at a rate 80 percent as well as the best-performing group. The groups, for purposes of the Uniform Guidelines, are (1) blacks; (2) American Indians (this term includes Alaskan natives); (3) Asians (which includes Pacific Islanders); (4) Hispanics (includes Mexicans, Puerto Ricans, Cubans, Central and South Americans, and others of Spanish culture or origin, regardless of race); (5) females; and (6) males.

For purposes of assessing whether there is an adverse impact, records are required to be kept not only by ethnic group, but also by sex. Although the

Uniform Guidelines do not specifically say so, it seems apparent that the federal agencies, by the manner in which they have required records to be kept, have retained the option of comparing the performances of, for example, black females, white females, Hispanic females, and each of the other female groups, as well as white males, Hispanic males, and each of the other male groups. There are thus 44 different analyses of adverse impact permitted for each selection device used. Since comparisons of whole groups, undivided by sex, can also be made, another nine different analyses are possible. Although the Uniform Guidelines do not require that each of these 53 (44 + 9) adverse-impact analyses be performed for each selection device, they do require that each entity using any selection device maintain and have available for inspection records or other information disclosing the impact that its tests and other selection procedures have upon employment opportunities. Other regulations proposed by EEOC would require that records be kept for a period of two years regardless of whether the selection devices have a demonstrated adverse impact. If there is such an adverse impact, the record keeping and required analyses become even more burdensome.

The failure of an employer to have the required records will permit the federal enforcement agencies to draw an inference of adverse impact of the selection process—assuming the user has an underutilization of a group in the job category as compared to the group's representation in the relevant labor market, or, in the case of jobs filled from within, the applicable work force. There is authority, under Title VII, to allow for such an approach, not only by a federal agency but also by the federal courts.

There is a tempting, but dangerous, alternative offered in the Uniform Guidelines to avoid some of the record-retention burden. Section 4(a) provides that "where there are large numbers of applicants and procedures are administered frequently, such information may be retained on a sample basis, provided that the sample is appropriate in terms of the applicant population and adequate in size." The reason this alternative is dangerous, for all but the most sophisticated and courageous of personnel officers, is that statistical sampling is a precise science and, if not done properly, it can ruin the data base and all possibility of defending the selection device. A decision describing the pitfalls of statistical sampling is *Dickerson* v. *U.S. Steel Corp.*[2]

Furthermore, sampling as permitted by the Uniform Guidelines is a dubious benefit: If the sampling does not demonstrate adverse impact, the sampler is still subject to attack; if it does, the sampler, by exercising this option, has effectively certified that the sample is "appropriate."

ADVERSE IMPACT CONSIDERATIONS

The Uniform Guidelines recognize that blind application of the 80 percent rule to determine adverse impact may create an unfair burden on users who undertake affirmative action. They also recognize that performance pursuant to an affirmative action program is another factor to be considered in determining who will be made the subject of enforcement efforts. Any optimism engendered by these recognitions, however, is tempered by the fact that it is virtually impossible for any user to compel or dictate how a federal agency will exercise its prosecutorial discretion.

The Uniform Guidelines adopt the "bottom-line" approach to assessing adverse impact. This means that if there are a number of selection criteria for making one employment decision, the federal enforcement agencies will look to the end result of all of them when assessing adverse impact. Thus, if hiring is determined by an interview, a number of minimum job requirements, and a skill test, these agencies will not ordinarily seek validation of the skill-test requirement, even though it may be having an adverse impact, if the results of that adverse impact are being negated by other parts of the hiring process so that there is no end-result adverse impact in hiring. This has generally been the law, although not the position previously adopted by EEOC.

The Guidelines, however, provide for two exceptions to the general rule that the government agencies will refrain from prosecuting a testing case unless there is bottom-line adverse impact. The first exception, which is understandable, is a situation in which the selection procedure is a significant factor in the continuation of patterns of assignment of incumbent employees caused by prior discriminatory practices.

The second exception is not understandable, since it refers to situations in which the weight of court decisions and administrative interpretations holds that a specific procedure (such as height or weight requirements) is not job-related. There is irony in this *per se* exception because where specific standards have been struck, it has always first been established that they had an adverse impact on minorities or females. The Uniform Guidelines, therefore, go against the great weight of authority by indicating that even if there is no bottom-line adverse impact, certain specific procedures could still be the subject of administrative or judicial action by the federal agencies.

Practical Approaches to Assessing Adverse Impact

Most users probably lack the resources to conduct 53 separate adverse-impact analyses for each selection device used in each employment unit. As a practical matter, federal agencies probably lack the desire and resources to monitor on such a broad scale anyway. Consequently, both the users and the agencies will probably concentrate the limited time and resources available on the most obvious and significant analyses first, and go on to the more esoteric analyses as time and resources permit.

The most obvious analyses will be comparisons of the performance of females against males and minorities against nonminorities. Generally, either Hispanics or blacks will constitute the largest of the user's minority groups, and an analysis of the larger of these two will be a minimum requirement.

The most obvious irony in the Uniform Guidelines is that so much detail is devoted to directing what must be done when a preliminary determination of adverse impact is made, and so little to assisting personnel officers in making the initial adverse-impact analyses. Given the monumental burden that is placed on users when an adverse-impact analysis is performed and confirms adverse impact, it can be anticipated that personnel officers without detailed instructions relating to the analysis will most frequently find no adverse impact, thereby obviating the bulk of the Uniform Guidelines.

For purposes of adverse-impact analysis,* a practical, relatively unsophisticated first step will be to establish job pools. The term *job pool,* as used here and hereafter, refers to the availability pool for purposes of adverse-impact analyses. It is a group of job titles, all of which have the same minimum entry qualifications. Thus, there might be a "clerical pool—skilled typing and shorthand," as opposed to a "clerical pool—unskilled." The very process of identifying the job pools will require consideration of the factors that will be used to identify the availability pool. That availability pool may be outside the user's work force, or inside, or both.

Once the job pool and availability pool have been established, adverse impact is determined by first arriving at the percentages of people by sex and ethnic background in the availability pool, then calculating the percentage of those by sex and ethnic background placed into a particular job pool, and then comparing these percentages. The lowest percentage should be 4/5 the highest percentage. Thus, for example, if there were 100 placements into the job pool (20 blacks, 10 Hispanics, 70 white; 40 females, 60 males) and 1,000 people in the availability pool (210 blacks, 118 Hispanics, 672 whites; 440 females, 560 males), the placement percentages for these groups would be 9.5 for blacks, 8.4 for Hispanics, 10.4 for white, 9.09 for females, and 10.7 for males. There would be no adverse impact by sex, (the ratio 9.09/10.7 is more than 80 percent), and no adverse impact by race or ethnic group (the relevant ratio for the worst-performing group, Hispanics, to the best-performing group, whites, is 80 percent or more).

It is noteworthy that the factors considered in determining a job pool for adverse-impact analysis are radically different from the factors used in determining a job group under Revised Order 4. The basic function of adverse-impact analysis is different from the utilization analysis under Revised Order 4, the former being designed to determine whether illegal discrimination has occurred, and the latter being oriented toward enhancing the employment status of minorities and females, even absent discrimination.

---

*Detailed descriptions of how to do adverse-impact analysis for each major component of the personnel system appear later in this book. For recruiting, interviewing, and hiring, the subject is covered in Chapter 4; for promotions, transfers, and assignments, in Chapter 5; and for discipline, discharge, and reductions in force, in Chapter 6.

There are two other practical aspects of adverse-impact analysis, both of which seem to have been resolved in favor of users. First, the Uniform Guidelines permit upgrading in job qualifications, except as to persons who have previously suffered discrimination. Thus, users may upgrade the qualifications for a job to include, for example, a high school diploma requirement, if that requirement does not have an adverse impact or can be validated. A second practical aspect that should be helpful to users is the recognition by federal agencies that users may test for skills not immediately required of the candidate as long as it is expected that the candidate will probably need those skills within a reasonable time. A reasonable time could be up to five years.

USER RESPONSIBILITIES

If There Is no Adverse Impact

If there is no "bottom-line" adverse impact, the user is nonetheless required to keep substantial records. However, the probability that government agencies will commence enforcement efforts against such a user is minimal, even for technical noncompliance with the record-keeping provisions.

Whether or not there is adverse impact, even small employers have heavy record-keeping burdens. Users with 100 or fewer employees are still required to maintain and have available records showing, for each year, (1) the number of persons hired, promoted, and terminated for each job categorized by sex and, where appropriate, by race and national origin; (2) the number of applicants for hire and promotion categorized by sex and, where appropriate, by race and national origin; and (3) the selection procedures utilized. When the Uniform Guidelines say "where appropriate," they mean that records should be maintained for each race or national-origin group that constitutes more than 2 percent of the labor force in the relevant labor area.

Employers or users with more than 100 employees are required to maintain and have available, for each job, records or other information showing whether the total selection process for that job, or any part of that selection process, has had an adverse impact on any of the groups for which records are required to be kept. Adverse-impact analyses for such groups are required to be made at least annually if such groups constitute at least 2 percent of the labor force in the relevant labor area, or at least 2 percent of the applicable work force. Perforce, the records required to be kept by an employer or user with more than 100 employees would include all those required of employers or users with 100 or fewer employees.

With respect to the adverse-impact analysis, both the employer or user with 100 or fewer employees and one with more are required to keep records or other information showing which components of the selection process are having an adverse impact. If there is no bottom-line adverse impact, then such information need not be maintained for the individual components except in instances where in the past that selection process has had an adverse impact. In those situations, the employer or user must maintain and have available information on the individual components of the selection process for the periods when the process was having an adverse impact and for at least two years after the adverse impact was eliminated.

Data Are Insufficient to Determine Adverse Impact

In situations where there are too few selections to determine whether a selection procedure is having an adverse impact, users must maintain and have available information on the individual components of the selection process. Such data must be collected until sufficient to demonstrate whether there is or is not adverse impact. The Uniform Guidelines do not address the problem—which could be significant in white-collar jobs—arising where, while the data are being collected, the job function being analyzed substantially changes so that the prior data lose their significance.

If There Is Adverse Impact

The user whose selection procedures are having an adverse impact will probably be the user most closely scrutinized to determine compliance with all parts of the Guidelines.

If there is demonstrated bottom-line adverse impact, the first thing the user must do is demonstrate the validity of the selection process. There are three basic methods for validation recognized by the Uniform Guidelines: criteria validity, content validity, and construct validity; but the Guidelines do acknowledge that "new strategies for showing the validity of selection procedures will be evaluated as they become accepted by the psychological profession."

The process for demonstrating validity is very complicated. Even the attempt to validate a typing test for a secretarial position, a content-validity exercise, places a substantial burden on the user. In such a situation, the user must first do a job analysis. A job analysis, pursuant to the Uniform Guidelines, entails developing a description of the method used to analyze the job. The tasks tangential to the job, the percentage of work time devoted to such tasks, the impact on the work product, and all other information relevant to the job must be compiled and, along with the remainder of the information being described, must be incorporated in a study. The various tasks involved in the job and the importance of these tasks must be weighed one against the other. The setting in which the work takes place, the manner in which knowledge, skills, or abilities are used, and the complexity and difficulty of the knowledge, skills, or abilities

The Uniform Guidelines

must all be described. The dates and locations of the job analysis must be identified, and the name, mailing address, and telephone number of the person who may be contacted for further information about the validity study must be given. The purposes of the analysis and the circumstances in which it was conducted must be provided. Existing selection procedures and cutoff scores must be described. Where the selection procedure purports to measure knowledge, skill, or ability, evidence must be provided that it does measure that characteristic *and* is a representative sample of that characteristic.

To the extent that they apparently require that the selection procedures for which a content-validity approach is adopted must measure the characteristic *and* be a representative sample of it, the Uniform Guidelines proceed far beyond the developed body of law concerning content validity. To the extent that the selection procedure purports to be a sample of the job, the study should make a comparison between the manner, setting, and level of complexity of the selection procedure and the manner, setting, and level of complexity of the actual work situation. If any steps are taken to reduce adverse impact on the basis of race, sex, or ethnic origin, these steps must be described. The measure of reliability of the selection procedure—for example, .05 reliability—should be indicated. The analysis must be conducted for each relevant race, sex, or ethnic subgroup, either *in toto* or on the basis of a statistically reliable sample.

Additionally, the user must demonstrate that alternative selection procedures having a lesser adverse impact have been investigated, and must indicate the available evidence of their impact. If the selection procedure has used a ranking system, the user must demonstrate that it has also considered a cutoff score with no ranking, as well as the adverse impact or lack of it shown by that procedure. The user must demonstrate what kind of work performance or proficiency it expects and accepts from persons in the job and have a selection procedure that relates to that expectancy. The user must demonstrate that it has considered the possibility of differential validity—that is, having one pass score for minorities and/or females and another pass score for nonminorities and males. The user must make these adverse-impact determinations at least annually for each group that constitutes at least 2 percent of the labor force in the relevant labor area, or 2 percent of the applicable work force. This must be done for each job title, and the user must maintain and retain all the records reflecting what it has done and what the result has been.

Even assuming that the validity of the selection procedure is established, the government enforcement effort requires more: It requires validation of each step in the selection process. It requires retesting. It requires continued exploration of alternative selection procedures for each step in the selection process to possibly identify selection procedures having a lesser adverse impact yet still predictive of successful job performance. And, if the job changes to any substantial degree, it requires that the entire process start all over again.

When one considers that the courts have uniformly adopted the content-validity approach without all these support data, it is possible to gain a perspective as to where the government is headed. The government does not propose to face head-on the logical, or apparently logical, defense an employer might assert—namely, that obviously a secretary must know how to type to get the job. Instead, the government orientation appears to be toward attacking the collateral issues surrounding the basic issue. It will not be contending that a secretary who is supposed to type need not type to obtain a job, but rather that the degree of proficiency required by this employer is not needed, or that other work behaviors involved in the performance of a secretarial job are equally important and not as heavily weighted by the validation procedure selected. Following this scenario, the fact that the user might not have validated the skill or speed proficiency required, or considered other skill criteria required, or kept the relevant records, will all be factors that might undercut the legitimacy of the user's defense. Whether the government strategy works depends a great deal upon its selectivity and that of its agents in choosing litigation vehicles. To enhance its position, the government should select for enforcement cases in which there is an egregious adverse impact, and where the employer has not even attempted to follow any of the Uniform Guidelines or kept the records the Guidelines indicate must be kept.

SUMMARY

In the light of the number of selection procedures used by employers and other users (hiring alone usually consists of at least three selection devices—a review of the application, an interview, and at least some minimal qualification), the number of groups or subgroups for which adverse-impact analysis could be required, the number of different ways in which an attempt can be made to establish validation, and the fact that all these considerations relate to each job in the employer's or user's work force, one can appreciate the pressure being exerted upon the users to develop and utilize selection procedures that do not have a bottom-line adverse impact.

FOOTNOTES

[1] Uniform Guidelines, Section 16Q.
[2] 17 EPD (CCH) ¶ 8528 (E.D. Pa. 1978).

Chapter 3

Techniques for Validation

INTRODUCTION

There are three techniques for validation recognized by the Uniform Guidelines on Employee Selection Procedures. These are criterion validity (predictive or concurrent), content validity, and construct validity. In addition, the Uniform Guidelines say that "new strategies for showing the validity of selection procedures will be evaluated as they become accepted by the psychological profession."

Validation under any of the authorized techniques is a multistep process. The improper implementation of any one of the steps negates the attempt at validity, and the test user or testing service must start over. If the incorrectness of one of the steps is established during litigation, it is too late to start over, and the test user loses the validation defense.

CRITERION VALIDITY

Criterion validity is the type of validation preferred by the Uniform Guidelines. There are at least eight separate factors to be considered if a test user proposes to rely upon criterion-validity studies. These are (1) technical feasibility, (2) analysis of the job, (3) criterion measures, (4) representativeness of the sample, (5) statistical relationships, (6) operational use of selection procedures, (7) overstatement of validity findings, and (8) fairness.

Technical Feasibility

Technical feasibility is the determination by the test user of whether criterion-validity studies are appropriate. There should be a large enough sample of people available so that the study can achieve statistical significance, a term discussed below under "Statistical Relationships." At least one expert in the field has said that a group of at least 300 people is required to enable a validation study to gain the necessary statistical significance. The Uniform Guidelines indicate that the test user can group jobs with substantially the same major work behaviors, but any user that does this is just creating another issue in the event there is litigation: whether the jobs the user grouped really did have substantially similar work behaviors.

Another aspect to determining whether this type of validation is technically feasible is whether the sample group available is sufficient to enable the user to obtain a wide enough range of scores. As will be seen later, if there is adverse impact, the user must consider alternatives. One alternative is lowering the test score for minorities or females. If, by doing this, the employer can achieve the same predictability for minorities and/or females as it does for whites or males, then it should do so. Another alternative is lowering the cutoff score to reduce adverse impact. If the sample is too small, these alternative means of implementing the selection cannot be properly established.

The third aspect to determining technical feasibility is whether the test user can devise unbiased, reliable, and relevant measures of job performance. Such measures may be relatively easily established in a garment factory, where workers are paid by the piece, quality-control standards are uniformly and consistently applied, and appropriate records are kept. However, such measures can be virtually impossible to establish for research chemists, where management makes the determination about which imaginative ideas will be researched further and which will not.

Analysis of the Job

In analysis of the job, the test user measures the duties of the job and weighs them according to importance. Thus, the pieceworker job in a garment factory may be measured by quantity of garments produced, number of garments rejected by quality control, absenteeism, tardiness, care and maintenance of machinery, and other work behaviors. Even assuming that the claimant in a lawsuit and the test user can agree on the identity of the work behaviors, it would be unusual if they agreed on the importance to be given to each of them.

The Uniform Guidelines indicate that each of these criterion measures and the methods for gathering the data must be examined for freedom from factors that unfairly alter the scores of any group. In other words, if nonminorities have significantly fewer garment rejections by quality control, but minorities have a higher production rate than nonminorities, one of the issues in a lawsuit will be how great a weight should be attributed to production and how great a weight to number of rejections.

Criterion Measures

Criterion measures are part of the analysis of the job discussed above. The issue at trial will be how the employer measures the criteria, once they are selected. Thus, assuming production rate is established as a proper criterion, how does the employer who is selecting pieceworkers for a garment factory measure the potential to produce? If the potential ability to produce work at a certain rate is measured by a dexterity test, then that test must almost invariably be able to predict who will be the productive employees. Furthermore, to the extent that the employer relies on a paper-and-pencil test, the Uniform Guidelines warn that such tests will be closely reviewed for job relevance.

To the extent that the test user relies upon success in a training program to predict success on the job, the relationship between the content of the training program and performance on the job must be established.

Representativeness of the Sample

Representativeness of the sample means that the candidates who are the subject of the test-validation study must be representative of the candidates normally available in the relevant labor market for the job or jobs in question. Furthermore, the test user is required to take into account the extent to which the specific knowledges or skills that are the primary focus of the test are those that employees learn on the job.

This is the factor that causes the difference between a predictive validation study and a concurrent validation study. It usually leads to the demise of the latter. Many employers, when a charge of discrimination or lawsuit has been filed and they realize their selection system has been having an adverse impact on minorities, try to validate that system. They can seldom do an adequate predictive-validity study, because this entails considering applicants as they apply and it would take too long to hire the requisite number that would constitute a large enough sample. Consequently such employers opt for concurrent-validity studies. They give the test at issue, which they have been using to screen out people from being hired, to those who are already on the job and attempt to validate by using these test scores.

Claimants attack these attempts at concurrent validation by arguing that this approach does not take into account the degree to which these employees are now good performers because they have been doing the job and learning along the way. The claimants also assert that the sample is not representative, since the older, established work force is generally more heavily white, or male, than the candidates available in the relevant labor markets. Using these kinds of arguments, claimants usually prevail when test users try to rely on concurrent-validity studies.

Statistical Relationships

Statistical relationships are the measures of how predictive the test is of success or failure on the job. The Uniform Guidelines state that the relationship between performance and the criterion measure is statistically significant at the 0.05 level of significance. This means that 95 times out of 100, the person who scores high enough on the test to receive the job will perform that job adequately, and that 95 times out of 100, the person who does not score high enough on the test to receive the job would not be able to perform the job successfully.

Because of the latter provision, defenders of tests face a dilemma. On the one hand, the Uniform Guidelines indicate that nothing in the EEO laws require an employer to hire someone who is not qualified. On the other hand, if the employer does not hire people it believes will not be able to perform a job successfully, claimants will attack the validation study because it does not demonstrate to any degree that people who fail the test would also fail in the job. A similar attack is made on concurrent-validity studies because they cannot establish to a statistically significant degree that the person who failed the test and never received the job would have failed in the job had it been awarded to him or her.

Operational Use of Selection Procedures

This is a euphemism meaning that even if the user has succeeded in its validation study thus far, it will not necessarily be legal to continue using the selection device. Even assuming the validity of the selection device, this provision requires that the test user consider alternative selection procedures that have a lesser adverse impact, yet can be validated. Thus, the test user must consider the alternative of lowering the cutoff score on a paper-and-pencil test, or abandoning a policy of hiring first the person who performs best on the test and hiring last the one who performs worst but still passes it.

Overstatement of Validity Findings

All this means is that it is desirable to perform a comprehensive validation study and that it is suspect to rely upon just a few selection criteria or a sample.

Fairness

Fairness means that even if the test user has validated its selection procedure, if that procedure has an adverse impact, the user must still consider other alternatives. Thus, if minority employees generally received lower scores on the test but performed at the same level as nonminorities on the job, the employer should consider lowering the acceptable score for minority candidates. Additionally, if the test results in adverse impact against any group that is a significant factor in the relevant labor market, the user is required to consider other alternatives that reduce adverse impact. Finally, the Uniform Guidelines indicate that a more stringent standard of review will be applied for tests that meet all the requirements and still have an adverse impact. The same kind of review used for validation purposes will be made to assure that each group was comparable in terms of the *actual* job the persons performed, the length of time on the job, and other factors that might have affected the performance rating. While conceding that a test user need not promote or assign people on the basis of group qualifications, the Uniform Guidelines advise that the "user has the obligation otherwise to comply with these guidelines," and then proceed to indicate that the fairness test requires considering "comparable groups."

CONTENT VALIDITY

Content validity is unique among the methods of validation. There is a huge gap between the kinds of tests courts generally find content-valid (and the technical support data they require to support such a legal conclusion) and the technical standards required by the Uniform Guidelines to establish content validity. Thus, an employer can argue that its tests are content-valid and submit no technical support data, and still have a fair chance of establishing the test as valid.

The content-validity approach is inappropriate for tests that rate personality, intelligence, or aptitude. Content validity is appropriate when the test is a representative sample of the content of the job for which the person is being tested. It is also appropriate when the test user can establish that the knowledge, skill, or ability is a necessary prerequisite to successful job performance and can be observed.

The Courts' Approach to Content Validity

Tests such as for typing or stenography are regularly found by courts to be piece-of-the-job tests and, as such, content-valid. Generally, the courts reject claimants' attacks on the collateral aspects of these tests. Thus, claimants will generally not argue that people being hired as secretaries should not be able to type, but rather that typing is just one aspect of the job and that the employer has not considered other aspects. They will also argue that, even though the ability to type is necessary, the proficiency level demanded by the test user has not been established, and that the test user has not considered whether the lowering of qualification scores would have a lesser adverse impact against minorities and/or females.

Such arguments would seriously undermine the validity studies if the test user were purporting to justify the test on the basis of criterion-validity or construct-validity studies, but these kinds of attacks generally do not succeed in court against the content validity defense.

Because there is a de facto lower level of validity proof required of test users to justify continued usage of content-valid tests, there has been an increased usage of such tests and an increasing expansion in the courts' recognition of the kinds of tests that are adaptable to content-validity studies. Thus, in *Hester* v. *Southern Railway Co.*,[1] the SRA verbal test was found to be content-valid. In *Wilson* v. *Woodward Iron Company*,[2] the trial court went a step further. In that case, an oral test was given for promotions; it related to the actual performance of the job and included questions relating to the tools that would be used for the job, the manner in which they would be used, and so forth. The court found the test acceptable as a content-valid selection procedure.

Some employers lack the resources to attempt validation studies and probably do not even know whether their selection procedures are having an adverse impact. Such employers, if they do nothing else, might want to abandon paper-and-pencil tests and consider implementation of simple piece-of-the-job–type tests, which will at least give them the possibility of arguing content validity. In undertaking such an effort, these employers should consider these factors:

1. It will be difficult to argue successfully that a test is content-valid, even to a court, if a training period is necessary to enable people to achieve the minimally acceptable level of performance.

2. If oral questions are asked, applicants should be allowed to answer all the questions, regardless of how poorly they perform on the first few. This is because the test user might want to consider lowering the pass score if it will reduce adverse impact.

3. The questions should relate not only to the ability to perform the job in the abstract, but also to the manner in which the job is performed at that particular user's premises. Thus, if the candidate is being considered for a plumber's job, it may very well be that plumbers generally know what a Stillson wrench is and how it is used, but it may not be necessary to use a Stillson wrench to perform the type of plumbing work that the test user expects the candidate to perform.

4. The same questions should be asked of all candidates. Of course, the questions will have to be changed periodically, but asking the same questions of

all candidates during a given time period will avoid arguments about the degree of difficulty of the questions and disparate treatment of minorities by asking them the harder set of questions. The potential for applicants to become testwise can be reduced by not allowing the test to be taken more than once in any set period of time.

5. Whenever it is feasible, the test user should consider allowing the person to actually do a piece of the work that he or she will be required to do if hired. Thus, if a person is being considered for a pieceworker job in a garment factory, the person might be set down at a machine on the floor, told how that particular machine works and what is to be done, and timed. Of course, the employer in such circumstances should not "test" the person too long or use the garments produced during the test, because that might create problems with the Wage and Hour Division of the U.S. Department of Labor.

If it is feasible, the employer should consider having the directions for machine operation or for completing the test written out. The written directions should also indicate that the employer representative administering the test will answer any questions the candidate has. Prior to the test, the candidate should sign on the bottom of the directions, acknowledging that they have been given and that any questions have been answered. This technique is further assurance against claims of disparate treatment.

Requirements for Content-Validation Studies

The Uniform Guidelines state nine factors that should be considered in creating a content-validation study: (1) appropriateness of content-validity studies; (2) job analysis for content validity; (3) development of selection procedures; (4) standards for demonstrating content validity; (5) reliability; (6) prior training or experience; (7) content validity of training success; (8) operational use; and (9) ranking based on content-validity studies.

Appropriateness of Content-Validity Studies

Appropriateness means that the test is a representative sample of the job, or that the knowledge, skill, or ability to be measured by the test can be "operationally defined" and is a prerequisite to successful job performance. "Operationally defined" means that there is a body of learned information used in the job and that one can observe the need for this knowledge by looking to the work done in the job; or it means that there are skills or abilities that can be observed to be a part of the job and that the test measures those skills or abilities.

The Uniform Guidelines advise that content-validity studies are not appropriate if the selection device purports to measure traits or characteristics such as personality, intelligence, aptitude, common sense, judgment, leadership, or spatial ability. Nor are they appropriate if the selection procedure is testing for knowledges, skills, or abilities that the candidate will be expected to learn on the job.

Job Analysis for Content Validity

The test user must identify the important work behaviors for successful job performance. If the work behaviors are not observable, the analysis should identify and analyze those that can be observed and the observed work products. These work behaviors should constitute most of the job.

This simply means that the test user must be able to demonstrate in some concrete way that the characteristics for which it is testing are essential to successful job performance and that the end result produced by the test can be seen and be seen to be related to successful job performance. Thus, a test user selecting a secretary could try to measure finger dexterity as an important characteristic for a typist, but it would be argued that the relationship between the finger-dexterity test given and the ability to type is not observable. In such situations the test user should rely on the observed work product, such as the sample letter the candidate has been asked to type.

Development of Selection Procedures

This means that the user can develop its own test specifically from the job and job analysis in question, or may rely on a test prepared by someone else.

If the test is one that was prepared by the user at some time in the past, procedures should be established to ensure that the work behaviors for which it tests are still necessary to successful job performance. In other words, the user should check to be sure its plumbers still have to use Stillson wrenches if it is going to ask questions about use of that tool.

While it may be easier to use someone else's test that purports to be content-valid, doing so creates issues. Such a test may be a good instrument for determining in a general way whether someone will perform well as a secretary, but the issue created is whether the same work characteristics for hiring a secretary generally are applicable to the performance of the candidate in the secretarial job the employer wishes to fill.

Standards for Demonstrating Content Validity

The user must be prepared to demonstrate (1) that behavior demonstrated in the test constitutes a representative sample of the behavior required to perform successfully on the job, or (2) that the knowledge, skill, or ability being measured is minimally necessary for successful performance on the job, and that the test used to measure the knowledge, skill, or ability actually does measure such characteristics.

Reliability

Under the Uniform Guidelines, this term does not mean that the validity studies must meet the 0.05 level of statistical significance for content-validity studies. It merely means that "whenever feasible, appropriate statistical estimates should be made of the reliability of the selection procedure."

Prior Training or Experience

Employers who require a certain number of years' experience in a particular field for a particular job are affected by this factor. Not only the necessity of experience, but the necessity of the number of years' experience required must be justified by demonstrating the relationship between the content of the learning or experience and the content of the job for which the training or experience is being required.

Content Validity of Training Success

This means that if the user is considering success in a training program as a selection device for determining whether someone should be hired or promoted, then a relationship between the content of the training program and the content of the job must be demonstrated.

Operational Use

This means that the selection device should not be a measure of duties tangential to the job but rather of those essential to the job.

Ranking Based on Content-Validity Studies

As in the use of criterion validation, the Uniform Guidelines advise users not to use a ranking system unless they can demonstrate that a candidate with a higher pass score on the test is more likely to perform better on the job.

CONSTRUCT VALIDITY

Construct validity is the least used and most complicated type of validation. The Uniform Guidelines require that four factors be considered for construct-validity studies: (1) appropriateness of the construct-validity studies, (2) job analysis for construct-validity studies, (3) relationship to the job, and (4) use of construct-validity studies without new criterion-related evidence.

Appropriateness of the Studies

The Uniform Guidelines warn users away from this type of validation study by advising that it is a relatively new and developing procedure in the employment field, and that the effort to obtain sufficient empirical support is an extensive and arduous effort involving a series of research studies. The Uniform Guidelines do not acknowledge that this type of validation is appropriate for any job or type of job.

Job Analysis for Construct Validity

The job analysis for a construct-validity study should establish the work behaviors required for successful job performance, the critical work behaviors, and the constructs believed to underlie successful performance of these critical work behaviors. Thus, the constructs must support factors found in content- and criterion-validity studies. The construct must be defined. If a group of jobs is being studied together, then they must have in common at least one critical work behavior.

Relationship to the Job

Assuming the user has developed a proper construct, then it must develop a way of accurately measuring that construct. If that is done, validity must be demonstrated by one or more criterion-related studies, proving the relationship between the construct and the work behaviors.

Use of Study Without New Criterion-Related Evidence

The Uniform Guidelines indicate that construct-validity studies will be accepted without the supporting criterion-related evidence only if certain conditions are satisfied: First, a criterion-validity study must have been conducted elsewhere; second, that study must have met the standards of the Uniform Guidelines; third, the incumbents in the user's jobs and the incumbents in the jobs on which the validity study was conducted must have performed substantially the same major work behaviors. This must be demonstrated by job analyses of both groups.

FOOTNOTES

[1] 497 F.2d 1374 (5th Cir. 1974).
[2] 362 F. Supp. 886 (N.D. Ala. 1973).

PART 2

STANDARDS AND SYSTEMS FOR PREVENTING LIABILITY

Chapter 4

Standards for Recruiting, Interviewing, and Hiring

INTRODUCTION

The minimum qualifications for hiring usually determine the manner in which recruiting and interviewing are conducted. If a standard is acceptable and legal for purposes of hiring, it can be made the subject of interview questions and recruiting requirements. On the other hand, if a standard is not legal, or is suspect for purposes of hiring, then the use of it in questions or discussions during any part of the hiring process renders such questions or discussions also suspect, and places upon the user the burden of defending that standard as part of the hiring, recruiting, or interviewing process. The basic rule is that any standard having an adverse impact, either generally or in the experience of a particular employer, union, or employment agency, might have to be defended.

In this chapter and the following three chapters, personnel actions are discussed in the chronological order in which they usually develop. Standards are identified that have been, or probably will be, subjects for contest and litigation. The analysis describes the manner in which courts or administrative agencies have treated these standards, and defenses that have been raised by employers, unions, or employment agencies, together with an indication of whether those defenses were successful or unsuccessful.

The fact that a standard has an adverse impact on some protected group does not automatically render that standard illegal. The employer, labor organization, employment agency or any other entity utilizing the standard still has the right to defend it on the basis of business necessity, or as a bona fide occupational qualification (BFOQ).*

An important factor to consider with regard to those standards identified in this and the following three chapters is that if the entity utilizing the selection device chooses to forego use of that device in assessing any particular group of candidates, such as minorities or females, it would be discriminatory for it to continue to use the device to screen out nonminorities or males. See *McDonald v. Santa Fe Trail Transportation Co.*[1]

SELECTION DEVICES AT ISSUE

The discussion that follows is of the selection devices most likely to be placed in issue by each of the protected groups.

Age Standards

The U.S. Department of Labor (referred to hereafter as "Labor") had indicated that questions about date of birth or age on an application form are suspect. It strongly suggested that, when such information is sought, there be a legend on that application form (or whatever form is used to seek such information) to the effect that "the Age Discrimination in Employment Act of 1967 prohibits discrimination on the basis of age with respect to individuals who are at least 40 but less than 70 years of age." Labor had indicated that certain other terms used in advertising are also suspect—"age 25 to 35," "young," "boy," "girl," "college student," "recent college grad," "age 40 to 50," "age 50," "age over 65," "retired person," and "supplement your pension"—because their use may have a chilling effect on the application for employment of people within the protected age group, or may indicate that certain people in that group are not as preferred as others in the group. Under the Age Discrimination in Employment Act of 1967 (ADEA), it is discriminatory not only to prefer people who are not between the ages of 40 and 70, but also to prefer one group within the protected age category over other groups in that category.

In a major lawsuit dealing with help-wanted advertisements and their impact on persons protected by the ADEA, the Fourth Circuit Court of Appeals ruled on a number of terms used in recruiting. In the case of *Hodgson v. Approved Personnel Services, Inc.*,[2] that court held that the following terms, when

---

*The terms *business necessity* and *BFOQ*, and their functions, were described in the Introduction preceding Chapter 1.

used in help-wanted ads, violated federal law: "recent college grad," "recent high school grad," "one/two years out of college," "any recent degree," "recent math grad," "prefer recent technical school grad," "recent sharp grad," "girls," "career girls," "school-age applicants," and "college-age applicants."

In the same case, the court held that the use of certain terms was nondiscriminatory for recruiting purposes in the context in which they were used. These terms are "junior," when used to describe the subordinate status of the job rather than the age of the applicant sought; "recent graduates," because it was interpreted to mean prospective customers of the employment agency coming into the job market (but the same words, if used to refer to the specific employment opportunity, would violate the ADEA); "returning military veterans," because the ads were timed to the end of the Vietnam War and not all returning veterans were young; "first job" or "excellent first job"; "young executive," when identifying the person for whom the applicant would be working, not the type of person who was being sought; "young office group," when identifying the group of people with whom the applicant would be working; "athletically inclined"; and "All-American type."

The use of the term "girl" in a newspaper ad was found to be discriminatory because the term meant that a young person was being sought, said the court in another case, *Hodgson* v. *Career Counsellors International, Inc.*[3] That term, if used as a recruiting or screening device, would also violate the provisions of Title VII. An unusual decision by a federal judge in New York held that the use of the terms "college students," "girls," "boys," and "June graduates" in ads was not violative of the ADEA. The court reasoned in that case, *Brennan* v. *Paragon Employment Agency, Inc.*,[4] that use of those terms was justifiable because it was grounded on "reasonable factors other than age"—namely, encouraging young people to work. That decision is without precedent and should be relied upon only if absolutely necessary, since the court had already ruled that the complaint was insufficient for other reasons, rendering its remarks about use of these terms gratuitous (dicta).

Recruiting at colleges is a selection device that may have an adverse impact on people in the projected age groups, because most of the people graduating from college are not within the protected group. Nevertheless, in a case where that device was placed in issue, *Mistretta* v. *Sandia Corp.*,[5] the court held that concentrated recruiting efforts on college campuses did not violate the ADEA. There was nothing inherently suspicious in campus recruiting, held the court, because the available labor market would be expected to come from recent graduates who are job hunting, rather than from protected-age-group people who would normally be established in more permanent positions, and because there was no evidence presented that would show whether applicants in the protected age group had less success in finding employment with the employer than applicants generally for that employer.

Despite that decision, it is possible that there are employers, such as law firms, who will not hire anybody other than those coming out of college or graduate school. These employers argue that they follow that practice because they want to train the new hires their way and not have to correct other employers' mistakes. It is very possible that such a practice, if it relies on such a rationale, would be held to be discriminatory. Employers who do recruit predominantly at college campuses, for the reasons given by the court in *Mistretta,* might consider also notifying the alumni associations of those colleges where it recruits that it would accept for consideration applications or résumés of alumni. It is very probable that such alumni are already earning more than what might be offered by the employer to candidates just starting out, but even so, the fact that the employer did notify such recruiting sources would be very helpful if this standard became the subject of litigation.

Physical-condition standards have been the subject of litigation. Some employers preclude from consideration people over a certain age because they feel that, starting out at such a late age in that career, such people could not adequately perform their jobs over the course of their careers. In *Usery* v. *Tamiami Trail Tours, Inc.,*[6] the company had refused to consider applicants over 40 for the position of bus driver. The company was able to defend the standard as valid by introducing evidence showing that it took a certain number of years to reach a certain level of proficiency as a bus driver, that the body inevitably suffered physiological degeneration when one became older, and that this degeneration would affect performance, possibly endangering the safety of passengers. The company was able to offer motor-vehicle accident records to support its position and medical testimony establishing that there was really no effective, practical way to distinguish the debilitating effects of old age on an individual basis. The age requirement for bus drivers was also sustained in another case, *Hodgson* v. *Greyhound Lines, Inc.*[7]

However, this selection standard was held discriminatory in another case, *Aaron* v. *Davis.*[8] The defendant had tried to terminate firemen who had reached the age of 62 because of the greater risk of injury to themselves and others that their continued work would impose. Similarly, in *Rodriguez* v. *Taylor,*[9] it was held that the city of Philadelphia had discriminated against the plaintiff on the basis of his age by refusing to consider his application for the position of security officer. There was a requirement that applicants for the position be less than 41 years of age, and Mr. Rodriguez was 46. Again, the city was not able to justify the imposition of this standard.

In a circuit-court case, *Arritt* v. *Grisell,*[10] the city had a requirement that candidates for the police force be not more than 35 years of age. The circuit court indicated that the city would have to show that people over 35 could not perform, or that it would be impossible to consider applications on an individualized basis and that people starting a career at an age over 35 would generally not be able to perform without endangering themselves and others.

In administering personnel policies, it is very important to remember that there are many state-law prohibitions against age discrimination. In New York, for example, the protected age group is the entire group from 18 to 65, and the employer cannot discriminate for or against any one on the basis of age. Consequently, any standard that might have an adverse and disparate impact against younger people would also have to be assessed. In California, on the other hand, there is no top limit on the protected age group. There, as in Alaska, Connecticut, Delaware, the District of Columbia, Hawaii, Illinois, Iowa, Maine, Maryland, Montana, Nevada, New Jersey, New Mexico, South Carolina, and West Virginia, it is unlawful to refuse to hire or employ, or to discharge, dismiss, reduce, suspend, or demote any person over the age of 40 on the basis of age. Consequently, employees cannot be involuntarily retired because of age.

The problem of the future for personnel administrators will be administering a nationwide personnel policy when there are states such as these, which have no top on the protected group. This might be made especially difficult when career paths take an employee from a state where there is no top on the protected group to another state where there is a top, and vice versa.

Transaction Analysis

In assessing compliance with the age standards not only for hiring purposes but also for promotion, termination, benefits, and other personnel practices, it will be helpful for employers to know exactly how the government is going to analyze their compliance. In the U.S. Department of Labor's *Field Operations Handbook,* available through the Freedom of Information Act, the Labor Department directed its compliance officers to follow a ten-step "transaction analysis."

First, the compliance officer is to examine the chain of events, circumstances, and decisions related to some particular aspect of a person's employment status. For example, hire, promotion, or discharge may be an end product for the person in the transaction being examined. Second, the compliance officer is then to examine the universe of people who may be positively or negatively affected by the transaction, examining each decision in the process leading up to the final event in the transaction and determining which employees went on to the next step in the process and which did not. Third, the officer is then to compare the source of those involved at the beginning of the transaction with those involved at the end of the transaction; for example, those who successfully completed the transaction, who were hired, promoted, or discharged. Fourth, if a pattern of age discrimination is then established, the compliance officer looks for possible defenses on the part of the employer. Fifth, having identified the decision point where age is a factor, the officer then looks at the criteria allegedly used in making the decision. Moreover, the compliance officer is supposed to examine the application of the criteria and how the criteria are being measured. Sixth, the officer will then determine whether the criteria have been uniformly applied without regard to age. Seventh, the compliance officer will determine whether the measurement of the criteria was slanted toward youth. Eighth, the officer will determine whether the criteria accurately measure qualities necessary for the performance of the job, or if they merely adversely affect older people. Ninth, the compliance officer is then advised to look beyond the source of the people involved to determine any other factors affecting the decision; for example, looking to ads placed in various newspapers to determine how the applicant pool was obtained. The tenth and final stage is a two-step process involving, first, identifying areas where Age Discrimination in Employment Act violations may appear and, second, defining particular transactions where discrimination has occurred.

The *Field Operations Handbook* suggests that the following groups usually reflect results of certain transactions:

1. Hires—by department, occupation, management, nonmanagement, trainees, full-time, part-time, men, women, minorities
2. Promotions—by department, occupation, management, nonmanagement, trainees, full-time, part-time, men, women, minorities
3. Terminations—by department, occupation, management, nonmanagement, trainees, full-time, part-time, men, women, minorities, quits, fires, retirements
4. Trainees—by department, occupation, management, nonmanagement, trainees, full-time, part-time, men, women, minorities

The *Handbook* also advises looking at other transaction groups, such as transfers between departments, jobs, or shifts; and it says that in regard to time periods, the years should be broken down into quarters, in addition to examination of whole years.

This approach to analyzing an age-discrimination claim is more thorough and more fair than the adverse-impact approach described in the Introduction to this book and now incorporated in the Uniform Selection Guidelines. Since the Guidelines have been adopted by the U.S. Department of Labor, and since EEOC has assumed jurisdiction of enforcing the ADEA as of July 1979, the continued viability of the detailed "transaction analysis" approach may be questionable.

Race and National-Origin Standards

In an EEOC decision, the commission held that it was improper to refuse to hire a Hispanic American as a store manager on the basis of his *appearance* and his *accent,* because his accent was peculiar to his national origin.[11] An EEOC decision does not have the precedential value of case law; it is simply EEOC's interpretation of what the law should be.

In the area of national-origin discrimination, EEOC has once before issued its interpretation of what the law should be, and has had that interpretation rejected. In *Espinoza* v. *Farah Manufacturing Co.*,[12] the Supreme Court rejected EEOC's position—namely, that it was discriminatory to refuse to hire somebody on the basis of lack of citizenship because this selection device was more likely to have an adverse and disparate impact on persons of foreign national origin. However, in *Espinoza,* the Supreme Court indicated that nothing in Title VII prohibits discrimination on the basis of citizenship. It certainly helped that in that situation, 92 percent of the employees at the facility were Mexican-Americans or Mexicans who had become American citizens. The person who was refused hire on the basis of lack of citizenship was a Mexican and not a citizen.

On the issue of accent, it can be expected that if the employer had a representative percentage of Hispanics in its work force and the charging party was Hispanic, the employer could successfully demonstrate that accent was not a subterfuge for national-origin discrimination, just as citizenship was held not to be a subterfuge for national-origin discrimination in *Espinoza.* On the other hand, if the employer did not have a representative percentage of Hispanics in its work force and the applicant rejected on the basis of accent was Hispanic, then the employer might have to come forward and justify the requirement that the candidate not have an accent on the basis of business necessity. In a decision issued by a federal trial court in New York, *Mejia* v. *New York Sheraton Hotel,*[13] it was held that a greater proficiency in the English language than that demonstrated by the claimant was a business necessity for a job the claimant sought in the cashier's department, and that the language *proficiency standard* did not operate to exclude minority candidates at a disproportionately high rate.

Arrest-record inquiries were made the subject of a court action in *Gregory* v. *Litton Systems, Inc.*[14] In that case, Gregory was rejected for hire because he had an arrest record. Gregory was black and claimed that the use of the arrest record as a standard for determining selection of candidates had an adverse and disparate impact on blacks. At about the same time that Gregory was litigating his case, UCLA was completing a study to determine the incidence of arrest for blacks and other minorities, as opposed to the incidence of arrests of whites. The study demonstrated that blacks and other minorities were arrested, without being convicted, far more frequently than whites. On that basis, the court struck down the arrest-record standard of the employer, after the employer had been given the opportunity to demonstrate that there was a business necessity for refusing to hire persons with an arrest record, and had failed to meet the burden of proof.

The use of *conviction information* has also been the subject of litigation. In *Green* v. *Missouri Pacific Railroad,*[15] the plaintiff, a black, was able to demonstrate that blacks were convicted of crimes far more frequently than whites. The defendant employer had a standard policy of refusing to hire anyone convicted of any crime for any job. In *Green,* the court struck down the standard, after giving the employer the opportunity to demonstrate that it was a business necessity to have this standard and the employer had failed to meet the burden of proof. The court did indicate that the employer could consider convictions for specific crimes in evaluating a candidate for specific jobs. Thus, in another case, *Richardson* v. *Hotel Corporation of America*,[16] the defendant successfully defended its refusal to hire Richardson, a black, because of his convictions. In that case, the job for which Richardson was being considered was that of bellhop, which required that the employee have keys to the rooms in the hotel. Richardson had been convicted of theft and receiving stolen property. The defense was probably helped also by the fact that although Richardson was rejected, the candidate who was ultimately hired was also black but had had no convictions. (Subsequent to the decision in *Richardson,* the U.S. Court of Appeals for the Fifth Circuit held that the award of the job at issue to a person of the same national origin as the complainant mooted the claim of the complainant. *DeVolld* v. *Bailor.*)[17]

The determination of what conviction will bar a person from what job will have to be made on a case-by-case basis. What is known, however, is that a standard policy of refusing to hire anyone with any conviction for any job may create liability under Title VII. Additionally, some states such as New York prohibit discrimination in employment against prior offenders.

Following through on the criminal aspect of selection standards, the use of information regarding the *type of military discharge* a candidate received may create litigation problems for an employer. In *Dozier* v. *Chupka*,[18] the plaintiff, a black, claimed that he had been denied a position because he had a dishonorable discharge and that use of that standard had an adverse impact against blacks. The court struck down the employer's hiring requirement because the plaintiff had proved that the standard had an adverse and disparate impact against blacks and no proof was offered by the employer that the criterion was related to job performance. This represents only one district-court decision; in another, the employer successfully withstood a motion for summary judgment, despite evidence that fewer whites than nonwhites received less than honorable discharges. *Lewis* v. *Western Airlines, Inc.*[19] Nevertheless, employers would probably be well advised not to automatically disqualify dishonorably discharged candidates for all jobs, but rather to pursue the reasons for the dishonorable discharge to determine how they relate to the job for which the candidate is being considered.

The use of *credit references, garnishment information,* or *financial-status information* is another subject that might have EEO implications. EEOC has indicated in its decisions that any policy that considers financial status violates Title VII because minorities have a lesser financial status than nonminorities.[20] EEOC has also held that a policy of screening job applicants on the basis of credit reference violates Title VII.[21] It decided that there was reasonable cause to believe discrimination occurred when an employer refused to hire a black as a computer operator, in part because the candidate had a poor credit rating, since the use of credit information discriminated against Negroes.[22]

And finally, EEOC has indicated that if prior-employer reference checks are made and a minority candidate is being rejected on the basis of a bad reference, the candidate should be given the opportunity to explain the bad reference, and that it is discriminatory not to afford that opportunity.[23] The rationale given by EEOC for this decision is that—although it cites absolutely no statistical support for such a theory—it is much more likely that a prior employer would give a bad reference to a former black employee, for discriminatory reasons, than to a former white employee. Of course, if an employer gives minorities the opportunity to explain bad references from prior employers, it must afford the same opportunity to nonminority candidates.

In court, EEOC has not succeeded in having the judiciary accept its positions on these subjects. In *EEOC* v. *National Academy of Sciences*,[24] the court held that EEOC had not been able to introduce any evidence to establish any disparity in the treatment accorded black and white applicants and had furnished no support for the theory that the use of reference checks had an adverse impact on black employment applicants. The employer in *National Academy of Sciences* had requested information from prior employers of candidates concerning the nature of an applicant's former employment, the term of service, an evaluation of the quantity and quality of work performed, attendance and punctuality, personal problems affecting the employee's work, particularly strong and weak points, and whether the applicant would be rehired by the former employer. The purpose of the form was to verify the information the applicant had provided relative to his or her credentials, and to provide additional information concerning the applicant's qualifications as reflected in prior jobs. The employer introduced a validation study that the court found to have established a significant relationship between the reference-checking procedure and the work behavior and turnover rate on the job. Additionally, the court noted that adverse references did not automatically screen out candidates and that the percentage of black and white candidates with adverse references who were hired was very close. It also noted that the U.S. Department of Labor used the same procedure in making qualification inquiries of applicants for employment from outside the department and that the form had been developed by the Labor Department's Office of Employment Policy and Standards.

In view of the facts that (1) the Department of Labor uses such a form; (2) the Office of Management and Budget, as was noted by the court in *National Academy of Sciences*, required the agencies to take care to ensure that persons hired were qualified and trustworthy; and (3) at least one court has sustained the policy of checking credit references—whether or not the candidate is given an opportunity to rebut such references—it would appear once again that EEOC's interpretation of the meaning of Title VII has been rejected. However, employers who intend to use such selection standards as credit references would be well advised to pattern their policy on that approved in *National Academy of Sciences.*

EEOC has also held that it is unlawful to refuse to hire or terminate an employee who has *lied on an application form* if the employee has lied about something that EEOC feels the employer should not be asking about. However, the courts have uniformly upheld employer policies that require termination for employees who lie on their application forms.[25]

Educational requirements have been the subject of constant litigation. As a general rule, an employer should be wary of having an absolute rule that one must have a high school diploma, or two years of college, or a college degree, for any job. The leading case on educational requirements was *Griggs v. Duke Power Co.,*[26] in which the Supreme Court struck down the high school requirement for certain jobs. In that case, the plaintiffs were able to demonstrate that 34 percent of the white males in North Carolina, where the employer was located, had high school diplomas, whereas only 12 percent of the black males had high school diplomas. Moreover, it was shown that prior to the effective date of Title VII, the employer had not required a high school diploma for these jobs, that there were people performing these jobs successfully even though they did not have a high school diploma, and that, after the effective date of Title VII, the employer had not only imposed that educational requirement but also instituted a paper-and-pencil testing system. The employer, in defense, could not establish the business necessity of requiring a high school diploma, and the standard was struck down. Subsequently, and in similar circumstances, the requirement was struck down in *Watkins v. Scott Paper Co.;*[27] *Stallworth v. Monsanto Co.;*[28] *United States v. Georgia Power Co.;*[29] *Pettway v. American Cast Iron Pipe Co.;*[30] and *Stevenson v. International Paper Co.*[31] See also *James v. Stockham Valves & Fittings Co.,*[32] in which a similar requirement was struck down as being discriminatory until the company could prove that it was essential to the safety and efficiency of the plant; *Donnell v. General Motors Corp.;*[33] and many other cases.

Municipalities, especially, have sought to defend educational requirements, with varying results. In *Dozier v. Chupka,*[34] the requirement of a high school diploma for firefighters was found to have an adverse impact against blacks as a group and not to be defensible on the grounds of business necessity. In *Castro v. Beecher,*[35] the high school diploma requirement for policemen was upheld, even though it had a disparate impact on minorities. The court found it a business necessity. In *League of United Latin American Citizens v. City of Santa Ana,*[36] the requirement of a high school diploma for employment as a fireman was struck down because it was found not justified by business necessity; such a requirement was sustained for the job of a policeman because it was justified by the business needs of that job.

College-degree requirements have also been the subject of court attention. In *Spurlock v. United Airlines, Inc.,*[37] the court upheld the college-degree requirement for the job of airline pilot. A main consideration was the fact that the safety of large numbers of people was involved. It is evident that when an employer can put forth a defense demonstrating that the job at issue places the safety of others into the hands of the candidate, the courts are less likely to require strict validation and more likely to permit the standard to be retained even though it might have a disparate impact on minorities.

There is a significant outstanding question still unresolved regarding educational requirements. Should the courts look to the experience of a particular employer or to external work-force figures for statistics in determining whether or not the standard has an adverse impact? Most of the cases rely on the latter.

Donnell v. *General Motors Corp., supra,* illustrates the general rule. There, statistics showed that 27.9 percent of the black males and 49.1 percent of the white males over the age of 14 in the relevant hiring area had completed four years of high school. The court held that requiring a high school diploma for admission to the company's apprenticeship training program had a disparate impact on blacks. The company attempted to justify the requirement by demonstrating that the skilled trades required specialized knowledge, especially in the area of mathematics, and that two studies it had performed validated the diploma requirement. The court rejected the validation studies, one reason being that the performance of the class of applicants that met the educational requirements had not been compared with the performance of the class of applicants that failed to meet the educational requirements. This was impossible, since the employer was not permitting people without high school diplomas to become apprentices. Therefore, the attempted justification by the company failed.

A significant case, which adopts an approach different from *Donnell* and the majority, is *Townsend* v. *Nassau County Medical Center.*[38] In *Townsend,* the Second Circuit found that plaintiff had not properly placed in issue the validity of the college-degree requirement for a laboratory technician's position because she had not demonstrated that the degree requirement had an adverse and disparate impact against minorities, based upon the experience of that particular employer. It held that plaintiff's introduction of general statistics showing the percentage of whites and the percentage of minorities possessing a college degree in the external work force was not sufficient to place in issue the validity of the college-degree requirement for the job in question.

The Supreme Court, by denying *certiorari* in *Townsend,* left the area muddled. At the very time that *Townsend* was being decided, the U.S. Court of Appeals for the Fifth Circuit decided *Payne* v. *Travenol Laboratories, Inc.,*[39] holding that general external statistics concerning potential adverse impact of educational requirements were sufficient to establish the plaintiff's case. In *Payne,* the employer had required a college degree for the position of systems, traffic, or scheduling analyst.

In the meantime, in *EEOC* v. *E.I. du Pont de Nemours & Co.,*[40] the district court sustained a high school diploma requirement for the position of laboratory technician and for other highly rated clerical and technical jobs, by approaching the issue from the back end. That court noted that, statistically, a high percentage of those who performed these jobs nationally had a high school diploma. Therefore, the court reasoned, there must be some correlation between education and ability to perform these jobs. The low percentage of minorities in these positions could be explained, said the court, by the fact that only 33 1/3 percent of the blacks in the Wilmington area had high school diplomas. Although the facts of this particular case might sustain the result on another theory, it would appear that the court's approach was inconsistent with developed law.

Unless an employer or some other selecting entity feels very strongly about the validity of a high school or college-degree requirement, it might be advisable to substitute the term "degree or equivalent experience" for a plain degree requirement and closely monitor applicant flow ratios to determine whether or not the requirement is having an adverse impact. Applicant flow ratios are discussed in more detail later in this chapter.

Considering their widespread use, it is surprising to find that there have not been more cases decided involving *experience requirements* as selection devices. This is not to say that some experience might not be fully justifiable, but it might be very difficult to validate a certain level of experience—say, one, two, or three years—as necessary for satisfactory performance of the job. Probably one reason there have not been greater attacks on the experience requirements is that there is very little demographic data to demonstrate that a substantial experience requirement is having a disparate impact on minorities and females. When experience requirements do develop in a context in which they can be attacked, the attacks can succeed. For example, in *United States v. Operating Engineers, Local 3*,[41] the U.S. Department of Justice had commenced an action against the union for refusing to permit minorities to become members. A consent decree was entered into by the government and the union, but some of the named private plaintiffs continued to prosecute on other issues.

One of the requirements left standing after the consent decree was that a person undergo 4,000 hours of training before becoming a journeyman. Because this included some classroom and some on-the-job training and was administered by the union itself, the private plaintiffs felt that it would be used as a continuing barrier to prevent them from becoming journeymen. When the union was called upon to defend the 4,000-hour program, it failed in its proof except with respect to one job, that of surveyor. The court indicated that it was inclined to modify the training requirement and reduce it to no longer than six months. There were no further decisions published in this case.

The court in *Operating Engineers* recognized that at least one court, in *Dobbins v. Local 212, IBEW*,[42] had ruled that objective criteria—such as two years' experience—must be the only criteria for referral, thereby de facto recognizing that experience was a valid job requirement. However, the length of experience and training were not at issue in *Dobbins*.

In *Taylor* v. *Safeway Stores, Inc.*,[43] the experience requirement was also upheld. There, the court held that the employer was not violating Title VII by giving preference to warehouse applicants with warehousing experience, despite the plaintiff's claim that whites were more likely to have such experience. In *Barnett* v. *W.T. Grant Co.*,[44] an experience requirement of two years and an age requirement of at least 23 years were upheld for road driving jobs, despite the claim of disparate impact.

When there has been, or can be offered, proof that minority-group persons are not as likely to have the experience because of prior discrimination, then the courts are more likely to strike down the experience requirement. Thus, in *Crockett* v. *Green*,[45] the requirement that applicants for "prevailing wage" positions in city or school-district skilled craft jobs complete a formal apprenticeship program and have a certain number of years' experience as journeymen was struck down because it had a disproportionate impact upon blacks and could not be justified on the basis of business necessity.

Because so many unions have had, or are alleged to have had, discriminatory practices against minorities, it may be wise for an employer who is seeking people with experience to relate that skill requirement not to union jargon, such as "journeyman," but rather to the basic skill or experience. It might even be advisable for the employer to give oral tests in which the applicant is asked questions about the fruits of experience—that is, the skill involved, the tools used, the manner in which they would be used, and so on. In doing so, the employer should be sure it is asking questions that test not only knowledge of the abstract skill but also knowledge of that skill as it is exercised in that employer's workplace. Under such circumstances, these oral tests have been sustained as being content-valid and permissible. See *Wilson* v. *Woodward Iron Co.*[46]

Grooming codes and appearance standards have generally been upheld, even though arguments have been made that some minority groups are more inclined to have mustaches than are nonminorities. *Willingham* v. *Macon Telegraph Publishing Co.*[47] Thus, in *Ramsey* v. *Hopkins*,[48] the court found no evidence that the wearing of a mustache was a cultural symbol for members of the Negro race. However, if the policy regarding grooming or appearance is being applied more stringently to blacks than to whites, it is, of course, a violation of Title VII. See *United States* v. *Leeway Motor Freight, Inc.*[49] Additionally, EEOC Decision No. 71-2444 states that an employer's hair standards should take into account the difference in texture of Negro hair.

A case involving *medical standards* shows how the pure and theoretical application of adverse impact analysis will sometimes be ameliorated with a sprinkling of common sense. In *Smith* v. *Olin Chemical Corp.*,[50] the plaintiff was a black who was hired as a probationary employee for a manual laborer job. At the end of his probationary period, he was given a physical examination that showed he had a bad back, which disqualified him from permanent employment, and he was discharged. The plaintiff claimed that his bad back was the result of sickle-cell anemia, a blood disease found almost exclusively in descendants of tribes living in malarial regions in Africa. The district court had dismissed this case, but a panel of the Fifth Circuit reversed, indicating that if plaintiff could prove what he claimed—that the standard had a disparate impact—then the employer would have to justify the medical standard on the basis of business necessity. Upon reconsideration, the Fifth Circuit sitting *en banc* (with all the active members of the court) reversed the decision of the panel and ruled that a job requirement that an employee have a good back is so job-related that an employer is not required to introduce evidence showing the business necessity for it. As an alternative basis for its decision, the full court sustained the employer's defense of business necessity because of the manifest relationship between having a good back and performing manual labor, indicating that it was obvious that this was not a situation in which the employer was asserting the medical standard as a subterfuge to screen out minority candidates and discriminate.

Height and weight requirements have also been the subject of litigation, basically because they have a disparate impact on Hispanics, Orientals, and females. They will generally be struck down or modified if the employer cannot demonstrate a relationship between the height requirement and performance of the job. Thus, in *Davis* v. *County of Los Angeles*,[51] the height requirement was struck down for the fire department because it disqualified 45 percent of the otherwise eligible Mexican-American applicants. Similarly, in *League of United Latin American Citizens* v. *City of Santa Ana, supra,* the height requirement for firemen and policemen was struck down because it was a substantial barrier to Mexican-Americans.

Nepotism rules or *grandfather clauses* have generally been struck down where there is proof that minority-group people have previously been excluded from entry into the organization. Most of these cases have arisen in situations where the union required that to become a member, one had to have a relative who was a member. See, generally, *Vogler* v. *McCarty, Inc.*[52]

Paper-and-pencil tests had been the subject of continuous litigation even before the Supreme Court's decision in *Griggs* v. *Duke Power Co., supra*. The general standard is that if a test has an adverse impact on a protected group, the employer will be required to justify continued use of the test on the basis of business necessity. Basically, this means validating the test—that is, showing that it is job-related. In Appendix B at the back of this book, there is a listing of cases in which various paper-and-pencil tests, and other named tests, have been the subject of litigation and court or administrative decisions. It would obviously be advisable for any entity that screens applicants for employment by means of a paper-and-pencil test to familizarize itself with court decisions addressing that test.

Sex Standards

The principles described in the Introduction to this book relating to the manner in which tests or other selection standards are assessed apply to sex standards just as much as to any other standards. However, the application of

Title VII and other employment discrimination statutes to the workplace has been most troublesome in matters relating to sex standards. This is at least partially because prior generations have grown up with male legislators and male executives seeking to "protect" females, and establishing sophisticated systems to do so. Just how deep and how pervasive these systems have become is realized only when the employer, or other entity selecting a candidate, faces a charge and investigation evolving from a sex-discrimination claim.

One of the earliest cases decided by the Supreme Court involving sex discrimination considered a company rule that precluded from hire women with school-age children. In that case, *Phillips* v. *Martin Marietta Corp.*,[53] the company sought to defend the rule by arguing that it did not preclude *all* women from consideration for the job, just those with school-age children, and that there was a business necessity for the requirement. Unfortunately for the employer, these arguments were based on stereotypes and were rejected. The employer was operating on the assumption that the obligation to care for children was imposed only on females, since it was hiring males with school-age children.

The clear implication of *Phillips* v. *Martin Marietta* is that no standard can be imposed only on females and not also on males. This means, specifically, that a woman cannot be precluded from consideration for a job because she is divorced, if a divorced man is not precluded; that a woman having an affair must be treated the same way as a man who is having an affair; that a woman who has illegitimate children must be treated the same way as the father of illegitimate children; that a female cannot be precluded from consideration for a job because it requires attending conventions, or socializing; and that an employer is not supposed to consider what a woman's husband does for a living if it does not consider what a male candidate's wife does for a living.

Some of these principles cause some professional consultants on employee selection to shudder. They would argue, for example, that the employer should know what a woman's husband does because the husband may be engaged in an occupation that would require him to relocate in connection with a subsequent move up his own corporate ladder. When one points out that this is an illegal consideration under Title VII, consultants argue that this country still has matrimonial rules and laws that create a legal obligation on, or certain presumptions against, the female who refuses to accompany her husband when he relocates for business.

Many of these conflicts have been resolved by the unanimous rejection of state protective laws. The employer who follows such rules now does so at its peril.

As in the area of race discrimination, the burden in a sex-discrimination claim will be on the plaintiff attacking the standard to demonstrate that it has an adverse and disparate impact on females or that it is applied only against females, not against males, the disparate treatment theory. Only then will the employer have to defend the standard as being necessary for the conduct of business. Thus, in *Coopersmith* v. *Rouderbush*,[54], a requirement of *recent ex-*

perience was placed in issue by the plaintiff. Plaintiff claimed that the requirement of recent experience had an adverse and disparate impact on females because they are more likely to suspend employment to raise children, and then return to school in preparation for a professional career or resume a career they had abandoned. The court rejected the argument and held that the employer's requirement that the candidate be a recent law school graduate or have recent experience in the practice of law did not violate Title VII—that this appeared to be valid job-related requirement.

Reasonable *appearance standards* are permissible under Title VII even if they differ as applied to males and females. Thus, an employer can require males to keep their hair a certain length but have no similar restriction for females. See, *e.g., Fagan* v. *National Cash Register Co.*[55] Similarly, an employer's policy forbidding female employees to wear pants in the executive office of the employer's business was upheld as not constituting sex discrimination. *Lanigan* v. *Bartlett and Company Grain.*[56] The *Lanigan* court rejected the argument that the dress code policy significantly affected employment opportunities for women by perpetuating a sexist, chauvinistic attitude in employment. The court concluded that since the plaintiff had failed to establish a prima facie case of discrimination, the employer was under no obligation to prove that there was a business necessity for the policy.

In an unusual case, it was held discriminatory to have a dress policy that requires female employees to wear "career ensembles" and permits male employees to wear business suits. In *Carroll* v. *Talman Federal Savings & Loan Association,*[57] a split court held that the imposition of two entirely separate dress codes constituted disparate treatment. The court explained that the dress code was demeaning to women because they had to wear "uniforms" and men did not. The court accepted the argument that persons who wear uniforms are generally subordinate to persons who do not wear uniforms. In addition, the court held that the employer had a variety of nondiscriminating alternative means of assuring good grooming. The court indicated that a dress code that required, for example, suits for males and females, would not be considered a violation of Title VII.

The *Carroll* decision is hard to reconcile with the decision of the U.S. Court of Appeals for the Ninth Circuit in *Fountain* v. *Safeway Stores, Inc.*[58] In that case the court sustained a requirement that male employees wear ties whereas female employees did not have to dress with ties.

In another case, an airline policy which prohibited only female cabin attendants from wearing *eyeglasses* was held to be discriminating. *Laffey* v. *Northwest Airlines, Inc.*[59]

Weight standards are permissible as part of an appearance code, even if they differ as applied to males and females, as long as they have no adverse impact on one sex which cannot be justified by business necessity. *Gerdom* v. *Continental Airlines, Inc.*[60]

Gerdom involved a complaint by a female flight attendant who had been terminated for failing to meet the standards of a weight control plan. The plaintiff claimed, *inter alia,* that her termination was unlawful because the standards of the weight control plan discriminated against female employees in violation of Title VII. In each instance, however, the court disagreed and upheld both the weight control plan and the termination on the basis of the following factors: weight control is not an immutable sex characteristic and does not involve a constitutionally protected activity; the weight control plan standards and sanctions applied to male as well as female flight attendants; the different standards applied to males and females were reasonable in terms of medical considerations and ability to comply; and, most importantly, the differing standards had not had a demonstrable disparate impact on the employment opportunities of female flight attendants.

Some courts have gone further and held that weight standards are lawful regardless of any demonstrable disparate impact because weight is neither an immutable characteristic nor a constitutionally protected category. See, *e.g., Cox* v. *Delta Air Lines.*[61] The *Cox* court held that the airline was entitled to summary judgment because the plaintiff could not successfully challenge the weight standards as being discriminatory under any set of facts.

A more recent decision suggests that weight might be treated as an immutable characteristic. In *Flight Attendants* v. *Ozark Air Lines,*[62] the airline moved for summary judgment on the ground that the weight standards challenged by the plaintiff were merely part of a reasonable appearance standard and therefore lawful under Title VII, without regard to their impact on males and females. The court denied the motion. While intimating no view as to whether the plaintiff could establish a *prima facie* case at trial, the court held that an issue of material fact as to whether the airline's weight control plan has a disparate impact on females had been raised by evidence that only female flight attendants had suffered adverse employment actions under the plan and that only female flight attendants have had to resort to special diets and drugs to comply with its requirements.

Though weight requirements have been sustained as part of an appearance standard, they have not been sustained as part of a job performance standard. Thus in *Meadows* v. *Ford Motor Co.,*[63] the employer had sought to impose a requirement that candidates for factory work weigh at least 150 pounds. The court found that the weight requirement had a disparate impact, did not have a valid relation to the ability of a person to perform the job, and was not a bona fide occupational qualification.

Minimum height standards have also been attacked under the claim of sex discrimination. The requirement that a police officer be a minimum of 5'6" tall has been successfully challenged. Female plaintiffs have established a *prima facie* case by introducing statistics showing the highly disparate impact of the requirement. See, *e.g., Dothard* v. *Rawlingson,*[64] and *Officers for Justice* v. *Civil Service Commission.*[65] When the same type of height requirement was attacked by a white male, however, the requirement was sustained since his group suffered no disparate impact. The court reasoned that Title VII does not prohibit height discrimination when it does not also entail discrimination based on race, color, religion, sex, national origin. See *Smith v. Borough of Wilkinsburg.*[66] It is important to note that when these height requirements are attacked by females utilizing Title VII, the height standards are generally held illegal; if they are attacked on constitutional grounds, however, they are not found illegal because there is some rational state purpose for the requirement. See *Smith v. City of East Cleveland.*[67] The proof of business necessity required for an employer is far greater than a mere showing that there is some reason for the rule. To demonstrate business necessity the employer virtually has to show it cannot operate without the standard.

In considering height and weight standards, the most recent movement by government agencies has been to rely on prohibitions against discrimination on the basis of disability or handicap.

In *N.Y.S. Div. of Human Rights v. Thomas J. Lipton, Inc.,*[68] the New York State Division of Human Rights sought to establish as law the premise that obesity, *per se,* is a disability. Previously, in *N.Y.S. Div. of Human Rights v. City of New York,*[69] an administrative law judge had ruled that obesity which was contributed to by glandular disorder was a disability.

The administrative determination that obesity was a disability which issued in the *Lipton* case was overturned by the appellate court in New York, but the basis for reversal was that the complainant could not perform the job in question. Consequently, the issue of whether obesity *per se* is a disability is still open in New York. The testimony put forth in the *Lipton* case by the State's medical experts was that persons who are 20% above normal body weight are obese. Those same medical experts further testified that about 80% of the U.S. population fits within this definition of obesity.

Another State FEP agency, for the State of Oregon, is seeking to establish that short people are "handicapped" and, therefore, protected by that state's statute prohibiting discrimination against the handicapped.

Marital status rules, especially in the airline industry, have been under almost continuous attack and have almost always been held discriminatory. Thus, it was held a violation of Title VII to require a female flight attendant to resign or be discharged upon her marriage. *Inda v. United Airlines, Inc.*[70] Similarly, in *Sprogis v. United Airlines, Inc.,*[71] the policy of discharging married stewardesses was held discriminatory where stewards were permitted to be married. The employer had sought to defend the policy by claiming that the standard distinguished between classes of employees, and that it was applied to the class denominated stewardess. A similar defense had been successfully asserted in an unusual case, *Stroud v. Delta Air Lines, Inc.,*[72] in which the company had applied its rule only to flight attendants and claimed it was not discriminating because the rule pertained to a class of employees, not a particular sex. *Stroud* is the minority viewpoint.

One court, in *Allen v. Lovejoy,*[73] has also held that it is a Title VII violation to suspend a newly married female employee because she refuses to comply with an employer's requirement that she change her name on her personnel form to that of her husband. Because there was no company rule requiring the man to change his name to the name of his wife on personnel forms after he got married, the court caused the employer to reinstate the female and correct the Title VII violation. This decision is clearly a minority viewpoint, since there are usually state statutes requiring the name change.

Another rule that has been the subject of litigation mandated that pregnant flight attendants no longer fly—that they either take a leave of absence or work at a ground job. The policy has been sustained as legal, basically because of the FAA requirement that airlines exercise the highest degree of care for passengers, and because of pertinent medical testimony. *Condit* v. *United Air Lines, Inc.*[74] However, the same rule has been held discriminatory by the U.S. Court of Appeals for the Seventh Circuit in *In re Consolidated Pretrial Proceedings in the Airline cases.*[75]

Nepotism rules have been sustained by the courts when these rules prohibit persons who are close relatives, including husbands and wives, from working either for the same company or in the same department. Such a rule against the employment of spouses within the same department was held lawful in *Harper* v. *TransWorld Airlines, Inc.*[76] Another rule, which prohibited spouses or relatives from working in supervisory-subordinate relationships, was sustained as nondiscriminatory in *Smith* v. *Mutual Benefit Life Insurance Co.*[77] A publishing-company rule that prohibited employment of close relatives in the same publication, *Tuck* v. *McGraw-Hill, Inc.*[78] In *Yukas* v. *Libbey-Owens-Ford Co.*,[79] a nepotism rule has been struck down by the District Court, but the U.S. Circuit Court of Appeals for the Seventh Circuit reversed and sustained the rule. The reasoning was unusual. Although the appeals court recognized that the rule had an adverse impact against females, it found it sustainable because, hypothetically, it could be related to job performance. The more important factor for the court was that the rule did not create a "built-in headwind" against progress by persons in the protected group and did not focus on personal characteristics that members of the protected group were not as likely to possess, given their environmental or genetic background, as other applicants.

While it may be a violation to discriminate against a female, it is not a violation to discriminate against a man who appears to be a female. In *Smith* v. *Liberty Benefit Life Insurance Co., supra,* the court held that the employer did not discriminate on the basis of sex when it refused to hire a male on the ground that he appeared to be effeminate. Title VII, the court indicated, does not prohibit discrimination based on affectional or sexual preference or affectation.

Standards for the Handicapped and Disabled

Claims of discrimination on the basis of disability or handicap usually arise under the Rehabilitation Act of 1973 or state and local statutes, and occasionally under the U.S. Constitution. There is not yet very much case law giving definitive direction to employers in this area. The major distinction between the state statutes and the Rehabilitation Act is that the former usually only prohibit discrimination, whereas the latter, rightly or wrongly, has been interpreted by the federal government as requiring not only nondiscriminatory treatment, and not only affirmative action on behalf of the handicapped, but also reasonable accommodation by employers.

Blindness has been the subject of litigation. In *Coleman* v. *Darden*,[80] the court rejected a claim by a blind applicant who was rejected for employment by EEOC as a legal research analyst. The court found that the applicant would require the services of a reader, that the physical requirement imposed by the government was job-related, and that sufficient visual accuity to enable the employee to read had a direct relationship to the ability to assist lawyers. The court did not consider, because the issue was not raised, whether circumstances could be developed in which it could be considered that the potential employer, EEOC, had not made reasonable accommodation to the handicap of the applicant.

In *Gurmankin* v. *Costanzo*,[81] an application by another blind applicant was at issue. In this case, however, the applicant had been issued a professional teaching certificate by the state, but the school district to which he had applied refused to permit him to take a qualifying examination. The court held that by doing so, the school district was illegally presuming that his blindness made him incompetent to teach sighted students, and that the school district had discriminated by not permitting him to take the qualifying examination.

Epilepsy has also been the subject of litigation. An outright policy of refusing to hire epileptics was struck down as being discriminatory in *Duran* v. *City of Tampa*.[82] The city had refused to hire anyone who had experienced an epileptic seizure less than two years before the date of application. In another case, however, which was brought under the U.S. Constitution, the U.S. Postal Service was found not to have discriminated by denying employment to an epileptic. Applying the strict constitutional standard, the court found that a rule conclusively presuming that epileptics are medically unfit for certain kinds of duties has a reasonable relationship to the achievement of proper governmental interests of guarding the safety of the Postal Service employees and the general public. *Counts* v. *U.S. Postal Service*.[83] It should be noted, however, that this defense, while satisfactory under the Constitution, would be inadequate under the Rehabilitation Act of 1973 or most disability statutes.

In *Davis* v. *Bucher*,[84] the court held that a person with a history of *drug abuse*, including anyone currently a participant in the methadone maintenance program, is handicapped within the meaning of the Rehabilitation Act of 1973. The court held that the outright refusal to consider such a person for employment was discrimination in violation of this act, and that the employer should have considered individual factors, such as recent employment history, successful maintenance on the drug program, and so on, rather than rejecting the applicant for having a drug history. However, in *New York City Transit Authority* v.

Beazer,[85] the U.S. Supreme Court sustained a rule that prohibited people on methadone maintenance from holding certain jobs, such as motorman. Yet, the basis for the claim was the U.S. Constitution and Title VII (because the rule screened out more blacks than whites). The Court found the rule rational and justified by business reasons, therefore rejecting the claim. While the decision did not directly interpret the Rehabilitation Act, in footnote 32 of the opinion, the Court implied that as long as an individual was on a maintenance program, he or she was not rehabilitated. This could mean that both alcoholics and drug abusers currently undergoing treatment would not be covered under the Rehabilitation Act, because of certain amendments made to the Act in 1978 regarding alcoholics and drug abusers, when read together with footnote 32 of *Beazer*.

At least one state, New York, is trying to establish that *obesity*, no matter why it exists, is a disability. This is discussed in detail on p. 62 of this chapter.

Alcoholism is already considered a disability in at least one state, Wisconsin, where it is discriminatory to refuse to hire persons with a history of alcoholism. The U.S. government has also adopted the position that alcoholism is a handicap within the meaning of the Rehabilitation Act of 1973, as long as the condition does not affect their work performance or place persons or property in direct danger.

A certain dilemma is created for employers who have employees who are alcoholics, or who are developing into alcoholics. On the one hand, in order to take any adverse action at all against the employee, the employer must be prepared to prove that the condition affects the work performance. On the other hand, however, if the employer does, for example, terminate an employee for whom the condition is affecting work performance, the claim will be made that the termination is violative of the law, because once it is determined that alcoholism is a handicap, the alcoholic being terminated because of the condition will claim he should be treated just like any other person under the company's disability-benefits program. The U.S. government, through OFCCP, will support him in this claim. Another irony is that many state disability-benefits programs to which employers subscribe do not cover alcoholism as a disability. Consequently, the employer, despite its payments and contributions pursuant to the state disability-benefits law, may have to make the payments to an alcoholic employee or former employee directly, without benefit of any insurance.

With respect to statutes prohibiting discrimination against those who are disabled or handicapped, there is a conflict on some basic issues. The first area of conflict is whether the debilitating characteristic, to qualify as a disability, must be permanent or long term, or whether it might be a temporary condition. The second area is whether an existing condition that does not currently impair a job candidate's ability to perform but will very likely do so in the future, or will very likely become aggravated if he is allowed to perform in the job he seeks, should constitute a disability. The third area of conflict relates to the burden of proof—whether the complainant must prove that his or her condition will not affect work performance in order to qualify as disabled or handicapped under statutory definition, or whether the burden of demonstrating inability to perform rests with the employer who has denied employment to the complainant.

On the first issue, long-term versus short-term nature of the disability. Wisconsin appears to be the most liberal and ready to find most maladies to be disabilities. For example, Wisconsin courts have found asthma, migraine headaches, alcoholism, diabetes, a deviated septum, and rheumatoid arthritis to be handicaps covered by the Wisconsin statute. On the other hand, Rhode Island courts require the handicap to be "a serious injury or impairment of more than a temporary nature," and therefore have held that "whiplash" is not a handicap. *Providence Journal Co.* v. *Mason.*[86]

The federal government position seems more in line with the Wisconsin approach than that of Rhode Island. In *OFCCP* v. *E. E. Black, Ltd.,*[87] an administrative law judge had held that persons who could perform most or many jobs did not suffer from a "substantial impairment;" therefore, they were not "handicapped." The Department of Labor, OFCCP, reversed this decision and the issue is now in the courts.

In the second area of conflict, present ability to perform versus possible future adverse effects to the employer or employee from permitting him to perform, some states permit the employer to look to the future. Thus, in Oregon a court has allowed an employer to consider whether the condition would prevent the person from performing or would increase the person's risk of incapacitation while performing. *Montgomery Ward & Co.* v. *Bureau of Labor.*[88] In Washington State, an employer may consider the candidate's present ability to perform, the safety of that person and his co-workers, and future deterioration. *Clark* v. *Milwaukee Road.*[89] In New York, because a candidate would eventually be unable to perform and because his preexisting condition, dermatitis, would be aggravated by exposure to work, it was held not discriminatory to refuse him employment. *Westinghouse Electric Co.* v. *State Division of Human Rights;*[90] see also *State Division of Human Rights* v. *County of Monroe*[91] (limited use of one leg affected ability to squat, which candidate would have to do later on). However, in affirming the *Westinghouse* decision, New York's highest court indicated the result may now be different because of a recent legislative change.

In Wisconsin, however, the law does not permit the employer to consider the increased possibility that a person would become incapacitated by performing the job being sought. *Chrysler Outboard Corp.* v. *DILAR.*[92] Again, on the basis of the OFCCP's actions in the *E. E. Black, Ltd.* case and the language of that case, it would appear that the federal government has adopted the Wisconsin approach.

On the third issue, burden of proof in establishing that the physical condition does not detract from the ability to perform the job and therefore is a protected disability, there is also a conflict between the law, as thus far developed, in New York and in Wisconsin. In New York, in order to have a disability trigger the operation of the statute, the disability must be unrelated to job performance, and the burden of proof in establishing this fact is on the complainant. Otherwise, the statute is inapplicable. Thus, a school-bus driver with a hearing defect who was refused rehire could not invoke the statute because his disability was job-related. *State Division of Human Rights* v. *Averill Park Central School District.*[93] This court holding is contrary to the interpretation by the New York State enforcement agency, which believes that all disabilities are protected and that the employee has the burden of demonstrating that the disability affects the ability to perform.

Wisconsin places on the employer the burden of proving that a disabled person cannot perform the job satisfactorily. *Connecticut General Life Insurance Co.* v. *DILAR.*[94] Moreover, the employer must show that the individual disabled person cannot perform; it is not allowed to make generalities. *Fraser Shipyard, Inc.* v. *DILAR.*[95] Thus, there is a two-step process in Wisconsin. First, a handicap is shown to exist; this triggers the operation of the statute. Then, in order to escape liability, the employer must demonstrate that the handicap prevents performance.

The doctrine of reasonable accommodation is also being developed in the area of discrimination based on handicap. Some states place a burden on the employer to make a person employable. For example, one court in Washington found that a company discriminated against an employee with cerebral palsy by transferring him to a job the company knew or should have known he could not perform. *Holland* v. *Boeing Co.*[96]

Though the OFCCP requires that employers undertake reasonable accommodation on behalf of handicapped people, this position has already been rejected in *Carmi* v. *St. Louis Sewer District.*[97] A similar attempt by the government to go beyond its authority under the Rehabilitation Act was rejected by the U.S. Supreme Court in *Southeastern Community College* v. *Davis.*[98]

SYSTEMS FOR ASSESSING AND MINIMIZING ADVERSE IMPACT IN HIRING

Background

As we have seen in Chapter 2, the entire governmental effort is oriented toward analyzing employment systems in terms of adverse impact. In fact, the federal regulations require that this term and this concept be the focal point for an employer's own analysis.

Adverse impact is really a relationship between two functions, availability and hires. Availability, for purposes of adverse-impact analysis in hiring, is generally considered to be applicant flow, and not just general external availability. See *Hazelwood School District* v. *United States.*[99]

Applicant flow, for legal purposes, is largely controlled or affected by the employer, union, or employment agency seeking candidates. It is such entities that notify recruiting sources, determine who will be denominated as an applicant or what job the candidate will be deemed to have made application for, and set the time period when applications will or will not be taken. What determines whether a person is "hired," for legal purposes, is also largely affected by the employer's input.

The manner in which adverse impact is analyzed is by the 80 percent rule, described in Chapter 2, or by the standard-deviation analysis formula that was approved by the Supreme Court in *Hazelwood School District* v. *United States, supra.* The formula, which can be two-tailed or one-tailed, is set set out below:

$$S.D. = \sqrt{\frac{\text{Total black applicants}}{\text{Total applicants}} \times \frac{\text{Total white applicants}}{\text{Total applicants}} \times \frac{\text{Total of persons selected}}{}}$$

The formula above is the two-tailed, standard-deviation analyses formula; it shows whether there has been discrimination against the protected group or the group being used as a basis for comparison. The expected number, based on direct ratios, plus or minus two standard deviations, constitutes the acceptable (safe) range for the employer.

An example will illustrate how the standard deviation analysis is utilized. For purposes of the example, let us assume that there were 1,000 applicants, 320 black and 680 white, and that 300 persons were hired, 75 black and 225 white. The standard deviation analysis formula used to ascertain whether the number of blacks selected was within the acceptable range would read as follows:

$$S.D. = \sqrt{\frac{320}{1000} \times \frac{680}{1000} \times 300}$$

$$S.D. = \sqrt{65.28}$$

$$S.D. = 8.08$$

$$2 \times S.D. = 16.16$$

The number of blacks one would expect to be hired, on a straight ratio basis, is $320/1000 \times 300 = 96$. Therefore, the Acceptable Range =

$$96 \pm 16.16 \text{ or } 79.84 - 112.16.$$

Stated conversely, if the number of blacks hired is less than 79.84 or more than

112.16, a statistician would testify that something more than chance was affecting the decision making.

Adverse Impact in Recruiting

Adverse impact in recruting is *not* a source of substantial exposure for any employer or other screening entity, and it is a relatively simple subject for adverse-impact analyses.

There is no legal obligation under Title VII to do recruiting or undertake any affirmative action. *Lewis* v. *Tobacco Workers International Union.*[100] Furthermore, even if it were a Title VII violation not to do these things, there is no practical way in which substantial liability could be assessed against a selecting entity for such a violation. Courts simply will not, after the conclusion of a case, order the publication of a newspaper advertisement advising protected-group persons who would have applied for a job had they heard about it to step forward and collect money in the form of back pay. Such a procedure is too speculative. Furthermore, the Supreme Court has already indicated that to recover back pay, one must have actually applied or, in limited circumstances, been deterred from applying. *Teamsters* v. *United States.*[101]

There is a possibility that the failure to take affirmative action in recruiting will be found to constitute noncompliance with the provisions of Executive Order 11246 and Revised Order No. 4. However, in most cases, the remedy sought by OFCCP for such a violation would be to require the contractor to become more aggressive in seeking out qualified minority and female candidates for employment. Nevertheless, aggressive recruiting efforts should be directed toward inducing quality, not quantity, in minority and female applications.

One of the most serious blunders of employers is to engage nonselectively in the solicitation of applications from minorities and females, and to equate a large number of applications with compliance with Executive Order 11246 and Revised Order No. 4. Most often, compliance officers reviewing a government contractor's status under these orders will indeed equate a relatively large number of applications from minorities and females as compliance, for recruiting purposes. The employer, however, in avoiding this relatively minor problem in recruiting, may have created a far more significant problem: Once a protected-group person becomes part of the applicant flow, he or she must also be considered for purposes of adverse-impact analysis. If an employer's minority and/or female applicants have not been as selectively recruited as the nonminority or male applicants, there is a far greater likelihood that there will be adverse impact in the total hiring process. And if the employer tries to avoid adverse impact in hiring by following a quota system for hiring, the problem will surface later in the employment system when and if minorities and females are not promoted as fast as others, or do not earn as much as others, or are involuntarily discharged at a higher rate than others.

To minimize the prospects for adverse impact at these later stages, it is critical that an employer recruit selectively. This does not mean turning away minorities or females; that would be blatant discrimination. It does mean, however, that the employer resist the temptation—and the pressure of compliance officers—to send out job notices to every female or minority referral source that happens to exist.

Such recruiting should be done scientifically. The number of such minority and female referral sources should not be so large that the plant or facility personnel director cannot establish some kind of personal relationship with those who will be referring minority or female candidates. If possible, these people should be invited for a plant or facility tour. It should be made known to them that it is the employer who has selected them and that the employer wants a long-term relationship; that there will be only a limited number of referral sources used; and that the employer does not want just "live bodies." If possible, the employer should monitor the performance of these referral sources (referrals versus hires from that source), and rate them, and discontinue using them if they are abusing the confidence of that employer. Many such referral sources are very reliable and helpful. However, there is no economic or practical sense in continuing to use sources that do not send people who can realistically be expected to qualify.

One of the best sources for qualified minority and female referrals is an employer's own minority and female employees. For reasons not discussed here, these employees are often reluctant to refer another female or minority member for consideration. Nevertheless, this group is a good first source for affirmative action in recruiting, and one where documentation is relatively easy.

If there is an adverse-impact problem in the hiring stage, one of the things an employer might do is monitor its recruitment pool—perhaps by the use of "gate cards." Gate cards, as the term is used here, are small index cards given at the facility gate to people who inquire about employment opportunities at a time when applications are not being taken. The person inquiring is given the card and asked to fill it out in case there are openings. The card merely asks for name and telephone number and the kind of job in which the person has an interest. The alternatives given on the card might be, for example, jobs requiring only light lifting (20 lbs. or less, occasionally); medium lifting (40 lbs. or less, occasionally); medium-heavy lifting (40 lbs. or less, frequently); or heavy lifting (50 lbs. or more, frequently). The card might also ask for skills (typing, machinist, plumber).

The purpose of the card is twofold. First, it serves the very legitimate business purpose of saving the employer from having to contact many people before finding one interested in the type of job available. Second, it is very helpful for adverse-impact-analysis purposes. When applications are being taken, there is an identifiable pool of people who can be contacted and who apparently have an interest. The employer avoids the necessity of having to count 20 females as part of the applicant pool for a heavy-lifting job, when only four out of the 20 have an interest in such a job. The employer contacts the four who indicated a predisposition to such work, not all 20.

For record-keeping purposes, EEOC would probably consider all gate cards to be applications; for adverse-impact analysis, however, EEOC would be hard-pressed to prove that the employer should be required to count people as part of the applicant pool for a particular job when they themselves indicated they were not interested in such a job.

Adverse impact in recruiting is assessed relatively easily, by comparing the percentage of persons with particular skills in the work force, and employed or unemployed, with the percentage of people with such skills who are applying. External availability is determined by first establishing the relevant hiring area, which may vary depending upon the job, and then looking to appropriate census or EEOC figures. The census figures can be obtained from the local state employment service, which is funded by the federal government to extract and furnish such figures to employers for purposes of affirmative action programs; or from a large public library; or from private groups—such as National Planning Data Corp., Ithaca, New York—for a relatively modest charge. The EEOC figures are compiled from EEO-1 forms submitted by employers and are more current than census figures. They are in book form and are available for inspection, pursuant to EEOC regulations,[102] at some 32 district offices of EEOC and its headquarters. The addresses of these offices are given in EEOC Regulation 41 C.F.R. § 1610.4.

If there is a serious problem involved, the employer may want to use what are called "Sixth Count" data. These are much more refined data and will relate much more directly to the employer's particular industry and the particular job involved. For example, general census data might give the number of females who are salespersons, but the refined data might give, say, the percentage of the salespersons in the railroad industry who are outside salespersons. These kinds of data are available from private companies, such as National Planning Data Corp.

Adverse-Impact Analysis for Hiring

The starting point for adverse-impact analysis for hiring is a simple comparison of applicant flow for a particular job to hires for that job. If there is just one entry point for unskilled or semiskilled production workers, the process is very much simplified. In such circumstances, the applicant flow for production jobs can be rated against the hire rates for production jobs.

A necessary ingredient for any adverse-impact analysis is the determination by the applicant of the job or job category he or she is seeking. Extreme care must be taken at this stage. There can be no "funneling"—pointing females to clerical jobs and pointing males to production jobs. The candidate should do the selecting, without coaxing. If there is coaxing—that is, indicating to a male applying for production work that there is a porter's job open—then that coaxing must be utilized in exactly the same manner for females. In fact, for affirmative action purposes, if there is an underutilization of females as porters, the employer might consider coaxing only the females. This is what the Department of Labor would want for compliance with Executive Order 11246, and it is apparent from the Uniform Selection Guidelines that EEOC would close its eyes, and its enforcement mechanism, to such a violation of Title VII. Whether such conduct would violate Title VII is questionable. However, for all practical purposes, employers can be sure the federal government is not going to prosecute them for reverse discrimination, because it has never done so. Whether such action is discriminatory would depend upon the employer's past practices, its existing workforce composition, and the manner in which the employer implemented the procedures. Compare *McDonald v. Santa Fe Trail Transportation Co.*[103] and *Kaiser Aluminum & Chemical Corp. v. Weber.*[104]

The greater the range the employer permits the applicant for making his or her designation of the job sought, the more difficult it will be to conduct adverse-impact analyses. In fact, a broad designation may require the employer to consider and assess the applicant for two, three, or more job titles.

Based upon the applicant pool, the employer compares the hire rates for each job title. If there are basic skill requirements held in common among a number of jobs, the employer might consolidate the applicant pool and the hires for those jobs.

Having established the groups, the adverse-impact analysis is conducted using the 80 percent rule or the standard-deviation analysis formula. If there is no net adverse impact, no further analysis need be conducted.

If there is a net adverse impact, then further analysis is required. The initial step is to segregate the hiring process into discrete segments. The hiring process will vary, depending upon the job and the employer, but most frequently will include the application form; the initial interview in the personnel department; a paper-and-pencil test or a skill test; an interview with the supervisor for whom the candidate would be working, if hired; an offer, conditional upon passing a physical examination; and a hire. At any stage of the process, the candidate can be considered as having precluded himself or herself from further consideration by failing to persevere in the procedure.

Once the hiring process has been divided into segments, those segments should be categorized. The categories are "Rejection by employer" and "Rejection by candidate." If the employee has failed to appear for an interview or a physical, and the employer has followed regular procedure in notifying and accommodating the candidate for this step, or if the candidate has received an offer and rejected it, this is a "Rejection by candidate." All other rejections are considered "Rejections by employer."

The purpose of the second adverse-impact analysis will be to correct for one distortion not within the control of the employer. Thus, if minorities and females are rejecting job offers at a higher rate, this second adverse-impact analysis will correct for that distortion.

The third type of adverse-impact analysis will take into account only those factors within the control of the employer. Thus, it will not consider actual hires, but rather actual offers made; it will not consider all applicants who initiated the hiring process, but rather all those who persevered in the process to completion.

An example indicating how these three types of adverse-impact analyses might be utilized follows, and following the example are some caveats for the employer engaging in such analysis.

Example

XYZ Corporation hired 300 people into unskilled entry-level jobs in 1977. Of these, 225 (75 percent) were white and 75 (25 percent) were black. XYZ Corporation had 1,000 applicants for these jobs, of whom 680 (68 percent) were white and 320 (32 percent) were black. All hires were within 30 days of application, and there were no hires in January 1977 and no applications received in December 1977. XYZ Corporation follows a policy of refusing to consider any application more than 30 days old and so states on the application form. The hiring process consists of application, interview by personnel director, interview by supervisor, hire subject to medical examination, and start of work if the medical examination is satisfactory. In 1977, offers of employment had been made to 400 people, of whom 295 were white and 105 were black. From the time of application to the time of acceptance or rejection by XYZ Corporation, 80 whites and 80 blacks had voluntarily withdrawn from further consideration by failing to appear for an interview or medical examination.

First type of adverse-impact analysis—hires/applicants:

1. The success rate for black applicants is

$$\frac{75 \text{ hires}}{320 \text{ applicants}} = 23.4\%$$

2. The success rate for white applicants is

$$\frac{225 \text{ hires}}{680 \text{ applicants}} = 33\%$$

3. Blacks are not achieving at a level equal to or exceeding 80% of the white success level, because

$$\frac{23.4}{33} = 70.9\%$$

Therefore, by straight adverse-impact analysis, there is discrimination, and the selection system must be validated.

Step 2 of the adverse-impact analysis—offers/applicants:

1. Black applicants received offers of employment at the rate of

$$\frac{105 \text{ offers to blacks}}{320 \text{ black applicants}} = 32.8\%$$

2. White applicants received offers of employment at the rate of

$$\frac{295 \text{ offers to whites}}{680 \text{ white applicants}} = 43.4\%$$

3. Blacks are not achieving at a level equal to or exceeding 80% of the white success rate on applications, because

$$\frac{32.8}{43.4} = 75.5\%$$

Therefore, by straight adverse-impact analysis of offers to applicants, there is discrimination.

Step 3 of the adverse-impact analysis—those given offers/those who persevered in the hiring process:

1. If 80 blacks voluntarily withdrew from consideration, then 240 blacks persevered to completion of the hiring process.
2. If 80 whites voluntarily withdrew from consideration, then 600 whites persevered to completion.
3. The percentage of offers to blacks persevering is

$$\frac{105}{240} = 43.75\%$$

4. The percentage of offers to whites persevering is

$$\frac{295}{600} = 49.1\%$$

5. Blacks who persevere in the hiring process are achieving at a level equal to or exceeding 80% of the white success rate, because

$$\frac{43.75}{49.1} = 89.1\%$$

These analyses are by no means all the different ways in which adverse-impact analysis can be conducted, but they demonstrate that there is nothing sacrosanct about the process. In engaging in any variety of analysis other than the first one given in the example, the employer should be mindful that the alternative methods selected will be closely scrutinized. It thus makes no sense to try to adjust the facts and numbers to fit the conclusion sought. Furthermore, the employer must be absolutely sure that the system determining who is to be considered a person receiving an offer, or a person persevering in the application process to completion, is uniformly applied.

It should be noted that in the example given, certain liberties were taken to avoid complications. One of these is the fact that XYZ Corporation specified a time period after which applications were no longer considered. Many employers have such a procedure and clearly state it on the application forms. It serves a few purposes. First, from a strictly business point of view, it saves the employer from contacting candidates who have probably been hired someplace else. The period does not have to be 30 days, and it does not have to be the same for all categories of jobs. After the time is up, the applicant should know that he or she must reapply. Neither the proposed new record-keeping requirements nor the existing requirements mandate how long applications must be kept active, but only how long they need be kept.

A second benefit of having a time period for active consideration of applications is to prevent stale charges of discrimination or unduly large class actions. Courts faced with questions regarding the timeliness of a charge for filing purposes with EEOC or state or local agencies are wont to interpret timeliness issues in favor of the complainant. If there is no clear indication of a time after which an applicant knew, or should have known, that he or she was not hired, the establishment of that date becomes a complicated fact issue very much dependent upon the subjective state of mind of the applicant. If, however, the statement is clearly indicated that "this application will only be considered for 30 days after it is filed; for consideration after that time, reapplication is required," then all fact issues are mooted, and the relevant periods for filing charges commence running 30 days after the application (which should always be dated by the applicant) has been filed. Similarly, since class actions in Title VII cases relating to hires can include all those who could have filed a timely charge of discrimination when the complainant filed his or hers, it is desirable to know who these people are.

A third benefit, even more significant in view of the new Uniform Guidelines, is that having a time period indicated facilitates adverse-impact analyses. There will be questions raised by the government reviewers concerning what applications and hires should be considered for purposes of an adverse-impact analysis. By having a cutoff time for active consideration of applications, and by doing the analyses for annual time periods, many of these factual issues can be avoided.

Another liberty taken in the example was to indicate that there had been no applications in December 1977. This avoids problems that arise when the employer compares likes to likes. In reality, an employer should utilize all applications in a given year and all ultimate hires, rejections, or dropouts relating to those applications. This might mean that adverse-impact analyses cannot be accurately conducted until February or March of the year following those applications, depending upon the cutoff time established by the employer for active consideration of applications. As can be seen, if there is no cutoff date for active consideration, it will be difficult even to establish conclusively the necessary variables—applicants and hires—to do adverse-impact analysis.

The second and third alternatives presented in the example are not yet accepted or rejected by the courts. They are believed to be realistic and soundly based, and when the legal principles embodied in these alternatives have been presented, they have been favorably viewed. Thus in *Hester* v. *Southern Railway Co.*,[105] in conducting its own adverse-impact analysis, the court found it very relevant to know and identify the people who had persevered in the hiring process. A very helpful, perhaps even necessary, support of the second or third alternatives would be an investigation into the reasons that the protected group might be rejecting offers or dropping out during the hiring process.

One problem not yet covered here but equally important is what to do if the adverse impact cannot be explained by any alternative. In such an event, each segment of the hiring process—that is, application review, first interview, second interview, and medical examination—must be separately analyzed to determine exactly where the adverse impact exists. Once that is determined, efforts must be undertaken to reduce that adverse impact to the acceptability range under the 80-percent rule, or validate that part of the selection process.

Avoiding Charges of Discrimination in Hiring

One of the simplest yet most effective ways of avoiding charges of discrimination that could lead to expensive investigations is to maintain fairness and, most important, the appearance of fairness in the entire hiring process. This might be accomplished at a minimal extra cost, but experience shows that it reaps large dividends.

The person who is applying for a job has little or nothing to lose by filing a charge of discrimination if he or she does not obtain that job. This is especially true in situations where the applicant is unemployed at the time of application. So many times, it is little things that have triggered major cases—the fact that a minority or female candidate was not interviewed in order, or did not get a response to a letter or telephone call, and similar instances. There may be a very good reason that the candidate did not receive a return call or letter, but that very good reason might surface only after an investigation has been triggered. Furthermore, as we have seen, the investigation may go far beyond the individual complainant's claim, exposing the employer to liability far beyond the parameters of that claim.

A procedure that can ensure the appearance of fairness is to have the actions of the company in rejecting or accepting a particular candidate justified before a company selection committee. This can be done periodically, reviewing applicants rejected over a two-week or four-week period in very brief fashion, and explaining the rejections to the selection committee. One benefit obtained from this procedure is to ensure consistency in the application of standards, consistency in the questions asked during interviews, and consistency in the weight given to various responses or lack of responses. Additionally, the selection committee could include minorities and/or females or other protected-group persons, either on a rotating basis or as permanent members. If an applicant who is rejected persists in wanting to know why, it might be helpful to convey to such a person not only the fact that the personnel department rejected him or her, but also the fact that the selection committee—which consists of people of the same race, color, religion, and sex—has reviewed the action, pursuant to regular company procedure, and approved it.

Another procedure used to avoid charges of discrimination is a training program for interviewers. In such training programs, interviewers observe a candidate in a mock interview; they rate the candidate on the basis of that interview and are asked to comment on the interview. In such a manner, the company can ensure that standards are being uniformly applied and weighted so that an applicant fares just as well or poorly with any interviewer.

Also, an employer should establish a policy of not giving reasons for rejection unless absolutely pressed. If it is the company policy to send a kind "letdown letter" rejecting a candidate, such a letter should not give reasons for the rejection.

Finally, it is advisable for an employer to avoid those areas of the hiring process that are "red flags" to compliance review agencies, government enforcers, and the applicant. Such a danger area is any kind of test or selection standard that rates personality, intelligence, or aptitude. The further the employer gets away from the actual duties and functions of the job, the more likely it is that the hiring process will be difficult or impossible to validate.

FORMS

Application Forms

Not every question on an application form requires comment, but some do. (See the sample application form that follows.)

Person to contact in case of emergency is an inquiry that the State of New York Human Rights Commission Guidelines find to be discriminatory. The rationale for the position is that the employer might find that the person to contact is a minority or Hispanic and thereby determine that the applicant is a minority or Hispanic. This is very farfetched logic; it has not yet been tested in court, and probably would not succeed in court.

Questions about *availability for shift work,* weekend work, or overtime are generally not asked of candidates for exempt jobs. However, these questions elicit necessary information for most production and nonexempt jobs. If a candidate indicates that he or she is not available for such work, but also explains that this is for religious reasons, then there is a requirement under Title VII that the employer make reasonable accommodation. If the candidate indicates he or she is not available for such work because he or she has a National Guard commitment, there are some states that have statutes prohibiting discrimination on that basis.

Questions about *handicaps,* such as those asked in this form, may cause problems with the government investigators and deserve comment for that reason. The federal and state agencies do not permit employers to ask about handicaps generally, but only to ask, "Do you suffer some handicap or disability which would affect your ability to perform the job you seek?" Employers who have restricted their inquiry to this question alone have had bad experiences. People are not known to admit that their handicap or disabilities will affect their performance.

Justification for asking the general question about handicaps might be found in the requirements of the Rehabilitation Act to take affirmative action. An employer cannot take such affirmative action with regard to hiring unless he knows whether the candidate has a handicap. There are also record keeping and reporting requirements to state agencies concerning the hiring of handicapped or disabled persons, which cannot be properly satisfied without learning of this information at some stage of the hiring process.

Information about *convictions* and type of discharge from military service is another danger area. The danger can be eliminated by indicating under such inquiries that "the information will be considered only in relation to the job being sought."

Education is an item most employers seek, especially because it tells the employer something about the candidate's minimum abilities to read, write, and understand. That does not mean that a high school education or a college degree should be required, but it does justify the request for education information. The firm requirement of a high school diploma or a college degree should not be imposed unless the employer concludes it is absolutely necessary. It is more advisable to indicate that high school or college training in a specific area is desirable, but that comparable experience is acceptable.

Asking the applicant to indicate the *job sought* is essential, to enable the employer to engage in any kind of adverse-impact analysis.

The manner in which the applicant came to apply at XYZ Corporation is necessary information for purposes of affirmative action programs and also to monitor the effectiveness of all recruiting sources, including those for minorities and females.

Asking about *relatives* working for the employer is justified if there is some provision in the employment rules that prohibits relatives of a certain degree of consanguinity from working in the same department or in the direct line of supervision. Such business practices have generally been sustained (see the discussion of this point earlier); the application form can provide the means by which to acquire such information.

Asking if a candidate is *bondable* can be justified. However, the impact of an inquiry rating bondability should be carefully monitored and abandoned unless absolutely necessary.

The *signature blank,* in which the applicant attests to the information on the application form, should clearly indicate that providing false information on the application form can be a cause for discharge. It frequently happens in cases of a charge of discrimination that the employer learns only upon close scrutiny that the complainant had lied on the application form, but by that time it is usually too late to do anything about it. It is advisable to establish some kind of policy with respect to false statements on the application form, including a period within which it will be cause for discharge. Thus, if a person is performing well for a period of, for example, two years, then it might be that the employer, not having learned of the falsification at the time of application, should consider its right to take adverse action against that applicant on the basis of falsification as having been waived. On the other hand, if the employer discovers the falsification within the initial two-year period, or some other period, the policy could be to terminate the person who falsified the application; if the falsification is a minor offense and the employer desires to have that employee, it should tell the employee to reapply.

XYZ CORPORATION

Employment Application

This application will be considered for thirty (30) days after it is filed. For consideration after that time, reapplication is required.

Date of Application _____

The company does not discriminate in hiring or employment on the basis of race, color, religion, creed, national origin, sex, ancestry, age, or handicap. No question on this application is intended to secure information to be used for such discrimination.

Personal

PLEASE PRINT OR TYPE

Last name	First name	Middle name	Area code and home phone number
Current address (street, city, state, and zip code)			Other phone numbers where you can be reached
Are you over 18? _____	Social Security No. _____		Are you a U.S. citizen? ___ Yes ___ No

If No, are you eligible to work in the U.S.? ___ Yes ___ No |

AN AFFIRMATIVE ACTION EQUAL OPPORTUNITY EMPLOYER M/F/H

Position

For what position or Type of Work are you applying?

_____

Are you interested in

___ Full-Time   ___ Temporary   ___ Part-Time   ___ Summer

Are you available for

Shift work ___   Weekend work ___   Overtime ___

Do you have any physical handicaps? ___

If answer is yes, will they affect your ability to perform the job you seek? ___

_____

Have you ever applied at this company before?

___ Yes   ___ No

If Yes, indicate date _____

Subsidiary and address where you applied

_____

Date available   Will you relocate?

                              Yes ___ No ___

_____

State geographic preference, if any   Wage or salary acceptable

_____

Who referred you to this company?

_____

List the names of friends or relatives employed by this company

_____

Person to contact in case of emergency

Name _____   Telephone No. _____

Mechanical Skills

Typing (Speed _____) ( )   Telephone switchboard ( )

Shorthand (Speed ____) ( )   Keypunch   ( )

Office machines (Type of equipment _____) ( )

Data processing (Type of equipment _____) ( )

Other skills and licenses _____

Have you ever been convicted of a crime? ___ Yes ___ No

If yes, describe place, crime, and date.
_____

Have you served in the armed forces of the United States? ___ Yes ___ No

Date of entry in service _____

Rank at entry _____

Branch of service _____

Date of discharge _____

Rank at discharge _____

Reason for separation _____

Special training/duties _____

(Adverse information relating to convictions or type of military discharge will be considered only in relation to the particular job being sought.)

Education

School or Institution   Location   From   To
_____
                Major course   Class standing
_____

Advanced education—college, university, vocational, or other. Applicants may be asked to furnish transcripts of school or college work.
_____
Name of institution   Location or address
_____

Dates attended: From _____ To _____

Did you graduate? __ Yes __ No

Degree granted   Major   Minor
_____

Gradepoint average _____

If you did not graduate, give reason.
_____
Name of institution   Location or address
_____

Dates attended: From _____ To _____

Did you graduate? __ Yes __ No

Degree granted   Major   Minor
_____

Gradepoint average _____

If you did not graduate, give reason.
_____

Employment

Are you presently employed? __ Yes __ No

May we contact your present employer? __ Yes __ No

Present employer

Employer	Telephone no.	Supervisor's name

Mo.　Yr.　to　Mo.　Yr.

Address　　　　　　　　Dates employed

Job title　　　　Salary: Start　　　End

Nature of duties

Reason for leaving

1st previous　　　Telephone no.

Employer　　　　Telephone no.　　　Supervisor's name

Mo.　Yr.　to　Mo.　Yr.

Address　　　　　　　　Dates employed

Job title　　　　Salary: Start　　　End

Nature of duties

Reason for leaving

Employer　　　　Telephone no.　　　Supervisor's name

Mo.　Yr.　to　Mo.　Yr.

Address   Dates employed
_____

Job title   Salary: Start   End
_____

Nature of duties
_____

Reason for leaving
_____

References

List professional references or personal references.

1. _____
    Name   Address   Tel.   Years known

2. _____
    Name   Address   Tel.   Years known

3. _____
    Name   Address   Tel.   Years known

General

All applicants should complete the remaining sections
_____

Were you ever bonded?   Has bond ever been refused or canceled?

Yes ___ No ___   Yes ___ No ___
_____

If Yes, give date and reason

Reason   Date
_____

Authorization

I authorize an inquiry to be made on the information contained in this application. Upon written request, the nature and scope of this inquiry will be made available to me.

Former employers named herein are authorized to give information regarding me. They are hereby released from all liability for issuing such information.

I understand that misrepresentation or omission of facts will be cause for cancellation of consideration for employment or dismissal if employed.

I understand that employment is conditioned upon a favorable health evaluation which may include a physical examination by a doctor. I agree to complete a health evaluation form as part of that physical examination.

_____   _____
           Date   Applicant's signature

Post-Hire EEO Form

Not many employers today utilize a post-hire EEO form, but there are substantial benefits to be gained by doing so.

The post-hire EEO form that follows asks for *race* and *national origin*. Such information is absolutely necessary for filing EEO-1 reports, for compiling data required under Executive Order 11246, and for performing adverse-impact analyses. A practical benefit gained by having the new employee identify his or her race and national origin is that the person cannot later change his or her mind without informing the employer. Especially in the area of national origin, there are many Hispanics who have been classified as other than Hispanic. This is because the employer guessed. Conversely, there have been females who are married to Hispanics who are not themselves Hispanic, but who have been classified as Hispanic because of their surname.

In one instance, a person had been employed by the company for 19 years. Since the mid-1960s, the company, which had thought he was Italian, had been reporting him on its relevant EEO forms as a person other than Hispanic. In 1976, he was denied a promotion and filed a charge of discrimination on the basis of national origin, for the first time identifying himself as Hispanic.

If the employer had used a post-hire EEO form and had new hires and existing workforce fill the form out, it would have been very difficult for the claimant to have asserted his claim, at least with any hope of prevailing.

The data requested concerning impairment is designed to elicit from laymen information necessary to determine whether they are covered by the

Rehabilitation Act of 1973. This information is necessary for record-keeping purposes. Just as important, it can serve as further evidence for an employer defending itself against a claim of discrimination under the Rehabilitation Act or state statutes prohibiting discrimination on the basis of disability.

People who have something adverse happen to them—be it termination, failure to be promoted, or a bad evaluation—more and more often look for a vehicle by which they can have that adverse employment decision reviewed. The Rehabilitation Act and state prohibitions of discrimination against the disabled are increasingly serving as the vehicle for such claims. Furthermore, the definition of who is covered by these kinds of statutes is continuously being expanded.

The employee who has not identified himself or herself as handicapped or disabled, or who has done so only after having had some adverse action taken, will have a more difficult burden in establishing that he or she falls within the protected group. Furthermore, especially if it is a latent handicap or disability, such a claimant will have difficulty establishing that the adverse action was taken because of the handicap or disability when the employer ostensibly, through this record, never knew that the handicap or disability existed.

Finally, if there is a claim of discrimination on the basis of handicap or disability, the employer who has a record such as this should more easily be able to demonstrate to the government investigators or the courts that there are other people with the same handicap or disability working in the job in question, so that could not have been the basis for adverse action against the claimant.

Post-Hire EEO Form

This information is requested for various government reports that must be filed. This document will not be kept in the employee's personnel file. It is kept with the records of the Director of Affirmative Action. Additionally, the information furnished on this document will not and legally cannot be used adversely against the person furnishing the information.

Some of the questions here relate to characteristics that cannot change, and others to characteristics that can change. If there is any change, you are required to inform the Director of Affirmative Action immediately. Our company is required to maintain accurate records and file accurate reports. We view this responsibility most seriously. Similarly, we will treat the making of false statements on this form, or the failure to properly have this information corrected if there is a change in status, in the same manner as we treat false statements made on an application form.

If you have any questions about what is meant by the terms used on this form, please ask the person who gave you this form for an explanation.

This information furnished on this form is provided on a voluntary basis.

You do not have to fill out this form. However, even if you do not fill out the form, we still want you to sign it at the end.

1. Name _____
2. Race _____
3. Sex _____
4. National origin _____
5. Date of birth _____
6. Do you have any relatives in the following categories working for the company presently in any capacity? (Mother, father, stepmother, stepfather, brother, sister, half-brother, half-sister, son, daughter, stepson, stepdaughter)

                      Ans. _____

7. If the response is "yes" to question number 6, please identify the relative(s) and the jobs held by him or her.

_____

_____

_____

_____

8. Are you a drug addict? Ans. _____
9. Have you been a drug addict? Ans. _____
10. If the response to question 8 or 9 is "yes," please indicate the drug you are or have been addicted to, your present status, and identify your doctor, if any.

_____

_____

_____

_____

11. Are you an alcoholic? Ans. _____
12. Have you been an alcoholic in the past?

Ans. _____

13. If the response to questions 11 or 12 is "yes," please indicate your present status and identify the person who is presently treating you, or has been the person who most recently treated you in the past, if you have been treated.

_____

_____

_____

14. Are you a person who (1) has a physical or mental impairment that substantially limits one or more of your major life activities, (2) has a record of such impairment, (3) is regarded as having such an impairment, whether or not you really have such an impairment?

Ans. _____

15. If the response to question 14 is "yes," please identify the impairment, indicate whether you are receiving or have received treatment, and, if so, identify the person who has most recently treated you, or is presently treating you.

_____

_____

_____

To the best of my knowledge the statements above are correct. I have understood the questions or obtained an explanation of the terms used from the person who handed me this form. I understand my obligation to inform the Director of Affirmative Action of any facts that might cause the response to these questions to change, and the seriousness of my failure to answer correctly or change the responses promptly if change is necessary. I have been informed that a copy of this form is posted on Bulletin Board No. 1 so that I can periodically reassess my status. I have been permitted to keep a copy of this form, with my answers.

If the form is not filled out, it is because I have chosen not to fill it out. I fully realize that by not filling out this form I may have made it difficult or even impossible for the employer to consider me for purposes of certain affirmative action purposes.

Signed _____

Name (Printed) _____

Date _____

Directions to the Person Giving the Post-Hire EEO Form to the New Hire (to be filled out immediately after receiving back the Post-Hire EEO Form from the person indicated above and affixed behind that person's filled-out Post-Hire EEO Form)*

Name of New Hire _____

1. Did you personally give the two-page Post-Hire EEO Form to the person indicated above?

    Check one   Yes ☐   No ☐

2. Did that person ask any questions of you?

    Check one   Yes ☐   No ☐

3. What were the questions, if any, and what were your answers?

    _____
    _____
    _____

Signed _____

Name (Printed) _____

Date _____

A DIRECTIVE TO THE FIELD TO SET UP A SAFE HIRING SYSTEM

Sometimes there is difficulty synthesizing obligations under affirmative action programs and other EEO laws and regulations with the essential purpose of the business, which is to earn a profit. Most major corporations now hire on a quota basis, and they hire the best-qualified people for the various jobs from the various groups.

---

*Note to Readers: This page is not part of the EEO Post-Hire Form. This is the direction sheet to be given to persons who are having employees fill out the EEO Post-Hire Form.

Standards for Recruiting, Interviewing, and Hiring

The directive that follows is a sample of how corporate headquarters of a large company might advise one of its operating facilities. The format used will probably not fit every corporation, but it should be adaptable by those it does not perfectly fit. The system described in the memo is believed to be safe under all existing EEO laws.

TO: Facility Personnel Manager

FROM: Corporate Director of Personnel

SUBJECT: The hiring system at Able Widget Company as it will
         be conducted pursuant to our Affirmative Action
         Program

    The hiring system will consist of the application process, the record-keeping system prior to the screening process, the screening system, and the offer system.

    The first step in the application process will be the contact with the person handing out applications at the reception area to persons who seek to be employed for Able Widget Company. Jane Doe presently does this. If anyone inquires about opportunities, be it a relative or friend of a present employee or otherwise, that person will be advised to file an application. Under the old system, employees might indicate they had a friend or relative who was interested in employment and try to find out if there were opportunities. If there were no opportunities, that person never appeared as an applicant. If there were opportunities, that person not only appeared as an applicant, but got the job also. Under the new system, all persons who are at all interested in obtaining employment at Able Widget Company will be required to fill out applications, and we should not indicate whether opportunities are available, but direct anyone who inquires to have the person who is interested fill out an application.

    People will fill out applications on the premises and return them to Jane Doe, or a person who serves her function. They will indicate on the application in the "Job Desired" area whether they are interested in sales, administrative, or plant work. If the application, upon being returned by the applicant to Jane Doe, is not filled in indicating the area of work in which the person is interested, then Jane Doe will advise the person that this has to be filled in and hand the person a copy of the general descriptions of the types of jobs in each category. If people want to be considered for a couple of categories, they can indicate on the application that they are interested in one or more categories and indicate the categories in which they are interested. We should consider them for all the categories for which they indicate an interest.

    There will be no interviewing immediately after the applications are returned except in unusual circumstances. For example, if there is a highly qualified member or female applying

page 2

for a skilled craft position, or some position we have been trying to fill for some time, then we might want to interview immediately.

When Jane Doe receives the application back and the person has left, Jane Doe will fill out the applicant flow log with all the information required there. The determination of whether a person is a minority member will be made by visual observation. While this may create some mistakes, we are not going to ask people what race or national origin they are.

Once Jane Doe has the application and has made the entry into the applicant flow log, there will be a standard means for keeping track of the application. The record-keeping system will require that Jane Doe make a duplicate of any application by a minority female. Furthermore, if a person has indicated an interest in more than one category, more than one copy of the application will have to be made.

Jane Doe will have to keep three separate sets of application files: for sales, administrative positions, and plant positions. Additionally, within each of these groups, she will keep, separately, applications by females, applications by minorities, and applications by others. An application by a minority female will be included in the female group and in the minority group.

When we want to hire for any particular category--that is, sales, administrative, or plant positions--the person in charge of the screening for such hiring will ask Jane Doe for the files for active applicants for those positions. An active applicant will be any applicant who has submitted an application within the prior 90 days. As is indicated on our application form, we will not consider persons for employment if their applications have not been filed within the preceding 90 days.

The person who is doing the screening for the position must be aware of the goals and timetables we have set for hiring minorities and females. We are going to meet those goals. Thus, if our goals call for hiring 25% females into a particular job group and we have four openings, one of those hires should be a female. If this means that we have to go through each application by a female for that category or position and interview each of these females to find that one, we will have to do so. However, in practice, we do not believe that will be necessary.

page 3

In determining who should be invited in for an interview, the person who is doing the screening for the job should be aware that the goal has to be met. If six people are being invited for an interview for four positions, and one of those four positions has to be filled by a female, then it will be best to have two or even three females among those six people.

When the candidates are invited in for an interview, first we should try to steer females to jobs not traditionally held by females, and males to jobs not traditionally held by males. Thus, if we have an opening for a racker-feeder position and a loader/shipper position, and we have a male candidate before us who had applied for a plant job, we should orient our interview toward offering the candidate the racker-feeder job. Second, if any candidate appears attractive for a job and we desire to make an offer, before making the offer we should show the candidate to whom the offer is about to be made the job for which he or she will be hired. This can be done as part of the interviewing process.

The candidate will not be told about any other opening that is available, at this stage. Thus, at this stage, the male candidate will not be told about the loader/shipper opening, and the female candidate will not be told about the racker-feeder opening.

After showing the candidate the job for which we want to hire him or her, we will return to the office.

If, as part of the interview or after viewing the job, the candidate indicates that he or she is not interested and will not take the job to which we are trying to orient him or her, then we will ask the candidate to sign a rejection form. We will tell the candidate that he or she can be considered for other positions, but that he or she must first sign the rejection slip.

We cannot refuse outright to consider any candidate for any position; if we did, we would be in violation of Title VII. However, our purpose in conducting our screening system in this way is to break up concentrations of male and female job groups.

On a monthly basis, Jane Doe will have to total the number of male and female, Hispanic, black, and Caucasian applicants for each category of job--sales, administrative, or plant. Although we have goals and we are treating those goals as quotas, that alone is not enough for us to be safe. If the applicant

page 4

flow rate of minorities or females for any particular type of job--sales, administrative, or plant--is higher than our goal percentage, then we must consider the applicant flow rate to be our goal. Thus, if our goal for hire of females into job group 8 is 25%, but our applicant flow rate of females for plant jobs generally is 35%, then our goal for hire of females into loader/shipper should be 35%. In no event should we allow our hire rate of females for any job group to fall below the applicant flow rate of females for the category of jobs within which that job group falls.

If there are any problems on implementing this system, or there is apprehension about failing to meet our goals for the affirmative flow, then John Goodfaith should be contacted immediately.

FOOTNOTES

[1] 513 F.2d 90 (1975), *reversed* 423 U.S. 923 (1976).
[2] 529 F.2d 760 (4th Cir. 1975).
[3] 5 FEP Cases 129 (N.D. Ill. 1972).
[4] 356 F. Supp. 286 (S.D. N.Y. 1973), *aff'd mem.* 489 F.2d 752 (2d Cir. 1974).
[5] 15 FEP Cases 1690 (D.N.M. 1977).
[6] 531 F.2d 224 (5th Cir. 1976).
[7] 499 F.2d 859 (7th Cir. 1974).
[8] 424 F. Supp. 1238 (E.D. Ark. 1976).
[9] 428 F. Supp. 1118 (E.D. Pa. 1976).
[10] 567 F.2d 1267 (4th Cir. 1977).
[11] EEOC Decision No. AL68-1-155E (May 19, 1969).
[12] 414 U.S. 811 (1973).
[13] 18 EPD ¶8701 (S.D. N.Y. 1979).
[14] 472 F.2d 631 (9th Cir. 1972).
[15] 523 F.2d 1290 (8th Cir. 1975).
[16] 332 F. Supp. 519 (E.D. La. 1971).
[17] 568 F.2d 1162 (5th Cir. 1978).
[18] 395 F. Supp. 836 (S.D. Ohio 1975).
[19] 379 F. Supp. 684 (N.D. Cal. 1974).
[20] See EEOC decision No. F4-02 (July 10, 1973), 6 FEP Cases 830.
[21] See EEOC decision No. 72-1176 (Feburary 28, 1972), 5 FEP Cases 960.
[22] EEOC decision No. 72-0427 (August 31, 1971), 4 FEP Cases 304.
[23] EEOC decision No. 72-0947.
[24] 12 EPD (CCH) ¶11,010 (D.D.C. 1976).
[25] See *Merriweather* v. *American Cast Iron Pipe Co.,* 362 F. Supp. 670 (N.D. Ala. 1973); *Lester* v. *Ellis Trucking Co.,* 10 FEP Cases 1036 (W.D. Tenn. 1975); *Jimerson* v. *Kisco Co.,* 542 F.2d 1008 (8th Cir. 1976).
[26] 401 U.S. 424 (1971).
[27] 530 F.2d 1159 (5th Cir.) *cert. denied,* 429 U.S. 861 (1976).
[28] 13 FEP Cases 825 (N.D. Fla. 1974).
[29] 474 F.2d 906 (5th Cir. 1973).
[30] 494 F.2d 211 (5th Cir. 1974).
[31] 516 F.2d 103 (5th Cir. 1975).
[32] 559 F.2d 310 (5th Cir. 1977).
[33] 576 F.2d 1292 (8th Cir. 1978).
[34] 395 F. Supp. 836 (S.D. Ohio 1975).
[35] 459 F.2d 725 (1st Cir. 1972).
[36] 410 F. Supp. 873 (C.D. Cal. 1976).
[37] 475 F.2d 216 (10th Cir. 1972).
[38] 558 F.2d 117 (2d Cir. 1977), *cert. denied,* 434 U.S. 1015 (1978).

[39] 565 F.2d 895 (5th Cir. 1978).
[40] 445 F. Supp. 223 (D. Del. 1978).
[41] 4 EPD (CCH) ¶7944 (N.D. Cal. 1972).
[42] 292 F. Supp. 413 (S.D. Ohio 1968).
[43] 524 F.2d 263 (10th Cir. 1975).
[44] 396 F. Supp. 327 (W.D. N.C. 1974), *aff'd in relevant part and rev'd in part,* 518 F.2d 543 (4th Cir. 1975).
[45] 388 F. Supp. 912 (E.D. Wis. 1975), *aff'd,* 534 F.2d 715 (7th Cir. 1976).
[46] 362 F. Supp. 886 (N.D. Ala. 1973).
[47] 507 F.2d 1084 (5th Cir. 1975).
[48] 320 F. Supp. 477 (N.D. Ala. 1970), *rev'd on other grounds,* 447 F.2d 128 (5th Cir. 1971).
[49] 7 FEP Cases 710 (W.D. Okla. 1973).
[50] 555 F.2d 1283 (5th Cir. 1977).
[51] 566 F.2d 1334 (9th Cir. 1977).
[52] 294 F. Supp. 368 (E.D. La. 1968), *aff'd sub nom. Local 53, International Association of Heat and Frost Insulation v. Vogler,* 407 F.2d 1047 (5th Cir. 1969).
[53] 400 U.S. 542 (1971).
[54] 517 F.2d 818 (D.C. Cir. 1975).
[55] 481 F.2d 1115 (D.C. Cir. 1973).
[56] 466 F. Supp. 1388 (W.D. Mo. 1979).
[57] 20 FEP Cases 764 (7th Cir. 1979); *cert. den.* 22 FEP Cases 315 (1980).
[58] 555 F.2d 753 (9th Cir. 1977).
[59] 366 F. Supp. 763, 790 (D.D.C. 1973), *modif. on other gds,* 567 F.2d 429 (D.C. Cir. 1976), *cert. den.* 434 U.S. 1086 (1978).
[60] 18 FEP Cases 1118, 430 F. Supp. 884, 891 (E.D. Va. 1977), *aff'd,* 577 F.2d 869 (4th Cir. 1978).
[61] 14 FEP Cases 1767 (S.D. Fla. 1976), *aff'd,* 553 F.2d 99 (5th Cir. 1977).
[62] 19 FEP Cases 1087 (N.D. Ill. 1979).
[63] 510 F.2d 939 (6th Cir. 1975), *cert. denied,* 425 U.S. 998 (1976).
[64] 433 U.S. 321 (1977).
[65] 395 F. Supp. 378 (N.D. Cal. 1975).
[66] 15 FEP Cases 365 (E.D. Pa. 1977).
[67] 520 F.2d 492 (6th Cir. 1975), *cert. denied sub nom. Smith v. Troyan,* 426 U.S. 934 (1976).
[68] A.D. 2d 1029 (3rd Dept. 1979); NYSDHR Case No. GCD-36562-75.
[69] NYSDHR Cases Nos. GCD-39208-75 and GCDS-34885-74.
[70] 405 F. Supp. 426 (C.D. Cal. 1975).
[71] 444 F.2d 1194 (7th Cir. 1971), *cert. denied,* 405 U.S. 991 (1972).
[72] 544 F.2d 892 (5th Cir. 1977), *cert. denied,* 434 U.S. 844 (1977).
[73] 553 F.2d 522 (6th Cir. 1977).
[74] 558 F.2d 1176 (4th Cir. 1977), *cert. denied,* 435 U.S. 934 (1978).
[75] 17 EPD (CCH) ¶8586 (7th Cir. 1978).
[76] 525 F.2d 409 (8th Cir. 1975).

[77] 13 FEP Cases 252 (D.N.J. 1976).

[78] 421 F. Supp. 39 (S.D. N.Y. 1976).

[79] 562 F.2d 496 (7th Cir. 1977).

[80] 15 FEP Cases 272 (D. Col. 1977), *aff'd,* 595 F.2d 533 (10th Cir. 1979), *cert. den.* 21 EPD ¶30,316.

[81] 556 F.2d 184 (3d Cir. 1977).

[82] 17 FEP Cases 914 (M.D. Fla. 1977).

[83] 17 FEP Cases 1161 (N.D. Fla. 1978).

[84] 17 FEP Cases 918 (E.D. Pa. 1978).

[85] 47 U.S.L.W. 4291, 19 EPD ¶9027 (1979).

[86] 13 FEP Cases 385 (R.I. 1976).

[87] Case No. 77–OFCCP–7–R OFCCP decision reported in 19 FEP Cases 1674 (1979).

[88] 280 Or. 163, 570 P.2d 76 (1977).

[89] 12 FEP Cases 1103 (Wash. 1975).

[90] 63 A.D.2d 170, 406 N.Y.S.2d 912 (3d Dept. 1978), *aff'd,* 18 EPD ¶8716 (1978), *cert. den.* 439 U.S. 1073 (1979).

[91] 64 A.D.2d 811, 407 N.Y.S.2d 281 (4th Dept. 1978).

[92] 14 FEP Cases 344 (Wis. 1976).

[93] 59 A.D.2d 449, 399 N.Y.S.2d 926 (3d Dept. 1977).

[94] 13 FEP Cases 1811 (Wis. 1976).

[95] 13 FEP 1809 (Wis. 1976).

[96] 12 FEP 975 (Wash. 1976).

[97] 20 FEP Cases 162 (E.D. Mo. 1979).

[98] 47 U.S.L.W. 4689 (June 11, 1979).

[99] 433 U.S. 299 (1977).

[100] 17 FEP Cases 622 (4th Cir. 1978).

[101] 431 U.S. 324 (1977).

[102] 41 C.F.R. ¶1610.18.

[103] 423 U.S. 923 (1976).

[104] 99 S. Ct. 2721 (1979) 20 EPD (CCH) ¶30026.

[105] 497 F.2d 1374 (5th Cir. 1974).

Chapter 5

Standards for Promotion, Transfer, and Assignment

INTRODUCTION

The principles described in the introduction to Chapter 4 for recruiting, interviewing, and hiring are equally applicable to promotions, transfers, and assignments. The courts and government enforcement agencies in the EEO area will examine the standards established and the impact of those standards on protected-group persons in the same manner as described in Chapter 4.

The scenario that most frequently develops to make promotion, transfer, or assignment an issue is (1) a claim of denial of promotion, transfer, or assignment by a person in a specific protected group, and (2) a statistically significant underrepresentation, when compared to the *apparent* availability, of people in that protected group in the job or category to which the claimant had aspired.

Defense is usually very difficult in these cases because the employer is placed in the position of having to explain the operations of what are really social phenomena. The developed EEO law presumes the neutral. It presumes that a job that pays more will be equally desirable to males and females, minorities and nonminorities, old and young; that a job requiring extensive retraining and learning is no less desirable to the old than to the young; that minorities would just as frequently as nonminorities prefer to be promoted and receive a higher rate of pay than stay in the same job and work more overtime; that females just as much as males desire jobs that require overnight travel, after-hours business/social engagements, dirty jobs, night jobs, jobs requiring heavy lifting, and jobs that require the operation of heavy machinery.

It would be blatant discrimination for an employer not to rely on these neutral premises in making a personnel decision. Nevertheless, practical experience has taught many personnel specialists that not all groups respond the same to a given opportunity. In an EEO promotion case, it often becomes the burden of an employer to prove as a matter of law that the neutral premise does not in fact exist; that a differential in assignments, promotions, or transfers has occurred through no fault of the employer; and that these social phenomena do account, in whole or in part, for a differential in rate of promotion, transfer, or assignment, and for a differential in earnings between males and females, minorities and nonminorities.

Employers will continue to have to explain or account for the impact of essentially social factors on their promotions, transfers, and assignments. For this reason, and especially in this area of employment, it is most advantageous for employers to have extensive documentation of the manifestation of these phenomena. Systems such as job posting and bidding, self-identification by employees of jobs to which they aspire, and other procedures permitting the personal predilection of the employee to be demonstrated are very important and helpful. Very frequently, it is only by developing evidence of this personal predilection that an employer can demonstrate that the *apparent* availability of people in a protected group is not the *real* availability. Just as it is crucial to adverse-impact analysis to have an applicant for employment identify the job sought, so also in the promotion and transfer area is it essential to have identification by an existing employee of the job that person seeks. Only in this way can a real adverse-impact analysis be conducted.

An extensive discussion concerning the establishment and implementation of such systems is described later in this chapter. First, let us describe standards that have been the subject of litigation and decision.

STANDARDS AT ISSUE

Age Standards

Promotion potential or *time left to retirement* is the most significant standard in the age-discrimination area. In *Marshall* v. *Board of Education of Salt Lake City*,[1] the court found that it was a violation of the Age Discrimination in Employment Act (ADEA) not to reappoint a qualified administrator because he would be able to work only one year before being mandatorily retired at age 65. The school administration had given this as the reason for not reappointing him.

In some of the most significant settlements involving age-discrimination charges, *promotion potential* was found to have been one of the factors established by management for purposes of assessing employees being considered for termination because of a reduction-in-force (RIF). Those administering the assessment programs were demonstrated to have given older employees less point credit on the evaluation sheet for promotion potential. Thus, employees 60 to 65 had received the least number of points for this factor, employees 56 to 59 had received the second least, and so on. (This approach of placing employees above the age of 40 into subgroups of progressive age is standard for the U.S. Department of Labor, and any adverse-impact analysis conducted by an employer to determine its own exposure should compare not only the effect of some personnel action on people over 40 and under 40, but also the effect of that action or policy on people within different age groups over the age of 40.) This type of evidence was felt to be so damaging by the employers involved that they settled the cases rather than litigate the issue of whether promotion potential, when it has a progressively disparate impact on people over the age of 40, is discriminatory. Such an assessment of the impact of such evidence is probably correct, as indicated by the decision of the court in *Marshall* v. *Board of Education of Salt Lake City, supra.*

Even though *Board of Education of Salt Lake City* did not involve promotion, only retention, and the cases settled involved the use of promotion potential as a factor in determining retention, not promotion, transfer, or assignment, it would seem clear that the principles involved are equally applicable to promotion cases.

Although it is discriminatory to consider promotion potential when that factor is having an adverse and disparate impact on people over 40, it is not a violation of the Age Discrimination in Employment Act to give *preferential consideration* to people over 40. For example, in *Gill* v. *Union Carbide Corporation,*[2] another layoff case, the company had established a policy regarding company service for reduction-in-force layoff purposes that personnel with less than three years of service would be considered first for the RIF unless the quality factors were exceptional; that personnel of less than 40 years of age with relatively short service would be considered next, with the quality factors being important; and that the last to be considered for layoff were personnel with long company service and who were over 40 years of age. Again, although this was a layoff case, it would seem that the principles involved were equally applicable to promotion and that under the ADEA, the U.S. Department of Labor would have approved of an employer's giving extra credit to those over the age of 40. In fact, in those large settlements referenced above, one of the conditions demanded by the U.S. Department of Labor was that the employer give extra credit to people over 40. However, in adopting such a policy, the employer should be wary of state laws, such as those in New York, that prohibit discrimination against people above the age of 18. Also, the employer should consider that giving extra points to people over 40 might have a foreseeable adverse impact against minorities and females; and that EEOC, not the U.S. Department of Labor, is enforcing the ADEA, and the sympathy of EEOC will very likely lie with enforcement benefitting the traditional Title VII protected groups.

In the *Gill* case, there were other standards that were noted approvingly by the court. These standards were *ability, effectiveness, versatility, uniqueness* (whether the employee possesses a specialty that is important), and the *existence of personal problems.* If these are legitimate factors to consider for purposes of RIF, they should also be legitimate for determining promotion, transfer, or assignment.

It would appear that *physical-fitness* requirements can be considered in determining whether or not employees should be considered for promotion. Again, the support for this comes from regulations involving layoff, rather than promotion cases. According to the U.S. Department of Labor,[3] it is a defense to an age-discrimination claim to consider physical fitness, because this is a "factor other than age" within the meaning of the ADEA, Section 4(f)(1). However, to gain the benefit of this exemption in the ADEA, the physical-fitness standard must be reasonably necessary for the work to be performed, must be uniformly applied to all applicants or persons under consideration regardless of age, and must not be based upon the assumption that every employee over a particular age becomes physically unable to perform the duties of a certain job. The fact that the Department of Labor feels that physical fitness must be only *reasonably necessary* for the work to be performed, as opposed to a business necessity, is significant. Under the developed Title VII law, if a claimant were able to demonstrate that the standard was having an adverse impact upon people in the protected age group, then the employer would be required to come forward and validate the standard. The proof necessary to establish that something is reasonably necessary is far less onerous than the proof necessary to validate.

Furthermore, it would seem that, at least in certain occupations, an employer might be able to rely upon certain assumptions concerning the effects of old age, without looking to the individual. Thus, in *Usery* v. *Tamiami Trail Tours, Inc.,*[4] and in *Hodgson* v. *Greyhound Lines, Inc.,*[5] the employer was able to sustain its compulsory age limitation without reference to the actual physical condition of an individual because there were no physical tests available to accurately assess the debilitating effects of old age on a case-by-case basis. Consequently, at least insofar as public carriers such as bus lines and airlines are concerned, such age requirements would appear permissible, based upon evidence that workers are generally less physically capable as they get older and that the carrier is required to exercise the "highest standard of care," the standard required by the FAA, to protect the public.

The *"youthful look"* or the *"mature look"* can be a legitimate job requirement, according to the Department of Labor, when the job entails promotion or advertising of products exclusively designed for and directed to appeal to either youthful or elderly customers.[6] EEOC will probably disagree with this interpretation.

It is illegal to consider the *cost of providing insurance benefits or other ancillary benefits* when considering someone over 40 for promotion, even though those benefits might cost more because the person is over 40. This is the administrative interpretation of the U.S. Department of Labor.[7] However, through another interpretation, Labor has indicated that employers do not have to fund their pension plans in such a manner as to increase the entitlement of an employee who stays beyond the age of 65. Also, Labor has indicated that an employer need not make increased insurance premium payments for anyone 65 or older if those increases are required solely because of the age of the employee.

Age standards for entrance into a *bona fide apprenticeship program,* whether by promotion or transfer, or even hire, are legal, according to the U.S. Department of Labor.[8]

Standards for Race and National Origin

In individual cases where charges of discrimination on the basis of race or national origin have been made regarding promotion, transfer, or assignment, even absent the introduction of any statistics by the claimant, the burden of proof is easily shifted by the claimant to the employer. A minority member who can demonstrate that he had the highest rating pursuant to the selection standard used by the employer but did not receive the job sought can establish a *prima facie* case and shift the burden of defense to the employer. See *Abrams* v. *Johnson.*[9] A minority person who can demonstrate that the supervisor who acted for the employer in determining who would be promoted, transferred, or assigned had a reputation for being prejudiced, and who can also demonstrate that there was preselection—that is, that the posting of the job was *pro forma* and the selection had been made before it was posted—can thereby establish a *prima facie* case. See, for example, *Haire* v. *Calloway.*[10] A minority member who can demonstrate that the employer did not give him or her the sought-after transfer, promotion, or assignment and, that in doing so, the employer did not follow established regular procedures or its own policies, can establish a *prima facie* case. See *Page* v. *Bolger.*[11]

Employers defending against class-type discrimination claims asserted by minorities regarding promotions, transfers, or assignments are in a most disadvantageous position. All the standards described in Chapter 4 would be applicable here. Additionally, the scenario would be the same; that is, the claimant would demonstrate adverse impact, that he or she was adversely affected by imposition of the standard, and the employer would have to come forward to show that the standard was validated. The big difference in these cases, however, is that most employers do not have the documentation to establish the actual availability pool from which the promotions, transfers, or assignments have been made, whereas in a hiring case, they generally have such documentation. Where the claimant can demonstrate that the system is keeping minorities from achieving promotion, transfer, or assignment at the rate one might expect, given their *apparent* availability in the pool from which the people to be promoted, transferred, or assigned are working, the burden also shifts to the employer. In such cases, the established case law indicates that there are certain standards (although the courts are not wont to say it) for assessing whether there has been discriminatory conduct. These standards, in promotion, transfer, or assignment cases, are in summary (1) *a job posting system;* (2) *a formal evaluation system for promotion, transfer, or assignment—written job descriptions;* (3) *written guidelines to be used by the persons who do the evaluations for selecting people to be promoted, transferred, or assigned;* (4) *a system for rating the supervisors who are doing the ratings to determine who will be promoted, transferred, or assigned;* and (5) *the race or ethnic composition of the group of people doing the rating or selection.*

Courts almost always look to the existence or nonexistence of a utilized *posting system* in assessing class claims of discrimination regarding promotion, transfer, or assignment. Thus, in *James* v. *Stockham Valves & Fittings Co.,*[12] the employer could not demonstrate that it had a job posting system that was utilized. Similarly, in *Stewart* v. *General Motors Corp.,*[13] there was no job posting system that was generally utilized. The employer, as an alternative, tried to demonstrate that offers of promotion had been made to minorities but that they had turned them down. The evidence proved unacceptable. In *Wells* v. *Meyer's Bakery,*[14] again, vacancies were not posted, and in the relief the court ordered that vacancies be posted.

The posting of vacancies is not in and of itself required by the law. But the absence of a posting system, together with an apparent underrepresentation of minorities among those being selected for promotion, assignment, or transfer, is powerful evidence of discrimination. Furthermore, the Office of Federal Contract Compliance Programs has adopted a policy of seeking to compel employers to implement and utilize job posting systems. Since the courts and the government are equating a posting system with equal employment opportunity, employers should seriously consider utilization of such a system.

Subjective, unstructured evaluation systems that result in a disparate adverse effect on minorities have been unanimously condemned by the courts and found discriminatory. See, for example, *Rowe* v. *General Motors Corp.*[15] As a remedy, the courts almost always order that *formal, written evaluation systems* be established and implemented. See, for example, *Baxter* v. *Savannah Sugar Refining Corp.*[16] However, even an unstructured, informal evaluation system, if it does not result in disparate adverse impact against minorities, is not illegal. (*Hester* v. *Southern Railway Co.*[17])

In addition, a necessary part of any formal, written evaluation system is that it *evaluate the people who are doing the rating.* *(Wells* v. *Meyer's Bakery, supra.)*

If posting jobs, having a formal written evaluation system, and having a system of evaluating the raters would assure an employer of having a court find its promotion, transfer, or assignment system to be fair, then should not employers be rapidly initiating such systems to insulate themselves from substantial liability?

The answer is (1) yes, employers should initiate such systems, but (2) such systems will not guarantee immunity from either prosecution or liability, and (3) what the courts generally mean by "fair" or "nondiscriminatory" is not what one generally thinks of when using those terms. The legal meaning of "fair," in the EEO promotion, transfer, or assignment context involving minority claims, generally is that the end result of the selection process does not have a disparate effect against minorities.

Some courts directly say that this is what they mean, as in *Patterson* v. *American Tobacco Co.;*[18] others do not directly say this but order the employer to establish such standards itself, and then reject such standards as inadequate when the employer proposes them, as in *Strain* v. *Philpott;*[19] others enjoin the use of any procedure that has a disparate impact and is not validated, with the net result that the employer engages in a quota system for promotions for a long period of time. This was the aftermath of *Rowe* v. *General Motors Corp., supra.*

Although nothing less than a promotion, transfer, or assignment system with no end-result adverse impact can guarantee an employer immunity (see, for example, *Robinson* v. *Union Carbide Corp.,*[20]) the standards described can enhance the likelihood of an employer's prevailing in a promotion case involving a class claim by minorities. See *Friend* v. *Leidinger.*[21]

An *oral interview* and a *prior record of unsatisfactory performance* were the standards at issue in *Blizard* v. *Fielding.*[22] In that case, the claimant had been the only person who passed a civil-service test for promotion. The court found that the commissioner had discretion to reject a civil-service list containing less than three candidates; that the claimant's interview demonstrated she was unsatisfactory for the job; and that her prior neglect of her work assignments demonstrated her poor attitude. In this case, the employer could establish these facts by ample oral testimony and memoranda to the file.

Sex Standards

A refusal to consider a female for promotion to a position because management feels it is "a man's job," since it is possibly unsafe or heavy work, is in and of itself discriminatory. In *Gillin* v. *Federal Paper Board Co.,*[23] management admitted that it did not consider the claimant for a position of truck dispatcher because the job required that the incumbent go out on the road to assist truck drivers whose vehicles had broken down. Frequently this required the person to go out at night, and management felt that Ms. Gillin would not be safe. The refusal to consider is *per se* discrimination, stated the Second Circuit. However, the fact that the claimant was not considered does not automatically entitle her to the job for which she was not considered. The Second Circuit remanded the case for the district court to determine whether or not claimant was more qualified than the male who was ultimately awarded the job. The Second Circuit noted that this male apparently had better qualifications, but that would be an issue of fact for the trial court to determine. Ultimately, the trial court found as fact that the person to whom the job had been awarded, a male, was better qualified than claimant, so she was found not to be entitled to any remedy.[24]

In *Gillin,* the claimant had applied for the job she knew was open. However, in *Huckeby* v. *Frozen Food Express,*[25] the court distinguished *Gillin* and found that the employer's failure to interview the claimant was not sex discrimination. There, the female employee had failed to ask for an interview or apply for the position in question, and the court found that she had not been denied any opportunity to be interviewed. It also found that despite the absence of females in supervisory positions, the claimant did not have the objective qualifications for the job she sought.

Refusing to consider a female for a position because the job requires *late-night entertaining* is also discrimination. In a case voluntarily settled after the commencement of a lawsuit, a New Jersey bank had been accused of refusing to award the position of branch manager to a female because she could not do the necessary socializing and late-night entertaining. The female had been the assistant branch manager at that branch and as such was the most likely candidate, and she had sought the position. The decision by the employer to settle rather than litigate was probably judicious.

Giving informal training to males but not to females is also discriminatory. Certain production plants have provisions in their collective-bargaining agreements, or at least a practice, that a person who bids on a job and is transferred into that job must demonstrate proficiency in it within a certain period of time. In such situations, if only males are given the opportunity to fill in on those jobs temporarily when the incumbent is absent or on vacation, they are, because of that advantage, more likely than females to demonstrate proficiency after bidding for and obtaining the jobs. Such a practice was found discriminatory in *English* v. *Seaboard Coast R.R. Co.,*[26] a race-discrimination case. To the extent that such practices exist today, however, they more frequently disadvantage females than minorities. Similarly, denying to females the opportunity to test and train so as to enable them to bid for jobs in a higher classification was found discriminatory in a situation where males, although not in the same job, were given that opportunity. See *Trivett* v. *Tri-State Container Corp.*[27]

Giving a *preview* of jobs that are dirty, or require heavy lifting or handling of heavy machinery, to females who bid for those jobs but not to males who bid for them is also discriminatory. Very often this "informal introduction" takes place without the knowledge of management, because a foreman who has seen a female bid for a job in his sector has made a personal determination that the female will not be able to perform, or will disrupt his crew.

Restrictive bidding or opportunity policies are also discriminatory—for example, telling only males about certain job openings and only females about other job openings.

Word-of-mouth recruiting for supervisory jobs, when coupled with prior discrimination against females in attaining those jobs as evidenced by an absence of females in those jobs, has been found to be discriminatory. *Nance* v. *Union Carbide Corp., Consumer Products Division.*[28]

One standard to be wary of, but that has not yet been ruled on in court, is the manner in which females who bid on and attain traditionally "male" jobs are portrayed. In one case, which settled, a woman who had bid into such a job and performed it successfully had been portrayed in the employer's monthly newletter to employees as a tomboy who had been the only girl in a family of five children and had liked to tinker with machinery from the time she was a child. Two psychologists were prepared to testify that this portrayal, which was truthful, had a chilling effect on other female employees who might otherwise have bid into the same job. Given the fact that pre-Title VII discrimination had existed in job assignments, this type of evidence might have established a continuity of the illegal practice. But see *Lewis* v. *Tobacco Workers Int'l Union,*[29] where the court indicated that there was no affirmative obligation on an employer to announce that it no longer discriminated.

Standards for the Handicapped and Disabled

There is as yet very little case law developed under federal and state statutes prohibiting discrimination against the handicapped or disabled, especially in the area of promotions, transfers, and assignments. Those standards noted in the preceding chapter regarding hiring and in the subsequent chapter regarding discharge are equally applicable to promotion, transfer, and assignment fact situations. Additionally, what little case law does exist indicates that the courts will approach employment discrimination claims under handicap and disability statutes in the same manner as other employment discrimination claims.

In *Smith* v. *Fletcher,*[30] the claimant established that people with a similar education and work background to hers had been promoted past her, for no apparent reason. She also established that she was a paraplegic confined to a wheelchair. This showing was sufficient, the court held, to demonstrate that she had suffered discrimination because of her handicap.

Another case, *McNutt* v. *Hills,*[31] although presenting many procedural issues unrelated to standards, is noteworthy because the hearing officer, whose ruling was enforced by this trial court, had found discrimination in the failure of the employer, the federal government, to undertake affirmative action on behalf of the claimant, thereby breaching its statutory and regulatory obligations.

ASSESSING AND MINIMIZING ADVERSE IMPACT IN PROMOTIONS, TRANSFERS, AND ASSIGNMENTS

There are two approaches available to employers who are seeking to avoid class-type liability because of their promotion, transfer, and assignment policies. The first, and most difficult, is to validate the selection procedures by which people are chosen for promotion, transfer, or assignment. If that selection procedure is validated, the employer can rebut a *prima facie* case of discrimination, and need not be concerned if the selection procedure is having adverse impact.

Popular literature such as *Psychology Today* and the *New York Times* have described selection attempts being made via batteries of tests and exercises administered at assessment centers. Large employers, such as AT&T and Eastern Airlines, as well as the EEOC itself, are using such techniques, which are described as "validated."

It is to be hoped that the day will come when such tests, if subjected to legal attack, are deemed validated by courts, and that they will be generally available to all employers at an affordable price. For the present, however, these tests have not been found validated by the courts. Furthermore, virtually every testing service has claimed its tests validated, yet these claims have not succeeded when subjected to the rigorous examination at trial. Appendix B, at the end of this book, lists many tests and the court or EEOC decisions in which they have been assessed.

The second approach available to employers for assessing and minimizing adverse impact can and must be utilized with any program purporting to validate a test. As was indicated in Chapter 2, even if an employer does have a validated selection procedure, if that procedure is having an adverse impact, the Uniform Guidelines impose upon the employer an obligation to continuously seek alternative selection procedures that have a lesser adverse impact and are also validated.

This second approach, and the ultimate elimination of statistically significant adverse impact in the selection process, is the only safe and practical manner in which to operate a business. Furthermore, the first approach, attempting to validate the selection device, is expensive and calls for continuous reanalysis, but the second approach can operate independently. If there is no adverse impact, not even a *prima facie* class case can be established by a claimant, and no validation of the selection devices need be demonstrated.

The key element in establishing systems for assessing and minimizing adverse impact in promotions, transfers, and assignments is generating the proper type of data and documenting such data. In Chapter 4 we saw that for purposes of adverse-impact analysis in hiring, the appropriate data to be compared are applicants and hires; so also in the area of promotions, transfers, and assignments, data should be generated to as closely as possible simulate an applicant/hire ratio. Thus, for purposes of analysis, placements into jobs through internal systems of promotion, transfer, and assignment should be viewed as hires, and the people seeking those promotions, transfers, and assignments should be considered the applicant pool.

Applying this approach requires an understanding of certain basic legal principles for purposes of adverse-impact analysis in promotions, transfers, and assignments. These principles relate to both sides of the ratio—"hires," people who were actually promoted, transferred, or assigned, or were offered such opportunity; and "applicants," those who placed themselves in the availability pool and remained in it until they were accepted or rejected.

On the hiring side of the ratio—that is, those promoted, transferred, or assigned—an important first step is establishing the relevant time period. Once an ongoing system of adverse-impact assessment is established, the period, for assessment purposes, can be a year. The employer can compare the number and composition of those who sought promotion, transfer, or assignment that year with the number and percentage of those who actually received, or were offered, such promotions, transfers, or assignments that year. In reviewing government contractors, OFCCP will be doing its reviews on that basis.

However, for the employer who has not had an ongoing system, and who wishes to know what its existing exposure might be if someone should file a charge of discrimination, the time period will be different. There are three different periods available, and all three have found some support in court decisions.

One alternative available is to look to the racial, ethnic, or sex composition of those who have been promoted, transferred, or assigned, whenever that might have occurred. This requires review of existing employees in the positions to be examined.

A second alternative in Title VII cases is to look at the promotions, transfers, or assignments subsequent to July 2, 1965, the effective date of Title VII. The rationale for this approach is that before that date, discrimination was not illegal; therefore, in analyzing the employment system, the courts should not charge against the employer responsibility for actions taken before that date.

The third alternative, again in Title VII cases, is to analyze activity that has occurred during the relevant period covered by the lawsuit. Under this approach, one looks to the date on which the charge of discrimination forming the basis for the lawsuit was filed, and then looks backwards either 180 days or 300 days, depending upon whether there was a state deferral agency and it was utilized. The rationale for this approach is that the only people who can be in the class are those who could have filed a timely charge at the time the class representative filed his or her charge. *Wetzel* v. *Liberty Mutual Insurance Co.*[32] Further support for this rationale comes from the Supreme Court's decision in *United Airlines, Inc.* v. *Evans.*[33] There, the Court ruled that "a discriminatory act which is not made the basis for a timely charge is the legal equivalent of a discriminatory act which occurred before the statute was passed. . . . [I]t is merely an unfortunate event in history which has no present legal consequences."[34]

As the case law develops, the third alternative will probably become the most prevalent in use, but evidence of discriminatory conduct prior to the relevant period of liability will probably be admitted into evidence for historical background purposes.

On the "applicant pool" side of a ratio involving assessment of promotion, transfer, or assignment policies, law unfavorable to employers has developed. In the absence of very strong evidence to the contrary, courts will presume that everyone in an employer's blue-collar work force wanted to become a supervisor, if that is where most supervisors come from. Some courts have even gone so far as to suggest that everybody in the population surrounding the facility is a potential supervisor for that facility, for purposes of determining what the percentage availability of minorities is for supervisory positions.

In the area of promotions, transfers, and assignments, all too frequently an employer's existing system does not allow for any kind of adverse-impact analysis other than a comparison between the gross placements and the gross pool. The fundamental step in establishing a system for assessing and minimizing adverse impact in promotions, transfers, and assignments is to correct this basic flaw.

Defining the Applicant Pool for Promotions, Transfers, and Assignments

Just as not everyone in the population surrounding a facility is literally an applicant for employment for purposes of hire analysis, so also, not every person in the workforce of an employer is an applicant for promotion to a supervisory position within that facility. It is to the advantage of the employer to establish its promotion, transfer, and assignment system in such a way as to reflect this truth. People should have to apply to be promoted, transferred, or reassigned. The process of applying for a promotion, transfer, or assignment is referred to in this book as "self-identification," to distinguish it from the actual applicant-hire situation.

There are substantial advantages to having a self-identification system in operation:

1. Such a system makes it much simpler to conduct adverse-impact analyses. The people who have identified themselves as wanting a particular job, whether it be by promotion, transfer, or assignment, will constitute the appli-

cant pool, and those who are awarded the promotions, transfers, or assignments will be the ones hired. Both EEOC decisions[35] and court decisions, such as *Hester* v. *Southern Ry. Co., supra,* would support this approach—assuming the proper data are available to support it.

2. Although the very process of self-identification may have an adverse and disparate impact against minorities and females, there is the significant difference that the employer is not responsible for that impact. This might occur because the personal predilections of the work force, whether molded by society or otherwise, are reflected—in a totally legal way. For example, I have observed self-identification systems in "clean" situations—that is, untainted by any illegal employer influence—reflecting that females choose less frequently than males to work in, or bid for, jobs requiring heavy lifting or night work, and that minorities are less likely than nonminorities to want to be promoted to the first level of supervision.

3. A self-identification system avoids significant proof problems if there is litigation. For example, in *Stewart* v. *General Motors Corp., supra,* the company tried to establish that tenders of promotion had been made to minorities. The proof was rejected, however. The main difficulties in such types of proof are that they require an extraordinary number of witnesses to establish the facts (courts are generally reluctant to have a large number of witnesses paraded to the stand during trial), and that each instance of a tender becomes in and of itself a mini-trial to establish whether the offer was sincere, clear, and unequivocal. Additionally, the employer faces the prospect of the plaintiffs' arguing that although these tenders might have been made to minorities or females, there were probably also tenders made to nonminorities and males, and plaintiffs should be offered the opportunity to have virtually every nonminority person or male testify as to whether or not he or she had been offered a promotion, transfer, or assignment and also turned it down.

4. A self-identification system also offers a purely business benefit. Especially in promoting people from the bargaining-unit ranks or blue-collar work force to the first level of supervision, employers usually face difficulty. Frequently, such a position might be offered to two, three, or even four people before one can be found who wants it. When someone is finally found to take it, there is an extraordinary peer pressure against, and even mockery of, that person because he or she took the position. By utilizing the self-nominating procedure, the employer avoids this possibility. The employer also has the opportunity, by knowing early enough who wants to be a supervisor, to try out different people, be they minority or nonminority, male or female, in the supervisory position to see how they function on a temporary basis and to give them the necessary training to enable them to perform effectively in the position once they attain it.

5. A self-identification procedure avoids another significant proof problem in large-scale discrimination cases: determining what are, or are not, desira-

ble jobs. In almost all these cases, the claim is made that minorities and females are restricted to the lowest-paying, least desirable jobs. The rebuttal by the employer requires proving that these jobs, just because they are low-paying, are no less desirable, and that the low pay might be more than counteracted by the fact that the people in them do not have to work overtime, or nights, or in high danger areas, or in dirty places, or doing heavy lifting, and so on. This frequently involves testimony by psychologists. Most frequently, these fact issues are resolved against the employer.

If there is a self-identification system, the issue of whether or not a job is desirable, or is more desirable than another, does not exist. Rather, the issue is, as it should be, one of equal employment *opportunity*. That is, when minorities and females sought opportunity, were they treated in the same way as nonminorities and males? The character of the jobs these people sought, and whether or not they were wise in selecting the jobs for which they were self-identifying, becomes a problem for the plaintiffs, not the defendant, to explain.

6. Another benefit from having a self-identification system is that it permits much more accurate analysis. For example, it may be that for some jobs, there is adverse impact against minorities or females who seek promotion, transfer, or assignment. However, there are probably going to be many jobs for which there is no adverse impact. Even if the employer does lose in litigation, therefore, the group to which it might be exposed, for purposes of damages and remedy, will be significantly smaller than the group to which it would be exposed if it does not have a self-identification system.

7. The final benefit for employers utilizing a self-identification system is also in the burden-of-proof area. There has been at least one U.S. Court of Appeals opinion, *Townsend* v. *Nassau County Medical Center*,[36] indicating that adverse-impact analysis is not to be conducted in the abstract, but rather based upon a particular employer's experience. Thus, it might be that an employer has a college-degree requirement for a certain supervisory job. If the plaintiffs are able to use external-work-force statistics, they will most surely be able to demonstrate that the requirement has an adverse impact. However, *Townsend* indicated that such external statistics would be inappropriate. It might also be that if the plaintiffs are able to use gross-work-force data of that employer, they can demonstrate that the college-degree requirement would have an adverse and disparate impact against minorities. However, if there is a self-identification system, properly structured, it could very well be that the college-degree requirement is not actually having an adverse impact on minorities with respect to that specific position, so no *prima facie* case can be established.

Concerns employers might have about minority or female employees exhibiting ambitions more unrealistic than those of whites or males have proved unfounded when self-identification systems have been put into effect. Such systems, I have observed, have demonstrated that females have no great desire to move into traditionally male jobs; that minorities are more likely than nonminorities to prefer to remain in the same job and work overtime to increase earnings, rather than bid for a higher-paying job that might not require or offer the opportunity for so much overtime; and that minorities are less likely than nonminorities to desire a job as first-level supervisor.

If an employer were to try to establish these premises as fact in trial, its burden of proof would be very difficult to meet. However, if the employer can allow for these predilections to be demonstrated as fact through the voluntary exercise of rights in a self-identification system, the employer is in a much better position to defend itself. Of course, the claim will be made by the plaintiffs that the employer has tinkered with the system, but that will be for the plaintiffs to prove. If the employer has proper safeguards around the system, it will be a very difficult proof by the plaintiffs.

Furthermore, effective use of the self-identification system, coupled with periodic counseling and a good evaluation system, can be an effective tool for affirmative action programs. It can also enable an employer to upgrade the status of its minority and female workers without exposing itself to claims of discrimination or reverse discrimination. Finally, it can have the very useful business benefit of creating for the employer a work force that is continually upgrading itself.

If the selection system, based upon self-identification through bids or otherwise, has no end-result adverse impact, the plaintiffs should not be recognized by courts or the government as having established a *prima facie* case. However, because there are so many different ways to look at the same statistics and reach opposite conclusions, employers would be well advised to include as many of the following additional safeguards as it can:

A detailed evaluation system, by supervisors, of employee performance.

A system for assessing the raters, to ensure consistency and propriety of criteria being utilized.

A means whereby minority or female input can be inserted into the evaluation process. Ideally, the number and percentage of minorities and females among the supervisory staff doing the ratings will reflect the minority and female representation in the general work force of the employer. Since this rarely occurs, however, an alternative means of assuring minority/female participation might be a review panel that does include minority members and females, and that reviews supervisory ratings either as a regular course of business or as an appellate tribunal acting if a claim of unfairness or discrimination is raised. Certainly, there is no legal requirement to have such a panel. However, it is one of the indicia of fairness that are persuasive to courts. In non-union facilities, such a panel also serves another function—providing a forum for grievances without having a union and a formal arbitration procedure.

Assessing Adverse Impact under a Collective-Bargaining Agreement with a Bona Fide Seniority System

The U.S. Supreme Court has indicated that even if a seniority system maintained pursuant to a collective-bargaining agreement is having an adverse disparate impact on minority or female transfers or assignments, maintenance of such a system is legally permissible. *Teamsters* v. *U.S.*[37] The qualification to this immunity, which rests upon Section 703(h) of Title VII, is that the system be bona fide—that is, not have discriminatory purpose at its origin.

Even though the section relied upon exists only in Title VII, for policy purposes it thus far appears that Executive Order 11246 and the Civil Rights Act of 1866[38] will have to be interpreted consistent with *Teamsters*. OFCCP refuses to follow *Teamsters* in this regard, but it has already been told by at least one U.S. Court of Appeals that it must do so.

Since age would seem to enhance bidding achievement in a seniority system, and since there is not likely to be significant impact on handicapped or disabled persons in a seniority system, employers having a bona fide seniority system do not face a serious problem in the area of transfers and assignments.

The type of adverse-impact analysis that could be feasible in such a system would be of all the exceptions—that is, instances in which the person with the greatest seniority, whether in the plant, department, or whatever, was *not* awarded the job he or she sought.

Another appropriate type of adverse-impact analysis would be to compare the minority/nonminority or male/female success rate in bidding, when the bidder had the most seniority, with respect to specific jobs. This would be especially appropriate if the employer had reason to suspect that minorities or females were not being successful in gaining that job, despite having the highest seniority when they bid for it.

Assessing Adverse Impact without a Seniority System

Unless an employer has a bona fide seniority system and utilizes it, the employer does not gain the protections afforded by Section 703(h) of Title VII.

In the absence of a bona fide seniority system, a self-identification procedure becomes imperative. This can be demonstrated by a comparison of the way the government and the courts might react to the example that follows, with and without a self-identification system.

Example

XYZ Co. is unionized, but it does not award positions pursuant to seniority. It has 110 positions in eleven different jobs. Its production work force is made up as follows:

Job Title	Salary Grade	Earning Rate Range	% Female
Operator A	1	10M–11M	50%
Operator B	2	11M–12M	45%
Operator C	3	12M–13M	40%
Operator D	4	13M–14M	35%
Operator E	5	14M–15M	30%
Operator F	6	15M–16M	25%
Operator G	7	16M–17M	20%
Operator H	8	17M–18M	15%
Operator I	9	18M–19M	10%
Operator J	10	19M–20M	5%
Operator K	11	19M–20M	5%
Supervisor	12	22M–25M	2%

With such a profile, an employer would be hard-pressed to defend itself against a charge of discrimination, in the absence of strong proof that the females were in the jobs they had chosen. Plaintiffs would not even have to prove whether this distribution existed because of discriminatory assignment or discriminatory promotion.

If the employer had a self-identification or even a bidding system,* it would have various defensive alternatives available to it. Through proper pleadings in use of pretrial discovery, it might nullify the plaintiffs' ability to even establish a *prima facie* case.

These alternatives, which would not otherwise be available, would be:

1. The employer could compare male to female success rates in bidding by job title; e.g., Operator A, Operator B.
2. The employer could compare male to female success rates in bidding by salary grade; e.g., salary grade 10 would include two job titles.
3. The employer could compare male to female success rates in bidding by salary grade bands, or earnings rate bands; e.g., all jobs in which the earnings rate is from 10M to 12M, 12M to 14M, etc.
4. The employer could compare male to female success rates in bidding by job group; i.e., jobs with similar function, earnings rate, and promotion potential.
5. The employer could isolate certain job characteristics, such as rotating-shift jobs, jobs that require some night work, etc., and do male/female comparisons on that basis.

All or some of these analyses might demonstrate that it is the free volition of the females that is causing the concentrations, and not the assignment or promotion policies of the employer.

*A bidding system is one kind of self-identification system. Other kinds might allow for the employee to designate his or her preference well in advance of an opening.

Since there will most assuredly be a claim by the plaintiffs or claimants that the self-identification or bidding system was tainted, the employer should make efforts to ensure that its system has as many of the following characteristics as possible.

1. Written job descriptions. In the absence of written job descriptions, courts or government agencies might argue that the right to bid loses its value.

2. A right to bid or self-identify for a job, even if the candidate feels that he or she does not have the qualifications in the job description, and a right to view different jobs in operation, under certain set conditions. In the absence of this characteristic, the claimant might allege that a job-description requirement—say, engineering background—although neutral on its face, has a disparate and adverse impact against minorities and females and is not really necessary. By indicating on job descriptions that the description is only the employer's attempt to characterize the job, that any employee can bid for any job, that any employee can observe any job in operation under certain set conditions, and that the employee will not be precluded from consideration for a job because he or she lacks certain job-description characteristics, employers can mitigate the expected argument of the claimants on this aspect. This will not lead to ridiculous bids, especially if the system also requires that the bidder take the job sought if it is offered. The incentive to bid prudently would be the knowledge that the job being vacated by the bidder might be filled and subsequently not available if the bidder is awarded the job sought, and fails to perform satisfactorily.

3. Stressing fair treatment and equal training for all successful bidders. This would reduce the impact of another frequent claim—namely, that minorities or females who do bid for a traditionally white or male job are programmed to fail. It is in the employer's interests to have such bidders succeed, for it is only when there are no concentrations of minorities or females that the employer can feel comfortable.

4. A clear, unequivocal notification to the work force of all the relevant openings, whether by posting or otherwise. This will reduce the impact of another common claim, that the employer used word-of-mouth recruiting and a buddy system. The regular course of business should include documentation of when, where, and for how long a job was posted or otherwise announced.

Future Prospects in Assessing Adverse Impact

Very often, an employer will have concentrations of minorities or females in certain work areas or job groups, and very few in most other work areas. Generally, a large number and percentage of the minority or female work force will be considered for and selected for supervisory positions where these concentrations exist. Thus, a female might be the supervisor of the secretarial pool

Standards for Promotion, Transfer, and Assignment

or clerical area, but there will not be females as supervisors in production, shipping, public relations, accounting, and so on. The female who is in charge of the secretarial area, furthermore, will probably earn substantially less than the other, male supervisors. In making their case, plaintiffs can graphically demonstrate this disparity by doing multiple regression analysis, using education and company seniority, or other such "neutral" factors—but not freedom of choice or personal preference. In rebuttal, it becomes very difficult for the employer to explain the earnings differential.

Employment systems can be completely computerized to include bid or self-identification history. Some day, such information will be computerized, and employees will receive with their annual W-2 forms a statement of their bid index—that is, an indication of how their bidding relates to achievement of optimum earnings. Bid or self-identification history will be rated against possible career pathways that would lead to achievement of these maximum earnings. In this way, employers will be able to document that employees make choices for reasons other than maximizing earnings.

This kind of system, which constantly reminds persons of the earnings lost by failure to seek other positions, may now be the only alternative to a much more ominous movement presently in progress in the sex discrimination area. That ominous movement is the comparable pay theory.

The comparable pay theory, usually utilized by females, is based not on a claim that a certain job or jobs were denied to females, but on a claim that the employer intentionally pays a lesser rate than it should for jobs in which females are concentrated. For example, it might be that a company pays its truck loaders, who are mostly males, at a rate of $5.00 per hour and its assemblers, who are mostly females, at the rate of $3.00 per hour. The claim by the women will be that the worth of the assembler's job, considering skill, effort, responsibility, and working conditions, is $5.00 per hour. They will claim discrimination not because they were denied the truck loader's position, but because they were paid at a lesser percentage of true job value—only 60%—than males, who were paid 100%.

The comparable pay theory has been considered, and rejected, by Congress on numerous occasions. It has been considered and rejected by numerous courts. Nevertheless, female groups keep pressing comparable pay claims, and they may ultimately prevail through judicial, administrative, or Congressional action.

In the judicial arena, the U.S. Court of Appeals for the Ninth Circuit has recognized that persons asserting a comparable pay claim state a cause of action and should be allowed the necessary discovery to enable them to attempt to prove the claim. This discovery may include having expert witnesses go into the workplace to observe and compare jobs. Because of the conflict in the Circuit Courts of Appeal, the Supreme Court will probably have to determine whether the comparable pay theory is cognizable under Title VII.

Regardless of how the Supreme Court rules in the Title VII context, it has become apparent that OFCCP proposes to implement the comparable pay theory in interpreting Executive Order 11246.

Even if judicial action or administrative action does not establish the comparable pay theory, it is very possible that there will be Congressional action on the subject.

Employers should be apprehensive about the impact of the comparable pay theory. They should now be developing documentary evidence, such as that described in this chapter, to prove that persons do have the right to move at will. They should be undertaking affirmative action efforts to dilute concentrations of minorities and females. Finally, they should be assessing the feasibility of undertaking job studies and adjusting pay rates, as necessary, especially for jobs not covered by a bona fide seniority system. In the long run, it will be far less costly to employers, and more productive for the national economy, to break traditional concepts of "male" or "female" jobs, than to raise pay rates for a huge segment of the workforce.

FORMS

Performance-Assessment Forms

A sample performance-assessment form for use in evaluating the performance of first-line supervisors of maintenance mechanics is below, preceded by the instructions to the person who will be doing the rating. As can be seen from the form itself, the evaluating procedure envisions that the person assessing the supervisor will in turn have his or her assessment reviewed by a supervisor.

One of the common problems in performance evaluations is that the form does not permit a wide enough range to allow the person doing the rating to weigh one person against another. It is to the advantage of the employer to have shades of excellent or poor performance. Additionally, few evaluation forms now used by employers allow for a weighing of the factors relative to the importance they have for a particular job. The sample demonstrates how this can be done.

Despite the detail in the sample form that follows, if there were to be adverse impact in the selection, promotion, or compensation given to the class of supervisors rated by this form, it is not likely that the form would be found "validated." Nevertheless, use of a form such as this can provide significant benefits for employers. First, even in a class-action-type situation, and even though the statistics are outside the acceptable range, it is possible that a court might find no discrimination, because of the employer's attempt to be as objective as possible—a kind of simplified "content" validity. See, for example, *Mastie* v. *Great Lakes Steel Corp.*[39] Second, use of a form such as this will definitely help in defending against individual charges of discrimination. It is an observed fact that supervisors generally do not want to rate any of their charges as poor performers or failures. As a result, when someone is ultimately discharged, it is not uncommon to find past performance appraisals indicating that the person discharged has been a "good" or "acceptable" employee. The rating form does away with the tags and lets the supervisor rate performance against that of other employees. Thus, even if a supervisor does not literally follow the directions on the form, the employer should be able to demonstrate that the employee is among the poorest performers. This will be of assistance, not only in determining whether a promotion or a salary increase should be granted, or the amount of that salary increase, but also to sustain a termination or a layoff. See *Mastie* v. *Great Lakes Steel Corp. supra,* and *Gill* v. *Union Carbide Corp., supra.*

Since a performance-assessment form should be as closely related to a specific job as possible, this book contains only one type of performance-assessment form, and that only as an example. However, here is a checklist employers should be aware of for the purpose of creating their own performance-assessment forms. The following factors should be considered:

1. Insofar as possible, the person who does the assessment should have that assessment reviewed by his or her supervisor. This is to assure uniformity in approach. Additionally, that supervisor, by reviewing assessment forms from a number of people, will be in a better position to assess objectivity and uniformity, and to determine whether the use of the forms might be having an adverse impact on some protective group.

2. The performance-assessment form should be as specific as possible.

3. Insofar as possible, employers should avoid having the performance review conducted in conjunction with an annual salary review. Instead, if possible, they should be six months apart. This will enhance the objectivity of the person doing the rating. In many companies, salary increases of a set percentage have become the norm, and holding the annual assessment in conjunction with the annual increase has become more or less *pro forma.* In such circumstances, much of the usefulness of performance assessment is lost.

4. At the time the performance assessment is given to and discussed with the employee, constructive suggestions should be made for enhancement of performance by the employee.

5. The weight to be given to the different factors that are a part of the performance assessment will vary, depending on the purpose of the assessment. The form that follows is oriented only toward performance evaluation and not specifically toward promotion potential. Otherwise, some of the factors, such as "Interaction with other managers and administrative personnel," might be weighted more heavily than they have been.

6. Instructions should be given to the person who is to do the assessment,

and those instructions should be a part of the assessment form. This is to enhance his or her objectivity and uniformity in approach.

The form that follows has been developed from an EEO perspective. There are other performance appraisal systems, such as BARS (Behaviorally Anchored Rating Scale), which have been developed primarily as a management tool for general productivity purposes. The BARS system has ratings, e.g.—0+ or 1, 2, 3, 4, 5—and a behavioral description of the rating.

Regardless of what kind of performance evaluation system an employer chooses, it is likely that implementation and refinement of the system will take years, and that the system will still be extremely difficult to validate under the Uniform Guidelines for Employee Selection.

ABC CORPORATION

Management Assessment Form—No. 1

Name of Manager
to be Reviewed _____   Reviewer's Name _____

Title _____   Reviewer's Title _____

Work Area/Facility _____

Date of Assessment _____

Purpose of Assessment
(annual review, other) _____

INSTRUCTIONS

Rating on the Individual Scales

This booklet contains a separate rating scale for each of 8 standards identified as important to a position at ABC Corporation. These standards will vary, and their relative importance will vary, depending upon the nature of the position being reviewed. The reviewer should have determined which form is appropriate for this managerial position by checking the Performance Evaluation Form Code Book.

The employee is being rated against the position description for the job which he or she holds. Before doing this rating, you should review the position description to assure that it is currently accurate. Directly below the title of each standard, a short paragraph appears elaborating on the standard as applicable to the managerial job in question. If in the course of your assessment you have reason to believe that the position description, the standards, or the weight given to each standard for review purposes, is no longer accurate or appropriate, you are asked to bring this to the attention of John Goodfaith, Vice-President, Personnel. The same procedure applies if the person being reviewed questions the standards or the weight attributed to a standard.

Rate the performance of the person on the items appearing in the paragraph, and enter the rating from 1 to 15 in the space provided. At the end you will follow the exercise indicated to turn the raw score into a weighted score. Each time you rate a person on a standard, try to determine his or her strengths and weaknesses on that standard. You may want to use fractions of a point in determining a person's rating on a standard.

A comments section follows each standard. Any time you rate performance at 5 or less, or at more than 10, this section must be filled out. This is not meant, and should not be interpreted as, an attempt to dissuade you from giving such a rating.

Rating on the Overall Performance Scale

The overall performance scale assumes a basic degree of satisfactory performance. You will be distinguishing between varying degrees of satisfactory performance.

Administration

The completed evaluations should be reviewed with your immediate superior and forwarded to the Vice-President, Personnel. Do not discuss the evaluations with the person being appraised at this time. After the forms are returned by the Vice-President, Personnel, you should discuss with the person being evaluated his or her strengths and weaknesses, and also the efforts necessary to enhance the person's achievement of his or her immediate career objective as established by the Employee Self-Identification Program. The appraiser and the person being appraised should then sign the front page of the form. The completed forms should be returned to the Vice-President, Personnel.

---

1. MANAGING THE WORK FORCE

Controlling efficiency of subordinates; making correct job assignments; minimizing and equalizing overtime (or having a good reason for not doing so); skillfully utilizing subordinates; meeting deadlines, maintaining adequate staffing skills; cross-training sufficient personnel to cover normal contingencies such as sickness, vacation relief, and bidding out, eliminating excess manpower on a project by reassigning personnel; administering policies according to appropriate collective-bargaining agreements and company rules; accepting overtime assignments to meet difficult deadlines.

Manager's Appraisal Rating on the above items is _____ .

LOW   HIGH
 1   2   3   4   5   6   7   8   9   10   11   12   13   14   15

_____   _____   _____   _____   _____

Comments: _____
_____
_____

2. MOTIVATING THE WORK FORCE

Providing study materials for staff; briefing staff on problems and deadlines in a manner that gets the job done correctly and on time; explaining to the staff how completion of their particular tasks contribute to the overall effort; utilizing motivational or beneficial competitive techniques effectively.

Manager's Appraisal Rating on the above items is _____ .

LOW   HIGH
1   2   3   4   5   6   7   8   9   10   11   12   13   14   15
___   ___   ___   ___   ___   ___   ___   ___

Comments: _____
_____
_____

3. ADMINISTRATIVE RECORD KEEPING

Maintaining accurate, current, and legible records, such as overtime, attendance, and vacation; scheduling vacation to avoid excessive needs for overtime; timely submitting of reports and correct authorizations; monitoring accuracy of routine/nonroutine cards for correct signoffs, missing names, lost time.

Manager's Appraisal Rating on the above items is _____ .

LOW   HIGH
1   2   3   4   5   6   7   8   9   10   11   12   13   14   15
___   ___   ___   ___   ___   ___   ___   ___

Comments: _____
_____
_____

4. COMMUNICATION REQUIRED TO COMPLETE WORK

Accurately, clearly, and timely informing staff, other shifts in work location, and supervisor where appropriate; discussing operational status of shift with outgoing supervisor and briefing the incoming supervisor; checking with other work areas to coordinate the delivery of units required in work; providing accurate estimates of time required to complete tasks; avoiding maintenance delays by thoroughly briefing staff; providing adequately for someone to act in employee's place when he or she is absent from work area.

Manager's Appraisal Rating on the above items is _____ .

LOW   HIGH
1   2   3   4   5   6   7   8   9   10   11   12   13   14   15
_____   _____   _____   _____   _____

Comments: _____
_____
_____

5. SAFE WORKING CONDITIONS AND HOUSEKEEPING

Monitoring equipment and operating techniques for safety; maintaining safe and orderly work area; conducting weekly work-area safety inspections; correcting potential hazards by reading trade publications and other manuals; immediately correcting any discrepancies discovered by insurance inspectors; keeping exits and fire lanes unobstructed; complying with OSHA and other government safety regulations.

Manager's Appraisal Rating on the above items is _____ .

LOW   HIGH
1   2   3   4   5   6   7   8   9   10   11   12   13   14   15
_____   _____   _____   _____   _____

Comments: _____
_____
_____

6. TECHNICAL EXPERTISE

Correctly analyzing and trouble-shooting problems; accurately analyzing complex problems, thereby reducing needs for factory experts; keeping self well versed on new repair or inspection procedures; knowing when other parts of a system should be checked before pulling the same unit out of service again; using ingenuity in utilizing alternate parts when possible or appropriate to avoid shutdown.

Manager's Appraisal Rating on the above items is _____ .

LOW   HIGH
1   2   3   4   5   6   7   8   9   10   11   12   13   14   15
_____ _____ _____ _____ _____ _____ _____ _____

Comments: _____
_____
_____

7. INTERACTION WITH OTHER MANAGERS AND ADMINISTRATIVE PERSONNEL

Timely informing superiors of problems calling for their attention; conveying helpful suggestions in courteous fashion to fellow managers and administrators; willingly assuming projects helpful to the corporation; being responsive to requests for necessary information from other departments or managers or administrators; demonstrating ability to obtain other managers' and administrators' cooperation.

Manager's Appraisal Rating on the above items is _____ .

LOW   HIGH
1   2   3   4   5   6   7   8   9   10   11   12   13   14   15
_____ _____ _____ _____ _____ _____ _____ _____

Comments: _____
_____
_____

8. MANAGEMENT-EMPLOYEE RELATIONS

Listening effectively to employee complaints; explaining company position when employee is wrong; discreetly undertaking corrective action when employee is right, seeking further information when necessary toward resolution; giving needed input for creation of Affirmative Action program; undertaking good-faith efforts toward meeting goals and timetables put forth in the Affirmative Action program; maintaining a work atmosphere free of antagonism based upon race, sex, national origin, or other EEO considerations; handling EEO grievances promptly and effectively.

Manager's Appraisal Rating on the above items is _____ .

LOW														HIGH
1	2	3	4	5	6	7	8	9	10	11	12	13	14	15

Comments: _____

_____

_____

Factor	Value	Score	Weighted Score
1. Managing the Work Force	25%		
2. Motivating the Work Force	15%		
3. Administrative Record Keeping	5%		
4. Communication Required to Complete Work	10%		
5. Safe Working Conditions and Housekeeping	5%		
6. Technical Expertise	15%		
7. Interaction with other Managers and Administrative Personnel	10%		
8. Interaction With Persons Supervised and EEO Performance	15%		

EMPLOYEE COMMENTS ON:

Position Description _____

_____

Evaluation Standards _____

_____

Weight Given to Standards _____

_____

Rating Against the Standards _____

_____

PROPOSED ENHANCEMENT ACTIVITIES FOR PERSON
SUBJECT TO THE REVIEW

___

FOOTNOTES

[1] 15 FEP Cases 368 (D. Utah 1977).

[2] 368 F. Supp. 364 (E.D. Tenn. 1973).

[3] Wage and Hour Administrator Opinion, July 31, 1968, FEPM Section 401 at 5208, entitled "Discriminatory Layoffs."

[4] 531 F.2d 224 (5th Cir. 1976).

[5] 499 F.2d 859 (7th Cir. 1974).

[6] 29 C.F.R. Section 860.102(e).

[7] 29 C.F.R. Section 860.103(h).

[8] See 29 C.F.R. Sections 521.2, 521.3, and 860.102(e).

[9] 534 F.2d 1226 (6th Cir. 1976).

[10] 17 FEP Cases 252 (8th Cir. 1978).

[11] 21 EPD ¶30,500 (4th Cir. 1979), 250 Daily Labor Report E-1 *et seq*, (December 28, 1979). But see also *Goodman* v. *Schlesinger,* 584 F.2d 1325 (4th Cir. 1978), 18 FEP Cases 191.

[12] 559 F.2d 310 (5th Cir. 1977), *cert. denied* 434 U.S. 1034 (1978).

[13] 542 F.2d 445 (7th Cir. 1976), *cert. denied* 433 U.S. 919, *reh'g denied* 434 U.S. 881 (1977).

[14] 561 F.2d 1268 (8th Cir. 1977).

[15] 457 F.2d 348 (5th Cir. 1972).

[16] 495 F.2d 437 (5th Cir. 1974), *cert. denied* 419 U.S. 1033 (1975).

[17] 497 F.2d 1374 (5th Cir. 1974).

[18] 8 FEP Cases 778 (E.D. Va. 1974), *aff'd in relevant part,* 535 F.2d 257 (4th Cir. 1976), *cert. denied* 429 U.S. 920 (1976).

[19] 4 FEP Cases 825 (M.D. Ala. 1971).

[20] 538 F.2d 652 (5th Cir. 1976), *mod. on other gds.* 544 F.2d 1258 (5th Cir. 1977), *cert. denied* 15 FEP Cases 1184 (1977).

[21] 18 EPD ¶8704 (4th Cir. 1978).

[22] 17 FEP Cases 146 (D. Mass. 1977).

[23] 479 F.2d 97 (2d Cir. 1973).

[24] 12 FEP Cases 1329 (D. Conn. 1975).

[25] 14 FEP Cases 1501 (N.D. Tex. 1977).

[26] 12 FEP Cases 75 (S.D. Ga. 1975).

[27] 7 FEP Cases 1292 (E.D. Tenn. 1973).

[28] 13 FEP Cases 211 (W.D. N.C. 1975).

[29] 17 FEP Cases 622 (4th Cir. 1978).

[30] 15 FEP Cases 1081 (S.D. Tex. 1975).

[31] 15 FEP Cases 1370, 1381 n. 32 (D.D.C. 1977).

[32] 508 F.2d 239 (3d Cir. 1975), *cert. denied* 421 U.S. 1011 (1975).

[33] 431 U.S. 553 (1977).

[34] *Idem* at 558.

[35] See EEOC Decisions, Case Nos. 68-8-257E and 68-9-329E (July 8, 1969), 2 FEP Cases 79.

[36] 558 F.2d 117 (2d Cir. 1977), *cert. denied* 434 U.S. 1015 (1978).

[37] 431 U.S. 324 (1977).

[38] 42 U.S.C. §1981.

[39] 14 FEP Cases 952 (E.D. Mich. 1976).

Chapter 6

Standards for Discipline, Discharge, and Reductions in Force

INTRODUCTION

The discussion in the prior two chapters concerning standards relating to hiring and promotions is also relevant to the present subject. Thus, for example, if it is illegal to require a high school diploma for hiring or promotion purposes, it would be just as illegal to terminate or force the layoff of employees, or restrict the bidding opportunities available to them as an alternative to layoff, because they do not have high school diplomas. This statement will not be repeated, but it is applicable to each subdivision of this chapter.

Claims of discrimination by discipline, discharge, or reduction in force are ordinarily less likely to create class-type exposure for employers than are hiring or promotion discrimination claims. This is because in the ordinary discipline or discharge-for-cause situation involving tardiness, insubordination, failure to perform, or the like, it is difficult for the complainant to establish that he or she was affected by an identifiable *policy* or *practice* that similarly affected many others, an essential ingredient to sustaining a class-type claim. See, for example, *East Texas Motor Freight Systems, Inc.* v. *Rodriguez;*[1] *Martinez* v. *Bethlehem Steel Corp.;*[2] and *Fernandez* v. *Avco Corp.*[3] In fact, the more specific and personal the claim is, or can be made to appear, the less likely that it can be prosecuted as a class-type case.

Conversely, reductions in force that are based upon criteria established by the employer at the corporate or facility level, or adverse personnel actions pursuant to the provisions of a seniority system, generally present the ideal vehicle for a class action by one person on behalf of all the protected group persons who suffer.

STANDARDS AT ISSUE

Age Standards

An employer taking adverse action against a person protected by the Age Discrimination in Employment Act of 1967 (ADEA) and anticipating a claim of discrimination based on age would be well advised to review the transaction-analysis approach set forth in the U.S. Department of Labor's *Field Operations Handbook,* discussed in Chapter 4 of this text.

Age-discrimination cases in general, and age-discrimination cases involving termination in particular, usually involve less exposure for an employer than do race or sex cases. Class-type cases by individuals pursuant to the ADEA are rare because of the various procedural requirements of the ADEA. (Class-action-type cases had been prosecuted pursuant to the ADEA only by the secretary of labor. EEOC assumed this power July 1, 1979, and will probably seek legislation to change these restrictive procedural requirements.) Additionally, a party attempting to establish age discrimination usually has a heavier burden of proof than does one trying to prove sex or race discrimination, because age discrimination is viewed by the courts as being less odious. Even statistics have lesser importance in age cases. See *Mastie* v. *Great Lakes Steel Corp.*[4] Furthermore, if an employer is operating pursuant to a collective-bargaining agreement in taking adverse action, the impact of that action is less likely to be against people protected by the ADEA. Thus, one of the main areas from which class-type claims of discrimination relating to layoff or discharge arise will generally not produce those claims on the basis of age.

Even though they are not likely to be class actions, age-discrimination cases, especially those involving discharge, present serious problems for employers for other reasons. One is that these cases are tried before a jury, and the claimant, by demonstrating long years of faithful and satisfactory service, immediately gets sympathy. Another reason these cases are troublesome is that the claimant is frequently earning the peak amount of his career at the time of termination and cannot find other employment, and thereby mitigate his damages. Also, if he or she prevails, the claimant is entitled by statute not only to lost earnings, but, possibly, to double the amount of the lost earnings, plus reinstatement.

Discharges have been sustained against age-discrimination claims by employers who demonstrated that the discharge was because of *unsatisfactory work performance* (*Brennan* v. *Reynolds & Co.*);[5] or because of *tardiness* (*Billingsley* v. *Service Technology Corp.*);[6] or because of *loss of business* (*Price* v. *Maryland Casualty Co.*);[7] or because *sound business judgment*, not the age of those involved, called for protected-group people to be terminated in a particular situation (*Cova* v. *Coca-Cola Bottling Co. of St. Louis, Inc.*);[8] or because there would be *higher labor costs* involved in keeping a particular older employee (*Mastie* v. *Great Lakes Steel Corp., supra*); or because the employee's *position was abolished*, even though other employees assumed some of the claimant's prior duties (*Moses* v. *Falstaff Brewing Corp.*).[9] It has been held not a violation of the ADEA for the employer to properly lay off an older employee for *lack of work*, then to recall him properly for a different job that is open and that he is entitled to have, and then terminate him because he could not physically perform the new job he was assigned. *Rhoades* v. *The Book Press.*[10] When an age-discrimination claim is presented, it is generally a minimum requirement that the claimant establish that he or she was replaced by a younger person. *Price* v. *Maryland Casualty Co., supra*, but see *Moore* v. *Sears, Roebuck & Co.*[11] However, even if the claimant does establish that he or she was replaced by a younger person, that does not mean the claimant automatically prevails. *Laugesen* v. *Anaconda Co.*[12] The claimant must establish that *the* determining factor in his or her termination was age, not just that age was *a* factor. See *Mastie* v. *Great Lakes Steel Corp., supra.* (Under Title VII, it is necessary only to establish that one of the prohibited bases—sex, color, religion, race, or national origin—had been *a* factor in order to establish a technical violation of the statute. *Gillin* v. *Federal Paper Board Co.*)[13]

Although it is difficult for age-discrimination claimants to prevail, they did in *Coates* v. *National Cash Register.*[14] There, they demonstrated that they had been denied training on electronics machines because of their age, and that they were then terminated because they had no training on electronics machines.

In class-type situations where there have been a number of layoffs or terminations pursuant to a reduction in force, the courts generally look to the standards that were utilized by the employer in achieving the reduction in force. In *Mastie* v. *Great Lakes Steel Corp., supra,* the court found it to be substantial evidence in favor of the employer that 17 factors had been considered in evaluating employees on the employer's standard evaluation form. These factors were *quality, quantity, knowledge, organization, dependability, initiative, resourcefulness, analytic ability, on-time record, cooperation with authority, cooperation with employees, attitude, advancement potential, appearance, acceptance of responsibility, development of subordinates,* and *delegation.* The court also found it significant that the people being considered for termination had been rated *prior to* the time the employer knew it would be required to reduce staff. Additionally, the evaluation program called for numerical totals on each rating sheet. Thus, although the claimants who were terminated had an acceptable performance rating, it was possible for the employer to demonstrate that their performance was at or near the bottom of the group being rated. Under such circumstances, the termination was sustained against a claim of discrimination under the ADEA. (A sample performance-evaluation form is included in Chapter 5.)

In considering using standards similar to those used by the employer in the *Mastie* case, it would be advisable to exclude the standard entitled "advancement potential," especially if the employer knows that a reduction in force is anticipated. This is because such a standard could be expected to have an adverse impact on people in the protected age group.

Other cases in which the courts sustained terminations against claims of age discrimination, based largely upon the type of evaluation forms used by the employer, were *Gill* v. *Union Carbide Corp.*[15] and *Stringfellow* v. *Monsanto Co.*[16] The *Gill* case and the criterion successfully relied upon by the employer in that case are discussed in Chapter 5 of this book.

An employer may consider the *labor costs* involved in terminating one person as opposed to another. However, it would be a violation of the ADEA to consider or act upon the general proposition that older employees cost more to the employer because of more frequent and higher medical costs, more significant pension contributions, or the greater likelihood of suffering debilitating injury than younger persons.[17] The courts have found that if labor costs are considered on an individualized basis, there is no violation of the ADEA. *Mastie* v. *Great Lakes Steel Corp., supra.*

In *Mastie*, the court found that an employer could consider the fact that one employee being considered for layoff was earning more than another who was also under consideration for layoff. Additionally, the record showed that one plaintiff's work required constant supervision and had to be rechecked, and that another of the plaintiffs lacked the ability to grasp new ideas. All these are factors that make it more costly to employ one person than another.

In considering individualized labor costs, the employer should be cautious, because some of the high-cost considerations, while not violative of the ADEA, may be in violation of other statutes. For example, it may seem perfectly justifiable to lay off one worker rather than another because the first worker has a high incidence of workmen's compensation claims. However, under many state workmen's compensation statutes, it would be illegal to take any adverse action where that was one of the considerations used.

In class-type cases, the claimants will almost always introduce evidence to show a statistical difference between the average age of the group before the reduction in force or layoff, and the age of the group that remains after it. However, in order for plaintiffs to prevail, this generally has to be a significant age difference. See *Hodgson* v. *First Federal Savings & Loan Assn.*[18] and *Schultz* v. *Hickok Mfg. Co., Inc.*[19] If the difference is only a year or two, absent other evidence, the plaintiffs will generally not prevail.

For purposes of considering the implication of the ADEA on a reduction in force, employers should review not only the cumulative effect of the reduction on protected-group versus non-protected-group people, but also its impact on various age strata within the protected group. Thus, the employer should consider the percentage of its employees scheduled for layoff who are, for example, between the ages of 50 and 55, 55 and 60, and 60 and 70. The Department of Labor traditionally took such an approach, and so does the EEOC. Evidence of a net reduction in the average age of the remaining work force, plus evidence of a more significant adverse impact against protected-group people as the age of the group increased, might be very difficult to rebut, regardless of what standards or evaluation forms are used by the employer for purposes of its reduction in force.

Race and National-Origin Standards

A most troublesome area, and one in which there is great monetary exposure, is race and national-original discrimination claims involving layoffs pursuant to seniority but not pursuant to a bona fide seniority system incorporated into a collective-bargaining agreement. A seniority system is bona fide if it was not set up with the sole or prime purpose of segregating employees on the basis of sex or race. The claims of minorities arise because they have generally been hired or promoted in greater numbers and percentages in the most recent past and are adversely affected if the least-senior employees are the first to be laid off.

The employer is usually best advised to lay off according to seniority—last hired, first fired—when there exists a bona fide seniority system incorporated into a collective-bargaining agreement. This is because there will most certainly be arbitration under the collective-bargaining agreement, and a violation of the agreement will be found if its provisions are not followed. Additionally, in *Teamsters* v. *U.S.*,[20] the Supreme Court found that Section 703(h) of Title VII protects bona fide seniority systems and, presumably, layoffs pursuant to such systems, even if such layoffs do have an adverse impact against minorities. Courts have also indicated that even though Executive Order 11246 does not have a provision similar to Section 703(h) of Title VII, the executive order must be interpreted consistently with Title VII on this subject. See *U.S.* v. *East Texas Motor Freight.*[21]

Many cases have sustained layoffs pursuant to the provisions of a collective-bargaining agreement despite the adverse impact resulting against minorities. See, for example, *Bryan* v. *California Brewers Association*,[22] *Croker* v. *Boeing Co.*,[23] and *Roman* v. *ESB, Inc.*[24] In *Croker,* the court sustained the layoff, pursuant to the provisions of a collective-bargaining agreement that was neutral on its face, despite the fact that the layoff had a disproportionate adverse impact against minorities. The court found this adverse impact was due to the fact that a large number of minorities had been hired in the late 1960s and had not yet achieved sufficient seniority to withstand the layoffs according to the seniority system called for by the labor agreement.

Note: To understand this and the following section, these principles involving collective-bargaining agreements, bona fide seniority systems, and the impact of the *Teamsters* decision should be understood:

1. The general rule is that layoffs pursuant to a bona fide seniority system are permissible no matter what the end result is. This is the meaning of the *Teamsters* decision. A system is bona fide unless it was set up with the prime or sole purpose of segregating males from females, blacks from whites, or the like.

2. Just because the system is sacrosanct does not necessarily mean that everyone in that system will have to be laid off according to the listed seniority date for each person in each department or line of progression. People can be entitled to "constructive seniority" if they can demonstrate that they personally would have had an earlier seniority date in a particular department or line of progression, except for discriminatory acts by the employer and/or the union. That "constructive" seniority date is the date the person would have been in that department or line of progression were it not for the discriminatory act(s). Everyone in the system is still laid off according to seniority—last in, first out— but those who have the "constructive" seniority date will be laid off on the basis of that date.

3. The person who wants to have a constructive-seniority date must have filed a charge of discrimination with EEOC, or be a member of a class whose representative had filed a charge with EEOC, within 180 days (or 300 days if there is a state or local FEP agency and statute involved) of the discriminatory act. In *United Air Lines, Inc.* v. *Evans,*[25] the Supreme Court had indicated that a charge must be filed within the relevant time period after the act of discrimination. Such a charge would not be considered timely if it only related for timeliness purposes to the consequences of the discriminatory act. Even though the Supreme Court has not ruled on the issue, it would probably construe the layoff as a consequence deriving from the initial discriminatory placement. Thus, if the employer had refused to hire any females into Department A, the time period started to run when that event occurred. If a woman was hired into Department B in 1975 because of this discriminatory practice and in 1977 she transferred to Department A and the employer relied upon departmental seniority for layoff purposes, the woman would have a 1977 seniority date in Department A. She would not be entitled to a "constructive" seniority date of 1975 unless (1) she had filed a charge within 180 days of the discriminatory act in 1975, or (2) the class representative had filed a timely charge after the discriminatory act against her. If there is a class representative who had filed a timely charge, then that person can represent herself and any other females who

could have still filed a timely charge at the time the class representative filed her charge.

Despite the case law noted above, the employer that lays off pursuant to the seniority provisions of a collective-bargaining agreement, and not race or national-origin quotas, may be subject to contest by EEOC. In one of its decisions, EEOC has already ruled that the use of seniority as a sole basis for layoffs could violate Title VII.[26] EEOC's position is that if there had been past discrimination against minorities that kept them out of the employment system, rendering them unable as a group to achieve as much seniority as nonminorities, then the use of seniority as the basis for layoffs is in violation of Title VII. It does not matter to EEOC that the minorities who suffered discrimination in the past by not being hired are not the same people who are scheduled for layoff.

Despite the possibility that EEOC might object, employers confronted with a conflict between a bargaining agreement and what EEOC claims is required by Title VII, are probably better advised to follow the bargaining agreement, if it incorporates a bona fide seniority system. The power of collective bargaining agreements was demonstrated in *Jersey Central Power & Light Company* v. *Electrical Workers (IBEW), Local 327*.[27] An employer was confronted with a conflict between achievement of its goals and timetables that had been established pursuant to a Conciliation Agreement with EEOC, and layoffs pursuant to the collective bargaining agreement. The company had hired a substantial number of minorities pursuant to the Conciliation Agreement with EEOC but then had a downturn in business and was forced to lay off employees. The union had demanded that the layoffs be pursuant to the collective bargaining agreement; EEOC had demanded that the percentage of minority employees that had been achieved through the affirmative action hiring effort be maintained and that some standard other than seniority be used to conduct the layoffs. The ultimate resolution was that the collective bargaining agreement provisions prevailed.

In order to resolve the conflict between Title VII and the collective bargaining agreements, the employer had taken the problem and the parties involved—the union and EEOC—to court and asked the court to issue a Declaratory Judgment as to what it should do.

The approach of proceeding by Declaratory Judgment is really the only sure way to correctly resolve a conflict, but even this approach has a drawback: final court adjudication may take years and during those years the employer has to conduct layoffs. In doing so, it can really only go by the last court decision that had been entered.

In instances when there is no bona fide seniority system controlling the layoffs, the general rules regarding adverse impact once again come into play. Thus, in *Randolph* v. *U.S. Elevator Corp.*,[28] the plaintiff was found to have established a prima facie case of discrimination in violation of Title VII by using statistics to demonstrate that the layoff in question reduced the number of black elevator construction helpers by 75%, while reducing the percentage of white elevator construction helpers by only 34%. The employer had tried to demonstrate that its layoff decisions were validated. However, the court found that the determination as to who would be laid off was based upon subjective evaluations, without reference to objective performance criteria, and without even any discussion with the plaintiffs' supervisors. The court noted that the employer did not have a system whereby it could gauge the plaintiffs' performance to the performance of employees who were retained.

In cases involving discipline, rather than layoff or discharge, the courts thus far appear less likely to apply the adverse impact analysis approach in strict fashion. Thus in *Friend* v. *Leidinger*,[29] the court considered a situation in which the adverse action, namely, the administering of discipline, had an adverse impact against minorities; nevertheless, the employer's actions were sustained.

In *Friend* v. *Leidinger,* the plaintiffs were black firefighters, who demonstrated that black firemen had been chargeable in 76% of the 22 accidents in which they had been involved, whereas whites had been chargeable in only 37% of the 76 accidents in which they had been involved. The trial court found that the sample used was too small to demonstrate adverse impact and that, in any event, the Fire Bureau could show a compelling business necessity for its procedures. Although the trial court did not specifically say so, it equated the business-necessity defense to a validation defense, under a "content-validity" approach. The circuit court sustained the district-court ruling.

A similar result was achieved in *Dickerson* v. *U.S. Steel Co.*[30] but a different rationale was used. In *Dickerson,* the court held that to recover in a class action for discrimination in discipline, the plaintiffs had to establish that racial harassment was the "standard operating procedure." Proof of isolated instances would be insufficient to establish the class claim.

If a minority member can establish that the employer *considered characteristics of the minority group* at all in reaching the decision to terminate him, then he will very likely establish a *prima facie* case and prevail. Thus, in *Thomas* v. *Parker,*[31] a black employee had been discharged, since he was nontenured and there was a reduction in force. The trial court found that an intent to discriminate could be inferred from the fact that the personnel file prepared by the plaintiff's supervisor contained a note indicating that the plaintiff had "bushy hair" and was "greatly concerned with minority rights." In *Saucedo* v. *Brothers Well Service, Inc.,*[32] the employer had a rule against the *speaking of a foreign language* while drilling or reworking an oil well. The rationale of the employer was that it was dangerous and highly technical work, and any failure of communication could be disastrous. The plaintiff had made an offhand remark in Spanish to a fellow Mexican-American and was discharged for that reason. The court found discrimination. In effect, it substituted its own judgment for the employer's judgment, and held that the utterance caused no danger or failure of communications. The court further relied on the fact that the remark was not made in the context of drilling or reworking, but rather when the plaintiff was bringing a part to the other Mexican-American to be straightened. Thus, the court did not invalidate the rule altogether but merely found that its application was discriminatory on the facts presented.

Standards that are *vague* and are relied upon by an employer as the basis for adverse action—termination or suspension of a minority employee—are also very suspect to the courts. In *McBride* v. *Delta Airlines*,[33] the plaintiff, a black employee, alleged racial discrimination when he had been fired for violating a company rule that mandated dismissal for "conduct unbecoming a Delta employee." The plaintiff had been discharged after being convicted of assault and battery. The trial court found the dismissal justified because of the plaintiff's conviction and his spotty work record. The court of appeals, although it affirmed the dismissal of the individual claimant, remanded the case to the trial court with instructions to consider how this vague policy affected the class. Most assuredly, if it were found that minorities were discharged or disciplined at a greater rate than whites, the standard would have been struck. However, in this case, the Supreme Court indicated that the class should be decertified, for a different reason, and that issue was never reached.

There is one standard that EEOC feels can be the basis for a finding of discrimination, but that has been rarely litigated. EEOC has been very concerned about the *move to the suburbs* by many major corporations, because the result is that many minorities are left in the urban centers and the work force of the employer becomes more nonminority. In one of the few cases in which the issue has been presented, the employer sustained its move to the suburbs for business reasons, despite the adverse impact against the minorities. In that case, *EEOC* v. *North Hills Passavant Hospital*,[34] the percentage of black employees had been reduced dramatically between 1964 and 1970 because the hospital had moved from the city to the suburbs. At trial, the hospital could demonstrate the financial necessity of moving. It could also demonstrate that it had guaranteed employment to all incumbent staff and that any incumbents who had sought to work at the new facility had, in fact, been granted the opportunity. The court held that the low representation of minorities on the hospital staff was the result of the move and the demographics in the area to which the hospital had moved, but that there was no discrimination.

Many employers still believe they should have the prerogative of firing whomever they want, whenever they want, and not have to give an explanation or defend that decision. Because of the manner in which equal employment opportunity law has developed, especially with respect to minorities, that belief is probably wrong. There have developed, through many court decisions, de facto rules of thumb in assessing whether action against minorities will be found to establish a *prima facie* case. If a person can demonstrate that (1) he or she is a minority member, (2) something bad had happened to him or her, and (3) "something else unusual" existed in the discharge or discipline, no matter how slight that "something else" might be, then that person probably will be able to establish a *prima facie* case, and the burden will be shifted to the employer to justify its action. The "something else" can be the fact that the employee was one of *long standing* (*Ficlin* v. *Sabatini*),[35] or the fact that there had been *no prior warnings* or *no prior complaints* against the minority person who was discharged for cause (*Harper* v. *General Grocer Company*),[36] or that, in terminating the minority employee, the employer had not specifically *followed its own regular procedures,* whether or not they were in writing.

The establishing of a *prima facie* case does not mean that the employer's actions will be found discriminatory, but it does mean that the employer that cannot present a reason for the action against the minority person will probably be found to have discriminated.

Sex Standards

The most serious problem respondents face regarding standards for adverse action against females arises in situations where there has been prior discrimination against females, causing them to be concentrated in certain jobs—say, packer jobs that require relatively light lifting—and were not hired into other jobs or lines of progression requiring substantially more lifting. In such circumstances, the employment system might have awarded advanced-level jobs to the person with the greatest job seniority in the next lower level in the line of progression. Such a system presents an equal employment opportunity problem when layoffs come and females are laid off out of the packing line of progression even though they have more company seniority than many males in other lines of progression.

A case in which this kind of problem was addressed was *Danner* v. *Phillips Petroleum Company,*[37] in which the court indicated that the company layoff policy was discriminatory in violation of Title VII. A similar result was achieved by decisions in *Chrapliwy* v. *Uniroyal, Inc.*[38] and *Bowe* v. *Colgate-Palmolive Company;*[39] but see *Trivett* v. *Tri-State Container Corp.*[40]

Another serious problem arises in situations in which the first, or one of the first, females to be awarded a particular job cannot perform according to the standard of performance required by the employer for that job. Thus, it might be that an employer has been pressed by the Office for Federal Contract Compliance Programs to hire, transfer, or assign women to particular job titles or lines of progression. When the employer does this, increasing its representation of females, one or more of the females cannot perform the job or a particular aspect of it. There is a strong tendency for an employer in such circumstances to make *accommodation* to the lack of performance by those females. For instance, if the job requires lifting 50-pound boxes on occasion and a female cannot perform that part of the job, when such boxes have to be handled, the employer might permit her to be assisted by another person.

The problem arises if the job title involved is covered by a collective-bargaining agreement. Neither Title VII nor Executive Order 11246 requires that an employer change the nature of the job just to accommodate females. However, Title VII does require that if the employer changes the nature of the job for any one particular group, such as females, then it can be required to change the nature of the job for all, including males. See *McDonald* v. *Santa Fe Trail Transportation Co.*[41] Contests on this issue can arise from grievance procedures under the collective-bargaining agreement or lawsuits by males under Title VII.

Employers instituting affirmative action programs or operating under such programs would be well advised to monitor their supervisors closely to ensure that they are not permitting job functions to change just to keep females in a particular job, as well as monitoring them to see that they are not making the nontraditional female jobs more difficult for females when they attain such jobs.

A complication related to this problem arises when a woman who has served in a job successfully for a considerable period of time finds that one of the incidental duties to that job is now required and cannot perform that incidental duty. At this point, she has already lost return rights to the job she vacated. An issue that will be raised by any agency or court reviewing the situation will be whether or not the job description pursuant to which the woman had bid for that job had indicated that this particular duty was part of that job. Although job descriptions should not unduly emphasize incidental duties that might discourage bids by females for particular jobs, they should indicate all the incidental duties that are required of the job. Another issue that will be raised will be whether there have been any prior exceptions, before females started to take those jobs, in which males were "accommodated" when they could not perform those incidental duties.

An employer may ultimately decide to change a performance standard (if only because female employees are injuring themselves and filing workmen's compensation claims). However, the employer should follow the close monitoring procedure described above to ensure that the performance standard is not being changed informally, without its knowledge, to become the rule of the workplace. If a decision is made to allow others to help a female on a particular duty, it should be a conscious decision. The employer must recognize that thereafter when that duty has to be performed, anyone doing it will be entitled to such help. Similarly, if a decision is made to use special equipment when females perform that duty, all employees will have the right to use special equipment when performing it.

Appearance standards and the differences allowed in dress codes for males and females have previously been discussed in Chapter 4, starting on page 60. Those standards and the discussion there relating to height, weight, hair length, the wearing of eyeglasses, pantsuits, ties, and career ensembles is just as applicable here. If the appearance standard can be legally used to make a hiring decision, then it can also be used to justify a termination decision.

General conduct standards or *general standards for performance* can be uniformly applied, even though particular females might suffer discharge because of their application. Thus, in *Batyko* v. *Pennsylvania Liquor Control Board*,[42] the plaintiff had had the highest grade on the civil-service exam for the position of liquor-store clerk. However, her duties included lifting heavy cartons of liquor, and the defendant was able to demonstrate, through written complaints from plaintiff's co-workers, her inability to perform, justifying her termination. That termination was sustained. In sustaining the standard, the court noted that the standard of physical strength was applied uniformly to the male and female employees.

In *General Electric Company* v. *FEPC*,[43] the claimant, a male, claimed he suffered a discriminatory discharge on the basis of sex. The Illinois State FEPC had found on his behalf, based upon the fact that he and a female had been involved in an altercation. However, the court found for the employer and sustained the discharge, because at the time the employer terminated the male, it had known that he had struck the female co-worker but had not known that she had also struck him. In *White* v. *Bailar*,[44] the discharge of a male nurse for *sleeping on the job* was sustained, since he could not demonstrate that females observed sleeping on the job were treated any differently. In *Lewis* v. *Ford Motor Co.*,[45] the discharge of a female because of her use of *vile language and unprofessional behavior* was sustained. The female could not prove that men who acted in the same manner were treated any differently.

Standards requiring that a person terminate employment upon *marriage* (*Sprogis* v. *United Air Lines, Inc.*)[46] or upon reaching a certain age, such as 32 years, or upon *becoming pregnant* will be struck as a violation of Title VII. However, in order to establish that these standards are a violation of Title VII, the claimant must establish that there are people of the opposite sex in the same job title and that they are not bound by the same standard. See, for example, *Stroud* v. *Delta Air Lines, Inc.*[47]

Present case law indicates that a female cannot be discharged because she refuses to *use her husband's name after marriage*. In *Allen* v. *Lovejoy*,[48] the plaintiff had refused to change her name on company personnel records after becoming married, and for that reason she was suspended. The court held that a rule that applies only to women, with no counterpart applicable to men, may not be the basis for depriving a female employee of the right to continue at work.

A termination after a person has had a sex change is not a violation of Title VII. In *Voyles* v. *Ralph K. Davis Medical Center*,[49] the court ruled that Congress was not seeking to protect change of sex, or sexual preference, when it legislated Title VII.

Many of the problems concerning adverse action against females are derived from the fact that males, and society in general, have preconceived notions about what the conduct of a proper female should be. These cases rest not on the adverse impact theory—that is, a neutral rule being uniformly applied but having a disproportionate impact against females—but rather on the disparate-treatment theory. This theory, quite simply, means there is a double standard. This is a violation of Title VII. Thus, it is discriminatory to terminate or transfer a female because she is having an extramarital affair unless the employer undertakes the same adverse action against males who engage in the same conduct. Similarly, women who curse should be treated the same as men who curse, and women who have drinking problems should be treated the same as men having those problems.

There are two significant areas that relate to the subject matter of this section but are more appropriately covered in the next chapter, which deals with standards for terms and conditions of employment. These areas are the treatment of maternity, and sexual harassment in the workplace.

Standards for Handicaps and Disabilities

The law regarding handicaps and disabilities, especially the law as defined by the Rehabilitation Act of 1973, is still in the embryonic stages. Procedural and definitional issues are still being litigated. Procedurally, the courts are still endeavoring to determine whether there is an independent right of action under the Rehabilitation Act of 1973, or whether it is only the government that can sue to enforce that statute. See *United Handicapped Fed. v. Andre*,[50] on this issue.

In the definitional area, there are still no definitive decisions defining "alcoholism," "reasonable accommodation," or "qualified handicapped person."

In the substantive area, the courts have addressed discharges involving physical maladies such as asthma, heart murmurs, alcoholism, and deafness.

In *Chicago, Milwaukee, St. Paul, & Pacific RR Co. v. State of Wisconsin, the Department of Industry, Labor, and Human Relations* (DILHR),[51] the issue was whether asthma was a handicap within the meaning of the Wisconsin Fair Employment Practice Code. The court held that it was, and further held that there was no evidence that the complainant's handicap impeded his performance in any way. Additionally, the court found that there was no proof that his having asthma would affect his performance in the future. On that basis, the company was found liable for discrimination because it had discharged the complainant. The court did not have to consider a factor that the employer might ordinarily consider—namely, that if the preexisting condition became aggravated, a workmen's compensation claim might be filed.

In the case of *City of Wisconsin Rapids v. Wisconsin Department of Industry, Labor, and Human Relations*,[52] after the complainant was hired as a firefighter, he was found to have a heart murmur. During his one-year probation period, he performed satisfactorily. However, the employer discharged him because medical reports indicated that he could possibly become disabled in the future. The holding of the court was that the possibility of a physical disorder's impeding an employee's performance in the future should not interfere with that person's opportunity to obtain gainful employment in the present. The court held that the employer has the burden of proving that a disability affects the employee's present output in order to lawfully discharge him.

In *Connecticut General Life Insurance Co.* v. *Department of Industry, Labor, and Human Relations*,[53] the issue was whether or not the complainant's drinking problem constituted a disability within the meaning of the Wisconsin Fair Employment Practices Act. In that case, the court found that the determination by the state that the complainant had a drinking problem did not equate with a determination that he was an alcoholic, and that only alcoholics were protected by the state statute. In order to establish that the complainant was an alcoholic, the court stated, the state would have to introduce medical evidence to establish that his drinking was not volitional. If it were volitional, he would not be handicapped within the meaning of the Wisconsin Fair Employment Practices Act.

Under the Rehabilitation Act of 1973, Congress wrote an amendment in 1978 to clarify an uncertain area involving alcoholism. The amendment made it clear that a person who has a drinking problem, whether that be defined as just "a problem" or as alcoholism, is not protected by the Rehabilitation Act of 1973 if his condition adversely affects his ability to perform the job or if his performance directly endangers the safety of persons or property.

Deafness was the issue in *State Division of Human Rights* v. *Averill Park Central School District*.[54] The complainant had been employed as a bus driver since 1962, and from 1971 on, he had used a hearing aid. He had been given a hearing test. Based on the results of that test, the employer determined that the disability made the complainant unqualified for his job and demoted him to the custodial staff. The New York State Division of Human Rights found that he had suffered discrimination. However, the court reversed, finding that although it is unlawful for an employer to discharge an employee on the basis of his disability, the disability must not be job-related. In this case, the court found, the disability was job-related, and so the defendant was justified in discharging him.

In *Southeastern Community College* v. *Davis*,[55] the Supreme Court addressed the area of disabilities and handicaps for the only time. The case did not involve employment, but it is helpful in assessing how the Supreme Court would act in an employment case. In that case, the complainant was a student who wanted to enter a college's nursing program. She had been tested and found to be defective in her hearing, and on that basis she was denied entry into the school. The test determined that although she met the educational requirements, she could not hear properly and depended in significant measure upon lipreading. The college said that because of the surgical masks worn in an operating room, the complainant would not be able to lip-read during surgery, and this could endanger the patient. The lower appellate court had indicated that in determining whether or not she should be admitted to the nursing-school program, the trial court should have considered only her educational qualifications. In reversing the lower appellate court, the Supreme Court ruled that "an otherwise qualified person is one who is able to meet *all* of the program's requirements in spite of this handicap."[56] The Court found that the complainant was not able to meet all the program's requirements.

Another important aspect of this Supreme Court decision was that it held that Section 501(c) of the Rehabilitation Act of 1973 imposed no exact duty upon federal-fund recipients such as the defendant to make reasonable accommodations for its handicapped students. Therefore, the court concluded, the refusal to do so was not discriminatory. This strict construction might be significant, because OFCCP, in its regulations implementing the Rehabilitation Act of 1973, has indicated that there is a requirement that employers make reasonable accommodation to the handicaps of employees or potential employees. However, neither the Rehabilitation Act nor the presidential executive order that implements it requires employers to make reasonable accommodation; they require only that contractors take affirmative action to employ and advance in employment handicapped people. Because of the approach taken by the Supreme Court in *Davis,* it is likely that the Court, if called upon to determine whether reasonable accommodation is required of government contractors, will find that there is no such requirement. Some lower courts have already indicated that there is no requirement to make reasonable accommodation under the Rehabilitation Act of 1973. See, for example, *Carmi* v. *St. Louis School District.*[57]

ASSESSING AND MINIMIZING ADVERSE IMPACT IN DISCIPLINE, DISCHARGE, AND REDUCTION IN FORCE

The preceding two chapters have demonstrated that the determination of whether there is adverse impact is dictated by the manner in which the groups being compared are defined. They also demonstrated that the greater the information available to the employer, the more options available it has in that determination. Thus, it was demonstrated in Chapter 4, involving hiring, that both sides of the ratio—that is, who would be considered an "applicant" and who would be considered a "hire"—were both concepts subject to a substantial amount of control by the employer. In Chapter 5, dealing with promotions, we saw that the group of people from which the persons were promoted could be defined and be considered an "applicant pool," and that those promoted could be considered the "hires."

In the area of terminations, there is at least as much flexibility. Quite simply, following through on the same approach, the pool from which the people terminated come is considered the "applicant pool," and those terminated are considered "hires."

It is obvious that the pool from which those terminated are chosen must be employees. However, for purposes of adverse-impact analysis, this pool might be employees in a particular department, job-classification, facility, work unit (administration, sales, or production), region, or the entire corporation. Similarly, there is opportunity for employer discretion in determining how terminations will be defined. To give just a few examples, there can be two overall termination categories: terminations by the employer's choice and terminations by the employee's choice. The first group would include people terminated for cause for a major offense (such as theft), people terminated pursuant to a progressive discipline system for a number of minor offenses (such as persistent tardiness), people who elect early retirement after being told they are about to be subject to a large-scale reduction in force, people who resign after being told they will be terminated if they do not resign, and possibly, people who quit after receiving a final warning under a progressive discipline system.

The second group, terminations at the employee's choice, includes retirements, those who quit for a better opportunity, or those who quit because they want to move.

Given all these options in determining what the groups will be, or could be, for purposes of conducting adverse-impact analysis, the employer facing a charge of discrimination or a lawsuit involving termination can use these groups as building blocks. The person who filed the charge of discrimination or lawsuit would be the nucleus, but different groups could be built around that nucleus. Thus, the charge or lawsuit might be by a person over the age of 40 who was terminated as part of a reduction in force. This person, therefore, is in the large group "terminated at the employer's option," and comparisons on that basis would be appropriate. However, such a person is also in the smaller group "terminated at the employer's option, but not for cause." The person is also in the still smaller group, "terminated as part of a reduction in force," but that group could be defined to include or not include people who took early retirement rather than risk being victims of the reduction in force.

In order for an employer to have the greatest number of options available for purposes of adverse-impact analysis in the area of terminations, proper record keeping is necessary. Employers who are government contractors will have some of the necessary records, because they are required by the regulations of OFCCP to keep lists of terminations.[58] However, quite frequently those lists, which are supposed to contain the reasons for termination, do not have the detail the employer might ultimately want. Nor is it advisable to put the detailed reasons for termination on such a list, since the government compliance officers can utilize different groupings to find adverse impact just as effectively as the employer might utilize them to rebut such a determination.

To ensure that the records are available to make the defense if it becomes necessary, the employer should establish systems requiring that when people are terminated, for whatever reason, a report giving the reasons for that termination be sent to some central source in the employer organization.

(If there are limited resources available to an employer, those resources would be better concentrated on the systems designed to ensure against hiring or promotion discrimination claims. This is because there is far less likelihood of a class action regarding terminations than there is of a class action involving hiring or promotion.)

One of the few areas of major exposure in cases involving terminations arises when there is a large-scale layoff of people not covered by a seniority system that is incorporated into a collective-bargaining agreement. The first step in establishing a system for assessing and minimizing adverse impact in layoff in such situations would be to identify the pool from which the layoffs will come. Generally, this can be done in the same manner that was used by the employer in determining how the payroll should be reduced. Thus, if it happens that the employer has determined to reduce the payroll across the board by 25 percent, then the pool is the entire work force. If the employer has determined to reduce its exempt work force by 25 percent, then the pool will be the exempt work force. Some further examples of the pools from which the layoffs might be coming would be professional or technical employees, employees at particular facilities, employees in particular EEO categories, employees above or below certain earnings rates, and employees by different regions within the employer's organization.

Once the pool from which the layoffs will come has been determined, then the race, sex, and national-origin composition in that group can be identified. Regarding age, the employer can identify people above and below the age of 40, but should also identify those who are between the ages of 40 and 50, 50 and 60, and 60 and 70.

The ideal, for EEO purposes, would be to have the percentage of the age groups in the work force who are laid off reflect the percentage those groups represent in the work force from which the layoffs are coming. Thus, if the layoffs are coming from exempt employees at a particular facility, and people over 40 represent 40 percent of the exempt employees at that facility, it would be desirable that the percentage of those laid off who are over 40, be no more than 50 percent. If this percentage is achieved, there will be no adverse impact according to the 80 percent rule.

Just as there might be four or five screening steps between the time of application and the time of hire, any one of which might have an adverse impact, so also in the area of large-scale reductions in force, there might be incidental steps, some of which are indicated below. However, every reduction in force is different, and no employment system is exactly like any other. Consequently, the main purpose of the following analysis of the interim steps that might take place is to demonstrate types of approaches to the problem of adverse-impact analysis in large-scale reductions in force.

One possible interim step, between the time of identification of the pool from which the layoffs will come and the actual layoffs, is identification of a subpool from which the layoffs will come. Insofar as possible, the people in this subpool would be identified by objective criteria. Thus, if it is employees from the sales region who are to be laid off, the employer might indicate that the pool would be all those who have not achieved their sales quotas for the last three years. If it is other than a sales district, it might be people who have had less than a satisfactory performance evaluation for the last three years. For purposes of illustration, this subpool can be identified as RIF List 1.

In comparing the total pool of employees from which the layoffs will come to the people on RIF List 1, it is not so important to know whether or not there is adverse impact. That is because adverse-impact analysis looks to the end result, not the interim steps toward achieving that result.

A subsequent step, after RIF List 1 is made out, might be to inform each unit supervisor how many people under his supervision must be "riffed" and let each unit supervisor pick those to be "riffed" from the list. The sum total of all these selections by all the unit supervisors would then come back to corporate headquarters. The percentage analysis could be conducted there—a comparison of the total employee pool of minorities, females, people over 40, and so on, to the total of those identified by the unit supervisors for reduction-in-force layoffs. If there is no adverse impact, then those identified by unit supervisors from RIF List 1 might be the ones laid off. If there is adverse impact at one facility or region that causes the gross statistics to result in statistically significant adverse impact against a particular group, then the exercise might be repeated at that facility or for that region. Alternatively, the employer might determine to give early-retirement opportunities to people at that facility or to employees generally, and reanalyze the remaining group on RIF List 1 after these opportunities have been exercised.

Early retirement is generally more attractive to long-term employees who are older. This group will usually be more preponderantly male and white than the regular work-force composition of the employer. Consequently, the employer offering early retirement can expect that people who are white and male and older will be more likely to take advantage of the opportunity.

One issue that has not yet been addressed by any court is how people who take early retirement in the face of a potential RIF should be counted: Should they be counted as people who were "riffed," or should they be counted as retirees, for purposes of adverse-impact analysis? Ideally, if the employer has an age-discrimination case brought against it, it would want those who took early retirement not to be counted as part of the RIF. Conversely, if an employer has a sex or national-origin or race case brought against it, it would probably want to count those who took early retirement in the face of the RIF to count as part of the RIF, for statistical counting purposes.

If an employer does offer early retirement and a considerable number of people take it, then the employer might want to compile a RIF List No. 2, consisting of those who are on the original RIF List No. 1, less those who took early retirement. With RIF List No. 2, the employer might go back to the unit supervisors and repeat the process described before.

For the employer not operating under a collective bargaining agreement which has a bona fide seniority system, who wants to lay off in such a way that the percentage of minorities and females remains constant before and after the RIF, there are certain benefits and protection. In fact, it is likely that an employer that determines to lay off on such a quota basis could immunize itself from all liability not only under Title VII, but also under the Age Discrimination in Employment Act of 1972.

The manner in which the employer could gain this protection is by utilizing and relying upon EEOC's Affirmative Action Guidelines. Since EEOC now enforces not only the prohibitions against discrimination on the basis of race, sex, and national origin but also those against age discrimination, it would be highly unlikely that, having immunized the layoffs pursuant to its Affirmative Action Guidelines, it would find them to be a violation of Title VII because of age.

Alternatively, the employer might actively seek review by EEOC, through its Office of Voluntary Programs, and have the Voluntary Programs Officer of the EEOC observe that the employer is proceeding by a quota layoff system. In this way, the employer might gain prior clearance and assurances from EEOC that the layoffs would not be found to be a violation of Title VII or the ADEA.

FORMS

One of the most useful sources for a frank appraisal of the employer's personnel system is the employee who is terminating employment. If the employer's personnel department has sufficient time and resources, it should seek to benefit from this source by having an exit interview.

Another benefit from the exit-interview process is that it memorializes the employee's reason for leaving. If at some later time the employee files a discrimination claim of constructive discharge, the statements made during the exit interview may be helpful in establishing that the charge is a makeshift attempt to obtain money improperly.

Finally, the exit interview can benefit the employer by indicating whether it is competitive with other, similarly situated employers, and if not, why not.

EXIT INTERVIEW FORM

Interviewer: _____ Date: _____

Employee name: _____

Supervisor: _____

Voluntary resignation:

1. When did you decide to leave the company?

2. What brought about this decision?

3. Do you plan to take another job?

    a. Where?

    b. Starting salary?

    c. Benefits?

    d. Opportunity?

    e. How did you discover the job was available?

    f. Why did you take this particular job?

    g. What made you look for another job?

(Ask persons who were discharged questions 4–18.)

4. How did you like your work?
5. What did you like most about your job?
6. What did you dislike most about your job?
7. How would you rate your own job performance?
8. What did you like most about working for this company?
9. What did you dislike most about working for this company?
10. Were you treated fairly?

11. If not, who treated you unfairly, and when?

12. Did you feel other persons were treated fairly?

13. If not, who or what group was not treated fairly? What was the unfair treatment? Who was the person not treating this person or persons fairly?

14. How did you like your supervisor?

15. How do others in your department get along with the supervisor?

16. How did you get along with the other people in your department?

17. Which one(s) did you not get along with, and why?

18. Would you recommend the company to your friends as a good place to work?

Additional comments:

FOOTNOTES

[1] 432 U.S. 395 (1977).
[2] 17 FEP Cases 113 (E.D. Pa. 1978).
[3] 14 FEP Cases 1004 (D. Conn. 1977).
[4] 424 F. Supp. 1299 (E.D. Mich. 1976).
[5] 367 F. Supp. 440 (N.D. Ill. 1973).
[6] 6 EPD ¶ 8879 (S.D. Tex. 1973).
[7] 561 F.2d 609 (5th Cir. 1977).
[8] 475 F.2d 958 (8th Cir. 1978).
[9] 550 F.2d 1113 (8th Cir. 1977).
[10] 18 FEP Cases 494 (D. Vt. 1978).
[11] 19 FEP Cases 246 (N.D. Ga. 1979).
[12] 510 F.2d 313 (6th Cir. 1975).
[13] 479 F.2d 97 (2d Cir. 1973).
[14] 433 F. Supp. 655 (E.D. Va. 1977).
[15] 368 F. Supp. 364 (E.D. Tenn. 1973).
[16] 320 F. Supp. 1175 (W.D. Ark. 1970).
[17] See 29 C.F.R. §860.103(h).
[18] 455 F.2d 818 (5th Cir. 1972).
[19] 358 F. Supp. 1208 (N.D. Ga. 1973).
[20] 431 U.S. 324, 97 S.Ct. 1843 (1977).

[21] 564 F.2d 179 (5th Cir. 1977).
[22] 588 F.2d 421 (9th Cir. 1978).
[23] 437 F. Supp. 1138 (E.D. Pa. 1977).
[24] 550 F.2d 1343 (4th Cir. 1976).
[25] 431 U.S. 553 (1977).
[26] See 16 FEP Cases 1813.
[27] 508 F.2d 687 (3rd Cir. 1975), *cert. den. sub nom. Jersey Central Power & Light Co.* v. *EEOC*, 96 S. Ct. 2215 (1976), *vac'd and rem'd sub nom. EEOC* v. *Jersey Central Power & Light Co.*, 96 S. Ct. 2196 (1976).
[28] 19 FEP Cases 368 (S.D. Fla. 1978).
[29] 588 F.2d 61 (4th Cir. 1978).
[30] 15 FEP Cases 752 (E.D. Pa. 1977).
[31] 19 FEP Cases 49 (D.D.C. 1979).
[32] 19 FEP Cases 91 (S.D. Tex. 1979).
[33] 551 F.2d 113, 14 FEP Cases 1137 (6th Cir. 1977).
[34] 19 FEP Cases 211 (W.D. Pa. 1979).
[35] 14 FEP Cases 1128 (E.D. Pa. 1977).
[36] 18 FEP Cases 1356 (E.D. Mo. 1978), *aff'd in relevant part, reversed in part*, 18 FEP Cases 1359 (8th Cir. 1979).
[37] 447 F.2d 159 (5th Cir. 1971).
[38] 458 F. Supp. 252 (N.D. Ind. 1977.
[39] 416 F.2d 711 (7th Cir. 1969).
[40] 368 F. Supp. 137 (E.D. Tenn. 1973).
[41] 423 U.S. 923 (1976).
[42] 450 F. Supp. 32 (W.D. Pa. 1978).
[43] 15 FEP Cases 1486 (Dist. Ct. Ill. 1976).
[44] 14 FEP Cases 383 (E.D. Mo. 1976).
[45] 17 FEP Cases 933 (E.D. Mich. 1978).
[46] 444 F.2d 1194 (7th Cir. 1971).
[47] 544 F.2d 892 (5th Cir. 1977).
[48] 553 F.2d 522 (6th Cir. 1977).
[49] 403 F. Supp. 456 (N.D. Cal. 1975).
[50] 558 F.2d 413 (8th Cir. 1977).
[51] 62 Wisc.2d 392, 215 N.W. 2d 443 (1974).
[52] 15 EPD ¶7846 (Cir. Ct. Wisc. 1977).
[53] 86 Wisc.2d 393, 273 N.W.2d 206 (1979).
[54] 17 EPD ¶8449, 59 App. Div. 2d 449, 399 N.Y. Supp.2d 926 (1977).
[55] 99 S.Ct. 236
[56] 47 U.S. L.W. at 4690.
[57] 20 FEP Cases 162 (E.D. Mo. 1979).
[58] See 41 C.F.R. §60–60.8.

Chapter 7

Standards for Terms and Conditions of Employment

INTRODUCTION

The principles set forth in the preceding three chapters are also applicable to treatment of employees in any aspect of the employment relationship. In this chapter, miscellaneous terms and conditions of employment are covered, with a detailed analysis of some particularly troublesome areas.

STANDARDS AT ISSUE

Age Standards

The Age Discrimination in Employment Act of 1967 (ADEA)[1] was amended by the Age Discrimination in Employment Act Amendments of 1978. Procedural and substantive changes were as follows:

1. The upper limit on the protected age group was raised, so that people less than 70 years of age are now protected.
2. The right to a trial by jury was clearly established.

3. The requirement that people give the secretary of labor notice of intent to sue prior to filing such a suit was removed.
4. There was established an automatic tolling period of up to one year of the statute of limitations if the U.S. Department of Labor is engaged in conciliation discussions.
5. Compulsory retirement at 65 was still permitted for high-level executives—that is, those who had a nonforfeitable annual retirement benefit equal to or exceeding $27,000—or for tenured faculty at the college level.

The ADEA Amendments of 1978 raised a number of issues concerning terms and conditions of employment. The Department of Labor has issued regulations interpreting the amendments;[2] however, although these interpretations are persuasive to a court, they are not binding on a court, and thus far there have been no definitive rulings by the courts concerning the issues covered by the Department of Labor's interpretations. Furthermore, many states have enacted their own age-discrimination provisions, and Labor has specifically said that neither the ADEA nor the Department of Labor interpretations of the ADEA preempts state statutes.[3] Additionally, both the ADEA amendments and state laws must be read in conjunction with the Employee Retirement Income Security Act (ERISA). Section 514 of ERISA may or may not preempt state laws, according to the Department of Labor.[4] Finally, EEOC has assumed jurisdiction over ADEA enforcement, and may or may not continue with the interpretations put forth by Labor.

One issue raised by the ADEA amendments is whether an employer with a retirement plan oriented toward retirement at age 65 or earlier is required to make contributions to that retirement plan for people who reach 65 and choose not to retire. The answer for most employers, if Labor's interpretation is followed, will be that no such contributions are required. This is because most employers have *defined-benefit plans.*

Defined-benefit plans are exactly what their name implies. Amounts are contributed by the employer, and sometimes by the employee also, toward achievement of certain benefits for the employee at a certain age. Employers who have defined-benefit plans can refuse to admit to them people who are, on the date of hire, less than five years younger than normal retirement age under the plan. Thus, if the plan calls for eligibility for retirement at age 65, and a person is 61 when hired, then that person can be excluded from the defined-benefit plan. However, if that person is 60 or younger at the date of hire, the person cannot be excluded at all, if the defined-benefit plan is subject to ERISA. He can be excluded if the plan is not covered by ERISA only if the employer is able to demonstrate that the exclusion is justifiable on the basis of costs, which is very difficult to demonstrate.

The employer that has a defined-benefit plan need not make contributions to that plan for people who work beyond the set retirement age, nor does the benefit to be received by the employee have to be actuarially adjusted when he does retire. Additionally, the employer does not have to pay the employee his pension amount at the established retirement age if the employee continues to work. The employer can amend the plan to postpone the date on which the retirement benefits will be paid, to coincide with the date the employee stops working.

The other kind of retirement plan covered by the Department of Labor interpretations is a defined-contribution plan, whereby the employer, and possibly the employee, contribute and the employee's retirement payment is determined by investment gains or losses. The employer that has only a defined-contribution plan need not make contributions for an employee who works beyond the normal retirement age. The plan may also provide that the employer need not contribute on behalf of someone who is older than the normal retirement age on the date of hire.

A second issue is whether a person who has retired on full pension at age 65 can reapply for the same job he or she just retired from, thereby gaining the pension *and* former salary. There has not yet been a definitive ruling on this, but there may be some direction provided by the experience under California state law. California had amended its age-discrimination act prior to the amendments to the ADEA. The state attorney general issued an Attorney General's Opinion that if someone had retired from a job and was on pension, the employer could legally refuse to hire that person for that job, or any job. However, the California experience has allowed employees to retire on full pension from one employer and seek to work for another employer in the same industry.

A third issue raised by the amendments deals with employer contributions to a sickness-and-accident plan for employees 65 or older. People 65 or older are entitled to Medicare and Medicaid benefits whether or not they are working. The issue is whether the employer can require such employees to utilize these benefits, merely supplementing the federal benefits to bring those employees 65 and over to par with all other employees. The answer is yes, according to the U.S. Department of Labor directives, although the issue has not been addressed by the courts.

There is at present under consideration by Congress legislation that would remove any top age limit for the protected age group. At least ten states have already done this. Consequently, employers in those states that are listed on page 49 of this book who want older people to retire to make way for ambitious younger people have only two alternatives to removing a person who is over 65: making retirement so attractive that it will be chosen, or terminating for cause.

Race and National-Origin Standards

One of the most troublesome problems for employers is maintaining a work environment free of racial or ethnic discrimination. The discussion of this problem is also applicable to maintaining a work environment free of sexual discrimination.

This area is troublesome because ethnic and racial bantering and joking have become almost a permanent part of the American work environment. Even if an employer tried to prevent such joking altogether, it could not succeed, short of terminating most of its work force. Furthermore, an employer rule banning such bantering absolutely might itself become the subject of ridicule and undermine the efficacy of other employer rules.

The court decisions issued thus far seem to recognize *sub rosa* this phenomenon of the American workplace. In *Cariddi* v. *Kansas City Chiefs Football Club, Inc.*,[5] the claimant had sued under Title VII complaining about discrimination on the basis of his national origin, Italian-American. The trial court found no such discrimination, and the appellate court affirmed. Even though the uncontradicted evidence was that the claimant's supervisor had called him a "dago" and had referred to other Italian-American employees as "the Mafia," no discrimination was found. The appellate court reasoned that the statements were just casual, and indicated that for such derogatory comments to rise to the status of Title VII violations, they must be excessive and opprobrious. In *Fekete* v. *U.S. Steel Corp.*,[6] the claimant was a Hungarian-born worker who became the butt of pranks from fellow employees. The court found that management did not know of these originally; that when it learned of them, it made an attempt to identify the perpetrators, to no avail; that the claimant's own odd conduct had precipitated some of these pranks; and that there was a substantial representation of ethnic backgrounds, including Hungarian, in the work force. On the basis of these findings, the court found the company not liable for a violation of Title VII.

Despite this "rule of reason" adopted by trial courts concerning such incidents and bantering on the job, the employer can be found liable under certain conditions. See, for example, *Kyriazi* v. *Western Electric Co.*[7]

Although the claim that the employer maintained a work environment that was discriminatory is almost never raised as a sole claim, it is frequently an added complaint when someone has determined to file suit for another reason, such as failure to promote. At trial, evidence concerning race or national-origin bantering, and the employer's reaction to it, is frequently highly persuasive. For that reason, it is advisable for the employer to establish standards for handling such conduct.

An initial step would be to post a statement such as this:

OUR COURTS HAVE DECIDED

THAT RACIAL, ETHNIC, RELIGIOUS, OR SEXUAL

HARASSMENT ON THE JOB

IS AGAINST THE LAW.

THIS COMPANY PROHIBITS VERBAL AND PHYSICAL

HARASSMENT OF ITS EMPLOYEES

BASED ON RACE, NATIONAL ORIGIN, RELIGION, OR SEX.

> Any employee subjected to such harassment
> should advise
> the Supervisor of Personnel.

Also, the employer should react, not initiate action, regarding bantering or pranks based on race or national origin. For the employer to unilaterally ban all such joking might easily cause it to go underground and become more vicious.

Nevertheless, if it appears to a supervisor that the joking is becoming excessive, or that any particular individual has become its target, even if that person has not made a complaint, it might be wise to talk to the person privately, advising him or her that there is a procedure available for redress if the person so desires. Such a private conference would be documented and a copy of the memo documenting it placed in the employee's file. As a general rule, it is best for the employer, as well as the employee involved, if the complaint procedure does not have to be used, since, if overt conduct is blocked, underground conduct frequently becomes more frequent, more vicious, and more difficult to prevent.

The general rules, however, do not apply to situations where a person of a particular sex or minority group is the first—or one of the first—of his or her kind to start working in a certain area. In such instances, the employer should make every attempt to prevent *any* pranks or joking about that person's race, sex, or national origin. If the person fails in that job, and can establish that he or she had been one of the first of his or her kind in that job, that there was such ridicule, and that the employer knew of the ridicule and did nothing, then that person will probably prevail in establishing a Title VII violation. All employer protestations about performance and introductions of performance ratings will be suspect in the eyes of the court.

The process of documenting the case against a particular person whom the employer wants to terminate, safely and legally, can itself be a discriminatory term and condition of employment. Thus, in *Francis* v. *AT&T, Long Lines Dept.*,[8] the employer had been found by the court to have documented scores of latenesses and petty work-rule violations against the plaintiff, a black. The supervisor who had done the documenting had, herself, been black. However, the company did not document against everyone similarly situated. The court held that the very process of faultfinding had been discriminatory and that the absence of similar documentation against other employees was evidence of an intent to discriminate against the plaintiff.

The courts and the EEOC have also found discrimination in terms and conditions of employment because of differential treatment regarding *working conditions,* such as unnecessarily prohibiting employees from speaking Spanish,[9] permitting other employees to harass a minority employee (*Brito* v. *Zia Co.*),[10] or reprimanding minorities in a manner different from that used for white employees (*U.S.* v. *Lee Way Motor Freight, Inc.*).[11]

It has been held a violation of Title VII by EEOC for an employer to maintain racially *segregated housing, recreational facilities,* and *church facilities* in a company town. EEOC considered the deeding of these facilities to the employees, or employee groups, to be a subterfuge and attributed responsibility for the segregation to the employer.[12]

In *Rogers* v. *EEOC,*[13] the Fifth Circuit sustained the right of EEOC to subpoena employer records concerning patients to determine whether patients had been segregated. Since the court felt this was relevant for the investigation, it would follow that such information would be relevant in a lawsuit.

OFCCP has set forth regulations that indirectly attack discriminatory practices of private clubs. They indicate that it is discriminatory for an employer to pay for the costs incurred by an employee for an eating club or recreational club, even though the club is used to conduct business, if the club discriminates on the basis of sex, race, or national origin in admitting people into membership or in granting them access as guests.

Sex Standards

Standards for Treatment of Pregnancy

The basic principle here, often enunciated but rarely understood, is that pregnancy must be treated just like any other disability. To understand how Title VII requires maternity to be treated for purposes of administration of benefits, it is helpful to note that there are six different stages of a pregnancy as far as Title VII is concerned. The first stage is conception; the second is that period of gestation during which the female's ability to work is not affected; the third is that period of gestation during which the female's ability to work is affected; the fourth stage is birth; the fifth is that period after delivery or miscarriage when the female is still physically unable to work; and the sixth stage is child-rearing, that period after birth when the female is physically recovered and physically able to work, but when she may desire to nurse or otherwise care for the child. Ordinarily, pregnancy runs in the chronological order of these stages, but it may be that a woman is physically unable to work during the second month of pregnancy, yet recovers and is able to work from the third through the last month of pregnancy. The chart below illustrates these various stages.

1	2	3	4	5	6
Conception	Pregnant and physically able to work	Pregnant and physically unable to work	Birth	Recovery— physically unable to work	Child-rearing— able to work

Benefits involving pregnancy relate to two basic areas—how the woman will be treated for purposes of salary maintenance, and how she will be treated

Standards for Terms and Conditions of Employment

concerning her medical expenses. A basic principle for properly treating pregnancy as a disability is the understanding that pregnancy is not *per se* a disability; it is a disability only during stages 3, 4 and 5 in the chart above. Furthermore, the time when the period of disability by reason of pregnancy commences and the time when it ceases vary among women and depend largely upon the person involved and her doctor. With this background, it is easier to address some specific situations.

1. It is discriminatory to condition on marital status an award of any benefit to a female who is pregnant. See *Leechburg Area School District* v. *Pennsylvania Human Relations Commission.*[14]

2. For purposes of salary maintenance, a female who is disabled by a pregnancy—that is, in stages 3, 4 or 5—must be treated in the same manner as a person disabled by a condition other than pregnancy. Thus, an employer who allows employees on sick leave to receive a certain number of weeks' salary, based upon seniority, must also grant salary continuation based on seniority to the female who is disabled by pregnancy.

3. There is no legal requirement to make reasonable accommodation to a female who is unable to perform her work in the ordinary manner because of her pregnant condition. However, if the employer has a policy or practice of making a reasonable accommodation to people who suffer from other disabilities, then that employer must also attempt to reasonably accommodate the female who has her capacity to perform affected by her pregnancy. Thus, if, during stages 2 and 6 on the chart above, a female wants to work, but in a less strenuous job, the employer is not required to attempt to find less strenuous work for her unless that employer would ordinarily attempt to accommodate a male suffering from a disability, or a female suffering from a disability other than pregnancy, under such circumstances. See *Roller* v. *City of San Mateo.*[15]

4. If an employer continues to pay the insurance premiums for an employee unable to work because of a medical condition other than pregnancy, then the employer is required to continue paying insurance premiums for a female who is unable to work because she has become disabled by her pregnancy.

5. For purposes of paying doctors' fees or hospital expenses, effective April 30, 1979, these fringe benefits must be equal for the female who is disabled by pregnancy to those that would be paid for an employee disabled by some condition other than pregnancy. Thus, it is a violation of Title VII to have a larger deductible for a doctor's fee relating to treatment of a woman for pregnancy than the deductible applicable to other medical conditions. Similarly, if insurance covers only a percentage of the costs incurred for a disability other than pregnancy, or if there is a cap on the amount that will be paid for doctors' expenses or hospital expenses for a disability other than pregnancy, only then can there be such a percentage limitation or cap for pregnancy disability.

6. The manner in which it is determined that a disability other than pregnancy has commenced or ended must be the same manner used to determine when a disability arising from pregnancy has commenced or ended. Thus, an employer cannot require periodic notes from the doctor of a woman who is disabled by pregnancy, certifying that she is still disabled, unless that employer requires similar notes from people receiving employer benefits for disabilities other than pregnancy. However, it is not a violation of Title VII, or any other statute, to institute a procedure whereby notes or certification of a disability is required, as long as the procedure is adopted for all disabilities, pregnancy being just one. The institution of such a policy is not a "reduction of benefits." See *Jones* v. *Klassen*.[16]

7. There is no legal requirement that an employer grant to a female a leave of absence for child-rearing after she has fully recovered from the delivery and is physically able to work. In fact, if such a leave of absence is granted, then Title VII might require that the employer grant a similar leave of absence to its male employees who have fathered children. See *Danielson* v. *Board of Higher Education*;[17] but see *Martin* v. *Dann*.[18] There is no legal requirement to permit a female to accrue seniority during the period of her disability caused or contributed to by pregnancy unless the employer also permits other employees, male and female, to accrue seniority during the period of their disability for a cause other than pregnancy. Conversely, if an employer—and many school districts do this—permits a female who has had a child to maintain her seniority and return to work at any time up to five years after the birth of her child, then that employer may be required to grant this option to anyone who has suffered a disability other than pregnancy.[19]

8. An employer generally cannot cause a female to discontinue work just because she is pregnant. There have been some cases involving airlines, which have a duty to maintain the highest standards for the safety of passengers, that are contrary to this general rule, but these cases have been decided in unique situations. Similarly, an employer cannot generally require the pregnant female who has delivered to remain out of work for a set period of time after the delivery. Again, there are airline cases decided under specific situations that are contrary to this rule. See *In re National Airlines, Inc.*,[20] but see *Condit* v. *United Air Lines, Inc.*[21]

9. Equalization of fringe benefits is required as of April 30, 1979, pursuant to the Pregnancy Amendments to Title VII. In this area there has been confusion, precipitated in part by EEOC's published guidelines, and specifically by "Q&A No. 29" to the EEOC Guidelines. This "Q&A" was first published on April 17, 1979, relating to benefits that were supposed to be equalized as of April 30, 1979. The "Q&A" in question read as follows:

29. *Q*: If an employer's insurance plan provides benefits after the insured's employment has ended (i.e. extended benefits) for costs connected with pregnancy and delivery where conception oc-

curred while the insured was working for the employer, but not for the costs of any other medical condition which began prior to termination of employment, may an employer (a) continue to pay these extended benefits for pregnancy-related medical conditions but not for other medical conditions, or (b) terminate these benefits for pregnancy-related conditions?

A: Where a health insurance plan currently provides extended benefits for other medical conditions on a less favorable basis than for pregnancy-related medical conditions, extended benefits must be provided for other medical conditions on the same basis as for pregnancy-related medical conditions. Therefore, an employer can neither continue to provide less benefits for other medical conditions nor reduce benefits currently paid for pregnancy-related medical conditions.

EEOC subsequently withdrew this interpretation insofar as it related to the treatment of pregnancy disability during the time period April 30, 1979, through October 31, 1979. However, EEOC has continued to maintain that if there are special benefits provided for pregnancy disability after October 31, 1979, then these special benefits must be extended to disabilities other than pregnancy. But it is also EEOC's position that after October 31, 1979, an employer can remove those special benefits that existed only for pregnancy disability without being in violation of Title VII. For most employers, the judicious approach would probably be to remove any special benefits it has for pregnancy disability and treat this as any other disability.

10. The general rule under Title VII concerning the return to work of the female recovered from pregnancy disability is that she is to be treated just the way anyone else is treated who is recovered from a disability other than pregnancy. However, OFCCP takes the position that a female who has taken time off for childbirth is absolutely entitled to return to her job or a similar job, regardless of whether the contractor has a leave policy, and regardless of the provisions of such a leave policy. This position of OFCCP is probably illegal and OFCCP proposes to change it.

One of the problems that frequently arises involving pregnant females and their returning to work stems from improper actions of supervisors. There is a great temptation for supervisors of females who are poor performers and who become pregnant to fail to do proper documentation concerning poor performance and hope the female never wants to return. When she does want to return, they refuse to take her back, citing poor performance. In such situations, the government agencies and the courts are likely to find discrimination. A pregnant female who is performing poorly should be treated exactly like any other employee who is performing poorly. If a pregnant female builds up excessive absences, she should be advised that if she is to continue working, she will be treated like any other employee and suffer the same discipline that other employees are subjected to if they do not meet attendance standards.

11. Under certain circumstances, an employer can require a pregnant

female to commence her disability leave at a certain time during the term of her pregnancy. The court will consider the time chosen and the business justification given. In *deLaurier* v. *San Diego School District*,[22] the school had a rule requiring pregnant teachers to take disability leave at the beginning of the ninth month of pregnancy; the rule was sustained.

Sex and Retirement or Annuity Plans

It has already been held that an employer cannot have a differential in retirement age based upon the sex of the individual. In *Rosen* v. *Public Service Gas & Electric Co.*,[23] the employer had a plan that permitted females to take full retirement benefits at the age of 62, but males had to wait until the age of 65 in order to retire with full benefits. The court found such differentials in retirement ages to be discriminatory.

In *Manhart* v. *City of Los Angeles, Department of Water & Power*,[24] the issue was whether an employer discriminated by paying out a lesser amount, on an annuity basis, to females than it did to males. In that case, the employer had funded annuities for retirement purposes, contributing the same amount to the fund for males as it did for females. However, because annuity tables showed that females lived longer than males, females generally received a lesser amount per month than their male counterparts.

Under the Equal Pay Act, such a procedure is legal, according to the Department of Labor, because under that act, there is no discrimination if either the contribution by the employer or the benefit to the employee is the same for both sexes. However, in *Manhart*, the Supreme Court held that such a plan was discriminatory because it was geared to *groups* of individuals rather than the individuals themselves. Title VII, the court indicated, prohibited employers from making employment decisions based upon group characteristics. See also *EEOC* v. *Colby College.*[25]

Sex and Hours of Work, Overtime, Rest, and Lunch Period

State protective laws that limit the number of hours women may work or weight they may lift constitute a violation of Title VII and have been uniformly struck down. See *Rosenfeld* v. *Southern Pacific Company.*[26] As a general rule, courts will strike down any state protective law as a violation of Title VII if it restricts the rights of a woman and damages her employment opportunities. However, if it is a state statute that creates a special benefit for females, then there is no uniform treatment. Thus, in such situations, the courts either take the benefit away from the woman (*Burns* v. *Rohr Corp.*)[27] or extend it to the men (*Hays* v. *Potlatch Forests, Inc.*).[28]

Sexual Harassment

Generally, employers are not liable, and need not fear liability, if there are sexual liaisons between male and female employees or if there is a sexual advance made by one employee to another. However, if one of those employees happens to be a supervisor, the circumstances change. An employer is liable for sex discrimination if it knows, or *should* know, that a supervisor made sexual advances to an employee of the opposite sex, then retaliated against that employee when the sexual advances were spurned. See *Garber* v. *Saxon Business Products*,[29] *Tomkins* v. *Public Service Electric & Gas Co.*,[30] *Barnes* v. *Costle*.[31] In fact, one appellate court has held that the employer is responsible for the actions of its supervisors, under the doctrine of *respondent superior,* even if the employer did not know that the supervisor was sexually harassing an employee of the opposite sex. *Miller* v. *Bank of America*.[32] Another factor that may cause the legal posture to change is the occurrence of repeated sexual propositions, even if they are not made by a supervisor. These may constitute conduct that "substantially interferes with an individual's work or creates a hostile, intimidating or offensive work atmosphere." If they do, EEOC, in its guidelines on sexual harassment, has indicated they would constitute sex discrimination.

Another problem employers face is sexual harassment that is not oriented toward sexual intercourse. Thus, the repeated statement by a supervisor that "all women are illogical" or similar statements can create a liability for the employer. This type of conduct would equate to statements made in the race and national-origin area, that "all Italians are Mafia" or "all Irish are alcoholics," a subject that was addressed by the court in *Cariddi* v. *Kansas City Chiefs Football Club, Inc., supra.*

To ensure against liability for such statements, the employer would be well advised to establish the policy described previously in this chapter in reference to race and national-origin terms and conditions of employment and extend that policy to cover complaints about sexual harassment.

FOOTNOTES

[1] 29 U.S.C. §623 *et seq.*
[2] 29 C.F.R. §860.120.
[3] 29 C.F.R. §860.120(g).
[4] *Ibid.*
[5] 568 F.2d 87 (8th Cir. 1977) 15 EPD ¶8014.
[6] 353 F. Supp. 1177 (W.D. Pa. 1973).
[7] 476 F. Supp. 335 (D.N.J. 1979).

[8] 55 F.R.D. 202 (D.D.C. 1972).
[9] EEOC Decision No. 71446 (1970), 2 FEP Cases 1127.
[10] 478 F.2d 1200 (10th Cir. 1973).
[11] 7 FEP Cases 710 (W.D. Okla. 1973).
[12] EEOC Decision No. YBI 9C-144 (1969), 2 FEP Cases 308.
[13] 454 F.2d 234, 238 (5th Cir. 1971), *cert. denied* 406 U.S. 957 (1972).
[14] 19 Pa. Commonwealth Ct. 614 (1975), 11 EPD ¶10,719, relying upon *Phillips v. Martin Marietta Corp.*, 400 U.S. 542 (1971).
[15] 572 F.2d 1311 (9th Cir. 1977).
[16] 389 F. Supp. 408 (E.D. Mo. 1974), 11 FEP Cases 767 *aff'd sub nom. Haire v. Calloway*, 526 F.2d 246 (8th Cir. 1975), 11 FEP Cases 769, *vacated and rem'd on other gds*, 537 F.2d 318 (8th Cir. 1976), 13 FEP Cases 1182.
[17] 358 F. Supp. 22 (S.D. N.Y. 1972).
[18] 9 EPD (CCH) ¶10,128 (D.D.C. 1975).
[19] EEOC's "Questions and Answers on Pregnancy Discrimination," an appendix to 29 C.F.R. §1604 *et seq.*; CCH Employment Practices Guide ¶3951. *But see paragraph 9, following in the text.*
[20] 14 FEP Cases 1807 (S.D. Fla. 1977).
[21] 558 F.2d 1176 (4th Cir. 1977), *cert. denied* 98 S. Ct. 1510 (1978).
[22] 588 F.2d 674 (9th Cir. 1978).
[23] 477 F.2d 90 (3d Cir. 1973).
[24] 435 U.S. 702 (1978).
[25] 589 F.2d 1139 (1st Cir. 1978).
[26] 444 F.2d 1219 (9th Cir. 1971).
[27] 346 F. Supp. 994 (S.D. Cal. 1972).
[28] 465 F.2d 1081 (8th Cir. 1972).
[29] 552 F.2d 1032 (4th Cir. 1977).
[30] 568 F.2d 1044 (3d Cir. 1977).
[31] 561 F.2d 983 (C.A. D.C. 1977).
[32] 600 F.2d 211 (9th Cir. 1979).

PART 3

GUIDELINES FOR PROPERLY PREVENTING INDIVIDUAL CLAIMS AND DEFENDING AGAINST THEM

Chapter 8

Individual Claims: Prevention and Defense

PREVENTION PROCEDURES

As we saw in the discussion of the various forums in Chapter 1, any employee or applicant for employment can trigger numerous independent EEO-related investigations by government agencies. Any of these investigations can be costly to the employer, regardless of whether the grievance is justified. In many of these forums, the investigations can expand to become a review of the entire personnel system. Furthermore, the very filing of the charge by an incumbent employee creates human-resources problems that might never have existed before. The employee who filed the charge starts "documenting" his or her case and frequently becomes suspicious and distrustful. The supervisor of that employee starts his or her own documentation and consults his or her manager before giving assignments to the employee. Frequently, other persons in the office or facility start taking sides, creating still further problems.

For all these reasons, it is smart business not to have charges filed, especially if these charges arose from misunderstandings and could have been avoided. The employer should make better use of early warning systems already available to it and make an investment in its personnel system to enable that system to prevent charges before they are filed.

Learning about a Claim before It Is Filed

One of the ironies of personnel law is that employers generally rely heavily on their first-line supervisors to advise them of possible union organizational activities, yet rely very little on them for forewarning about possible EEO charges. If the employer is surprised by the submission of authorization cards for an election, one of the first questions asked is, "Why didn't we know about this sooner?" The employer asks the first-line supervisors if they knew about any dissatisfaction and, if they did, why they did not bring it to the attention of upper management immediately.

In the EEO area, however, employers generally do not require first-line supervisors to be aware of dissatisfaction and report it before it results in a charge being filed. This is a mistake; it represents an improper utilization of a valuable resource. First-line supervisors are generally the part of management that is closest to the general work force, and therefore the part that is most likely to know about dissatisfaction that may lead to a charge of discrimination. Regardless of what else an employer does, it should require of its first-level supervisors the same sensitivity to potential EEO problems as to potential organizational campaigns or potential grievances under the collective-bargaining agreement.

Many employers already realize that it is to their benefit to have more formal mechanisms to enable them to become aware of employee dissatisfaction before it leads to a charge of discrimination. These employers utilize a posting system, or an "open-door" policy, or the personnel office—or a combination of all three—to learn of such dissatisfaction.

Employer "Posting" Systems

A posting system, using a posting similar to that in Chapter 7, will advise employees of the availability of an internal grievance system. The posting is the first step in the handling of an EEO-related grievance. Here is a flow chart indicating how such a grievance might be handled:

1. Post notice of policy.
2. Complaint ⟶ made to proper department/party
   ↘ made to supervisory personnel and referred to proper department/party
3. Investigation:
    a. Interview complainant—get the grievance and set a date for reporting back to grievant.
    b. Interview people who could have relevant information, including those of same race, sex, national origin, etc., as complainant.
    c. Check of personnel files:
        (1) Evidence of prior friction between parties

Individual Claims: Prevention and Defense

(2) Previous complaint

(3) Work records

    d. Check the statistics for the pertinent department or work unit to ascertain whether the grievance may have class implications and whether there is possible exposure to a class.

    e. Post-investigation oral discussion of facts, as ascertained, with complainant; allow for further input from complainant.

    f. Make short written report disposing of grievance to complainant and person accused, giving the disposition and *facts* that support it.

4. (Possibly) Appeal of determination by grievant or the person accused.

Employer "Open-Door" Systems

An "open-door" policy frequently originates because the employer is concerned about union activity and wants the employees to know they can complain about anything, including EEO-related claims, without the necessity of having a union. The term "open door" generally means that any employee can go to any level of management with any kind of grievance. One stricture on the policy is that before going to one level of management, the employee should go to the next-lower level first. (Of course, if the complaint is about a particular supervisor, that level of supervision can be skipped.) Thus, in the ordinary course, an employee using the open-door policy can go to his or her foreman, the department manager, the facility manager, and then the company president and the chairman of the board. If anyone in the line of supervision is not at the facility where the grievance arose, the employee is allowed to proceed by letter.

A necessary part of the open-door policy is that every employee who grieves on any matter will receive a response promptly. Sometimes, there are times periods set within which the initial complaint under the open-door policy must be made and time periods within which the manager addressed must respond.

Use of the Personnel Office

Some employers use the personnel office as an "ombudsman" to handle EEO-related grievances. For those employers, some general guidelines should be followed.

The fact that a grievance has been filed should not be held against the employee, except in situations where the person is a chronic complainer and has absolutely no basis for his complaints. Similarly, the fact that a grievance has been filed against a supervisor should not be held against the supervisor, unless the grievance proves to be justified.

The personnel office investigating a grievance should be assured of independence and noninterference. The function of investigator and ombudsman for internal grievances is generally a distasteful job. Furthermore, the results of the investigation, and the weight the report carries, usually bear a direct relationship to the status of the person who has done the investigation. For these reasons, the duty should be assigned to a responsible person and should be rotated to others as a regular function of the entire personnel department.

Management might also consider this ombudsman role within the personnel department as a training position toward a very high management position. More and more corporations are realizing that human resources is one of the most crucial concerns for management and consequently that it is advantageous for the chief executive officer, or those immediately below him or her, to be aware of human-resources concerns. One of the best ways of achieving such an awareness is to serve in this ombudsman position. The very fact that the person who is serving is seen as being groomed for a very high management function will lend greater credibility to the position and to the function it serves.

The importance of totally integrating the EEO function into the personnel system cannot be overstressed. There is developing, however, a practice that is antithetical to that principle. Many large employers are hiring people into personnel slots with titles such as "Manager of Affirmative Action." Frequently, these people are minorities and/or females. And frequently, they have prior experience in government enforcement agencies. These people are serving the personnel department, but solely for handling the disposition of EEO grievances.

One of the problems inherent in this situation arises from the fact that this is a dead-end job. Another problem is that the people in these slots, because the job is dead-end, and because their function frequently requires finding fault with personnel actions by those of higher rank in the employer organization, often come to feel they are isolated and view their role as the in-house government enforcer. Also, although they know the EEO laws and regulations, they have not been acclimatized to know the company and company "politics"; consequently, they may be viewed as lacking diplomacy by others in the corporate structure, and this can reduce their effectiveness. Finally, regardless of how effectively these people function, there are always going to be those of the same race, sex, or national origin as they are who view them as "Uncle Toms." This creates a psychological pressure on them that white male managers find difficult to appreciate.

These EEO slots provide an ideal entry into employer organizations at high-ranking positions for minorities and females. However, that entry point should not also be the end point for career advancement.

For the employer that does not integrate the EEO function and personnel into its system, the possibility arises that the EEO person or persons will become alienated—and themselves file EEO charges with the appropriate government agencies. This creates a horrible situation for the employer. At the very least, it usually leads to a broad-scale EEOC investigation or an EEOC commissioner's charge. At worst, it can substantially reduce the ability of the "Manager of Affirmative Action" to continue to function effectively within the employer organization.

Regardless of what kind of internal mechanism an employer establishes for handling EEO-related grievances, there is a tangential benefit. Under the Rehabilitation Act of 1973, which is enforced by OFCCP, if there is a charge of discrimination on the basis of handicap made to OFCCP, and if the employer has an internal grievance procedure for addressing complaints about violation of the Rehabilitation Act, then before investigating that charge, OFCCP may refer it to the employer. The employer is allowed 60 days to investigate and handle the charge pursuant to its internal system. Only if the charge is not resolved in that manner to the claimant's satisfaction will OFCCP assume jurisdiction.

Handling the Internal Investigation

If an employer is going to advertise to its employees that it does have an internal grievance procedure, then the employer must make that procedure meaningful. To be meaningful, the employer's internal investigation mechanism should incorporate some or all of the following aspects:

1. There should be an interview with the person who is making the complaint or filing the grievance, and a careful notation of the facts as alleged.

2. The person who is assigned to investigate the grievance should act promptly and set a deadline on his or her report. At the interview with the employee at the very first stage, the employee should be told what the deadline set by the internal investigator is. If it turns out that further time is needed to complete a thorough investigation, that can be handled by notifying the employee before the expiration of the original deadline that further time will be needed.

3. As part of the investigation, every attempt should be made to interview persons of the same race, sex, or national origin as that of the person who filed the complaint. Even if these people have only tangential knowledge, it is almost a certainty that they will report back to the complainant that they have been questioned. This, in and of itself, lends credibility to the neutrality of the investigation.

4. As part of the investigation, the internal investigator should check the facts, as alleged, against the employer's own regular procedures. As indicated in other parts of this book, the employer facing an EEO-related grievance will immediately be on the defensive and hard-pressed in a court trial if, when adverse action was taken against a protected-group person, the employer's own established procedures had not been followed. Because of the importance of following regular procedures, managers and supervisors should be advised that procedures must be followed before personnel action is taken. They should also be advised, and the employer should ensure, that extraneous procedures that are overtechnical and not generally followed are abolished. Once the employer has established the bare-bones procedures necessary to operate, those procedures should be strictly followed. There should be no exceptions except as provided

for in the procedures themselves. In this regard, employers should realize that they can change procedures and disavow precedents under the prior procedures. If this is to be done, it is probably advisable to republish procedural guidelines *in toto* rather than piecemeal.

5. When the investigation is completed, there should be an oral presentation to the employee of the facts as determined by the investigation. This will give the employee the opportunity to add his or her further comments and have them considered prior to the time the results of the investigation are memorialized in writing. If new facts are brought to the attention of the investigator by the complainant during the oral presentation, they should be investigated. Finally, a written document should be furnished to the complainant showing the results of the investigation and the reasons for those results.

6. It is vital to an internal grievance procedure that the employer not retaliate against the grievant. The more an employer or supervisor tries to dissuade or deter a person from filing a grievance by threatening adverse consequences, the more likely it is that the grievance system will fall into disuse. Employees will then use external channels, including government agencies, to get what they feel is a fair hearing.

7. It is essential also that the internal grievance procedure not be compromised. If the result of the investigation leads to a certain conclusion, the personnel action to implement that conclusion should regularly be taken.

If an employer intends to institute an internal investigation system, the entire system should be explained before it is implemented—first to supervisors, and then to employees. In implementing the system, the manner in which a person has been treated in similar circumstances in the past should be considered a precedent, much as prior arbitration decisions are considered precedents.

Some employers provide for an appeal from the conclusion reached as a result of the internal investigation. The benefits to be gained by such an appeal procedure should be weighed against the time and cost of it. If there is an internal appeal procedure established, it is probably advisable to have a tribunal of three to five persons to act as the reviewing authority. If among them there is a person of the same race, color, religion, sex, or national origin as the person who filed the grievance, the credibility of the appeal process is enhanced.

Advantages of an Internal Grievance System

The employer that has an effective internal grievance system establishes its reputation for fairness and the appearance of fairness. Since its system will most assuredly be swifter than the procedure of any government organization for addressing EEO-related charges, it can become the preferable way for addressing these kinds of claims.

To the extent that charges of discrimination to government agencies arise from misunderstandings or misinformation on the part of the claimant, the number of charges filed should be reduced. Furthermore, to the extent that the end result of filing a charge of discrimination with an agency is no different from that achieved by the internal investigation system, there should be a further reduction in charges filed. Filing charges with a government agency does take time for the employee, and if he pursues the claim through litigation, it takes time and money. If such an expenditure becomes perceived by employees as useless, they are less likely to pursue the government-agency and court alternatives.

Another important benefit for employers is that the internal grievance system gives them an opportunity to correct mistakes while the cost is still relatively low. If an employee was improperly denied a job assignment or promotion, the earnings differential should be relatively little if calculated for a few months, and by that time the internal grievance system should have determined the merits of the claim. However, if the employer has to wait for government agencies to conduct their investigation, years might have passed and the total of the earnings differential could be substantial.

Perhaps the most important benefit of an internal grievance system is that it recognizes the employee's right to a reason from the employer for its actions. Concomitantly, the employer's supervisors will feel it a duty to have a reason for their actions, and will be prepared to give that reason if a complaint is filed. The employer organization benefits because personnel cannot be arbitrary or capricious. It also benefits because the employees have less tendency to feel they need outside help, either from a government agency or a labor organization, to be treated fairly.

It is a mistake to view the establishment of an internal grievance system as the surrender of management's right to exercise "discretion." Because of the many EEO laws in existence, management has already lost the right to make personnel decisions that do not have a rational basis. Thus, to the extent that management discretion is exercised in a rational way, it will remain, and to the extent that it is exercised based on nonbusiness considerations, it will not remain.

The argument that management will be surrendering the right to consider "the equities" is also faulty. Courts have already recognized that the equities can be considered. See, for example, *Wilson* v. *Sharon Steel Corp.*[1] A properly structured set of employee work rules and procedures for administering them can allow for equitable factors to be considered.

DEFENSE PROCEDURES

In order for the employer to know how to defend against the individual charge, it should first understand the burden of proof that must be satisfied to establish a *prima facie* case.

An evolution has taken place in the burdens of proof for an individual to establish a *prima facie* case and for the employer to rebut that claim. The first pronouncements on the subject from the Supreme Court came in *McDonnell Douglas Corp.* v. *Green*,[2] in which the Court stated that a claimant, a black, could establish a *prima facie* case by showing (1) that he belongs to a racial minority; (2) that he applied and was qualified for a job for which the employer was seeking applicants; (3) that despite his qualifications, he was rejected; and (4) that after his rejection, the position remained open and the employer continued to seek applicants from persons of complainant's qualifications.

The burden on the employer, according to the *McDonnell Douglas* standard, is then to articulate some legitimate, nondiscriminatory reason for the claimant's rejection. The burden is then shifted back to the employee to show that the employer's stated reason was in fact just pretext, and the real reason was discrimination.

In *Board of Trustees of Keene State College* v. *Sweeney*,[3] the Supreme Court clarified what it meant by the employer's burden. The Court noted that the U.S. Court of Appeals for the First Circuit had interpreted *McDonnell Douglas* to mean that the defendant employer must *prove absence of discriminatory motive*, because it was the party having greater access to the evidence. The Supreme Court rejected that interpretation of *McDonnell Douglas*. It stated:

> While words such as "articulate," "show," and "prove" may have more or less similar meanings depending upon the context in which they are used, we think that there is a significant distinction between merely "articulat[ing] some legitimate nondiscriminatory reason" and "prov[ing] absence of discriminatory motive."[4]

The Supreme Court said that the burden on the employer was the former, not the latter.

Other court decisions indicate that the fourth element of the employee's initial burden of proof under the *McDonnell Douglas* standard may be heavier than it appears. Although the claimant's proving that the employer continued to seek people for the job may be enough to establish the *prima facie* case for a technical violation of Title VII, in order to recover damages the claimant may also have to establish that the job was actually filled, and that he or she would have been awarded the job if it had not been for discrimination, *and* that the person who was awarded the job was not of the same sex, race, or national origin as the complainant.

In *Gillin* v. *Federal Paper Board Co.*,[5] the U.S. Court of Appeals for the Second Circuit had acknowledged that the claimant had met the *McDonnell Douglas* standard for a *prima facie* case but found that she was not entitled to any relief unless she also established that she was better qualified for the position than the male who received it. Thus, she has to establish that, absent discrimination, she would have been awarded the job. On remand, the trial court found that even if there had not been discrimination, the claimant still would not have received the job.

In *De Volld* v. *Bailar*,[6] the U.S. Court of Appeals for the Fifth Circuit found that because the employer had awarded the job in question to a person of the same national origin as the claimant, Mexican-American, it could not be found that she had been denied the job on the basis of national origin. She might have been treated unfairly, the court reasoned, but that unfair treatment could not have been because of national origin; therefore there was no violation of Title VII.

The same reasoning used in *De Volld* has been adopted by U.S. circuit courts of appeal under the Age Discrimination in Employment Act of 1967 (ADEA), with courts holding that the claimant must show that the person who was awarded the job was younger than the claimant. See, for example, *Price* v. *Maryland Casualty Co.*;[7] contra, *Loeb* v. *Textron, Inc.*[8]

Some employers have already translated the reasoning of these cases into their personnel practices to ensure against liability when they suspect that a charge of discrimination may be filed. When these employers suspect that, say, a black will file a charge, they award the job in question to a black and they document that this job is, in fact, the one that would have been awarded to the claimant had he or she been successful. They follow the same pattern if they suspect the basis of the claim will be sex discrimination or national-origin discrimination. If the potential claimant is protected by the ADEA, then they make sure that the person awarded the job is older than the potential claimant. Such defensive action is legal.

Some employers, if they suspect that a discrimination claim will be filed regardless of the person chosen to fill a position, will extend their search and delay filling that position until they have found a candidate who they are sure can be established and demonstrated as more qualified than the potential claimant on the basis of objective criteria. It has not been determined by courts whether this kind of defensive action is legal or illegal. However, courts seem disinclined to require that a job be taken away from one person and given to another if the former is clearly more qualified. In *Gillin, supra,* the male was clearly more qualified than the claimant, and she was denied the traffic manager's job that he had been awarded. The employer had admitted that it refused to consider any female for the job because it felt it was unsafe for a woman to perform some of the duties, such as going out to assist truck drivers whose rigs had broken down on the road in the middle of the night. The employer also testified that it had a promotion-from-within policy. The trial record established that the employer had spent considerable time and effort to recruit the male who ultimately received the job. Although in theory it could be argued that the male never would have been found if the employer had considered the claimant, as a practical matter the court compared their qualifications and found the award of the job to the male to be justified.

Still other employers, if they suspect that a discrimination claim will be filed, purposely do not fill that job, or they restructure the job so that the prospective claimant is no longer qualified for the position. This kind of action is illegal.

The best way to prepare for a defense against an individual charge of discrimination is to ensure, prior to the time the personnel action is taken, that there is documentation, such as written memos, evidencing the reasons for the personnel action, *and* that this documentation was made as part of a documentation system. Most employers are careful about having the former, but are less attentive to the latter.

The case of *Francis* v. *AT&T, Long Lines Dept.*[9] illustrates the necessity that the documentation be part of a system. In that case, even though the tardiness of the claimant was well documented, she was the only one of her group for whom such records were kept. The court found that the very documentation the employer sought to rely upon was, in fact, evidence of an intent to discriminate. Thus, the supervisor who wants to "build a record" to justify termination would be best advised to document similar abuses by similarly situated employees.

Another kind of documentation helpful in justifying a personnel action is one reflecting the fact that the employer's precedents had been considered and followed prior to the time the personnel action was taken. The facts of the precedent should be noted in detail in such documentation.

Finally, and most obviously, there should be a rational, nondiscriminatory reason for the personnel action taken, and this should be expressed in a document. Thus, the supervisor would be well-advised to write out in a memo why the promotion is being awarded to the person receiving it, indicating that the prospective grievant has been considered and giving the reasons for not awarding the promotion to the prospective grievant. This should satisfy the Supreme Court's standard in *Board of Education of Keene State College* that the employer articulate a legitimate, nondiscriminatory reason for the personnel action. The fact that the memo was created and the reason stated at a time prior to initiation of the personnel action should make it difficult at a trial or hearing for the claimant to show that the stated reason was a post hoc rationalization.

Unfortunately, trials on individual claims rest on the adequacy of the documentation by the employer of the facts surrounding the claim. Often, too, the written documents are absolutely necessary, because the supervisors involved in the personnel action are not available as witnesses. If it is the regular business practice of the employer to create documentation about particular types of personnel actions, then generally these documents will be admissible into evidence when such a personnel action occurs, whether or not the person who created the document is available to testify.

The contemporaneous documentation also serves another purpose. It reduces the possibility that the person who initiated the personnel action at issue might be a hostile witness to the employer by the time of the trial.

The rule that the employer's burden of proof (even assuming a prima facie case of discrimination is established) is merely to articulate some legitimate, nondiscriminatory reason for the personnel action has been frequently overemphasized or misunderstood. This rule is applicable when there is an individual charge and there is no standard at issue or no statistical disparity claimed by the plaintiffs. This rule is applicable, even if there is a statistical disparity claimed by the plaintiff, if the employer can rebut the statistical claim. However, this relatively light burden of proof for employers is not available when the claimant can demonstrate a statistical disparity, say, between applicants and hires, or when the claimant can demonstrate that some neutral selection standard that screened him out also has the net effect of screening out others of the same race, national origin, et. al., disproportionately. In those situations, the employer generally has to validate the system or the standard, not just articulate some business reason for rejecting the claimant. See *Griggs* v. *Duke Power Co.*,[10] but see also *EEOC* v. *United Virginia Bank*,[11] and *Yukas* v. *Libbey-Owens-Ford Company*.[12]

FOOTNOTES

[1] 19 FEP Cases 336 (W.D. Pa. 1979).
[2] 411 U.S. 792 (1973).
[3] 95 S.Ct. 295 (1978).
[4] *Idem* at 296.
[5] 479 F.2d 97 (2d Cir. 1973).
[6] 568 F.2d 1162 (5th Cir. 1978).
[7] 561 F.2d 609 (5th Cir. 1977).
[8] 600 F.2d 1003 (1st Cir. 1979), 20 EPD ¶ 30,028, 20 FEP Cases 29.
[9] 55 F.R.D. 202 (D.D.C. 1972).
[10] 401 U.S. 424 (1971).
[11] 21 FEP Cases 1405 (4th Cir. 1980).
[12] 562 F.2d 496 (7th Cir. 1977).

Chapter 9

Handling the EEOC Charge and Investigation

INTRODUCTION

The Equal Employment Opportunity Commission enforces and administers Title VII, the Equal Pay Act, and the Age Discrimination in Employment Act (ADEA), having assumed jurisdiction over the latter two statutes in 1979. EEOC acts on the premise that if there is any validity to the claim, it is EEOC's responsibility to find the evidence to support that claim, because the person who has filed the charge is "unlettered in the law" and at a disadvantage in dealing with the employer.

This philosophy is evident at every stage of the administrative proceedings. It means that EEOC will assume jurisdiction over a charge even though its authority to do so might be questionable, and that it will try to "save" charges that appear untimely. It means that when a respondent makes a request to see the EEOC investigation file pursuant to the Freedom of Information Act, only limited access might be granted, whereas when a charging party or his attorney seeks to review the file, or even investigation material obtained as the result of other investigations, broader access will generally be granted. For this reason, the employer-respondent should realize that it will bear the burden of proof to justify the action taken, at least during the investigation.

Below is a chart giving the overview of the EEOC administrative proce-

Handling the EEOC Charge and Investigation

dures, with the time sequence involved and the employer's position at each stage of the administrative process. The exhibits cited in the chart are samples of forms and correspondence, which are grouped at the end of this chapter. The discussion that follows the chart relates to the administrative steps in the chronological order in which they develop, elaborating on the ways in which the employer can preserve and present its defense effectively. There are references in both the chart and the discussion to the Code of Federal Regulations (C.F.R.). EEOC frequently amends its regulations, and publishes the amendments in C.F.R.. Services such as the Bureau of National Affairs' (BNA) *Fair Employment Practice Manual* and Commerce Clearing House's (CCH) *Employment Practices Guide* also publish these amendments.

The chart summarizes general practices. Some offices or even employees of EEOC follow slightly different procedures. Furthermore, in some states, there have been agreements made between EEOC and the state deferral agency, and those agreements modify the general procedures.

A Summary Chart of the EEOC Administrative Process

Administrative Step	*Timetable*	*Comments, Respondent's Reaction*
1. Charge filed (see Exhibit A)	Within 180 or 300 days of the alleged act of discrimination	The respondent will not know that a charge has been filed and cannot do anything at this point.
2. Charge deferred to state agency (see Exhibit B)	Immediately after charge if applicable	This step applies only in states with local FEP laws and agencies. Respondent can do nothing at this point.
3. Assumption of jurisdiction by EEOC (see Exhibit C)	60 Days after Deferral	Respondent can do nothing.
4. Sending of Form 131 notice (see Exhibit D)	Within 10 days of assumption of jurisdiction by EEOC	The respondent will receive this notice within 10 days after EEOC assumes jurisdiction. As can be seen from Exhibit D, the information on it is sparse.
5. Receipt of charge form (Exhibit A)	Within days of agreeing to attend the "no-fault" conference	The charge is much more informative than the Form 131, and it is wise for the respondent to try to obtain it as soon as possible. The respon-

(continued)

A Summary Chart of the EEOC Administrative Process (Continued)

Administrative Step	Timetable	Comments, Respondent's Reaction
5. Receipt of charge form (Exhibit A)	Within days of agreeing to attend the "no-fault" conference	dent can obtain it early by agreeing to attend the no-fault conference; or, if the respondent does not want to attend the conference, then it can agree to attend the conference, receive the charge, and then cancel its attendance at the conference; or, the employer can inform EEOC that the Form 131 contains insufficient information to enable it to know what records are to be preserved and can ask for a copy of the charge.
6. Preinvestigation settlement attempt ("no-fault" settlement)	Within 3 months of receipt of Form 131 notice	This process was started within EEOC as a means of clearing up its backlog. It is referred to in EEOC's regulations as "Negotiated Settlement," 29 C.F.R. §1601.20. At this step, respondent will receive a copy of the charge. If the respondent believes it is at fault, there is no way it can handle the case more effectively than by settlement at this stage.
7. Notice from the investigator assigned, and questionnaire (see Exhibit E)	Between 6 months and 2 years after EEOC has assumed jurisdiction of the charge	The EEOC backlog is the reason for this delay, and the alacrity of the investigation depends upon the backlog in the appropriate district office. The only way to have a faster investigation on a particular charge would be to have it consolidated with a charge already pending against the same facility.
8. Letter or telephone call from investigator for appointment to visit the facility	Generally, within 30 days of the respondent's response to the questionnaire	The respondent should attempt to determine what the investigator will want to review *before* the commencement of the on-site investigation.

A Summary Chart of the EEOC Administrative Process (Continued)

Administrative Step	Timetable	Comments, Respondent's Reaction
9. Request for respondent's position letter and respondent's response (see Exhibit F for a sample response)	Requested as part of investigation or after investigation	The respondent should always submit a position letter and supplement it with favorable facts that develop subsequently.
10. Determination (see Exhibit G)	Generally, within 60 days after investigation is completed	If "no-cause" determination is issued, the time for suit by the charging party starts immediately upon receipt of the determination, and if the respondent is not sued within 90 days thereafter by the charging party, it will not be sued on the basis of that charge. If a "cause" finding ensues, further administrative steps will occur.
11. Notice of conciliation endeavor (see Exhibits H and I)	With the "cause" determination or soon thereafter	The respondent will not receive as good a proposal at this stage as it did during the no-fault settlement stage. However, it may still be advantageous for it to settle at this stage in view of facts uncovered during the investigation.
12. Case referred for litigation consideration (see Exhibit J)		Area field litigation units review all "cause" cases that have failed conciliation. In considering whether or not the EEOC should litigate, they evaluate (a) size of group affected; (b) previous evidence of recalcitrance of employer; (c) satisfaction of conditions precedent; (d) novelty, or lack thereof, of the legal theory. If the case is recommended for litigation, a presentation memo and a draft complaint are forwarded to the EEOC's general counsel, requesting authorization to commence suit in that case.

THE EEOC ADMINISTRATIVE PROCESS FROM RESPONDENT'S VIEWPOINT

Receipt of the Charge or Notice of Charge

Usually, the respondent first learns that it has been charged with discrimination when it receives a charge or a notice of charge. In the early days of Title VII enforcement, EEOC traditionally sent only what is called a Form 131. This form did not identify by name the charging party or give any specifics of the allegation. It merely identified the basis for the discrimination of which the employer had been accused, the company and/or the facility, and the date of the charge. Subsequently, EEOC changed its procedure so that at the initial stage, it would send the actual charge form it had received. The charge form is much more helpful to the respondent in identifying the specifics of the claim. The latest position by EEOC is a reversion to its prior policy of sending only the notice-of-charge form. This latest change has taken place in conjunction with the initiation of a new step in the administrative procedure: the "no-fault" conference, officially called the *negotiated settlement*.[1]

Under current procedures, the respondent will receive a copy of the notice-of-charge form and then, soon after, a telephone call or letter from an officer of EEOC inviting the respondent to the "no-fault" conference. If the respondent agrees, the official will ask the respondent to suggest a date and promise to send a copy of the actual charge prior to that date. However, without such agreement, the EEOC official will inform the respondent that it will not receive a copy of the charge at this time.

There is no legal obligation on the respondent to attend the no-fault conference; but the procedure gives the EEOC official the kind of leverage and trading material necessary to obtain the cooperation of the employer in attending the conference. If the respondent agrees to attend, it will receive a copy of the actual charge in a few days. If the respondent does not agree to attend the no-fault conference, there will be no conference.

For the respondent that does not wish to attend the no-fault conference but does want a copy of the charge at this stage, there are two alternatives. The first, and simplest, is to agree to attend and then, after receiving the charge, cancel the conference. The second alternative is to inform EEOC that the Form 131 notice does not provide sufficient information to enable respondent to identify the records that might be pertinent, so that respondent might inadvertently destroy documents relevant to the investigation and its defense; and to ask for a copy of the charge. If EEOC does not send a copy of the charge in the face of such a letter, it will be risking the possibility that the respondent can make an effective laches argument at a later stage. Laches is a defense to an action based upon inexcusable delay by the person or agency prosecuting the action, plus prejudice to the respondent or defendant, such as the loss of necessary records, because of the delay. Respondents in Title VII actions will find that there is frequently inexcusable delay by EEOC. For a discussion of laches in this context, see *EEOC v. C&D Sportswear Corp.*[2] Actually, the more appropriate defense, since laches cannot be asserted against government agencies, would be for failure to proceed as required by the Administrative Procedures Act. See 5 U.S.C. §706; *EEOC v. Westinghouse Electric Corp.*[3]

A common problem for respondents that have facilities at many locations is an internal system that is inadequate to ensure that headquarters is quickly informed of a charge of discrimination filed against one of its facilities. EEOC has indicated that it will help alleviate this problem by sending a copy of any charge against any facility of a respondent directly to headquarters. The respondent, to avail itself of this service, must notify EEOC of the location and name of all its facilities for which the accommodation copy of the charge or notice of charge is to be sent to headquarters, and give the name of the person at headquarters who is to receive these accommodation copies.

Action to be Taken on Receipt of the Charge

Examination for Jurisdictional Requirements

Acting from the premise that its actions should be oriented toward the benefit of the charging party, EEOC will liberally construe in favor of the charging party any kind of procedural requirements. For that reason, it becomes even more incumbent upon respondents to carefully examine the EEOC action at every stage of the investigatory process. When the respondent receives the charge form from EEOC, the charge should be examined to determine whether it satisfies at least the following five procedural requirements:

1. Standing
2. Deferral to the state or local agency
3. Timeliness
4. Stating a claim
5. Joinder of necessary parties

Standing. In examining a charge to determine whether or not the charging party has standing, the employer should be aware that there are three different types of persons who can file a charge. A charge may be filed by a person aggrieved, by a third person on behalf of a person aggrieved, or by an EEOC commissioner. If a charge is filed by a third person on behalf of an aggrieved party, then the underlying aggrieved party must be identified to EEOC and, as part of the investigation, EEOC is required to assure itself that this underlying aggrieved party does want the charge to be filed on his or her behalf.[4] Consequently, random charges by organizations are not valid unless the organization indicates to EEOC that it is filing on behalf of some underlying aggrieved party.

Deferral. When a person walks into an EEOC office and indicates that he or she wishes to file a charge of discrimination, EEOC will have that person fill out an EEOC charge form. However, that charge cannot legally be deemed filed with EEOC until after it has been deferred to the state or local agency. Deferral to a state or local agency is required by Title VII of any charge arising in the jurisdiction that has an agency and a statute that allows for the handling of claims of discrimination arising from the same basis as that indicated in the EEOC charge. Thus, EEOC will physically take the charge, send it to the state or local agency, and suspend further processing of it. The state or local agency must have at least 60 days of exclusive jurisdiction over the charge. This 60-day period can be reduced if the agency terminates proceedings on that charge in less than 60 days, or if it waives jurisdiction. After 60 days, or after the state or local agency has waived jurisdiction or has completed processing, whichever is earlier, EEOC will assume jurisdiction over the charge. During the time it was with the state agency, as far as EEOC was concerned, the charge was in a state of "suspended animation."

A respondent examining a charge form it receives from EEOC can ascertain whether or not the charge has been deferred to the state or local agency, and whether deferral is necessary, by noting the date on which the charge was filed and the date on which the respondent received a copy of the charge or notice of charge form. If the time period between the charge and its receipt is less than 60 days, then either EEOC did not defer to the state or local agency or the agency waived jurisdiction or terminated its investigation and proceedings in less than 60 days.

If there has not been a deferral by EEOC to the state or local government agency or a waiver of jurisdiction by the agency, then EEOC may not have jurisdiction and cannot even investigate. See, for example, *Motorola, Inc.* v. *EEOC.*[5] Whether or not that charge can ultimately be "saved" is another question, and one that has not been definitively addressed by the courts, although it was the issue in *Crosslin* v. *Mountain States Tel. & Tel. Co.*[6] In *Crosslin*, the defendant employer had moved to dismiss a court complaint filed by the plaintiff. The basis for the motion was that the charge had never been filed with, or deferred to, the Arizona Civil Rights Commission; for this reason, the employer argued, EEOC could never have assumed jurisdiction of the charge; since EEOC could never have assumed jurisdiction of the charge, there was legally no charge ever filed with EEOC, and in order for there to be a lawsuit pursuant to Title VII, there first has to be a valid charge to EEOC.

The district-court decision rejected the employer's motion, reasoning that the charge did not have to be deferred, because the Arizona Civil Rights Commission did not have authority to obtain remedies as broad as those permitted under Title VII.[7] On appeal, the U.S. Court of Appeals for the Ninth Circuit reversed and ruled for the employer, holding that the relief available through the Arizona Civil Rights Commission was sufficient to qualify it as a deferral agency within the meaning of Section 706(b) of Title VII. The case then went to the U.S. Supreme Court. The Solicitor General filed a brief in that case suggesting that the case be remanded so that the charge could be deferred by EEOC to the Arizona Civil Rights Commission. The Supreme Court vacated the Ninth Circuit order and remanded the case for treatment as outlined by the Solicitor General's brief.[8] The charge was then deferred to the Arizona Civil Rights Commission, EEOC assumed jurisdiction, and the case continued. The employer then moved again to dismiss the court complaint, claiming that the charge had not been timely filed with EEOC, since more than three years had passed between the date of the alleged act of discrimination and the date EEOC assumed jurisdiction. The district court denied this motion[9] because it would mean that the U.S. Supreme Court had told the plaintiff and EEOC to undertake a useless act. There were no subsequent proceedings in the case.

In a subsequent decision, involving an age-discrimination claim, where the charge had not been initially deferred to or filed with the state agency, the Supreme Court held that the appropriate action for the trial court to take was to retain jurisdiction of the case but suspend proceedings for 60 days to allow for deferral and reassumption of jurisdiction. *Evans* v. *Oscar Mayer & Co.*[10] However, in *Mohasco Corp.* v. *Silver*,[11] the Supreme Court held that under Title VII, the state or local agency must be allowed 60 days to process the charge, and this 60-day period—or a lesser time, if there is a waiver or completion of the investigation within such lesser time—must be completed before 300 days has run from the alleged discriminatory act, otherwise the charge is invalid because it is untimely.

Timeliness. The manner in which the charge to EEOC is treated by EEOC —that is, whether or not it is deferred—relates also to another jurisdictional aspect of the charge. A claimant has 180 days after the alleged act of discrimination to file a charge with EEOC. However, if the alleged discriminatory act occurred in a jurisdiction that has a state or local agency with authority to act upon such a charge, then the possibility exists that the person may have 300 days from the alleged act of discrimination within which to file a charge to EEOC. In order to gain the benefit of the 300-day filing period, the charging party must have filed its charge in timely fashion with the state or local agency. Similarly, if it is EEOC deferring to the state or local agency, EEOC has to get the charge to that agency within the period specified under the state or local statute or ordinance. Thus, if the claimant comes to EEOC 190 days after the act of discrimination and has not previously gone to the state or local agency, and the state or local agency has a requirement that charges of discrimination be filed within 180 days after the act complained of, there can be no timely charge of discrimination and no jurisdiction to EEOC, since the person could not have filed a timely charge with the state or local agency. And the person is in no better position by having EEOC act on its behalf in having that charge filed with the agency. Since the claimant could not have filed a timely charge with the state or local agency, there is no reason to allow EEOC up to 300 days to take jurisdiction of that charge. This reasoning has been adopted by appellate courts. *Olson* v. *Rembrandt Printing Co.*[12]

The purpose of the extended 300-day filing period is to allow EEOC to receive a charge, defer it to the state or local agency for the 60-day deferral period, and then assume jurisdiction of the charge, all before 300 days have passed from the alleged act of discrimination. Another possible timeliness defect can exist in the charge if the person comes to EEOC more than 240 but less than 300 days after the alleged act of discrimination. EEOC is required by statute to allow the state the full 60-day deferral period unless the agency waives jurisdiction or terminates its investigation in less than 60 days. Thus, if a person comes to EEOC 241 days after the alleged act of discrimination, not having previously gone to the state or local agency, the charge cannot be timely filed with EEOC, absent some extraordinary action. That is because when EEOC defers the charge to the state or local agency, the required 60 day period, when added to the 241 days that have elapsed between the time of the alleged act of discrimination and the time the person first came to EEOC, comes to 301 days. The date when EEOC assumes jurisdiction will be the 301st day, at the earliest, and this will be outside the statutory filing period. See *Mohasco Corp.* v. *Silver, supra.*

EEOC at one time had regulations directing its officers to defer for the full 60-day period charges that first came to EEOC at a time more than 240 days after the alleged act of discrimination. However, these regulations directed the officers to assume jurisdiction on the 299th day after the alleged act of discrimination, regardless of whether or not the statutory 60-day deferral period had expired. In this way, EEOC, acting on behalf of the claimant, had attempted to "save" what might be otherwise stale charges. This procedure has since been struck down as being in violation of the statute (*Moore* v. *Sunbeam Corp.*),[13] and EEOC subsequently amended its regulations.

There are procedures EEOC can use that can "save" what might be otherwise an untimely charge to EEOC. For instance, when EEOC defers to the state a charge that was filed more than 240 days after the act complained of, EEOC can either orally or in writing request the state agency to waive jurisdiction. If the agency does so, then the proceedings of the agency have been terminated in less than 60 days, and EEOC can assume jurisdiction prior to the expiration of 300 days after the act complained of.

Probably the most common way to attempt to save untimely charges is by labeling them "continuing violations." For example, in the case of a failure to promote, perhaps someone else already received the job more than 300 days before the charge is filed, but the charging party's claim is that as long as he is earning a lesser amount than he would have earned had he received the promotion, then he suffers from the continued effects of that prior discriminatory act.

The U.S. Supreme Court, in *United Air Lines, Inc.* v. *Evans*,[14] rejected the "continuing violation" theory. EEOC then issued its own memorandum "interpreting" *Evans* in such a way as to attempt to repudiate it. But the EEOC memorandum was noted and rejected in *Cates* v. *TWA*.[15]

Stating a Claim. Reviewing the charge to see that it states a claim can save an employer a substantial amount of time. For example, a charge that claims discrimination because the employer terminated the claimant after the claimant had a sex-change operation does not, at least insofar as EEOC is concerned, state a claim. Rather than going through an entire investigation, which might possibly turn up other acts of discrimination, the employer might raise the question of jurisdiction, because the charge does not state a claim, at the initial stage of the administrative process. See, generally, *National Organization for Women, Inc. (NOW), St. Paul Chapter* v. *Minnesota Mining and Mfg. Co.*[16]

Joinder of Necessary Parties. Another consideration when examining the charge is whether all the necessary parties have been joined. If the claim relates to an act of discrimination that is covered by a collective-bargaining agreement provision, then the union, which is signatory to that collective-bargaining agreement, should also be joined in the charge. It is standard operating procedure for the intake officer at EEOC to question the claimant, and if the intake officer ascertains that a labor organization is also a necessary party, the officer will have the claimant file against the labor organization also. However, more and more frequently, labor organizations are providing so-called "free services" to their members and encouraging members who wish to file claims of discrimination to come to the local union office, or go to the local shop steward, where they are assisted in filling out the charge form. Naturally, in the course of this assistance, the claimant is not told to include the union as respondent also. The union representative then takes the charge and sends it to EEOC, and EEOC frequently does not talk to the charging party until sometime much later.

The failure to identify a labor organization on the charge form does not preclude the claimant or EEOC from naming the labor organization as a necessary party, and therefore a defendant, in an ultimate suit. However, the procedure available at the time of suit does not permit the recovery of damages against the labor organization in such a Title VII suit if it is joined only as a necessary party. For it to be a full party defendant in a Title VII action, and liable directly for monetary damages, all the jurisdictional requirements of Title VII must be satisfied against it. One of these requirements is that a charge has been filed naming the labor organization as a respondent. Therefore, in certain circumstances, the employer may want to notify EEOC that the allegations in the charge relate to the substance in a collective-bargaining agreement and that not all necessary parties have been named in the charge.

Other Action on Receipt of the Charge

In addition to examination of the charge to see whether it satisfies jurisdictional requirements, receipt of the charge should trigger two other actions by the respondent: it should make sure that records relating to the charge are preserved; and it should commence its own internal investigation of the claims made in the charge to determine their veracity.

Record keeping is covered in Chapter 11, but there are specific record-keeping requirements when an employer is informed that a charge has been filed against him. At that time, the employer is under a duty to maintain all the relevant records; the destruction of those records subsequent to such notice can be construed as evidence that the material, if it were available, would have presented evidence damaging to the employer/respondent.

Receipt of the charge or notice of charge should trigger an *internal investigation* because the earlier the employer determines that there is potential liability because of improper action, the more easily the effects of that action can be corrected. In fact, the very first stage of the face-to-face contact with EEOC is the no-fault conference, and that is the easiest place to correct a mistake. If the employer does not know about its side of the story at the time of the no-fault conference, then this valuable opportunity for settling the case with minimal damages, and without an EEOC investigation, may be lost.

The Negotiated Settlement, or "No-Fault" Conference

Commencing in September 1977, the EEOC instituted on a trial basis new procedures for expediting resolution of charges of discrimination under Title VII. These procedures were slightly modified after the trial period, and they were incorporated into EEOC's procedural regulations, effective January 23, 1979. To date, approximately 40 percent of all EEOC charges are being disposed of as part of the negotiated-settlement procedures. For that reason alone, it is advisable for respondents to understand the procedures clearly. The heart of the procedures appears in 29 C.F.R. §1601.20 and §1601.19(e). Section 1601.20 (as amended in 1979) reads as follows:

> (a) Prior to the issuance of a determination as to reasonable cause the Commission may encourage the parties to settle the charge on terms that are mutually agreeable. District Directors, Area Directors, the Director of the Office of Field Services and the Director of the Office of Systemic Programs, or their designees, shall have the authority to sign any settlement agreement which is agreeable to both parties. The Commission shall limit its undertaking in such settlements to an agreement not to process that charge further. Such settlements shall note that the Commission has made no judgment on the merits of the charge. Such an agreement shall not affect the processing of any other charge, including, but not limited, to a

Commissioner charge or a charge the allegations of which are like or related to the individual allegations settled.

(b) In the alternative, the Commission may facilitate a settlement between the person claiming to be aggrieved and the respondent by permitting withdrawal of the charge pursuant to §1601.10.

Section 1601.19(e) states:

(e) Where a respondent has made a settlement offer described in §1601.20 which is in writing and specific in its terms, the Commission may dismiss the charge if the person claiming to be aggrieved refused to accept the offer: *Provided,* That the offer would afford full relief for the harm alleged by the person claiming to be aggrieved and the person claiming to be aggrieved fails to accept such an offer within 30 days after actual notice of the offer.

The negotiated-settlement procedure involves a three-step process:

1. Intake/investigation
2. Fact-finding conference: investigation/settlement
3. Postconference actions

At Step 1, after a charge is filed, the investigator is authorized to obtain a detailed statement from the charging party, focusing on each specific harm the person alleges and the factual background involved. The purpose of this statement is to draft a precise charge and to prepare a request for information from the respondent directed to the specific issues of the case. The request is then sent to the respondent with a copy of the Form 131 notice of charge. Accompanying these will be an invitation to settle on a no-fault basis.

If initial settlement attempts fail, the case moves to Step 2. This step is initiated by a telephone call from the EEOC official designated to handle the case at this stage. He or she will explain the no-fault process, invite the respondent to attend, and ask for some available dates. The official will tell the respondent that EEOC will forward a copy of the actual charge prior to the no-fault conference and that the respondent is expected to have in attendance at the conference any witness who can support its position and refute the charge. The EEOC official will also indicate that prior to the no-fault conference, the respondent will have to supply the information sought by the interrogatory, and that attorneys will not be allowed to become part of the fact-finding session.

EEOC judges the success of the no-fault conference by whether or not the case has been disposed of. This depends largely upon the skills of the EEOC representative at the conference. Generally, EEOC assigns senior, experienced staff members to this function.

At the no-fault conference, the EEOC representative hears the charging party and his or her witnesses, then the respondent and its witnesses. A value judgment is made on the merit or lack of merit in the charge. Usually, there is a strong attempt to negotiate a settlement. Thus, in a case where the claim is discriminatory discharge and the charging party has already obtained reemployment, the EEOC representative may seek to resolve the case by gaining some monetary amount from the respondent, without requiring an offer of reinstatement.

Occasionally as a result of the no-fault conference, the EEOC representative will find the claim to be without merit and after the conference will draft a "no-reasonable-cause" determination for signature by the area director, and dispose of the case in that manner. Even if the respondent does not agree to come to the no-fault conference but submits a detailed, effective rebuttal statement to the charge, it is possible that a "no-reasonable-cause" determination will be issued at this stage.

If settlement is not achieved, the case moves to Step 3. If the information obtained from the conference is not sufficient to make a reasonable-cause determination, the commission will employ the traditional investigative techniques, such as witness interviews, interrogatories, field visits, and examination of documents. At this stage, a determination is made as to whether to expand the investigation to "like and related" charges. After this investigation is completed, a "no-cause" or "reasonable-cause" determination is made. "Reasonable cause" is supposed to mean a case worthy of litigation. At all three of the steps, the emphasis is on effecting a settlement.

The fact-finding conference is an important innovation, because it focuses on the individual charge. Only after the failure of settlement efforts in the conference will the commission attempt to expand its investigation to encompass, for example, other departments of an employer.

This procedure represents a significant policy change. Complaints are construed as relating to the harm the individual has suffered. Although statistics of the employer may be examined, this will be done by a sharply focused investigation of the general activities of the employer and the activities in the particular unit in which the discrimination has occurred.

There are supposed to be no adverse consequences to a respondent because it refuses to attend a no-fault conference. However, in inviting the respondent to the conference, the EEOC representative will emphasize the possibility that the regular investigatory process will be far more time-consuming and comprehensive than the no-fault conference. In practice, that possibility usually becomes a probability. Consequently, if there are potential class implications to the charge or areas of severe vulnerability at the facility, a respondent might want to at least attend the no-fault conference and possibly even settle at that stage.

If resolution is achieved at the conference, the respondent should seek to have the charge withdrawn, and the withdrawal approved by EEOC, as part of the resolution. If there is no no-fault conference, or a failure of resolution at the conference, there will probably be subsequent investigation, but this may not be until from six months to two years later.

From a legal point of view, the respondent who agrees to a no-fault conference should have its representatives as thoroughly prepared for the conference as they would be for trial, since statements made at this stage will be recorded by the EEOC representative and can be used later by EEOC or the charging party at a trial.[17]

Also from the legal point of view, if an agreement is signed as a result of the no-fault conference, that agreement is enforceable. See, for example, *EEOC v. Mississippi Baptist Hospital.*[18] However, if the conciliation-agreement provisions conflict with provisions of a collective-bargaining agreement already in effect, and a court finds that the remedial provisions of the conciliation agreement were not minimally required by Title VII, then those provisions may be voided. See, for example, *W.R. Grace & Co. v. Rubber Workers, Local 759.*[19]

The Nature of the EEOC Investigation

The role of the personnel director in handling the EEOC investigation is crucial. If it is handled improperly, the respondent might be exposed to a broad-scale lawsuit that might otherwise have been prevented.

The U.S. Court of Appeals for the Ninth Circuit issued a decision in *EEOC v. Occidental Life Ins. Co.*[20] that shows the dilemma facing a personnel director who wants to cooperate with EEOC but also wants to properly serve his employer. In the *Occidental* case, the original charge was brought by a female who had charged discrimination on the basis of sex because the employer refused to provide her with maternity leave, other pregnancy benefits, insurance, vacation benefits, and seniority rights. During the course of the investigation, EEOC found apparent discrimination not only against the charging party, as she claimed, but also against other females, and against males, for totally unrelated reasons. These other subjects were made part of the EEOC determination, attempt at conciliation, and failed conciliation, and were included in the court complaint ultimately filed by EEOC. When the employer sought to have these other allegations dismissed from the complaint, its motion was denied, and that denial was affirmed by the Ninth Circuit. That court exhibited no sympathy for the employer's position, stating:

> Had Occidental believed that the EEOC's investigation exceeded the permissible statutory scope, it could have refused the EEOC's demand for access, and sought adjudication of its rights. [Citations omitted here.] Occidental did not do so. Thus we can only conclude that the EEOC investigation was reasonable and that the information supporting the allegations in subparagraphs 8(b) and 9(c) was acquired during that reasonable investigation.[21]

The lessons to be learned from this case are these: (1) If the respondent gives over information on a subject during the course of an investigation, it may have waived its right to object if and when suit is commenced on that subject. (2) The representatives of a respondent should make an independent assessment, on the basis of the charge, of what is relevant and restrict the investigation to what is relevant. (3) When giving over information that collates data about different subjects, such as affirmative action program materials, all materials not directly relevant to the subject of the charge should be sanitized before the investigator is given access to them. (4) The EEOC investigator should not be allowed unfettered opportunity to talk to employees or tour the facility; if the investigator does attempt to exceed the permissible bounds of a legitimate investigation concerning the subject charged, the employee interview should be curtailed. (5) Since the employer of the personnel director who cooperates with EEOC in its overexpansive investigation will possibly suffer because of it, there should be no hesitancy, when necessary, in forcing EEOC to go through the almost impossible administrative burden of compelling the information if its investigator attempts to exceed permissible bounds. Although there is legal authority contrary to the *Occidental* decision, see, for example, *EEOC* v. *Bailey Co., Inc.*;[22] a personnel director should not risk an *Occidental* conclusion.

Whether or not access to certain information should be allowed is frequently a subject of disagreement between EEOC's investigators and respondent's representatives. It is very helpful, therefore, to know what the strategic position of the investigator is when there is such a confrontation. A sample scenario, from the investigator's point of view, follows.

The first step in the development of the confrontation usually arises when the EEOC investigator sends the questionnaire for the respondent to answer or seeks to review documents on-site, and the respondent refuses to answer or grant access. In this scenario, let us assume that there were 14 questions asked and the respondent refused to answer all of them.

The second step is the investigator's drafting a subpoena for signature by the district director and justifying the need for all 14 items to the district director. However, the investigator may not be able to justify all 14 to the satisfaction of the director; the director may issue the subpoena for only twelve of the items sought.

When the subpoena is issued, the respondent still does not have to furnish the information. However, it does have to make objection to the subpoena in order to preserve its defenses to it. This is the third step. The respondent must file its objections within five days of receipt of the subpoena (not including Saturdays and Sundays). The objections must be in writing, they must be made to the EEOC Director of Compliance in Washington, D.C., and a copy of them must be sent to the director who issued the subpoena.[23] The Director of Compliance is supposed to make a decision concerning the validity of the subpoena in view of the objections, within eight days of receipt of the objections or as soon thereafter as practicable. That decision will be reviewed by the EEOC commissioners and, unless they decide otherwise, the decision becomes final three days after their review. In practice, the Director of Compliance can rarely make his decision within eight days. It is more likely that 60 days pass before his decision issues, because of his backlog. When the decision does issue, notice of it is sent to the respondent and the appropriate district director. As a result of the decision by the Director of Compliance, the respondent's objections to two of the twelve items sought by the subpoena might be sustained. Thus, the original 14 items could very well be down to ten, at least 90 days would probably have passed since the original request for information, and very little effort would have been required by the respondent.

The fourth step requires no immediate action by the respondent, who can still refuse to furnish the information. This means that the district office from which the subpoena issued must forward all the materials relating to the subpoena to the EEOC area attorneys for their consideration. It has been held that not only is the respondent not required to file a legal action for a protective order, but also that the respondent has no legal right to commence such an action at this stage. This is because EEOC still has the option of considering whether it will seek legal enforcement and, if so, for what information. If EEOC does determine to file a legal action to compel enforcement, then the respondent can capitulate and turn over the information, or contest access in court.

From the EEOC's investigator's position, this exhaustive administrative process is quite unacceptable. He is under pressure to produce a certain number of completed investigations, such as three per month. He is also under pressure to get rid of aging cases. Even if the effect of the particular case on his performance can be explained, it becomes a burden to explain it continuously. Once having followed the subpoena enforcement route, he usually never wants to use it again. Consequently, the investigator usually tries alternative techniques.

One of these is the strong bluff. The investigator might cite to the respondent legal authority for his being able to obtain the information sought and *threaten* the subpoena route. Alternatively, he might indicate that he will make an adverse inference against the respondent because of its refusal to turn over the information sought in a voluntary manner. However, in view of the fact that there is a legal procedure available to the investigator to compel this information, and a legitimate controversy about the relevance of such information, he cannot refuse to make use of that procedure and still make the adverse inference.

A second approach the investigator might follow is the "wrap-up" approach. The investigator will say he has almost all the information he needs and that he is inclined to recommend a "no-reasonable-cause" determination, but that he needs the other information he seeks to "wrap up" the case. In reality, he might be recommending a "cause" determination and want the other data for additional support, or to allow for a broader "cause" determination.

A third approach that a good investigator might follow is to search for alternate sources for the information. This might mean review of investigatory files involving that respondent at the Office of Federal Contract Compliance Programs, or the state or local FEP agencies.

A fourth and, unfortunately, too frequently used approach is for the investigator to recommend, and the district director to issue, a reasonable-cause determination on subjects for which there has been no investigation, and for which there is no evidence. These determinations that are issued without supporting evidence generally lead to no legal action whatsoever. When they are reviewed by the EEOC attorneys, they are rejected for litigation because there is no file evidence to support the conclusions. And when reviewed by private attorneys, who have little chance of getting their fee unless they prevail, they are also rejected.

Occasionally, these EEOC determinations do form the basis of legal action by EEOC, but if the respondent handles the case properly—and has some luck— this absence of evidence or reason to bring the suit can be exposed, and the suit will be dismissed. See *EEOC* v. *Anchor-Continental, Inc.*[24]

The Legitimate Scope of the EEOC Investigation

The leading case, frequently cited for identifying the general parameters of the EEOC investigation, is *Sanchez* v. *Standard Brands, Inc.*[25] Ironically, this case was actually addressed to the legitimate scope of a court complaint arising from a charge to EEOC.

In *Sanchez,* the court ruled that the scope of the judicial complaint is limited to the scope of the EEOC investigation that can reasonably be expected to grow out of the charge of discrimination. The court indicated that the proper subject to review in determining the nature of the charge is not the boxes checked on the charge form, but the allegations made in the body of the charge; that the purpose of the charge is to trigger an investigation; and that a subsequent court action is much more intimately related to the EEOC investigation than to the words of the charge that originally triggered that investigation.

In another appellate case, *Circle K Corp.* v. *EEOC,*[26] the court said that the filing of charges by one claiming to be aggrieved authorizes the EEOC to investigate the charge for the purpose of determining the existence of reasonable cause to believe the charge is true. This means EEOC can require the charged party to submit information that is *relevant and material,* even if it does not directly relate to the particular discriminatory practice that the charging party claims affected him or her.

Finally, placing some perspective on the parameters of the EEOC investigation, in *Graniteville Co. (Sibley Division)* v. *EEOC,*[27] the U.S. Court of Appeals for the Fourth Circuit indicated that the investigatory powers of EEOC are *at least* as broad as those of the National Labor Relations Board.

In sum, EEOC is certainly not restricted in its investigation to comparing the qualifications or performance of the person who filed the charge to that of the person who might have been selected by the employer (*Georgia Power Co.* v. *EEOC*),[28] and the legitimate scope of the investigation will be dependent in large degree upon the nature of the charge to EEOC.

Expansion of the Investigation from one Basis to More than One

EEOC believes that it has the right to investigate concerning multiple bases even though the charge specifies only one basis for discrimination.[29]

Generally, when the issue is clearly presented, the courts will find that when one basis, such as sex discrimination, is charged in the complaint, a reasonable investigation that ensues may *not* encompass another basis, such as race. See *EEOC* v. *Quick-Shop Markets, Inc.*,[30] *Fix.* v. *Swinerton & Walberg Co.*,[31] *EEOC* v. *U.S. Fidelity & Guaranty Co.*,[32] and *EEOC* v. *Bailey Co., Inc.*[33]

However, many times the issue is not clearly presented, and different, collateral issues are raised. In such circumstances, EEOC may be permitted to investigate on multiple bases even though only one basis has been charged. This might be because the body of the charge put the respondent on notice that multiple bases were at issue; see, for example, *Sanchez* v. *Standard Brands, Inc.*, *supra;* and *Latino* v. *Rainbo Bakers, Inc.*[34]

Most frequently, however, the issue is raised only after EEOC has impermissibly expanded the scope of its investigation from one basis to another without objection by the respondent. On such occasions, it is usually found that it is too late for the respondent to object. See *EEOC* v. *Occidental Life Ins. Co.*, *supra.*

Lateral Expansion of the Investigation

Whether the permissible scope of the investigation should be expanded beyond the particular department, facility, or job group where the charging party works, or sought to work, depends upon the nature of the respondent's personnel system, the nature of the charge, the number of people working in the department or facility from which the charge emanated, and, to a lesser degree, the burden that compliance would place on the respondent.

Based upon the facts involved, courts have restricted EEOC investigations to the particular facility in which the charge arose (*Joslin Dry Goods Co.* v. *EEOC*),[35] or to the particular job about which the charge arose (*U.S. Steel Corp.* v. *U.S.*).[36] See also *EEOC* v. *Packard Elec. Div., General Motors Corp.*[37]

However, in another case, the appellate court permitted an investigation into the personnel activities of the respondent's motel, even though the charging party worked only in the restaurant; *Parliament House Motor Hotel* v. *EEOC*.[38] Where the charge alleged that the respondent segregated its waiting rooms for clients, EEOC was sustained in its demand for access to patient applications; *Rogers* v. *EEOC*.[39] Additionally, EEOC has had its demands for access to records in all departments of a college sustained; *EEOC* v. *University of New Mexico*.[40]

Although there are many court decisions sustaining, or not sustaining, an expansive lateral investigation by EEOC, it is probably more fruitful to examine the facts and reasoning in some decisions than to list the many cases that have been decided.

In *Joslin Dry Goods Co.* v. *EEOC, supra,* the charge was that respondent discriminated on the basis of race by reason of discharge, and that respondent discriminated against blacks and Mexican-Americans generally in hiring. EEOC sought extensive records for seven stores.

An affidavit from one of respondent's executives established that the seven Joslin stores maintained separate personnel records, that there was no master file of employee records, and that to comply with EEOC's investigation demand would require a substantial amount of monetary expenditure. The appellate court found that there was nothing in the record in the court below to indicate that there were any hiring or discharge practices and procedures that were applicable to all the stores. On this basis, the appellate court sustained the limitation of the investigation to just one store, but did rule that both hiring and firing practices at that store could be investigated.

In *U.S. Steel Corp.* v. *U.S., supra,* the charge that triggered the investigation had already been the subject of grievance under the applicable collective-bargaining-agreement provisions. The trial court found that the charge was not couched in broad or general terms but specifically complained about nonpromotion to a welder position after submission of an application; that although the charge alluded to a requirement that complainant would have to enter an apprenticeship program, the facts showed that he did not; and that nothing in the charge, pleadings, or affidavits suggested any departmental or plantwide policy. On that basis, EEOC was restricted to an examination of all employees classified as welders during a set time period. This is probably as narrow as a respondent might reasonably expect to restrict the investigation, and there is substantial authority that the investigation should be broader. See, for example, *EEOC* v. *Blue Bell Boots, Inc.*[41]

One of the key considerations in assessing whether an investigation should be expanded laterally is the frequency of similar occurrences in the particular job group, department, or facility where the charging party worked. Thus, where the claim is discriminatory discharge because of race, if there have been a large number of people working in the charging party's department (say, 500), a large number of discharges in the period from two years before the charge was filed to the time of investigation (say, 50 discharges), and a fair representation of blacks in that department (say, 50), then there should be no need to go beyond that department to obtain a statistical sample.

On the other hand, if the charge is from a middle-manager minority employee, claiming discrimination in promotion to position of store manager, then it would be illogical to restrict the investigation to that one store. It would be necessary to determine the number of store managers in the region or perhaps nationally, and the number of those who were minority members, in order to obtain a statistical picture.

Occasionally, the personnel manager will be faced with a dilemma. Statistically, the respondent's representation of minorities or females might be far greater if it gives the investigator figures for the region, such as Southwest U.S. Regional Sales Area, rather than the local area, such as Dallas District Office. If the larger-area figures show a significant representation of minorities or females, it is more likely that a "no-probable-cause" determination will issue from EEOC. On the other hand, if EEOC disagrees with the respondent as to whether minorities or females are properly represented in the larger area for which figures have been supplied, it is very likely that a "probable-cause" determination will issue, and that it will be against the respondent on a regional basis, not just locally.

Nevertheless, the possibility of such a dilemma illustrates a defensive technique available to respondents. That technique is the respondent's identification of the relevant area of inquiry for purposes of the investigation, after examining its own statistical profile and determining which of its profiles, regional or local, shows statistical parity.

Expansion From One Policy to More Than One

In substantive legal actions under Title VII, courts will generally permit the person who is aggrieved by one particular reflection of an alleged broad-scale practice to attack all areas where that person might encounter other reflections of that policy. See *Johnson* v. *Georgia Highway Express Co.*[42] The rationale is that it would be foolish and unduly time-consuming to have that person come back to court time after time, as he might encounter first hiring, then assignment, then training, then promotion discrimination.

For purposes of investigation, EEOC has been permitted to investigate practices that are charged, even though they may not have affected the charging party. See *Joslin Dry Goods* v. *EEOC, supra* (hiring charged, but charging party had been hired and discharged).

However, if a particular aspect of employment—say, promotions—has not been charged as being discriminatory but EEOC seeks to investigate that aspect anyway, then, because this aspect has not been the subject of a charge, the possibility that the respondent will be successful in preventing an investigation into that aspect is enhanced. See *U.S. Steel Corp.* v. *EEOC, supra.*

As a practical matter, if EEOC really desires to investigate multiple aspects of a personnel system, it will search the charge, or the affidavit in support of the charge, to buttress its claim that the charging party had been complaining about the particular aspect of employment it seeks to investigate. Alternatively, EEOC will have the charging party file an amended charge to include the other aspects, or it will consolidate the charge it has involving one aspect of employment with others concerning other aspects. Additionally, or alternatively, if EEOC is really serious in its desire to broaden the investigation to other aspects, it can cause a Commissioner's Charge to be filed, involving all aspects of employment.

The Time Period

The relevant time period for the investigation depends greatly upon the nature of the charge. As a general rule, a respondent should be successful in restricting the EEOC investigation to the period from two years before the charge was filed to the time the investigation commences. This is because, regardless of what kind of policy is at issue, no one who was adversely affected by that policy can recover monetary relief unless the date he or she was adversely affected was within the two-year period prior to the filing of the charge.[43]

If controversy develops between a respondent's representative and an EEOC investigator on this issue, the respondent's representative can find support for its position in the decision in *EEOC* v. *Occidental Life Ins. Co., supra.* There, the Ninth Circuit stated:

> Third Section 706(g)[44] provides: "Back pay liability shall not accrue from a date more than two years prior to the filing of a charge with the Commission [EEOC]." *Thus, an employer need not produce records except for a period of time the charge is pending, and the preceding two years.* (emphasis added by author)[45]

There have been cases sustaining an EEOC request for information going back to more than two years before the charge was filed, as in *Georgia Power Co.* v. *EEOC*[46] (sustaining a demand for information from five years before the charge was filed). However, most of those cases are outdated because of a legislative change and some legal changes since the time they were decided.

The legislative change was the 1972 Amendments to Title VII (effective March 24, 1972), prior to which claimants could go back to the effective date of Title VII (July 2, 1965) to recover back pay. Because of this change, the period of recovery was restricted to two years prior to the time the charge was filed.

The legal changes were effected by the U.S. Supreme Court decisions in *Teamsters* v. *U.S.*[47] and *United Air Lines, Inc.* v. *Evans, supra.* Prior to *Teamsters,* it had generally been accepted that people could use Title VII to correct for the continued effects of prior discrimination and thereby supersede existing collective-bargaining-agreement provisions. For this reason, it would be necessary to have a charging party's employment history from the date of the initial discriminatory assignment through the time of the investigation. This usually covered more than two years prior to the time the charge was filed. In *Teamsters,* the Supreme Court rejected the "continued effects" theory insofar as it related to bona fide seniority systems.

By its decision in *Evans,* the Court upset the "continued effects" theory on procedural grounds. There, it held that the person must file a charge within the relevant time period (180 days or 300 days) after the act that was the subject of the charge.

Private Interviews with Respondent's Employees

It inevitably happens that during the course of an investigation the EEOC investigator will ask for private interviews with respondent's employees, on respondent's premises, and with the employees paid for the time by respondent. Very frequently, the respondent is strongly tempted to permit such interviews because the investigation thus far has been going well and it has no desire to "offend" the investigator. However, it is generally advisable for a respondent to permit interviews with its employees on its premises on its own time *only* when there is a representative of the respondent present during the interview. If a respondent persists in this position, the only alternative available to the EEOC investigator will be to seek out employees privately off premises and attempt to speak to them there and on their own time. Generally, the investigator will not pursue this alternative, and will conduct the interview in the presence of the respondent's representative.

There are a number of good reasons that a respondent should insist on having a representative present during interviews with employees. None of these reasons is even remotely connected with the purpose of intimidation, which is the reason EEOC claims it wants the interview to be private.

The first reason the respondent would want to have a representative present is that, during the course of the interview with the employee, EEOC's investigator may attempt to expand the investigation beyond the scope of the initial charge. This may arise intentionally, precipitated by questions from the investigator, or it may arise from the employee's using the interview as a forum for different types of gripes. As we have seen, once the investigation has gone beyond the charge, the respondent may ultimately be faced with a lawsuit that goes far beyond the charge.

A second reason for having a representative present is that the investigator may be, knowingly or unknowingly, pushing a point of view and misconstruing facts to support a predetermined conclusion. If this is the case, it is very easy for information given to the investigator to be misconstrued. Thus, in one actual situation, it was discovered that the investigator had determined, and the government concluded, that the employer had handed out job applications for certain jobs only to females and applications for other jobs only to males. This conclusion, which the investigator had reached on the basis of a private employee interview with a receptionist, was discovered by the respondent from documents obtained pursuant to the Freedom of Information Act.

When the respondent finally contacted the employee involved (she was no longer employed and had moved overseas), it was found that what she had told the investigator was that most females ask for applications for certain jobs and most males ask for applications for other jobs. Thus, although the end result was the same—that is, females generally apply for one series of jobs and males generally apply for another—the way that result was achieved was far different from what had been found by the government. The difference was crucial.

If there is a respondent's representative present during the private interview, that person should be one who is familiar with respondent's personnel practices and will be in a position to correct any misassumptions by the investigator immediately. That person will also be in a position to keep the interview restricted to the issues being investigated, regardless of whether it is the EEOC investigator or the employee being interviewed who is going astray.

The EEOC *Compliance Manual,* which gives direction to the EEOC investigators, recognizes the right of a respondent to have an attorney or a representative present during employee interviews that occur on respondent's premises and respondent's time. The manual provisions, as last amended in March 1979, deal with situations where the respondent wants to have an attorney present and those where it wants just a representative present.

Regarding the presence of an attorney, the manual, under the heading "Problem Areas," states:

> (3) *Attorney's Presence*—R may insist on having their attorney present during the interview with R, as well as with any R witnesses. It is R's right to have counsel present during their own interview. However, distinguish between salaried and hourly paid employees. Those on salary are usually part of management and therefore "Respondents." Consequently, R's request for an attorney to be present should be honored even when it requires setting up a new appointment. Hourly paid employees, on the other hand, are not part of management; if R remains adamant in their request for an attorney, make arrangements to talk with these persons at another time, away from R's premises, if possible.[48]

Regarding the presence of a representative, the manual states:

> On occasion R may insist on having a representative present during an on-the-job interview. Politely resist this condition, but if R is adamant, the following remarks may be used: "The Commission seeks to obtain any information that will facilitate an understanding of the facts surrounding a case of alleged discrimination. I serve the Commission in a fact finding capacity. The Commission believes that the best interests of all parties can be served by the free flow of information during the investigative stage of the Commission's proceedings. We feel that an employee's loyalty to his company will not be affected by the presence or absence of Company officials during an interview. However, if you insist upon being present during such interviews, I will be obligated to note your presence when I report to my office and the statements in such interviews will be weighed accordingly.[49]

There have been no cases in which EEOC sought to compel a respondent to allow a private employee interview on respondent's time and respondent's premises.

Access to Computer Tapes

When cases initiated by the commission are charged, it is very possible that the EEOC seeks computer-tape information in order to conduct its investigation. In such situations, the need for the information and the usefulness it will serve is weighed against the burden that compliance will impose on the respondent. The right of the EEOC to obtain computer-tape information during the investigation was sustained in *EEOC* v. *National Electric Co. Benefit Fund.*[50] In this area, the courts generally look to the law established under the Federal Rules of Civil Procedure. These rules have generally found that computer storage of data is now a commonly used practice and that discovery of such information is permissible.

Furnishing Documents or Access to Documents

In the early days of Title VII enforcement, EEOC took a different approach to its investigations. Generally, when a charge was filed, EEOC attempted a broad investigation as part of which it frequently called upon employers to assemble information in a form in which it was not otherwise kept for business purposes. When EEOC sought to compel the employer to rearrange or compile the information into the form in which it had been requested, its efforts met with only modest success. In *Georgia Power Co.* v. *EEOC*[51] and *Monsanto Company* v. *EEOC*,[52] the courts refused to require respondents to compile lists, especially when the process of compilation would be expensive and time-consuming. However, there were some cases in which EEOC's demand that the employer compile lists was enforced by courts. See, for example, *New Orleans Public Service, Inc.* v. *Brown*;[53] *Motorola, Inc.* v. *EEOC*;[54] and *Sheetmetal Workers, Local 104* v. *EEOC.*[55]

At present, EEOC uses standard questionnaires, which are generally not very burdensome, in seeking information from employers. The type of questionnaire a respondent will receive is determined by the nature of the charge. In fact, the questionnaires relating to each type of charge are published in the EEOC *Compliance Manual.* Under such circumstances, it is very likely that EEOC would be successful in compelling responses to the questions. However, if EEOC is conducting a broad-scale investigation, or seeks broad-scale information in a form in which the employer does not keep such information, it is very likely that the courts will not require such compilation. In making its assessment, the court will weigh the burden on the respondent against the benefit and necessity to EEOC of having the information in that form. Since the courts are very familiar with the procedures in the Federal Rules of Civil Procedure, especially Rule 33, they have become accustomed to expecting defendants in any kind of action who are requested for large amounts of information to comply by furnishing to the other side access to records that contain the information, rather than answer the questions specifically. Since this is such a common practice under the Federal Rules of Civil Procedure in the litigation context, it is very probable that a court confronted with the same issue, although in an investigation context, would find that such a respondent, having furnished the documents containing such information, had complied with the requirements of the subpoena.

Causing Investigation of Other Areas

Occasionally, a respondent undergoing an investigation by EEOC feels that testimony or documents submitted by some third party will be relevant to the investigation and helpful for its position. In such circumstances, that respondent might ask EEOC to contact such persons, or examine such records.

The basis for the right would be Section 710 of Title VII, 42 U.S.C. §709. That section provides that subpoenas should follow NLRB regulations. The National Labor Relations Act provides: "The Board or any member thereof shall, upon application of any party to such proceedings, forthwith issue to such party subpoenas requiring the attendance and testimony of witnesses or the production of any evidence in such proceeding or investigation requested in such application."[56] Contrary to the rules of the National Labor Relations Board, an EEOC procedural regulation specifically provides that subpoenas will *not* issue at the request of any party.[57] But because this EEOC regulation conflicts with the statutory language, it is probably invalid.

The manner in which this request is treated, and whether or not EEOC is required to pursue it, will depend not so much on EEOC's procedural regulations as on the relevancy of the information the respondent seeks to have considered as part of the investigation.

The Respondent's Position Statement

Content and Time of Submission

Many respondents have indicted themselves by prematurely protesting their innocence of a discriminatory practice about which EEOC knew nothing. They have done this by using unwisely the right to submit a respondent's position statement.

EEOC procedures provide for the right of a respondent to submit its side of the story and to have it considered before the EEOC determination or decision is issued.[58] EEOC's investigator and the district director who issues the determination usually consider this position statement quite seriously. And whether they do or not, it is considered at the time the case is being reviewed for litigation potential either by a private attorney or by the EEOC's own legal staff.

It is very difficult to submit a rebuttal statement to a charge without knowing specifically what the charge is and what the EEOC investigation has uncovered. For that reason, it is advisable for a respondent to submit its position statement when the investigation has been concluded—after the on-site investigation, if there has been one, or after the EEOC has completed its investigation by interrogatories.

There are at present respondent companies achieving a "no-probable-cause" determination rate of 90 percent on charges against them, largely by making effective use of the opportunity to submit a respondent's position statement. The statements submitted by these respondents marshal the relevant facts, and relate the relevant facts to the relevant law. Where possible, they rely on EEOC commission decisions as precedent for the proposition they are arguing, and they submit affidavits in support of that position.

Supplementing the Position Statement

Even if there has been a "reasonable-cause" determination against the respondent as a result of the investigation, if favorable facts—such as the recent hiring of many more minorities or females into a particular job group or department—become known to the respondent, then the respondent should immediately call them to the attention of the EEOC. If the administrative processes have already advanced past the determination stage, it is most unlikely that the determination will be reversed; however, these supplemental facts will be helpful to a respondent in other important ways, because whatever information is submitted by the respondent will be forwarded to the person in possession of the case file and be included in it. EEOC or private plaintiffs' attorneys litigate only a small fraction of the cases that have resulted in a reasonable-cause determination. In doing that, they use the standards described later in this chapter. Thus, for litigation purposes, the question is not only whether there has been a violation of Title VII, but also whether, given the limited resources of EEOC or the private plaintiffs' bar, this is the type of case to which those resources should be devoted.

The EEOC Determination or Decision

When a Commission Decision is Appropriate

When Title VII was first enacted, the five commissioners appointed by the president rendered every decision after investigation by EEOC. This became burdensome and caused severe backlogs. Therefore, the commissioners assigned to the District directors the right to issue commission determinations. A commission decision differs from a commission determination in that it is issued by the EEOC commissioners themselves, whereas a determination is issued by the District director. Additionally, a commission decision will be rendered only on a matter that has not been ruled upon before the commission, whereas a determination can issue only if there is a commission decision precedent (CDP) to support the finding in the determination.

Originally, EEOC had not followed the requirements of the Administrative Procedures Act in granting authority to District directors to issue determinations and for that reason, some courts found that determinations issued by the district directors were invalid. However, EEOC subsequently amended its procedural regulations in conformance with the requirements of the Administrative Procedures Act, and it is clear now that the area directors do have authority to issue commission determinations.[59]

There is one area where EEOC has directed its District directors to defer to the commissioners themselves in issuing decisions. That is when a respondent questions the jurisdiction of EEOC over the matter and raises a serious jurisdictional issue. In such instances, there are specific procedures for a District director to follow. Perhaps some day, the director will be authorized to issue a determination on the subject because EEOC determines that it is not a novel issue, but at present, the District director must contact the headquarters office when such a question is raised.

When a commission determination issues, there must be a CDP to support it. In the EEOC file, the Investigator's Memo, which EEOC will not make available to the public or the respondent, will note the CDPs relied upon to support the findings proposed to be made in the determination. Additionally, when a determination is sent out to the parties, EEOC is supposed to retain a copy of it and note on it the particular CDPs relied upon to support each of the findings made in that determination.

There is not supposed to be a determination on an issue that has not been investigated. However, occasionally, with only slight evidence in the file, a determination will issue on a subject. It is very difficult, once that happens and a court complaint is filed including an allegation on that subject, to claim that EEOC did not investigate that issue. The courts generally will not permit respondents to attack the determination, since the courts find that a determination in and of itself has no legal significance because it does not cause the respondent to have to do anything. Since it merely sets the framework for an endeavor in conciliation, it is not subject to court review.

The standard used by EEOC in determining whether reasonable cause exists to believe discrimination occurred is that the case is worthy of litigation.

The Significance of the Determination or Decision

The determination or decision defines the parameters for conciliation and, eventually, for suit, if one is to be commenced. If a legal action is ultimately to be commenced by EEOC, it cannot exceed the bounds of the determination in regard to facilities, bases, or subjects.

In theory, a charging party who obtains a right-to-sue notice after a determination may sue on items not covered in the determination, but generally the courts will find that the parameters of the determination by EEOC and the parameters of a lawsuit resulting from the filing of the charge are the same. See *Sanchez v. Standard Brands, Inc., supra.*

The Significance of a "No-Cause" Determination or Decision

If the results of the investigation are that there is "no cause" to believe that discrimination occurred, then EEOC will issue a determination to that effect, and at the same time send out to the charging party a copy of a right-to-sue notice. The "no-cause" determination and the issuance of the notice terminate the EEOC administrative process on that charge. Furthermore, even if EEOC fails to send out the right-to-sue notice with the determination, court decisions have indicated that the time for filing suit—that is, the 90-day filing period—commences upon the receipt of the "no-cause" determination, because that filing period follows immediately upon the end of the EEOC administrative process.

Even if there is a legal action filed on the basis of a "no-cause" determination, a respondent is in a much more favorable position than if the suit followed a "cause" determination. Usually, it will be very difficult for a charging party who has received a "no-cause" determination to obtain counsel willing to take the case, since private counsel usually take these cases on a contingency basis and receive an attorney's fee only if the plaintiffs prevail. A private plaintiff's attorney would generally not want to take the case if EEOC had not found reasonable cause, because that means it will be difficult to prevail. Furthermore, once a "no-cause" determination has issued, it will be very difficult, as a practical matter, for the charging party to become certified as a class representative.

The EEOC Conciliation Attempt

If reasonable cause is found to believe that discrimination has occurred, at the time a copy of the determination or decision is sent to the respondent and the charging party, there will also be enclosed an invitation to participate in conciliation. That invitation will ask the parties to notify EEOC within a certain period of time, usually five days, whether they wish to participate.

Generally, the charging party wishes to participate in conciliation. In fact, EEOC is authorized to engage in conciliation attempts even without the cooperation of the charging party, and it is theoretically possible that the case will be administratively closed by EEOC based upon an agreement reached between EEOC and the respondent. In such an event, the charging party will be issued a right-to-sue notice to seek his or her personal relief in court.[60]

Respondents can benefit from engaging in conciliation attempts, and it is usually fruitful for them to do so. First, the conciliation attempt will offer the respondent an opportunity to learn in even greater detail the evidence that has been used against it. Second, it enables the respondent to know what remedy the EEOC will seek. Sometimes, the remedy is not as onerous as the respondent expected, and the case can be resolved. Third, if the conciliation is successful and is embodied in a conciliation agreement, it is very possible that the agreement will offer to the respondent certain protections against claims by unions or whites or males that the remedy requires reverse discrimination. A respondent who engages in conciliation and achieves such an agreement is not liable, according to EEOC's guidelines, for monetary damages incurred by whites or males as a result of the remedy imposed.

Legally, too, the conciliation proposal by EEOC has significance. EEOC will draft a proposed conciliation agreement if the respondent wishes, and the agreement will almost always contain a remedy for all violations found in the determination. However, to the extent that the conciliation agreement does not seek remedy for violations found in the determination, those issues might be considered legally abandoned by EEOC. This is because EEOC, prior to filing its own lawsuit, must engage in an investigation, determination, and conciliation attempt on each of the issues it proposes to raise in its complaint in court.

Almost always, if the respondent provides a remedy satisfactory to the charging party, then EEOC also will sign a conciliation agreement embodying that remedy. However, EEOC retains the right to obtain a remedy above and beyond that which is satisfactory to the charging party and does not have to sign a conciliation agreement or close the case just because the respondent has satisfied the charging party.

Most conciliation agreements contain certain standard clauses. One of these is the statement that the agreement does not constitute either an admission of guilt or evidence of guilt by the respondent. If a proposed conciliation agreement omits such a provision, a respondent should seek to have it included. Another standard provision is for reporting requirements. Generally, these requirements are modest and easily fulfilled. The reports will be sent periodically to the EEOC office from which the conciliation agreement arose. One of the present weaknesses of EEOC, however, is that the review of conciliation agreements is not generally monitored with a great deal of diligence. Nevertheless, the agreement itself and the reporting requirements pursuant to it are legally enforceable by EEOC. In enforcing the conciliation agreement, EEOC does not have to prove the underlying violation.

Failure of Conciliation

EEOC Procedures

When EEOC believes that conciliation has failed or is about to fail, the EEOC regulations provide that EEOC is to notify the respondent and the charging party of that opinion.[61]

Actions by the Respondent

There have been various attempts, all unsuccessful, to impose a strict time requirement on private action under Title VII. Instead, the courts have indicated that after the exhaustion of the administrative process, EEOC is supposed to

Handling the EEOC Charge and Investigation

issue the right-to-sue notice to the charging party, and the charging party must file a court complaint, if one is to be filed at all, within 90 days of receipt of this notice. EEOC itself has indicated in its procedural regulations that after a "reasonable cause" determination, if the commission has decided not to bring a civil action against a respondent, it will issue a right-to-sue notice to the charging party.[62] Nevertheless, EEOC's offices are not uniformly following this procedure. It is not unheard of, and in fact it is quite common, for the administrative procedure to continue indefinitely, and it has happened that charging parties, ten or twelve years after having filed a charge of discrimination, notify EEOC that they desire a right-to-sue notice. Thereafter, they commence a legal action within 90 days after receipt of the notice.

Although a respondent can at that time claim laches, laches is a very difficult defense to make. It requires the respondent to demonstrate that the charging party waited an inordinate time and that the respondent will be prejudiced in its defense because of this delay in time.

When there is a failure of conciliation, the administrative procedure is *supposed* to move rapidly. The case file is *supposed* to be forwarded to the appropriate center for consideration as a litigation vehicle immediately, and that center is *supposed* to determine whether or not litigation will be initiated on the basis of that investigation file and determination within 30 days after receipt of the file. (See Exhibit K, a letter to the charging party conveying that information.)

However, the EEOC attorneys cannot and do not follow this timetable. They frequently take as long as two years to determine whether or not to proceed with litigation. Furthermore, even when they decide to reject a case file for litigation by EEOC, they do not issue a right-to-sue notice to the charging party at that time. Instead, they send the file back to the appropriate district office, which is *supposed* to issue the right-to-sue notice. But it frequently does not, preferring to make one last attempt to conciliate the case.

Because the charging party has 90 days to file a lawsuit, if he is to file one at all, from the end of the administrative process, it is in the best interests of the respondent to have the administrative process terminated and have the date of that termination clearly defined. To effectuate the triggering of the 90-day filing period, it might be advisable for a respondent, once it is notified of a failure of conciliation, to send a letter to the charging party describing the remainder of the administrative process. A sample letter that might achieve the intended result is Exhibit L, at the end of this chapter. Whether or not this tactic will prove successful depends a great deal upon the fact situation of a particular case. However, respondents have nothing to lose by following such procedure, and they may even be successful in preventing a stale suit many years later.

The procedural regulations of EEOC once allowed the issuance of a right-to-sue notice at the request of either party, but EEOC changed its regulations and withdrew from the respondent the right to demand it. As Title VII grows more mature, the problem of the indefinite time period allowed for private suits will become more acute.

Administrative Process after the Failure of Conciliation

Referral for Litigation Review

After the failure of conciliation, the case file will be put together with a cover memo and forwarded to the appropriate area litigation center for review for litigation purposes. That review, as indicated previously, is supposed to take place and be completed within 30 days after receipt of the file. If the District director has a particular reason for wanting the commission to litigate upon a case, he or she can so indicate in the cover memo that is forwarded with the file.

The Nature of the Litigation Review

Since EEOC cannot possibly sue on every case file forwarded to it, a decision is made at the area litigation section as to the relative merits and value of that particular case for litigation. In weighing these, the commission considers (1) the number of other charges outstanding against the respondent; (2) the egregiousness of the conduct complained about; (3) whether all conditions precedent have been followed during the administrative process; (4) the novelty of the theory or issues in the case; (5) the number of people to be benefited by litigating on that case; and (6) the degree of cooperation by the respondent during the course of the investigation or conciliation attempt.

Administrative Action if Litigation is Contemplated

If litigation by EEOC is contemplated, a complaint will be drafted and the EEOC attorney will prepare what is called a "presentation memo," addressed from the litigation center to the general counsel of EEOC. The presentation memo will outline the facts of the case, the evidence to support litigation, the reason litigation is appropriate in that particular case, possible jurisdictional problems, possible defenses of the respondent, and the legal issues involved. After the review by the general counsel and the obtaining of further information if necessary, the general counsel will determine whether or not the case is appropriate for litigation. If it is, the general counsel will approve it for litigation and present it to the commission itself for litigation approval.

After litigation approval, the case file and the approved complaint are sent back to the appropriate litigation center. Occasionally, there will be a telephone communication or a letter from the EEOC to the respondent prior to the initiation of the lawsuit, attempting to settle the case once again. More frequently, however, the complaint will just be filed and the respondent will become a defendant.

Administrative Action if Litigation is Not Contemplated

If the case is rejected for litigation, the case file is sent back to the area office with the reasons for the rejection. The district director can appeal the decision not to litigate, but that appeal procedure is rarely utilized. Once the case is back in the area office, the office is supposed to notify the parties that the case will not be litigated by EEOC and issue a right-to-sue notice immediately to the charging party.

Request for a Right-to-Sue Notice by a Charging Party

Ordinarily, when a right-to-sue notice is requested by a charging party, no matter what the stage of the investigation at that time, EEOC will issue the notice and, usually, close the case at that time. However, EEOC does not have to close the case file. It can determine that it should continue its investigation and administrative process in the interests of justice.

USE BY RESPONDENTS OF THE FREEDOM OF INFORMATION ACT AND COMPLIANCE MANUAL

The EEOC *Compliance Manual* provides that parties may obtain certain materials from the EEOC investigation file if they so request.[63] Additionally, the Freedom of Information Act also permits access to EEOC files.[64]

Access to the EEOC file can be invaluable for several purposes: for submitting the rebuttal statement of the respondent, for conciliation, or for defending oneself in a legal action after a complaint has been filed. As far as the rebuttal statement is concerned, access to the EEOC file is helpful in enabling the respondent to know what EEOC already knows and orient its response precisely against the evidence given against it. In regard to conciliation, the same might be true. For purposes of litigation defense, if there is any kind of procedural or jurisdictional defect, the EEOC file is an invaluable document to have.

Aside from the uses indicated above, access to the EEOC file will enable the respondent to know what employees have told EEOC, and to have a detailed affidavit from the charging party. As part of the investigation, EEOC will require the charging party to give a detailed statement enumerating all the allegations and the basis for believing that they arose because of discrimination. For the respondent who can point out to the EEOC investigator that the charging party has been misrepresenting the facts on numerous items in his affidavit, the chances of obtaining a "no-cause" determination will be enhanced.

The cost of obtaining the EEOC investigation file is minimal. A sample letter by which one would request the file under the *Compliance Manual* and under the FOIA is shown in Exhibit M.

Exhibit A

CHARGE OF DISCRIMINATION

(PLEASE PRINT OR TYPE)

APPROVED BY GAO
B — 180541 (RO511)
Expires 1-31-81

IMPORTANT: This form is affected by the Privacy Act of 1974; see Privacy Act Statement on reverse before completing it.

CHARGE NUMBER(S) (AGENCY USE ONLY)
☐ STATE/LOCAL AGENCY
☐ EEOC

Equal Employment Opportunity Commission and _____ (State or Local Agency)

NAME (Indicate Mr., Ms. or Mrs.)
HOME TELEPHONE NUMBER (Include area code)
STREET ADDRESS
CITY, STATE, AND ZIP CODE
COUNTY

NAMED IS THE EMPLOYER, LABOR ORGANIZATION, EMPLOYMENT AGENCY, APPRENTICESHIP COMMITTEE, STATE OR LOCAL GOVERNMENT AGENCY WHO DISCRIMINATED AGAINST ME. (If more than one list below).

NAME
TELEPHONE NUMBER (Include area code)
STREET ADDRESS
CITY, STATE, AND ZIP CODE

NAME
TELEPHONE NUMBER (Include area code)
STREET ADDRESS
CITY, STATE, AND ZIP CODE

CAUSE OF DISCRIMINATION BASED ON MY (Check appropriate box(es))

☐ RACE ☐ COLOR ☐ SEX ☐ RELIGION ☐ NATIONAL ORIGIN ☐ OTHER (Specify)

DATE MOST RECENT OR CONTINUING DISCRIMINATION TOOK PLACE (Month, day, and year)

THE PARTICULARS ARE:

I will advise the agencies if I change my address or telephone number and I will cooperate fully with them in the processing of my charge in accordance with their procedures.

I declare under penalty of perjury that the foregoing is true and correct.

NOTARY — (When necessary to meet State and Local Requirements)

I swear or affirm that I have read the above charge and that it is true to the best of my knowledge, information and belief.

SIGNATURE OF COMPLAINANT

SUBSCRIBED AND SWORN TO BEFORE ME THIS DATE
(Day, month, and year)

DATE: CHARGING PARTY (Signature)

EEOC FORM 5B MAR. 79   PREVIOUS EDITIONS OF ALL EEOC FORM 5'S ARE OBSOLETE AND MUST NOT BE USED

CHARGE FILE COPY

Exhibit B

EQUAL EMPLOYMENT OPPORTUNITY COMMISSION

DATE _____

EEOC CHARGE NO. _____

706 AGENCY
CHARGE NO. _____

TO:

SUBJECT: CHARGE TRANSMITTAL

Transmitted herewith is a charge of employment discrimination initially received by the:

☐ EEOC ☐ _____ on _____
      (Name of 706 Agency) *(Date of Receipt)*

☐ Pursuant to the work-sharing agreement, this charge is to be initially processed by the EEOC.

☐ Pursuant to the work-sharing agreement, this charge is to be initially processed by the 706 Agency.

☐ The work-sharing agreement does not determine which agency is to initially process the charge.

  ☐ EEOC requests a waiver ☐ 706 Agency waives
  ☐ No waiver requested   ☐ 706 Agency will process the charge initially

Please complete the bottom portion of this form to acknowledge receipt of the charge and, where appropriate, to indicate whether the 706 Agency will initially process the charge.

Typed Name of EEOC Office Director or 706 Agency Director Signature

Exhibit B   (Continued)

To whom it may concern:

☐ This will acknowledge receipt of the referenced charge.
☐ The 706 Agency will process the charge. Please refrain from processing until we have reached a final disposition.
☐ The 706 Agency will not process the charge.

TO:

DATE _____

EEOC CHARGE NO. _____

706 AGENCY
CHARGE NO. _____

EEOC FORM 212-A
    DEC 78

Exhibit C

EQUAL EMPLOYMENT OPPORTUNITY COMMISSION

Charge No.: 000099101
Respondent: XYZ Corporation

Ms. Lara C. Smith
1832 24th Street
Anycity, North Carolina   99999

Dear Ms. Smith:

Your charge of employment discrimination has been received by the EEOC and assigned the above charge number. A copy of your charge or notice of your charge will be provided to the respondent within ten days of the date your charge was received by this office, as required by law. Your identity will not be made known to the respondent unless you authorize us to do so.

You need do nothing further at this time. We will contact you if we require further information or other assistance from you.

Our regulations require that you notify us of any change in your address and keep us informed of any prolonged absence from your current address.

Sincerely,

Exhibit D

EQUAL EMPLOYMENT OPPORTUNITY COMMISSION	Person Filing Charge
	This Person (Check One)
	Claims to be Aggrieved
TO:	Is Filing on Behalf of a Person Claiming to be Aggrieved
	Date(s) of Alleged Violation
	Place of Alleged Violation
	Charge Number

NOTICE OF CHARGE OF EMPLOYMENT DISCRIMINATION

(See Notice of Non-Retaliation on Reverse)

You are hereby notified that a charge of employment discrimination under Title VII of the Civil Rights Act of 1964, as amended, 12 U.S.C. Section 2000e et. seq., has been filed against you. Information relating to the date, place, and circumstances of the alleged unlawful employment practice or practices is provided herein.

If you wish to submit any information in writing, it will be made a part of the file and will be considered when this charge is investigated. Telephone communications cannot be made a part of the record. Section 1602.14 of the Commission's Regulations *(See attachment)* requires the preservation of all personnel records relevant to this charge, as described below, until it is resolved.

You will be contacted when investigation commences.

Exhibit D (Continued)

BASIS OF DISCRIMINATION

☐ Race or Color   ☐ Sex   ☐ Retaliation   ☐ Religion   ☐ National Origin

NATURE OF CHARGE

Hiring	Discharge	Layoff	Recall
Wages	Promotion	Demotion	Seniority
Job Classification	Training/ Apprenticeship	Exclusion	Union Representation
Segregated Locals	Referral	Qualification/ Testing	Advertising
Benefits	Segregated Facilities	Intimidation/ Reprisal	Tenure
Terms and Conditions	Other/Explain		

Date   Typed Name/Title of Authorized EEOC Official   Signature

---

EEOC Form 131   RESPONDENT'S COPY
Sep 77

I hereby certify that I mailed the original of this Notice to the addressee herein above.

Date   EEOC Employee (Signature)

EEOC Form 131   FILE COPY
Sep 77

Exhibit E

EQUAL EMPLOYMENT OPPORTUNITY COMMISSION
PHILADELPHIA DISTRICT OFFICE
127 N. FOURTH STREET
PHILADELPHIA, PENNSYLVANIA 19106

June 18, 1979

Our Reference: Charge Number

Kenneth McCulloch, Esq.
Townley & Updike
Chrysler Building
405 Lexington Avenue
New York, New York 10017

Dear Mr. McCulloch:

The information described and requested in this letter is necessary to the United States Equal Employment Opportunity Commission's investigation of the above cited charge. If alternate documents are available that will satisfy the purpose of some item requested and can be supplied with greater convenience or less expense, please supply them as an alternative. The requested information is requested within fifteen days of receipt of this letter.

We appreciate your cooperation in supplying the following:

1. Explain in detail (or submit documents) that reveal(s) the nature and structure of the educational institution named in the instant charge. Include such information as the name and type of governing body controlling the institution, the source of funding, types of contracts issued to teaching personnel (listing the requirements) and types of education provided by the institution (primary, secondary, college, technical, etc.)

2. Supply an organizational chart, statement, or documents that describe your corporate structure, showing the relationship between it and the various types of schools supervised by the corporation.

3. Supply copies of rules, regulations, or policies in effect as of August 1, 1977 that determine how contracts are awarded to teaching personnel.

Exhibit E (Continued)

page two

4. Submit a listing or printout of all former and current teachers by name, sex, marital status, date of hire, name of institution and location, type of contract, for each school located outside the Continental United States, since August 1, 1976, to include the respondent.

5. Submit the following documents for all current and former teachers who were assigned to the respondent's facility for each year since August 1, 1976:

   A. Job Application/Resume

   B. Contracts

   C. W-2 Forms or yearly payroll period

6. Provide the same information requested in item 5 for teachers assigned to other facilities.

7. Submit a listing (with supporting documentation) of employees by name, sex, marital status who were denied a contract with respondent since August 1, 1975, stating the reason for the rejection.

8. Explain the benefits awarded to respondent's teachers and give the dollar amount for each, such as insurance, transportation, housing, utilities, retirement, etc.

9. In addition to any of the information requested herein, submit a written position statement on each of the allegations of the charge, accompanied by documentary evidence, affadavits, and other written statements, where appropriate, including any additional information and explanation you deem relevant to the charge.

Thank you for your cooperation. If you have any questions, please call me at (215) 555-3164.

Sincerely,

Equal Opportunity Specialist
(Employment)

Exhibit F

TOWNLEY & UPDIKE

CHRYSLER BUILDING

405 LEXINGTON AVENUE

NEW YORK, N. Y. 10017

TELEPHONE
(212) 682-4567

CABLE: TUCARRO
TELEX: 12-7815

TELECOPIER
(212) 697-3061

JOHN R. SCHOEMER, JR.
JOHN J. LEIGHTON
HOCH REID
EDWARD M. MAHER
ANDREW L. HUGHES
PHILIP D. PAKULA
RONALD S. DANIELS
RICHARD J. BARNES
RICHARD R. LUTZ
JOHN PAUL REINER
PHILIP S. OLICK
MARK D. GERAGHTY
JOHN D. CANONI
RICHARD C. KULLEN, JR.
LEONARD F. BINDER
ROBERT C. MANGONE
WILLIAM O'C. HARNISCH
KENNETH J. McCULLOCH
DOUGLAS C. FAIRHURST
ELLIOT PASKOFF
PEREZ C. EHRICH
JOHN C. SABETTA
JAMES K. LEADER

J. JEROME MADDEN
COUNSEL

MICHAEL S. BELOHLAVEK
FREDERICK D. BERKON
ROBIN BIERSTEDT
JEFFREY L. BOAR
CARL P. BOWEN
JESSE H. BRENNER
CARL J. CHIAPPA
JEROME P. COLEMAN
MARY D. FAUCHER
KENNETH M. HART
PHILIP L. KIRSTEIN
TERENCE J. LYNCH
JAMES D. MADIGAN III
ROBERT LLOYD RASKOPF
NEIL J. ROSINI
NINA SHREVE
MICHAEL S. STONE
SHERRI VENOKUR
ROGER E. WILLIAMS
HARRY H. WISE III

CERTIFIED MAIL
RETURN RECEIPT REQUESTED

July 23, 1979

Equal Employment Specialist (Employment)
Equal Employment Opportunity Commission
Philadelphia District Office
127 N. Fourth Street
Philadelphia, Pennsylvania 19106

Re: ABC Educational Foundation

Dear Sirs:

In response to your letter of June 18, 1979 with respect to the above entitled matter, wherein you requested information and the Position Statement of ABC Educational Foundation ("ABC") concerning the above entitled matter, it is the position of ABC that the Equal Employment Opportunity Commission ("EEOC") is without jurisdiction to process this charge. This position is set forth more fully below. Because ABC contests EEOC's jurisdiction, information requested in your June 18, 1979 letter will not be forthcoming. ABC requests that if EEOC still wishes to process this charge after studying the bases of ABC's position below, that EEOC subpoena records of ABC so that jurisdiction of this charge may be contested in court. In essence, it is the position of ABC that Jane Doe has not filed a timely charge of discrimination with EEOC. Because she has not satisfied a jurisdictional prerequisite, EEOC has no jurisdiction to process this charge.

TOWNLEY & UPDIKE
Equal Employment Specialist
page two

ABC is a private, nonprofit service agency that supports and advances the education of American elementary and secondary school children outside the United States. It is a service organization working by contract with overseas governments or corporations. The services it provides are educational consultants, school operations, educational staffing, purchasing, procurement, and financial management.

The manner in which ABC manages schools is determined by the contract entered into between ABC and the host country or industrial client operating in that country. There is no standard contract between ABC and the host country or industrial client, and each of these contracts is separately negotiated.

The school at issue here is the XYZ School of Brisbane, Australia. It is set up pursuant to a contract between ABC and the Widget Manufacturing Company. The rights and obligations of Widget under this contract with ABC are exercised pursuant to authority it has conveyed to the Brisbane School Board.

There are two categories of teacher contracts at ABC. Teachers hired by ABC in the United States to teach in Australia contract with ABC and receive one-year contracts. The School Board also hires a certain percentage of the teaching staff. These "local hires" (residents of Australia) contract with the School Board, and not ABC to teach at the Brisbane School. The School Board sets the salary for "local hires." Only the School Board recruits locally. The contract between Widget and ABC requires that there be a certain fixed number of local hires; ABC is only allowed to hire a fixed number of teachers.

Jane Doe held teaching contracts with ABC to teach at the Brisbane School for the academic years 1973-1974, 1974-1975, and 1975-1976. In late 1975 or early 1976 Ms. Doe was informed that she would not be getting an ABC contract for the academic year 1976-1977. In February or March 1976 she was refused an ABC contract. In May 1976 she signed a contract with the Brisbane Scnool Board for 1976-1977. Subsequently, she contracted with the School Board to teach as a local hire for the 1977-1978 and 1978-1979 years. Ms. Doe is presently a resident of Australia[*].

---

[*] Ms. Doe's husband held an ABC teaching contract for 1975-1976. In December 1975 he quit his employment at ABC and commenced other employment in Australia. He is still employed in Australia.

TOWNLEY & UPDIKE

Equal Employment Specialist
page three

Jane Doe's charge of discrimination involves the failure of ABC to renew her contract in 1976.

She has already made this failure the subject of an EEOC charge (Charge No. 75-0331 TNY3), filed with the New York District Office of EEOC). Ms. Doe requested and obtained a right to sue notice on this charge. She filed suit on this charge on June 27, 1978 in the United States District Court for the Southern District of New York, entitled Doe v. ABC Educational Foundation, Civil Action No. 75-1221 (Wisdom, J.). Ms. Doe was dismissed from that complaint by order entered November 13, 1978 (amended December 8, 1978) because the court lacked subject matter jurisdiction over her complaint (order attached hereto as Exhibit A). The transcript of Judge Wisdom's oral opinion dismissing Ms. Doe from the suit is attached hereto as Exhibit B.

As is clear from the opinion of Judge Wisdom, the act of discrimination of which Ms. Doe complains, failure to hire, is not a continuing violation of Title VII. A failure to hire is an isolated act and not a continuing violation. Smith v. Office of Economic Opportunity, 538 F.2d 226 (8th Cir. 1976); Hilkman v. Queen, 15 FEP Cases 953 (S.D. Ohio 1976); Gautam v. First National City Bank, 425 F. Supp. 579 (S.D.N.Y. 1976); Kennedy v. Braniff Airways, Inc., 403 F. Supp. 707 (N.D. Tex. 1975).

Ms. Doe cannot revive her already judicially determined stale claim by subsequently requesting employment by ABC. Masco v. United Airlines, Inc., 574 F.2d 1127 (3d Cir. 1978); see also, United Airlines v. Evans, 431 U.S. 553 (1977). She appears to argue that the act of which ABC is accused, failure to rehire her in 1976, will continue until she is employed again by ABC. As the court in Kennedy v. Braniff Airways, Inc., supra stated when faced with a similar argument,

> [t]he problem with the plaintiffs' position is that it proves too much. Virtually any violation may be construed as a continuing one. [Citations omitted.] For example, a refusal to hire may be characterized as an act that continues until the person is hired ... the doctrine, if not sharply circumscribed, may be used to undermine the statutorily imposed limitations.

Id. at 709.

Exhibit F (Continued)

TOWNLEY & UPDIKE

Equal Employment Specialist
page 4

Because Ms. Doe has not filed her charge of discrimination in a timely manner, EEOC is without jurisdiction to process this case. 42 U.S.C. §2000e-5(e); <u>United Airlines</u> v. <u>Evans</u>, supra; <u>Olson</u> v. <u>Rembrandt Printing Co.</u>, 511 F.2d 1228 (8th Cir. 1974); <u>Turnow</u> v. <u>Eastern Airlines</u>, 13 FEP Cases 1227 (D.N.J. 1976).

                                        Very truly yours,

                                        Kenneth McCulloch

Exhibit G

EQUAL EMPLOYMENT OPPORTUNITY COMMISSION

Charge Number: 099003000

Ms. Mary Smith
1818 Even Street
Somewhere, Texas 98988   Charging Party

Sample Corporation
3232 Short Street
Somewhere, Texas 98988   Respondent

DETERMINATION

Under the authority vested in me by the Commission's Procedural Regulations, I issue on behalf of the Commission the following determination as to the merits of the subject charge.

All jurisdictional requirements have been met. Charging Party alleged that she was discriminated against by being denied a promotion because of her race (Negro). Examination of the evidence in the record indicates that there is not reasonable cause to believe that this allegation is true. No determination is made as to the promotion of Negroes as a class or any other issues which might be construed as having been raised by this charge.

This dismissal concludes the Commission's processing of this charge. Should the Charging Party wish to pursue this matter further, she may do so by filing a private action in Federal District Court against the Respondent named above, within 90 days of her receipt of this letter and by taking the other procedural steps set out in the enclosed NOTICE OF RIGHT TO SUE.

On Behalf of the Commission:

_____   _____
Date   Jane Evans, District Director

Enclosures: (2)
    Notice of Right to Sue
    Copy of the Charge

Exhibit H

EQUAL EMPLOYMENT OPPORTUNITY COMMISSION
NEW YORK DISTRICT OFFICE
90 CHURCH STREET, ROOM 1301
NEW YORK, NEW YORK 10007
264-7161

CONCILIATION AGREEMENT

In the Matter of:

    U. S. EQUAL EMPLOYMENT OPPORTUNITY COMMISSION

    and

                                    Charge No.

    Charging Party

and

    Respondent

***

Charges having been filed under Title VII of the Civil Rights Act of 1964, as amended, with the U.S. Equal Employment Opportunity Commission, by the Charging Party against the Respondent, the charges having been investigated and reasonable cause having been found, the parties do resolve and conciliate this mastter as follows:

Exhibit H (Continued)

Charge No.

TABLE OF CONTENTS

Section		Page
I	General Provisions	1
II	Charging Party Relief	2
III	Affected Class	3
IV	Affected Class Relief	3,4
V	Affirmative Action Plan	4,5,6
VI	Reporting Provisions	6,7
VII	Signatures	8

Page No. 2

Charge No.

II. CHARGING PARTY RELIEF

1. Respondent agrees to immediately reinstate the Charging Party as an employee in good standing without loss of seniority.

2. Respondent Company will reimburse the Charging Party the amount of back pay which the Charging Party would have received had he not been dismissed, less sums earned elsewhere during the period after discharge. The amount to be paid shall include 6% interest on the base salary.

3. Respondent Company will make those contributions that would normally have been made to the Charging Party's Group Life Insurance Plan, Company Savings Plan, Retirement or Pension Plan, and will restore to the Charging Party all other fringe benefits which would have accrued had he not been dismissed.

4. The Respondent agrees to remove from its records and files any notations, remarks, or other indications evidencing that the service performed by the Charging Party prior to termination were other than or anything less than satisfactory. The Company further agrees that, in furnishing oral or written references concerning the Charging Party as may be requested by same or by prospective future employers, it will mention only the nature and duration of Charging Party's employment.

5. Respondent agrees not to engage in or allow any of its employees to engage in any retaliatory conduct against the Charging Party or any Party to or participant witness to any unlawful employment practice.

6. Respondent will submit to the EEOC any warnings or reprimands given to the Charging Party during the next one (1) year following the effective date of this Agreement and notify the District Director prior to taking any adverse action against Charging Party.

7. Respondent affirms that Charging Party will not be penalized in future considerations for transfers, promotions and other terms and conditions of employment because of these proceedings and that no other potential employers will be advised in any way of the facts or circumstances of these proceedings.

Exhibit H (Continued)

Page No. 3

Charge No.

III. AFFECTED CLASS

The Affected Class shall be defined as all minorities employed with Respondent Company.

IV. AFFECTED CLASS RELIEF

1. Respondent agrees that it shall cause its equal employment policy to be reemphasized to all employees particularly those who perform in a supervisory or lead capacity. The emphasis will go to the extent of requiring all employees to sign a stipulation that the policy has been read and understood.

2. The Company agrees that all minority employees who are in the affected class, as defined herein, will be given the right to transfer into any other department of the Company for which they are qualified or may qualify through training prior to the hiring of new employees into such departments.

3. The Company shall give notice of all job vacancies to all members of affected class by posting in conspicuous places throughout the physical environs a list of all job vacancies together with a description of each job. This notice shall specify the kinds of duties performed and predict as accurately as possible the number of such vacancies for a period of six months immediately following the effective date of this Agreement. The Company will continue to post such job vacancies as they occur in the future.

4. Each such employee who accepts a transfer will be counselled every three months as to necessary additions to his/her skill and experience which are required to entitle him/her to promotion. He/she will be afforded training opportunities on Company time, at Company expense, and at his/her regular rate of pay, which are necessary to qualify him/her for higher position. On the basis of these quarterly reviews, each such employee will be promoted as rapidly as his/her skills and ability permit until such time as he/she reaches the classification and pay of those employees possessing similar qualifications who were initially hired into that department. The results of all quarterly reviews will be in writing.

Exhibit H (Continued)

Page No. 4

Charge No.

5. Upon acceptance of such a transfer, each such employee's job security against layoffs will be maintained. This protection will take the form of transferring his/her seniority developed in the prior department into his/her new department and of continuing to accrue his/her seniority in the prior department for bump back purposes or layoff so that he/she is employed no less frequently while serving in the new department than he/she would have been in the old department.

6. Each member of affected class shall have the right to bid for any entry level job in any department and for any higher level job for which experience in the next lowest job is not needed in order to provide the necessary training to perform the duties required in the higher-rated job.

7. The Company will not require members of the affected classes to spend any period of residence in any job which exceeds the period actually necessary to qualify for movement to a higher-rated job. Further, the Company will not require such employees to spend any residence period longer than that spent by the employee who spent the shortest period of time in residence during the last five years.

8. Respondent agrees to:

    (a) Subsidize any training necessary to prepare members of the affected class for promotion.

    (b) Allow the affected class time off during normal working hours without penalty to attend such training.

V. AFFIRMATIVE ACTION PLAN

Statement of Policy

1. It is the policy of   , to seek and employ qualified personnel in all of its facilities and at all of its locations, to provide equal opportunities for the advancement of employees, including upgrading, promotion and training, and to administer these activities in a manner which will not discriminate against any person because of race, color, religion, sex, or national origin.

Exhibit H (Continued)

Charge No.

Dissemination of Policy and Plan

2. (a) The Statement of Policy and the Affirmative Action Plan will be communicated to all employees through Company publications and communications. It will also be distributed to new employees upon employment.

   (b) Copies of this Plan will be made available to various unions representing employees.

   (c) To insure understanding and continuing implementation of this program, the subject of Equal Employment Opportunity will be discussed during management and supervisory meetings.

   (d) Recruiting sources, community organizations and agencies, secondary schools and colleges will be informed of our nondiscriminatory policy.

Responsibility for Implementation

3. (a) The implementation of the policy is the responsibility of the _____ (title of official) _____ of each facility who shall report directly to the (title of official of) _____

   (b) Supervisory personnel throughout the Company will be responsible to implement the Equal Employment Opportunity Plan at their respective levels.

   (c) Each supervisory will prepare a regular report for top equal opportunity and/or management officials which will cover the E.E.O. Plan in their respective areas of responsibility describing any promotions, selection of new employees and their hourly wages, broken down by race, sex, and national origin.

Selection and Placement

4. (a) Selection of applicants for employment will be the responsiblity of the Personnel Department. Acceptance for actual job placement will be the responsibility of the supervisor, but if the supervisor rejects a referred applicant, a report will be forwarded to personnel outlining in detail the reason for rejection which will be recorded in writing and placed in the individual applicant's file.

Page No. 6

Charge No. TNY

(b) Any hiring standards used for selection such as height, weight, educational levels, previous employment records, etc., will be realistically related to job and progression requirements and will be applied without regard to race, color, religion, sex, or national origin.

(c) Any testing procedures used in the selection placement and upgrading will be validated in accordance with the existing laws.

Training of Employees

5. Supervisors are responsible for on-the-job training related to the immediate job assignment of the employee. Appropriate records of accomplishment will be maintained. Whenever specific on-the-job, as well as off-the-job training programs, are established by management for training in job skills not related to the immediate position, supervisors will encourage minority group and female employees as well as other employees to participate.

6. Importance of the Policy Penalties for Non-Compliance - The importance of fulfilling this policy will be brought to the attention of ___(title of company official)___ for appropriate action including, but not limited to, suspension or discharge.

VI. REPORTING PROVISIONS

1. The Respondent agrees to report in writing to the District Director, Equal Employment Opportunity Commission at _____ concerning the implementation of this Agreement. The first Compliance Reports shall be submitted not later than ninety (90) days from the date of this Agreement. Compliance Reports will be submitted every three (3) months thereafter for a period of two (2) years.

2. The Company shall maintain for at least two (2) years records of personnel assignments and actions and shall allow the Commission, upon reasonable notice, to inspect and copy any or all of such records. The records maintained shall include

Exhibit H (Continued)

Page No. 7

Charge No. TNY

all applications for employment with the Company and any action thereon, all postings of any vacancies, all bids or requests for transfer submitted and the action thereon, all personnel folders, and all periodic reports.

3. Three months after the entry of this Agreement, the Company shall file a report with the EEOC, setting forth the following information:

   (a) A detailed summary of the steps taken in implementation of the program.

   (b) With respect to each member of the affected class who submitted a request to transfer or bid for promotion:

   (1) The name of the employee making the request and choice of department;

   (2) If the action taken on the request is not granted, the reason(s) therefore;

   (3) The jobs worked by the employee during the two-week period following transfer or promotion;

   (4) A report on any disqualifications or elections to return which have occurred with respect to the employee and the reason(s) therefore.

4. Ninety days after the effective date of this Agreement and every three months thereafter for the duration of the Agreement, Respondent will submit a report detailing progress in attaining its hiring, transfer, and promotion goals. Each quarterly report will contain the following information:

   (a) A list of persons transferred identifying each person by name, race, national origin, and sex, showing date of transfer, job transferred from, job transferred to, and the hourly, weekly, or monthly pay rate of both jobs.

   (b) A list of persons promoted, identifying each person by name, race, national origin, and sex, showing date of promotion, job promoted into, job promoted from, and the hourly, weekly, or monthly pay rate of both jobs.

Exhibit H (Continued)

Page No. 8

Charge No. TNY

VII. SIGNATURES

I have read the foregoing Conciliation Agreement and I accept and agree to the provisions contained therein:

Date _____   _____
                              Respondent

Date _____   _____
                              Charging Party

I recommend approval of this Conciliation Agreement:

Date _____   _____
                              Conciliator/Investigator

I concur in the above recommendation for approval of this Conciliation Agreement:

Date _____   _____
                              Supervisor of Conciliations

Approved on behalf of the Commission:

Date _____   _____
                              District Director

Exhibit I

EQUAL EMPLOYMENT OPPORTUNITY COMMISSION

Pleasantville District Office
333 Treelined Street
Pleasantville, Utah 12345

November 30, 1977

In Reply Refer to:
099771234

Ms. Roberta S. Hartley
Director of Industrial Relations
Sample Corporation
1977 Sample Lane
Pleasantville, Utah 12345

Dear Ms. Hartley:

The Commission has determined that its efforts to conciliate this charge have been unsuccessful.

This letter constitutes the notice required by Section 1601.25 of the Commission's Procedural Regulations, which provides as follows:

> "Where the Commission is unable to obtain voluntary compliance as provided by Title VII and it determines that further efforts to do so would be futile or non-productive, it shall, through the appropriate District Director, the Director of the Office of Field Services and the Director of the Office of Systemic Programs, or their designated representatives, so notify the respondent in writing."

No further efforts to conciliate this charge will be made by the Commission.

Sincerely,

Henry Drake
District Director

Exhibit J

PRESENTATION MEMORANDUM
(Direct Suit)*

I. Introductory Information

1. Parties

   a. Respondents (in administrative process)
   b. Defendants (in proposed suit) (identify necessary party defendant by noting: "Necessary Party"; the jurisdiction for same should appear in Part VIII below)
   c. Charging Parties

2. Commission Case No(s). (Only those on which suit is based)
   Commission Charge No(s). (Only those on which suit is based)

3. Location of Facility(ies) (included in the scope of this proposed suit

4. Size of Work force (approximate) (for facilities noted above)

5. Summary of Nature of Proposed Suit (by each basis and issue) (separately for each proposed defendant other than necessary party defendants)

II. Nature of Respondent's Business

1. Business (product, service, etc.)

2. General Scope (describe generally Respondent's _entire_ operations, including total size)

III. Administrative Record

1. Summary Case Processing Chronology (_Dates_ _only_)

   a. (Date) _Charge_ (Filed) (_Not_ received or logged in or deferred, but the exact _filing_ date)

   b. (Date of) _Decision_ or _Determination_ (identify which)

   c. (Date of) _Notification_ _of_ _Conciliation_ _Failure_

   d. (Date) _Right-to-Sue_ (Issued) (if any) (treat _expired_ right-to-sue notices)

* The parenthetical notations herein are included for guidance only and should not be included in Titling.

Exhibit J (Continued)

2. Administrative Record _Narrative_

   a. Charge (if "on behalf of," treat compliance with procedural regulations for same)

   b. Deferral History (or, for Commissioner Charge - Referral)

   c. Decision/Determination (use appropriate one only) (also include "substantial weight" treatment)

   d. Conciliation (treat separately for each Respondent: (1) failure and (2) notification of failure; brief history, noting particularly the date of Respondent('s) last rejection or unacceptable counteroffer, as well as date of _notification_)

      Respondent 1
      Respondent 2, etc.

IV. Comparative Scope of Decision/Determination and Suit (Narrative Style)

   1. (Bases/Issues/Facilities in) Charge

   2. (Bases/Issues/Facilities) Unalleged but _Determined_ or _Decided_ "Cause" [1]

   3. (Bases/Issues/Facilities to be included in) Proposed Suit [2] (If same as #2, simply note "same")

      NOTE: In treating facilities in #1-#3 above, include:

      a. size of work force, of each
      b. (local) unions representing employees and whether the unions are defendants or not; and
      c. treatment of reasoning for expansion to facilities _arguably_ included in scope of Decision/Determination

      Also, where "issue" expansions are proposed, note related charges pending and note whether such issues were treated or arguably treated in conciliation endeavors.

---

[1] Specifically cite separately all "no cause" findings for informational purposes.

[2] Note briefly here, and specifically justify in Section VII, Proof, the _non_-inclusion in the proposed suit of all "cause" findings _not_ recommended for inclusion in the proposed suit.

Exhibit J (Continued)

V. Other Related Action

1. Contract Compliance Check

2. Affirmative Action Plans (include treatment of relative progress or absence of progress)

3. Other Suits against Respondent (private and/or Commission suits whether pending or closed)

   a. Class or individual action

   b. Nature of suit

   c. Present status

4. Pending Charges

   a. Total (for facilities included in *this* proposed suit)

   b. Effect of Suit (here note the pending charges that involve or appear to involve issues raised in this suit and thus are potentially subject to disposal by the resolution of this suit)

5. Prior Conciliation Agreement
   NOTE: also treat:

   a. Related or unrelated to this case?

   b. Present Compliance?

VI. Issues (each legal issue in order appearing below)

1. Alleged Bases/Issues

2. Unalleged But "Cause" Bases/Issues

3. Additional Issues (not treated, or only arguably treated, in the Decision/Determination)

4. Poster-Display Failure (if any) (note whether the failure is referenced in the Decision/Determination)

VII. Proof

1. General EEO Profile and SMSA Data (include historial development of profile) (only for *Bases* covered in proposed suit)

Exhibit J (Continued)

  2. Proof of Issues for Suit (follow exact order of VI, above)[3]

VIII. Unions (Narrative)

  1. Union Respondents (named in charge)

   a. Administrative Treatment (all steps?)

   b. Collective bargaining relationships and agreements

  2. Non-Respondent Unions

   a. Collective bargaining agreements

   b. Necessary Party Defendants (here treat reasons for inclusion or non-inclusion as a necessary party of each uncharged union representing employees of the respondent)

  3. Charging Party Union Names as Necessary Party Defendant (treat reason for realignment, or non-realignment, of union as necessary party defendant)

  4. Referral Unions (here treat justification for inclusion or exclusion of Joint Apprenticeship Committee, contractors' associations, etc.)

IX. Conclusion

---

[3] See n. 2, supra, re justification in this section for non-inclusion in suit of alleged or unalleged "cause" findings.

Exhibit K

EQUAL EMPLOYMENT OPPORTUNITY COMMISSION

Point Barrow District Office
1515 Snowy Street
Point Barrow, Alaska 99999

September 23, 1977

In Reply Refer to:
YPB4-101

Mr. Clifford Party
1818 Open Street
Point Barrow, Alaska   99999

Dear Mr. Party:

Your case has been referred to the Commission's General Counsel for review to determine whether the Commission will bring a civil action in Federal District Court based on your charge. An initial determination should be forthcoming within 30 days.

If the Commission decides to bring a civil action, you have the right to intervene in such an action. If the Commission decides that it will not bring a civil action based on your charge, you will be notified and receive a Notice of Right to Sue, which will entitle you to sue the respondent on your own behalf.

Sincerely,

James Doker
District Director

Exhibit L

XYZ CORPORATION
1495 Main Street
Newtown, New York 10990

Dear Ms. _____:

Sometime ago you filed a charge of discrimination with the Equal Employment Opportunity Commission against our company. Recently we were informed by EEOC that conciliation had failed after the EEOC had investigated your charge and found reasonable cause. A copy of the notice informing us that conciliation failed is enclosed.

As you may have already known, at any time during the course of the administrative process you could have independently filed suit. However, at the time the EEOC administrative process ends, then you will have ninety days to file suit or will be barred from filing suit at all.

The only step which remains before the entire EEOC administrative process is completed is the referral of the case file on your charge by the EEOC District Office to the appropriate office of EEOC to determine whether or not EEOC will litigate on your behalf. The EEOC Procedural Manual indicates that a determination as to whether or not litigation should be undertaken on your behalf by EEOC should be made within thirty days. We have enclosed a copy of the EEOC form letter which you should have received at the time the EEOC District Office referred your charge to the appropriate section for consideration for litigation.

Consequently, thirty days from now, or soon thereafter, the administrative process will have been completed by EEOC, and your ninety-day filing period under Title VII will have commenced.

Sincerely,

Personnel Director
XYZ CORPORATION

Exhibit M

TOWNLEY & UPDIKE

CHRYSLER BUILDING

405 LEXINGTON AVENUE

NEW YORK, N.Y. 10017

TELEPHONE
(212) 682-4567

CABLE: TUCARRO
TELEX: 12-7815

TELECOPIER
(212) 697-3061

JOHN R. SCHOEMER, JR.
JOHN J. LEIGHTON
HOCH REID
EDWARD M. MAHER
ANDREW L. HUGHES
PHILIP D. PAKULA
RONALD S. DANIELS
RICHARD J. BARNES
RICHARD R. LUTZ
JOHN PAUL REINER
PHILIP S. OLICK
MARK D. GERAGHTY
JOHN D. CANONI
RICHARD C. KULLEN, JR.
LEONARD F. BINDER
ROBERT C. MANGONE
WILLIAM O'C. HARNISCH
KENNETH J. McCULLOCH
DOUGLAS C. FAIRHURST
ELLIOT PASKOFF
PEREZ C. EHRICH
JOHN C. SABETTA

J. JEROME MADDEN
COUNSEL

MICHAEL S. BELOHLAVEK
FREDERICK D. BERKON
ROBIN BIERSTEDT
JEFFREY L. BOAK
CARL P. BOWEN
JESSE H. BRENNER
CARL J. CHIAPPA
JEROME P. COLEMAN
MARY D. FAUCHER
KENNETH M. HART
PHILIP L. KIRSTEIN
JAMES K. LEADER
TERENCE J. LYNCH
JAMES D. MADIGAN III
ROBERT LLOYD RASKOPF
NEIL J. ROSINI
NINA SHREVE
MICHAEL S. STONE
SHERRI VENOKUR
ROGER E. WILLIAMS
HARRY H. WISE III

October 10, 1978

CERTIFIED MAIL
RETURN RECEIPT REQUESTED

Abner Sibal, Esq.
General Counsel
Office of the General Counsel
Equal Employment Opportunity Commission
2401 E Street, N.W.
Washington, D.C. 20506

Re: Freedom of Information Act Request

Dear Mr. Sibal:

We represent   , Charge No.
with respect to the charge of
and Civil Action No.

Pursuant to the United States Freedom of Information Act, 5 U.S.C. Section 552 et seq., and the Regulations of The Equal Employment Opportunity Commission, Title 29, Chapter XIV, Part 1610, and Section 83 of the EEOC Compliance Manual, I request personal access to all Charges, files, reports, investigation documents, and other such written materials retained by the EEOC for the Charge which forms the basis of the above referred legal action. I understand that charge to be the one filed by John Q. Doe, as referenced above.

I request to see the entire EEOC case file or other such documents relating to the Charge of Discrimination, including, but not limited to, the following:

Tab A.   Charges and written materials submitted by the charging parties relating to the subject of their charges.

237

TOWNLEY & UPDIKE

Abner Sibal
page two

Tab B.   Jurisdictional items including:

        1. the initial written communication from charging parties;

        2. receipts for service of the charge;

        3. deferral correspondence, if any;

        4. the EEOC Form 131; and

        5. receipt for service of the Form 131 as registered mail for each charge.

Tab C.   Statements of each charging party, including the affadavit, report of initial and subsequent interviews, report of exit interviews, and any follow up letters from the charging parties.

Tab D.   The statements and/or affadavits of each witness interviewed at the request of the charging party or who supported charging party.

Tab E.   The statements and/or affadavits of each of the respondent's witnesses who were interviewed, and any explanations for unsigned statements or incomplete interrogatories.

Tab F.   The written statements of respondent's position and documentation with these written statements.

Tab G.   The documentary evidence gathered from the respondent.

Tab H.   Affadavits and/or statements of any additional witnesses interviewed and copies of any documents submitted by them.

Tab I.   Items listed under "Tour of Facilities," including but not limited to:

        1. observations of any apparent discriminatory pattern in the assignment of jobs or the use of facilities;

        2. summaries of comments made by employees as the investigator passed through various work areas;

Exhibit M (Continued)

TOWNLEY & UPDIKE

Abner Sibal
page three

        3. brochures, pamphlets, etc., explaining the operation and describing the product of the respondent;

        4. organizational charts; and

        5. any diagrams which were made of the respondent's facilities

Tab J.   The EEO-1 forms of the respondent which were available to the District Director and in the investigation file before each Determination and the EEO-1 forms which are available to the Commission presently.

Tab K.   The community background data for each geographic region where a facility of respondent embraced in the proposed suit is located.

Tab L.   Subpoenas where were not issued but for which issuance was contemplated by the District Director, including the circumstances and reasons.

Tab M.   If the Commission contemplated seeking preliminary relief, the memo indicating the reasons such action was contemplated.

Tab N.   All investigator's notes taken during the investigation.

Tab O.   The analysis of the data, including a review of all interviews and pertinent data.

Tab P through X   Any additional materials not covered by the above sections.

Tab Y.   A list of all persons contacted in connection with any of the investigations, including their name, address, race, job connection, and telephone number where they can be reached.

Tab Z.   Any additional evidence which was not included in any other part of the file because the investigator did not feel it was relevant.

Exhibit M   (Continued)

TOWNLEY & UPDIKE
Abner Sibal
page four

    If any documents or materials are not being released, please identify each of these documents, stating a brief description of the document, the date it was prepared, the number of pages of the document, the drafter of the document, and the present custodian of the document, and briefly state the reason(s) why each such document is being withheld from disclosure. Thank you.

                              Very truly yours,

                              KENNETH McCULLOCH

FOOTNOTES

[1] 29 C.F.R. §1601.20.
[2] 398 F. Supp. 300 (M.D. Ga. 1975).
[3] 17 FEP Cases 904 (E.D. Mo. 1978); see also *EEOC* v. *Bell Helicopter Co.*, 426 F. Supp. 785 (N.D. Texas 1976), *aff'd* F.2d (5th Cir. 1980).
[4] 29 C.F.R. §1601.7.
[5] 460 F.2d 1245 (9th Cir. 1972).
[6] 422 F.2d 1028 (9th Cir. 1970), *vacated* 400 U.S. 1004 (1971).
[7] 1 FEP Cases 803 (D. Ariz. 1969).
[8] 400 U.S. 1004 (1971).
[9] 4 EPD (CCH) ¶7577.
[10] 99 S.Ct. 2066, 60 L.Ed. 2d 609 (1979).
[11] 48 U.S.L.W. 4851 (June 23, 1980), 23 FEP Cases 1.
[12] 511 F.2d 1288 (8th Cir. 1975).
[13] 459 F.2d 811 (7th Cir. 1972).
[14] 431 U.S. 553 (1977).
[15] 561 F.2d 1064 (2d Cir. 1977).
[16] 14 FEP Cases 829 (D. Minn. 1976).
[17] See 29 C.F.R. §1601.26(b).
[18] 11 EPD (CCH) ¶10,822 (S.D. Miss. 1976).
[19] 565 F.2d 913 (5th Cir. 1978).
[20] 535 F.2d 533 (9th Cir. 1976), *aff'd* 432 U.S. 355 (1977).
[21] *Idem* at 541.
[22] 563 F.2d 439 (6th Cir. 1977), *cert. denied* 435 U.S. 915 (1978).
[23] This procedure is described in 29 C.F.R. §1601.16.
[24] 74 F.R.D. 523 (D.S.C. 1977).
[25] 431 F.2d 455 (5th Cir. 1970), *reh'g en banc den.* 431 F.2d 455 (5th Cir. 1970).
[26] 501 F.2d 1052 (10th Cir. 1972).
[27] 438 F.2d 32 (4th Cir. 1971).
[28] 412 F.2d 462 (5th Cir. 1969).
[29] EEOC Decision No. 71-332 (Sept. 28, 1970), 2 FEP Cases 1016.
[30] 526 F.2d 802 (8th Cir. 1975).
[31] 320 F. Supp. 58 (D. Colo. 1970).
[32] 420 F. Supp. 244 (D. Md. 1975). See Case Index for subsequent history not related to the decision.
[33] 563 F.2d 439 (6th Cir. 1977).
[34] 358 F. Supp. 870 (D. Colo. 1973).
[35] 483 F.2d 178 (10th Cir. 1973).
[36] 6 EPD (CCH) ¶8980 (W.D. Pa. 1973), *aff'd* 353 F.2d 545 (3d Cir. 1973).
[37] 569 F.2d 315 (5th Cir. 1978).
[38] 444 F.2d 1335 (5th Cir. 1971).
[39] 551 F.2d 456 (D.C. Cir. Ct. of Appeals 1977).

[40] 504 F.2d 1296 (10th Cir. 1974).
[41] 418 F.2d 355 (6th Cir. 1969).
[42] 417 F.2d 1122 (5th Cir. 1969).
[43] Title VII, Section 705(g), 42 U.S.C. §2000e-5(g).
[44] 42 U.S.C. §2000e-5(g).
[45] At 536.
[46] 412 F.2d 462 (5th Cir. 1969).
[47] 431 U.S. 324 (1977).
[48] EEOC *Compliance Manual,* Section 23.2(c)(3).
[49] *Op. cit.,* Section 23.3(b).
[50] 12 FEP Cases 1006 (D. C. Cir. 1976).
[51] 295 F. Supp. 950 (N.D. Ga. 1968), *aff'd* 412 F.2d 462 (5th Cir. 1969).
[52] 2 FEP Cases 50 (N.D. Fla. 1969).
[53] 507 F.2d 160 (5th Cir. 1975).
[54] 5 FEP Cases 1379 (D. Ariz. 1973).
[55] 303 F. Supp. 528 (N.D. Cal. 1969).
[56] 29 U.S.C.A. §161(1), Section 11.
[57] See EEOC Procedural Regulations, 29 C.F.R. 1601.15(b).
[58] 29 C.F.R. §1601.14.
[59] 29 C.F.R. §1601.21(d).
[60] 29 C.F.R. §1601.28(b)(2).
[61] 29 C.F.R. §1601.25.
[62] 29 C.F.R. §1601.28(b).
[63] At Section 83.
[64] 5 U.S.C., Section 552 *et seq.*

Chapter 10

The OFCCP Compliance Review or Complaint Investigation

INTRODUCTION

The Office of Federal Contract Compliance Programs (OFCCP) has jurisdiction over three substantive areas. The first is Executive Order 11246, which prohibits discrimination by federal government contractors and subcontractors on the basis of race, color, religion, sex, or national origin. This is the executive order that forms the foundation for affirmative action compliance programs; its actual language requires that "the contractor will take affirmative action to insure that applicants are employed, and that employees are treated during employment, without regard to their race, color, religion, sex, or national origin."[1] It is OFCCP's interpretation of this executive order that has required employers to make decisions that are cognizant of race, color, religion, sex, or national origin.[2]

The second substantive area of OFCCP's jurisdiction involves the handicapped. The Rehabilitation Act of 1973 required that "in employing persons to carry out such contract the party contracting with the United States shall take affirmative action to employ and advance in employment qualified handicapped individuals. . . ."[3] The regulations of OFCCP[4] have interpreted that statute to mean that the employer must make reasonable accommodation for the handicapped, and that all employees of a government contractor are protected by the provision, not just those employees working on a government contract.

The third substantive area of OFCCP's jurisdiction was created by the Vietnam Era Veterans' Readjustment Act of 1974.[5] This prohibits discrimination against, and requires affirmative action on behalf of, disabled veterans and veterans of the Vietnam era under certain circumstances.

A discussion of these three substantive areas is included in Chapter 1. In this chapter, the procedures implementing these laws and regulations are addressed.

The OFCCP is an agency unique in the civil-rights enforcement field. The reasons for its uniqueness must be understood to enable the government contractor to deal with it effectively.

The first reason is that OFCCP cannot really rely upon a well-developed body of substantive law. OFCCP does have a compliance manual, published by BNA as *Affirmative Action Program Guidelines*. Although the manual does make extensive reference to case law as developed under Title VII or under the Civil Rights Act of 1866,[6] OFCCP accepts legal developments under these statutes only to the extent that they have advanced what OFCCP perceives as favorable principles in employment discrimination law. When unfavorable developments, such as the Supreme Court's decision in *Teamsters* v. *U.S.*,[7] have been established under Title VII, the OFCCP has disavowed these developments. Although some courts have indicated that the basic substantive law as developed under Title VII is equally applicable to Executive Order 11246 (see *U.S.* v. *East Texas Motor Freight, Inc.*),[8] OFCCP has refused to acknowledge this reasoning or follow it. As a consequence, a certain tension has developed in the compliance-review field. On the one hand, when there are favorable legal decisions under Title VII, supporting the position OFCCP desires to put forth, it will cite those cases; on the other, when those principles support the contractor, OFCCP will remind the contractor that its position is that Title VII legal principles do not apply to the executive-order program.

A second way in which OFCCP is unique is that significant procedural and substantive changes are effected by OFCCP only through memos to its representatives in the field. These memos are not ordinarily made known to the contractors. To further complicate the problem, these OFCCP internal directives often allow for a great deal of inconsistent interpretations by its compliance officers. Thus, it is quite possible for a contractor, having conformed to the demands of an OFCCP representative conducting a review—having set up his program, job groups, and so on in a certain way—to see that entire program rejected by another compliance-review officer who comes in the next year.

OFCCP is also unusual in not being a charge-oriented agency. It may initiate a compliance review on the basis of a charge filed with it, but it does not have to have a charge in order to demand access to records or submission of the affirmative action compliance program (AACP), or to conduct an on-site review.

This makes it very difficult for the contractor to orient the compliance review or the complaint investigation.

A fourth uncommon characteristic is that OFCCP is frequently required to commence negotiations only in crisis circumstances, because of the pre-award compliance-review regulations it has established. Situations arise in which a contractor must be awarded a government contract very shortly or not at all. Under such circumstances, OFCCP might demand radical substantive changes, including the payment of back pay for "affected classes," as a condition for finding the contractor awardable. Even though the contractor might vehemently disagree with the legitimacy of the OFCCP claims, it faces the possibility of forfeiting the government contract if it does not comply with the demands.

THE ADMINISTRATIVE STRUCTURE OF OFCCP

The OFCCP field offices report to regional offices and the regional offices report to OFCCP headquarters in Washington, to the director of OFCCP. The director reports to the assistant secretary of labor, Employment Standards Administration, who in turn reports to the secretary of labor. In the event that there is an administrative hearing, the ultimate decision will be made by the secretary of labor. (The secretary has decided few cases under Executive Order 11246—and in the OFCCP compliance manual, Section 14, reserved for "Decisions and Opinions," is empty.) Ultimately, there can be court review of the secretary of labor's decision.

OFCCP involvement can be precipitated in three ways: When a contractor bids for and is awarded a contract of $1 million or more, this automatically triggers a pre-award compliance review; or a contractor can be subjected to a compliance review by OFCCP on a random basis; or OFCCP becomes involved when a complaint is filed by an individual employee or applicant for employment.

Ultimate enforcement of Executive Order 11246 can be initiated by a referral to the Justice Department or EEOC for court-enforcement purposes; or by issuance of an administrative complaint, triggering an administrative hearing before an administrative law judge; or by a "hearing" before the director of OFCCP.

TYPES OF REVIEWS CONDUCTED BY OFCCP

OFCCP frequently changes its procedures, and even the procedural rules and timetables it has set are very loosely interpreted. It has three different review procedures under Executive Order 11246, depending upon whether it is conducting a pre-award review, a complaint investigation, or a regular review. It also has different procedures under the Rehabilitation Act and under the Vietnam Era Readjustment Act. For these reasons, it is difficult to give a detailed chart of the OFCCP administrative process. Any given here might be outdated by the time it reaches the readers. Instead, in this section a summary of each administrative procedure is set forth.

The *pre-award compliance review* is required only under Executive Order 11246. It is initiated only after it is otherwise determined that the contractor is due to be awarded a federal government contract of $1 million or more. The awarding agency notifies OFCCP that the contractor is sure to be awarded such a contract and requests OFCCP clearance for it. If there has been a compliance review by OFCCP within twelve months prior to the request for clearance, and the contractor has been found to be in compliance, there need not be another compliance review and the approval can be given without it.[9] But that is OFCCP's option, not the contractor's right.

Within 30 days of the request for clearance by the agency letting the contract, OFCCP is supposed to find the candidate contractor awardable or nonawardable.[10] Before OFCCP makes that decision, the following procedures take place:

1. A request for the contractor's AACP, to be submitted within 10 days of the request
2. An on-site review
3. If necessary, a deficiency notice and conciliation agreement

As part of the pre-award compliance review, OFCCP will not specifically review compliance with and the existing AACP for the Rehabilitation Act and the Vietnam Era Readjustment Act. However, if there are apparent violations of these statutes uncovered as part of a pre-award compliance review under Executive Order 11246, the compliance officer is supposed to note these deficiencies so that the contractor may be scheduled for a subsequent review on these subjects. It is possible to receive a contract even though the OFCCP review is not yet completed, but in such instances the award is subject to OFCCP's ultimately finding the contractor awardable.

The *complaint investigation* is triggered by a charge, which must be filed within 180 days of the alleged discriminatory act. OFCCP indicated in documents filed in *Reynolds Metals Co.* v. *Rumsfeld*[11] that if the charge has only individual implications, it will be referred to EEOC pursuant to a Memorandum of Understanding between EEOC and OFCCP, and that it will be a charge deemed filed with EEOC and administratively handled *only* in the EEOC forum. It further indicated to that court that it handles only class charges. However, in practice, a charge to OFCCP, be it class or individual, frequently triggers both OFCCP *and* EEOC investigations. A complaint investigation by OFCCP will not only relate to the individual's allegations but also be a regular compliance review.

A *regular compliance review* consists of the same three basic steps in a pre-award compliance review and covers the same areas. However, the regular compliance review is supposed to be completed within 60 days after it has been commenced, the commencement date being the day the affirmative action program was received by OFCCP.[12] Also, the request for the AACP will give the contractor 30 days to submit it,[13] not ten days or less as in a pre-award compliance review. Additionally, the regular compliance review will cover compliance with the Rehabilitation Act and the Vietnam Era Readjustment Act.

Although OFCCP as a rule will grant extensions of time to submit supplemental information after a compliance review has commenced, or allow an extra five days if informed that the AACP is already mailed, it will not generally extend the 30-day time period within which the AACP itself must be submitted. Furthermore, if the proper information is not furnished in timely fashion, a 30-day show-cause notice may be issued at that time.[14]

Even though OFCCP does have part of its resources now devoted to what it calls its "National Programs,"[15] its future plans promise to be far more effective in identifying potential targets for regular compliance reviews. Specifically, OFCCP plans to require that government contractors file detailed annual reports with information regarding not only work force, but also hires, applicants, promotions, and so on, set forth in summary fashion for computer scanning. Computer programs will define the acceptability ranges and determine whether a particular contractor will be selected for a compliance review, if the present intention of OFCCP is accomplished.

THE OFCCP ADMINISTRATIVE PROCESS IN A REGULAR COMPLIANCE REVIEW

Information to be Forwarded by the Contractor

The contractor investigation usually focuses on such areas as recruitment, hiring, selection, placement, adverse effect, testing, selection, promotion, transfer, and termination. A contractor that has a contract or subcontract in an amount of less than $50,000 does not have to have an affirmative action program. Such a contractor will generally be reviewed only if a charge of discrimination has been filed against it.

The Federal Reports Act provides some limitation on the types of information OFCCP can ask contractors to provide. The act requires that a federal agency must have approved by the Office of Management and Budget any reporting requirements that involve requests for the same or similar information from ten or more respondents. Another federal statute that limits OFCCP's authority, but in the substantive area, is Executive Order 11821, dealing with Inflationary Impact Statements. (OFCCP had not complied with this executive order prior to issuing its regulations dealing with backpay and affected classes.)

The basic information sought by OFCCP as part of a compliance review is a copy of the contractor's AACP under Executive Order 11246, including the work-force analysis and supporting data for the AACP, and a copy of the contractor's affirmative action program under the Rehabilitation Act of 1973.

The essential ingredients for an AACP under Executive Order 11246 can be seen in the table of contents to such a program:

(1)	41 C.F.R. §60-1.40(c)	Report of Results of Prior Year's AAP
(2)	41 C.F.R. §60-2.13(a)	Development or Reaffirmation of EEO Policy
(3)	41 C.F.R. §60-2.13(b)	Internal and External Dissemination of Policy
(4)	41 C.F.R. §60-2.13(c)	Establishment of Responsibilities for Implementation of the AAP
(5)	41 C.F.R. §60-2.11(a)	Work Force Array
(6)	41 C.F.R. §60-2.11(b)(1)	Minority Availability Analysis
(7)	41 C.F.R. §60-2.11(b)(2)	Female Availability Analysis
(8)	41 C.F.R. §60-2.13(d)	Identification of Problem Areas by Organizational Units and Job Group
(9)	41 C.F.R. §60-2.12(d)	Establishment of Goals and Timetables
(10)	41 C.F.R. §60-2.13(f)	Action Programs to Attain Goals and Objectives
(11)	41 C.F.R. §60-2.13(g)	Internal Audit and Reporting Systems
(12)	41 C.F.R. §60-2.13(h)	Compliance of Personnel Policies and Practices
(13)	41 C.F.R. §60-2.13(i)	Support of Programs to Improve Employment Opportunities of Minorities and Women
(14)	41 C.F.R. §60-2.13(j)	Consideration of Women and Minorities Not Currently in the Work Force
(15)	41 C.F.R. §60-50	Compliance with Religion or National Origin Discrimination Guidelines

and "Appendices and Exhibits, including collective bargaining agreements, to Support the AACP."

Items 2 and 3 in such programs are fairly standard. Later in this chapter, there is a commentary on these subjects, checklists showing what should be included in the AACP under these headings, and samples of how these subjects can be covered. Items 5 through 9 are discussed below, under "The OFCCP Administrative Process for a Complaint Investigation."

The requirements for an affirmative action program in compliance with the Rehabilitation Act of 1973 or the Vietnam Era Readjustment Act are far less onerous. Such programs must include (1) a statement of purpose and policy, (2) provisions for dissemination of policy, (3) provisions for notice to labor organizations, (4) assignment of responsibility for implementation of the policy, and (5) a statement regarding recruitment, facilities, and subcontracts. There are no goal and timetable requirements imposed by these statutes.

The Desk Audit

The compliance officer will evaluate the data supplied by the contractor during the desk audit. The OFCCP compliance manual advises compliance personnel to focus on jobs in which minorities or women appear to be underutilized as well as those in which protected groups appear to be concentrated. If minorities or women are inordinately and consistently absent from a particular job title in relation to their availability, the contractor may be requested to set specific goals and timetables for protected-group employment in that job title, separate from the goals for broader groups. Other areas that are reviewed include the applicant flow data; hiring, promotion, and transfer if the analysis represents underutilization of protected groups; and testing and selection procedures, including qualifications requirements that may have an inhibiting effect on the initial hire or transfer of women or minorities. The compliance officer may also look at the collective-bargaining agreement, which may provide evidence that protected group members had the opportunity to advance freely.[16]

During the desk audit, potential problem areas will be identified, and the compliance officer may request additional information in those areas in preparation for the on-site review.

The On-Site Review

At the second stage of the compliance review, a notice that gives the scheduled time for the on-site review and requests additional information is sent to the contractor. The contractor is required to supply the information requested.[17] However, both the C.F.R. and the OFCCP compliance manual caution compliance personnel to limit requests for information to that which is relevant to the preliminary problem determinations made during the desk audit. On occasion, it may be necessary to request information in areas not previously identified in order to properly review problem areas; but the request for information should not usually exceed the scope of the problem areas identified during the desk audit. Furthermore, requests for additional data during the on-site review should be limited to information that is directly related to pertinent issues discovered during the on-site review. Also, compliance officers should not request validation studies for tests or selection processes if they do not have an adverse impact on protected groups.[18]

Attempts by the compliance officer to expand the scope of the investigation beyond those areas identified as potential problems are very difficult to counteract. One of the least defensible positions a contractor has is refusal to permit access to documents or information. The contractor that attempts this risks a show-cause notice and contract debarment. Even though neither the C.F.R. nor the OFCCP Compliance Manual authorize compliance personnel to examine areas not identified as reflecting potential problems, the fact is that they are entitled to examine what they feel is relevant.

Before meeting with the contractor's representatives, the compliance officer is supposed to note apparent violations that become evident during the desk audit, canvas the community for information about the contractor, contact the local EEOC office to determine whether there are outstanding any pending issues involving the contractor, and also contact other federal and state agencies to determine their experience with the contractor. Then the officer conducts an initial meeting with corporate CEO or person designated by the CEO and advises about the nature of the compliance review.[19]

If apparent deficiencies require further analyses after the on-site review is completed, the compliance officer indicates the areas of concern and obtains any additional information necessary for a final compliance determination. After the officer completes the review, the contractor receives written notification of all the apparent violations. If this is a deficiency notice, the compliance officer then incorporates any commitments the contractor makes to take corrective action into a conciliation agreement signed by the contractor.[20] If the deficiencies are minor, however, the contractor may correct them merely by sending a commitment letter.

The compliance review should usually be completed within 60 days from the date the OFCCP received the affirmative action program and work-force analyses. This includes the desk audit, on-site review, off-site analysis if conducted, and notification of compliance or issuance of a show-cause order.[21]

The Period Covered and the Records to be Made Available

As in EEOC cases, the relevant time period will vary, depending on the facts of the particular case and the issues involved. If the contractor underwent a compliance review in the recent past, the period covered by the current review may be only a year or two.

Although there is no set time period to determine relevancy, it is helpful to know that OFCCP considers a violation of Executive Order 11246 to be a breach of contract having a six-year statute of limitations. However, OFCCP has also indicated that it will seek back pay only for a period of two years prior to the finding of noncompliance, or, in the case of willful violations, for a period of three years. These two- and three-year limitation periods were adopted for consistency with the other segments of the U.S. Department of Labor, which had administered the Fair Labor Standards Act.

Ironically, there is no requirement under Executive Order 11246 for a contractor to keep past affirmative action programs and the support data for such programs. The contractor need only have its current AACP and the AACP for the preceding year. The contractor that keeps past AACP's unnecessarily does so at its peril, because those records may identify "affected classes."

OFCCP regulations require the contractor, or an applicant for or recipient of federal assistance involving a construction contract, to maintain and supply on request records that are necessary for the administration of Executive Order 11246. Furthermore, OFCCP can specify the form in which such records must be kept, within reasonable limits. The limitation on this power is the Federal Reports Act, described previously in this chapter. Failure to file the reports requested accurately, completely, and timely can constitute noncompliance with the contractor's obligation under the equal-opportunity clause and is grounds for the imposition of sanctions.[22]

The data that must be made available to the compliance officer are whatever is needed for an in-depth analysis of apparent inadequacies in the contractor's utilization of minorities or women, any relevant information necessary for a compliance determination in accordance with Executive Order 11246 that is not adequately treated in the affirmative action program, and any information that is necessary for a thorough appreciation of data that are a part of the affirmative action program or offered in support of it.[23]

It is important to note that the C.F.R. specifically provides that the request to maintain and furnish records in a specified form must be "within reasonable limits." This phrase acts as a limitation upon the record-keeping demands (including format) that can be made on a contractor.

There is an ongoing attempt by OFCCP to pressure contractors to computerize AACP data, and write special programs to assist the compliance officers as part of a compliance review. But there is no legal requirement to computerize the data, and a contractor who does not do so is not in noncompliance—despite the fact that it might take weeks for a compliance officer to analyze the data—as long as the necessary data are kept.

Private Interviews with Contractor's Employees

The compliance officer will ask to speak to the contractor's employees privately, during working hours and while they are being paid by the contractor. It is inadvisable to permit this, for the reasons discussed in Chapter 10. The compliance officer will point out that 41 C.F.R. §60-1.32 prohibits the intimidation of witnesses and will claim that the presence of a contractor's representative will have an inhibiting and intimidating effect on the employee. However, the employer can insist on the right to have a representative present at the interview. The OFCCP regulations and compliance manual instruct compliance personnel to develop mutually agreed-upon procedures for interviewing witnesses;[24] there is nothing in any of the OFCCP regulations or compliance manuals that prohibits a contractor from having a representative present, and there is no known instance where the contractor's insistence at having its representative present led to issuance of a show-cause notice. The compliance officer may advise the contractor that it may be necessary to interview some of the witnesses after hours; however, it is unlikely that the officer will conduct very many after-hours interviews.

The Deficiency Letter

When the on-site review and off-site analysis are completed, the compliance officer schedules an "exit conference." At this time, the compliance officer gives the contractor a copy of the deficiency letter, a written summary of all the deficiencies discovered during the compliance review.[25] Frequently, the deficiencies will be discussed orally and the letter will follow.

During the exit conference, the compliance officer explains and discusses the violations contained, or to be contained, in the deficiency letter. Possible alternative solutions to the problems are also discussed. The compliance officer tries to persuade the contractor to agree to the proposed remedial action within a specified time. Any agreements reached where the violation had involved back pay, affected classes, or the refusal to produce documents or information will be included in a written conciliation agreement.

The Show-Cause Letter

Whenever a compliance agency contemplates administrative enforcement action, it must issue a show-cause letter to the contractor involved unless a conciliation agreement has been violated, in which case a show-cause letter does not have to be issued.[26] The show-cause letter gives the contractor 30 days to show cause why enforcement proceedings should not be initiated. The letter advises the contractor of those sections of Executive Order 11246, and of the regulations, that the contractor is allegedly violating and contains a summary of the corrective actions the contractor must take to be found in compliance. Where appropriate, the show-cause letter will advise the contractor of the principles and concepts of an acceptable remedy or the results that are expected.[27]

The show-cause letter also requests that the contractor respond in writing to the findings. The response may include commitments to undertake corrective action as well as opposing facts and evidence.[28] The contractor should present evidence rebutting the compliance agency's findings, but should be careful to limit its rebuttal to those allegations contained in the letter. The show-cause letter frequently contains also a suggested date for a conciliation conference.

If a contractor fails to show that enforcement proceedings should not be initiated, the compliance agency will ask the director to begin enforcement proceedings.

The significance of the show-cause letter is that it signifies to awarding agencies that the contractor is not awardable. This is discussed later in this chapter.

The Conciliation Agreement

The conciliation agreement is a written document signed by the contractor that specifies the contractor's areas of noncompliance, the exact action that must be taken to correct the violations, and the dates by which corrective action must be taken. The time period involved will be the minimum needed to effect the necessary action. After the agreement is approved, the contractor may be considered in compliance as long as it faithfully adheres to the terms of the agreement.[29]

The emphasis in OFCCP regulations is on achieving compliance through informal conciliation meetings. This means that the contractor will usually have a better chance to reach a favorable agreement through conciliation than would be possible if the violations were the subject of enforcement proceedings. However, a conciliation agreement will not preclude a future determination of noncompliance if there is a finding that the commitments made are not sufficient to achieve compliance.[30]

The attempted resolution of deficiencies through the creation of a conciliation agreement often causes an impasse to be reached, not because the parties disagree on the substantive provisions, but because OFCCP insists that certain standard language be incorporated into the conciliation agreement. In fact, hundreds of thousands of dollars have been committed by contractors for distribution to persons in "affected classes," but that money has never been distributed because the parties have been unable to agree on language. Because this is such a troublesome area, some direction to contractors may be helpful concerning certain of the standard provisions of a conciliation agreement. Thereafter, we discuss ways to try to avoid having to enter into a conciliation agreement.

As a general rule, it is inadvisable for contractors to enter into conciliation agreements without knowing exactly what their commitments are: the exact amount of money to be paid out, the specific identity of the persons who are to receive that money, the way those persons are to be notified, and the disposition of the money if they cannot be notified.

OFCCP has a standard "Part I" for every conciliation agreement. The area director, or the compliance officer, is not authorized to change this standard Part I. Nevertheless, the problems which this situation creates can be addressed by other means.

The first provision of "Part I" that creates a problem is that paragraph of the conciliation agreement which reads as follows:

> This agreement does not constitute an admission by (Name of Contractor) of any violation of (Executive Order 11246, as amended/ Section 503 of the Rehabilitation Act of 1973, as amended/Section 402 of the Vietnam Era Veterans Readjustment Act of 1974).

Not only is this provision mandatory, according to the OFCCP Compliance Manual, for every conciliation agreement, but it is in and of itself a fallback position for the compliance officers. They are actually directed to "always endeavor to have the contractor admit the violation(s) set forth in Part II of the conciliation agreement."[31]

A contractor should not admit that it has discriminated because that admission can be used against it in a different forum. Nothing prevents persons from receiving money under the conciliation agreement *and* filing a suit under Title VII or some other statute to seek to recover even more money.[32]

The problem with this standard paragraph required by OFCCP is that the non-admission clause does not go far enough. It does not say that the agreement also does not constitute an admission of violation of "any other federal, state, or local law, rule, or regulation." The contractor should get that language into the non-admission clause. It can accomplish this by contacting OFCCP's legal department in Washington, D.C. and asking them to authorize the Area Director to include this language in the non-admission clause.

The second standard provision of "Part I," which causes a problem states:

> The provisions of this agreement will become part of the (Name of Contractor) AAP.[33]

This provision is a problem because it means that the conciliation agreement must be made available to the employees, unions, and the public through the Freedom of Information Act. In fact, there is a specific regulation of OFCCP that requires that conciliation agreements *must* be made available to the public through the Freedom of Information Act.[34]

The third standard provision that creates a problem is that mandatory portion of "Part I," which states:

> However, the (Name of Contractor) is advised that the commitments contained in this agreement do not preclude future determinations of noncompliance based on a finding that the commitments are not sufficient to achieve compliance.[35]

Read literally, this means that a contractor could pay out $1,000 to each person identified as a member of an affected class, have a full waiver and release from these persons, and still have OFCCP return six months later and claim that $1,000 each was not enough, that the contractor should have given $1,500 each, and that if it does not it will be found in noncompliance.

The Area Director or the compliance officer cannot change this language. The OFCCP will not change this language. However, the OFCCP will give the contractor a side agreement, in the form of a letter, stating that no further relief will be sought by OFCCP for the deficiencies noted during the course of the compliance review.

The fourth and fifth provisions of the standard OFCCP conciliation agreement are contained in one long paragraph which provides as follows:

> If at any time in the future, OFCCP believes that the (Name of Contractor) has violated any portion of this agreement, (Name of Contractor) will be promptly notified of that fact in writing. This notification will include a statement of the facts and circumstances relied upon in forming that belief. In addition, the notification will provide the (Name of Contractor) with 15 days to respond in writing except where OFCCP alleges that such a delay would result in irreparable injury. It is understood that enforcement proceedings for violation of this agreement may be initiated at any time after the 15-day period has elapsed (or sooner, if irreparable injury is alleged) without issuing a show cause notice. It is recognized that where OFCCP believes that the (Name of Contractor) has breached the conciliation agreement, evidence regarding the entire scope of the (Name of Contractor) alleged noncompliance which gave rise to the show cause notice from which this conciliation agreement resulted (where no show cause notice was issued, delete the words "which gave rise to the show cause notice") in addition to evidence regarding the (Name of Contractor) alleged violation of the conciliation agreement, may be introduced at the enforcement proceedings. It is further recognized that liability for violation of this agreement may subject the (Name of Contractor) to sanctions set forth in Section 209 of the Executive Order and appropriate relief.[36]

This paragraph is a problem because it does not make clear what rights the contractor is waiving. For example, does it mean that if OFCCP thinks the agreement has been breached that it can deny future government contracts to the contractor without offering it the opportunity for a hearing? This paragraph is also a problem because it leaves unclear what the remedy would be if OFCCP feels there is noncompliance with the agreement. Can it seek relief above and beyond that to which the contractor has committed in the conciliation agreement, or is it restricted to seeking specific performance?

Though OFCCP will not change this language, it will give the contractor a side agreement which indicates that even if OFCCP does feel there has been a breach, it will only seek specific performance of the agreement and that the only procedural right being waived is that to the show cause notice prefatory to other administrative action. Since the show cause notice is really only a last chance notice to conciliate, and since other provisions of the standard OFCCP conciliation agreement provide for notice to the contractor prior to any action in the event the OFCCP feels there has been a breach of the agreement, this is not a waiver of a substantial right for most contractors.

In addition to the problems noted above regarding the standard provisions of "Part I" of OFCCP Conciliation Agreements, there is a requirement that a standard paragraph regarding "ETA Linkage" be included in any conciliation agreement, regardless of the nature of the deficiency found during the course of a compliance review. The paragraph is as follows:

> The contractor will hire qualified minority and female applicants referred by the State Employment Service in sufficient numbers to meet the goals and timetables established in their Affirmative Action Program. In addition, if disabled veterans, Vietnam Era veterans, and handicapped persons are referred, and openings exist, the contractor will agree to hire from these protected group members so as to comply with their affirmative action obligation under existing regulations at 41 C.F.R. Section 60-250 and 741.

The letters "ETA" stand for Employment Training Administration. This standard paragraph is dangerous. In the beginning of this book we indicated that there was a general movement by the government to have private employers assume public functions. Thus, in the ideal world envisioned by the government, there will be no "hard-core unemployables" because these persons will be on the payrolls of private employers as part of "affirmative action programs."

The "ETA Linkage" paragraph is dangerous because it literally requires that the employer not only hire minorities and females to achieve its goals and timetables, but that the employer hire those particular minorities and females whom the State Employment Service refers to it.

This government program is rather simple. Through conciliation agreements, have government contractors committed to hiring those persons (minorities, females, handicapped, and Vietnam era veterans, for the present) who are referred by the state employment services. Through the federal funding mechanism (state employment services receive substantial federal funds, provided they fulfill certain conditions), establish the priorities the state should follow in referring persons to employers operating under affirmative action programs. It becomes quite simple, then, for the federal government to substantially determine the identity of those persons who will be employed and the jobs in which they will be employed. Furthermore, a change in the priorities can be accomplished without legislation, but merely through the administrative rules making process.

Because of all the problems raised by the conciliation agreement process, it is best to resolve deficiencies in some other way. One way to do so is by a *letter of commitment*. A letter of commitment must be dated, signed by the authorized official of the contractor, specify the deficiencies, specify the corrective actions that will be undertaken, and indicate when they will be completed.[37] It does not have to contain all the problem provisions previously described.

Generally, OFCCP will not permit deficiencies to be corrected by a letter of commitment if (a) there has already been a show cause notice issued; (b) an affected class has been identified; or (c) the deficiency was the failure to submit an AAP at all.

Occasionally there will be a particular complainant who has been identified by OFCCP as the victim of discrimination and, as such, entitled to backpay and other remedial relief. This situation would normally call for a written conciliation agreement. However, it is feasible for the contractor to settle with the complainant, with the approval of OFCCP, and have this settlement cause the withdrawal of the complaint. Thereafter, other deficiencies noted during the investigation may be susceptible of resolution by a letter of commitment rather than a conciliation agreement.

THE OFCCP ADMINISTRATION PROCESS FOR A PRE-AWARD COMPLIANCE REVIEW

Pre-award compliance reviews are basically the same as a standard compliance review, with some minor variations. In addition to those differences previously noted in this chapter, the other basic differences are that there does not have to be a desk audit,[38] and a show cause letter cannot be issued without the specific approval of the Director of OFCCP.[39]

THE OFCCP ADMINISTRATIVE PROCESS FOR A COMPLAINT INVESTIGATION

When the OFCCP receives a complaint, it may either process the complaint or, in appropriate circumstances, refer it to the Equal Employment Opportunity Commission for processing under Title VII. If it elects to refer the complaint to the EEOC, the OFCCP promptly notifies the complainant and the contractor of the referral.[40]

When the OFCCP retains the complaint, it thoroughly evaluates all the allegations and develops a case file, which contains such information as the names of persons interviewed, their statements, copies of relevant documents, and reference to at least one covered contract. If the OFCCP investigation does not show a violation of the equal-opportunity clause, it must notify the director of the OFCCP of this. The director may review the findings and request further investigation.[41]

If the investigation reveals a violation of the equal-opportunity clause, attempts will be made to resolve the matter informally through a compliance conference. If the violation is not resolved by informal means, the director may begin administrative enforcement proceedings to enjoin the violation, obtain appropriate relief, such as back pay, and impose appropriate sanctions.[42] However, 30 days before the OFCCP starts administrative enforcement proceedings, it will issue a show-cause notice that provides the contractor with the opportunity to show why enforcement action should not be taken.[43]

DEALING WITH OFCCP WHEN ISSUES CANNOT BE RESOLVED

As we have seen, a contract award of over $1 million must be approved by OFCCP only after review of the contractor's affirmative action program. When the award or disallowance of any contract, whether or not it is over $1 million, is imminent, OFCCP and the compliance agencies have been able to "negotiate" for innovative programs, higher goals and improved timetables, back pay for affected classes, and so on. This is because without approval of the AACP, OFCCP can and will cause the contractor to be "passed over," or declared "unawardable" or "nonresponsible." Agency executives within OFCCP have indicated that they do not enjoy this "crisis" negotiating, but it has become a common practice.

Three basic approaches have been followed successfully to retain the status of an awardable contractor under Executive Order 11246 while the case is awaiting hearing. The first approach, and the simplest, is to tender compliance and on such basis be found awardable. This is called "comply and contest."[44] The result will be that while the contractor is awaiting a hearing, no adverse contract actions will be taken against it. Ironically, tendering compliance does not have to equate to complying. For example, in *American Cyanamid Co. v. Roudebush*,[45] the issue presented was whether or not American Cyanamid discriminated against a particular individual. OFCCP claimed that it had and demanded $5,000 in back pay. In affidavits submitted to the court by the acting director of OFCCP, Diane Graham, OFCCP claimed that the provisions of the C.F.R. could be fulfilled by placing the money in escrow rather than giving it over to the employee.

A more common usage of "comply and contest" involves the setting of goals, or acknowledgement of underutilization. In these instances, the contractor submits a program that satisfies OFCCP and has this program accepted. Thereafter, within ten days after submitting the acceptable program, the contractor indicates that it disagrees with the demands of OFCCP as they had been incorporated in the affirmative action program, and demands a hearing. During the intervening period, between the "comply and contest" letter and the hearing, the contractor need not perform according to the commitments included in the affirmative action program.

One problem with the "comply and contest" approach, from both the contractor's and OFCCP's viewpoints, is that it takes a long time to receive a hearing. Some cases in which the "comply and contest" were initiated in 1976 have still not been set for a hearing, and the whole affirmative action effort of the contractor is in a state of suspension. In fact, the author knows of no cases in which there has ever been a hearing when the contractor has utilized the "comply and contest" alternative.

A second matter in which a contractor can avoid being denied a government contract while it is awaiting a hearing is by seeking a letter of "substantial issue of law or fact."[46] This approach requires extensive preparation of the presentation to the director of OFCCP, indicating the reasons that the issue of conflict between the contractor and OFCCP justifies the issuance of such a letter. If such a letter is issued, OFCCP will find the contractor to be awardable until the issue can be resolved by hearing or otherwise. The most common situation in which these letters are granted is one in which there is an "affected class," OFCCP is demanding back pay, and the contractor refuses to pay such back pay. Unfortunately, these letters of substantial issue of law or fact are not published, and it is very possible that the director will deny such a letter to one employer, yet grant it to another on the same basis and similar facts.

The OFCCP Compliance Manual specifically recognizes the "comply and contest" and "letter of substantial issues" approaches for contractors in a preaward situation.[47]

The third, and least desirable alternative is to proceed with an action for a preliminary injunction, as in *Pan American World Airways, Inc.* v. *F. Ray Marshall et al.*[48]

Maintaining status as an awardable contractor pending an administrative or judicial hearing on the merits is especially important because of the long time lag between issuances of an administrative complaint and the ultimate determination by an administrative hearing officer. This time lag varies from one to three years, depending upon the area of the country in which the contractor is located. During this period, unless the contractor has proceeded in one of the three ways indicated above to ensure its awardability status, not only will the contractor be unawardable for direct government contracts, but its status as a government subcontractor will also be jeopardized. In fact, under certain rules and regulations published by the General Services Administration, it is very possible that a contractor under "show cause" will not even be notified of possible contracts on which it might be interested in bidding. The same might occur, in a much more informal manner, in the private sector, with the result that the employer will not be considered for subcontracts on major government contracts let to other employers.

Given the seriousness of the situation, it is noteworthy that the issue of whether a contractor can be de facto debarred pending administrative hearing has never been passed on by a circuit court of appeals. One reason is that the Department of Labor has been able to gain substantial benefit by its threat of pass-over. Rather than seek reversal of the numerous lower-court decisions enjoining it from the practice, the department has persisted in the practice even in jurisdictions where a district court had previously enjoined it in a particular case. OFCCP has lost in court more than 40 times on this issue. One case in which the OFCCP had tried to have a contractor debarred de facto did go to the U.S. Court of Appeals for the Seventh Circuit; ironically, OFCCP did not appeal the lower-court order restraining it from causing the contractor to be denied contracts pending hearing. In that case. *Illinois Tool Works* v. *F. Rav Marshall*[49] the appellate court granted the contractor's request that OFCCP be restrained from publishing its name as a contractor not in compliance with Executive Order 11246.

SUBSTANTIVE PROBLEM AREAS

The heart of any affirmative action program under Executive Order 11246 is the goals-and-timetables concept. There are three discrete steps in this process: the establishment of job groups, the utilization analysis, and the establishment of goals and timetables for those job groups for which the contractor must acknowledge underutilization.

Job Grouping

The first step in establishing goals and timetables is job grouping. The OFCCP compliance manual[50] says that job groups should be composed of one or more jobs having similar content, wage rates, and opportunities. A fourth factor that must also be considered in job grouping is the availability, to the government and the contractor, of demographic data for the job group as a whole. Thus, even though bookkeepers may, in a particular situation, meet all three criteria to be grouped with accountants, if the external availability data are quite different for a bookkeeper and for an accountant, then it would be difficult to group bookkeepers with accountants. Finally, one more factor to be considered in grouping jobs (although it more frequently arises as an affected-class problem) is difference in utilization patterns. Thus, predominantly male clerical jobs should not be grouped with predominantly female clerical jobs.

As can be expected, grouping jobs is quite often very subjective, and the manner in which jobs are grouped can very substantially affect the entire utilization analysis and the goals and timetables for the OFCCP. Thus, if a contractor has a substantial number and percentage of minorities and females who are bookkeepers but a very low representation of minorities and females among its accounting staff, it is very likely that the contractor would want to group bookkeepers with accountants. In this way, the representation of minorities and females in the job group will be substantially enhanced, and the contractor may show no underutilization. In such a situation, there will not have to be a goal and timetable set for that job group; alternatively, there may be a minimal underutilization, and the contractor can make relatively modest commitments for hiring and promotion to correct it.

The government compliance officers are well aware of the importance of proper job grouping and the abuses that can occur in job grouping. In fact, the officers are required to note concentrations of minorities and females and, on no other basis than that, require that a particular job title be taken out of that job group.[51] Once that is done, the absence of minorities and/or females in that job group will become apparent, and the government compliance officers will identify it as a "focus job group" and mandate that special affirmative action be taken on behalf of minorities and/or females for that job group.

In job grouping, the contractor should very definitely use a systematic basis or method. Thus, as a first step, contractors might break down all job titles into the various EEO categories (those identified on the EEO-1 form). Then they will not put a job title from one EEO category into a job group with job titles from another EEO category. Although this is not required by the government regulations, it is a generally accepted practice, as is establishing job groupings through the use of salary grades or earnings ranges, and function.

A compliance officer reviewing job groupings is very likely to ask that jobs be grouped differently. When faced with such a request, the contractor should ask for a rationale for the proposed grouping. If that rationale applied to other job groups would cause irrational groupings, it can be shown to be unreasonable.

A contractor that has had its job groups approved during the course of a prior compliance review should be very apprehensive about changing those approved job groups. An exception might be a situation in which the essential nature of a job title has changed, so that it would be more appropriate in a different job group. In such a situation, the compliance officer who wants the job groupings changed will be at a distinct disadvantage and should have to explain why he or she feels the modification is necessary.

If a contractor has many similar facilities in different parts of the country, at one of which a compliance officer has approved job groupings, and the contractor feels the groupings are reasonable and beneficial, then it is probably advisable to apply the approved groupings to the other facilities that have the same function. If there is a review of the other facilities, the job groupings approved by the compliance officer in the first review should control for the other facilities if they are essentially the same as the first. At a minimum, following such an approach will require OFCCP to resolve its own conflicts internally. If necessary, the contractor should push OFCCP to be consistent. Thus, if the director of one OFCCP office insists that jobs be grouped in a certain way, and they have been grouped differently in an affirmative action program previously approved by a different office, the contractor may find it advisable to ask that the directors of the areas in which the two facilities are located contact each other and reach agreement. OFCCP has had various "national" programs to achieve such uniformity for large employers throughout all their facilities, but these programs have been spottily pursued. By inducing the contacts indicated, the contractor can achieve what it and OFCCP would ultimately desire.

A sample job grouping that was approved and commended by OFCCP is shown below.

Batch Bread Job Groups

		Total	Minority	Female
1A	General Manager	1	–	–
	Accounting/Administration Mgr.	1	–	–
	Operations Manager	1	–	–
	Office Manager	1	–	–
		4	–	–
1B	Data-Processing Supervisor	1	–	1
	Accounts Receivable Supervisor	1	–	1
	Production Superintendent	1	–	–
	Assistant Superintendent	1	1	–
	Assistant Supervisor	1	–	–
	Garage Superintendent	1	–	–
	Engineer Supervisor	1	–	–
	Assistant Supervisor Engineer	1	–	–
	Management Trainee	1	–	–
		9	1	2
4A	District Sales Manager	4	–	–
	Sales Supervisor	8	–	–
	Route Sales Representative	66	2	–
	Special Delivery Driver	6	–	–
		84	2	–
4B	Thrift Store Manager	6	–	6
	Thrift Store Clerk	4	–	4
		10	–	10
5	Accounts Payable Clerk	1	–	1
	Executive Secretary	1	–	1
	Order Clerk	2	1	2
	Accounts Receivable Clerk	3	–	1
	Payroll Clerk	1	–	1
	Keypunch Operator	2	–	2
	Settlement Clerk/Cashier	1	1	1
	Receptionist	1	–	1
	Purchasing Agent	1	–	–
		13	2	10
6A	Floor Leader, Lead Checker	14	7	–
6B	Mechanic	6	–	–
	Assistant Mechanic	3	1	–
	Mechanic Helper	2	–	–
		11	1	–
6C	Dough Mixer	6	–	–
	Sponger (Dough Mixer)	3	1	–
	Oven Operator	5	1	–
		14	2	–

Batch Bread Job Groups

		Total	Minority	Female
6D	Bread Wrapper, Machine Operator	16	4	–
	Bench Hand, Machine Operator	13	4	–
		29	8	–
7	Transport Dock Checker	5	1	–
8	Loader/Shipper	10	2	1
	Packer	5	1	1
	Driver	2	–	–
	Freezer Operator	3	–	–
	Sanitor	13	6	1
		32	9	3
9	Racker Feeder[a]	14	5	10
10	Truck Washer[a]	5	–	–

[a]In submitting these job groups, the contractor had originally included the "racker feeder" and the "truck washer" job titles within job group 8. OFCCP had demanded that they be listed separately because racker feeders have substantial concentrations of females, and truck washers have substantial concentrations of males.

The Utilization Analysis

Once jobs have been grouped, it becomes necessary to compare the percentage of minorities and females in those job groups with the percentage available to the employer to be utilized in them. This comparison is called the utilization analysis, or sometimes, underutilization analysis.

Like the grouping of jobs, the utilization analysis allows for a certain amount of discretion. The OFCCP regulations describe what factors are to be considered in determining whether there is an underutilization of minorities or females.[52] In the case of minorities, the government regulations say the contractor should consider (1) the minority population of the labor area surrounding the facility; (2) the size of the minority unemployment in the labor area surrounding the facility; (3) the percentage of the minority work force, as compared with the total work force, in the immediate labor area; (4) the general availability of minorities having requisite skills in the immediate area; (5) the availability of minorities having requisite skills in an area in which the contractor can reasonably recruit; (6) the availability of promotable and transferable minorities within the contractor's organization; (7) the existence of training institutions capable of training people in the requisite skills; and (8) the degree of training the contractor is reasonably able to undertake as a means of making all job classes available to minorities.

In determining whether or not females are underutilized, the government has indicated that eight slightly different factors are to be taken into consideration: (1) the size of the female unemployment force in the labor area surrounding the facility; (2) the percentage of the female work force as compared with the total work force in the immediate labor area; (3) the general availability of women having requisite skills in the immediate labor area; (4) the availability of women having requisite skills in an area in which the contractor can reasonably recruit; (5) the availability of women seeking employment in the labor or recruitment area of the contractor; (6) the availability of promotable and transferable female employees within the contractor's organization; (7) the existence of training institutions capable of training people in the requisite skills; and (8) the degree of training the contractor is reasonably able to undertake as a means of making all job classes available to women.

The utilization analysis is crucial to the affirmative action program concept because it is the percentage figure achieved as a result of the analysis that will determine, first, whether the contractor is underutilizing minorities and/or females, and second, the percentage goal that must be established by the contractor to correct that underutilization. Thus, if, as a result of consideration of the eight factors, for either minorities or females, the contractor acknowledges an availability of 25 percent minorities or females for a particular job group, then the contractor must have 25 percent. If it does not, it must acknowledge underutilization and set an ultimate goal of 25 percent minorities or females.

In practice, questions are raised most frequently between the contractor and the compliance-review officer concerning the weight to be given for each factor OFCCP requires to be considered. From the contractor's point of view, if there is a collective-bargaining agreement that requires promotion according to seniority, the contractor would realistically like to have the availability of minorities and females determined solely by the availability of those who are eligible to bid for the positions in a particular job group. However, the government traditionally rejects this concept and requires the contractor to go through the exercise of considering the figures relating to the external work force, the unemployment rate in the area, and so on, even though these are totally irrelevant. This is because the regulations of OFCCP are not oriented the same way normal corporate goal setting is established. OFCCP requires, for example, that "current occupations of employed persons . . . should at no time be considered the only basis for utilization, but must be expanded by evaluation of opportunities through training and recruitment."[53] This term "training and recruitment" is the hook that compliance officers are advised to use in pressing contractors for goals for each job group that are at least as high as the representation of minorities and females in the area *population*. The rationale for this is that "*because of past discrimination,* for most job groups, the number of minorities and women who at this time possess the requisite skills for these jobs may not equal the percentage of minorities and women in the population or labor force from which the jobs are filled."[54]

A standard approach adopted by many contractors to a utilization analysis is to give a minimum percentage weight to those factors that are irrelevant, or only minimally relevant. For instance, the existence of training that can be undertaken by the contractor, if the contractor does not do any training, might be given a weight of 5 percent. However, it can readily be appreciated how this use of the real, when OFCCP is demanding the ideal, can lead to conflict.

Another cause of conflict between compliance officers and contractors relates to the relevant hiring area. Many contractors are now located in suburban areas and recruit from a suburban work force, which generally has a lower representation of minorities than urban areas have. Compliance officers traditionally require such employers to include urban areas within the relevant hiring area, even though these areas might be up to 60 miles away from the facility. The sole purpose is to increase the percentage of minorities. A compromise often negotiated in such a situation is to consider the suburban county where the facility is located and the urban county where the city is located, but to give the suburban county greater weight in the calculation of availability.

The OFCCP has already lost in court in its efforts to have contractors extend the relevant hiring area. In *Timken Company* v. *Marshall*,[55] the contractor had indicated that its relevant hiring area was only 16 miles because, in practice, that is as far as it did recruit. The OFFCP had said that the contractor should recruit beyond 16 miles and set goals on that basis, because there was a greater representation of minorities beyond the 16-mile radius from the facility. The court held that the 16-mile radius was a legitimate relevant hiring area and that the contractor could not be forced to expand its relevant hiring area.

Internal guidelines of OFCCP indicate that if the availability of minorities or females for a particular job group is 2 percent or less, then a contractor, even though it has less than the availability, need not acknowledge underutilization or set goals and timetables for that gorup.

As can be seen, the utilization analysis is a negotiated document derived in part from very subjective factors. Nevertheless, plaintiffs in Title VII litigation frequently try to make use of it. These plaintiffs endeavor first to have the defendant employer admit, for purposes of litigation, that the availability of minorities and/or females for particular job groups is as indicated in the AACP Failing that, they try to introduce the utilization analysis as evidence that the employer had acknowledged a greater availability than it will acknowledge for purposes of the litigation.

To counteract this possibility, it is advisable for employers to submit, within the AACP and immediately before the utilization analysis, a disclaimer. The purpose of the disclaimer is to enable the employer to argue later, in the event of litigation under Title VII, or some other statute, that the utilization analysis is irrelevant and should not be admitted into evidence. Alternatively, if the utilization analysis is admitted into evidence, the disclaimer should reduce the evidentiary weight it is given by the court.

A sample disclaimer notice, which might precede the utilization analysis, might read as follows:

Note on Utilization Analysis

The "Utilization Analysis" which follows as part of this AACP has been constructed solely for purposes of compliance with Executive Order 11246 and the rules and regulations implementing it. It is not relevant for any other purpose and its use for any other purpose would be irresponsible.

The "Utilization Analysis" represents a statistical comparison between a real figure, which is the present utilization of minorities and females in a particular job group, and a non-existent, unreal figure. This second figure is *not* the actual availability of minorities and females for a particular job group. As the OFCCP regulations require, this second figure is established when the contractor and the OFCCP "estimate what the availability of minorities and women *will be* by the date of the ultimate goal. The estimate should take into account *potential* increases in the number of skilled minorities and women, including what can be done through promotion and training of present and future minority and female employees." OFCCP Comp. Man., Sec. 2-160.1c.

This second hypothetical figure is *not* one which management would use to establish regular production goals. It is not one which could be used for purposes of determining whether the contractor had discriminated. Consequently, when one compares this contractor's actual utilization to what is "available," it should be understood that in establishing this "availability" figure the OFCCP required that certain other facts *must* be considered. Some of these facts are:

1. there had been past discrimination in this country that has caused the percentage of minorities and females to possess the requisite skills for jobs in numbers that may not equal their representation in the population or labor force. OFCCP Comp. Man., Sec. 2-160.1d1.

2. minorities and females are learning the requisite skills for jobs faster and more generally, so their availability presently is not the same as it was the last time they were counted (in the 1970 Census). OFCCP Comp. Man., Sec. 2-160.1d2.

3. in assessing present availability the contractor has been required to consider "what the workforce would be had historical discrimination not occurred." OFCCP Comp. Man., Sec. 2-160.1f.

4. in determining what the geographic area should be for availability purposes, the contractor has been required to consider an area "broad enough to encompass the greatest availability of minorities." OFCCP Comp. Man., Sec. 2-160.5b.

5. OFCCP has refused to accept the federal government's own figures on availability, as established by the most recent census, unless the contractor can independently establish that those figures are correct. OFCCP Comp. Man., Sec. 2-160.6b.

6. the availability of minorities and females for jobs covered by collective bargaining agreements should be no less than the percentage of minorities and women in the population and overall labor force. The theory behind this is that they will be hired by the contractor in these numbers, and they will progress through the seniority system in these numbers; therefore, they are "available."

OFCCP Comp. Man., Sec. 2-160.7ez. The same is required for many white-collar jobs. OFCCP Comp. Man., Sec. 2-160.7e3.

This contractor is committed to affirmative action and in establishing "availability," this contractor has acted in good faith on these and other hypotheses for purposes of trying to enhance the availability of minorities and females. However, anyone who purports to use these "availability" figures set forth in this utilization analysis for any purpose other than that of Executive Order 11246 would be relying upon thousands of speculative occurrences which may or may not come to pass and which can only occur if government, industry and our country's population work together.

To illustrate how the "Utilization Analysis" can be presented, there follows a portion of one that was presented and commended by OFCCP. In this "Utilization Analysis" there were a total of 12 job groups. The job groups which covered all managerial jobs were denominated "1a" and "1b," because the first EEO category on the EEO-1 reporting form which is filed annually to the Joint Reporting Committee (EEOC and OFCCP) is "officials and managers." In the sample only the utilization analysis as it appeared for EEO-1 category 1 (Officials and Managers) is set forth.

Sample Utilization Analysis

Introduction

The figures used for the Utilization Analysis were part of the most recent U.S. census and consist of three basic types of figures. These are the basic census figures, 6th Count Data, and ORC Special Tabulation. All the figures used follow the Utilization Analysis and constitute part of the Utilization Analysis. An explanation of the figures is included. All the figures were procured through use of National Planning Data Corporation. Whenever refined figures were available, they were used.

In doing the Utilization Analysis, all eight factors were used. However, one of the eight factors, availability of minorities and females in the area in which the contractor might be expected to recruit, does not enhance minority or female availability figures.

The Denver SMSA at the time of the census is not the same as the Denver SMSA now. Two suburban counties, containing approximately 10,000 people in one and 1,000 in the other, have been added to the Denver SMSA since the census. The figures for the most populous of these counties, Douglas County, are included. However, the addition of these two counties does not enhance, and in fact reduces, the percentage availabilities of minorities and females. Consequently, we have used the basic Denver SMSA figures.

Although we actually calculated the availability for females and minorities (other than blacks), for blacks we estimated to achieve the derived availability because the numbers for blacks were so small. We believe that all our estimates for blacks are actually higher than the derived availability would have been, so this did not harm that group.

In the statistical material on pages 269-271, source materials for percentages used are shown in the footnotes. Page references are to NPDC materials.

Goals and Timetables

The purpose of the goals and timetables is to correct any underutilization that might exist for any job group. There are some basic guidelines for establishing goals and timetables. First, there must be an annual goal and an ultimate goal. The ultimate goal must be designed to completely correct any underutilization and generally should not exceed a five-year time period. The annual goal should be at least equal to the ultimate goal. Thus if the contractor has acknowledged, in its Utilization Analysis, that of all the persons available for a particular job group, 25 percent are females, then the ultimate goal of the contractor would be to have females hold 25 percent of the jobs in that job group and in its annual personnel activity at least 25 percent of the persons who are promoted or hired into job titles within that job group should be females.

Second, goals and timetables should be presented not only as a percentage, but also as a number for a particular year.

Third, even though a contractor does not expect any hiring activity in a job group for a particular year, the contractor must still set a percentage goal, even though it need not set a numerical goal. The percentage goal is set as a contingency, in the event that openings come in that job group.

Fourth, if the contractor achieves its goal, or even 95% of its goal, there will be no question raised about the contractor's good faith efforts. (There will probably be higher goals set for the next years.) In the event the contractor fails to meet its goal, the compliance officer will assess the efforts the contractor has exerted toward achievement of those goals and timetables. Thus, the first issue will be whether the contractor met the goals and timetables; if it did not, the second will be what efforts the contractor made to attempt to meet those goals. It is the contractor that has not met its goals *and* has not taken affirmative action to meet them that will be found not to be in compliance.

Fifth, separate goals generally need not be set for separate minority groups—Mexican-Americans, blacks, Orientals, Pacific Islanders, American Indians. However, if the compliance officer has reason to believe that one particular minority group is in need of special affirmative action, the officer can require that a separate utilization analysis be performed and special goals and timetables set for that group.

Occasionally, management of a corporation thinks that OFCCP is being unreasonable in the goals and timetables it is requiring, yet OFCCP refuses to accept an affirmative action program without those goals and timetables. One

Job Group 1a

Factors Required for Analysis	Raw % Availability			Percentage Weight Given This Factor For This Job Group	Net	
	Females	Minorities Except Blacks (MEB)	Blacks		F	MEB
1. Population[a]	51.35	12.69	4.09	5%	2.56	.63
2. Unemployment force[b]	37.8	.06	.03	5%	1.89	.003
3. Requisite skills—immediate area[c]	16.3	4.7	1.5	25%	4.07	1.1
4. Requisite skills—aff. action recruiting area[d]	16.3	4.7	1.5	25%	4.07	1.1
5. Internal availability[e]	22.2	11.1	-0-	25%	5.5	2.0
6. Existence of training institutions—external[f]	22.2	11.1	-0-	5%	1.1	.5
7. Contractor training[g]	20.4	5.9	1.9	5%	1.02	.2
8. Special aff. action efforts availability[g]	20.4	5.9	1.9	5%	1.02	.2
					21.23	5.73

Derived Availability		Present Utilization	Underutilization
Females	21.23	Females 0	Females Yes
Minorities (ex. Blacks)	5.73	Minorities (ex. Blacks) 0	Minorities (ex. Blacks) Yes
Blacks	1	Blacks 0	Blacks Yes

[a]From p. 1, NPDC.
[b]From p. 12, NPDC, unemployed civilian managers.
[c]From p. 2, NPDC, civilian managers.
[d]Includes Denver SMSA, plus Douglas and one other suburban county. Since these counties are predominantly white, the percentages do not change upwards to help females or minorities, and, in fact, go down slightly. Therefore, for this reason, in this entry we kept the same percentage as indicated for the Denver SMSA.
[e]Looking to the next lowest job group, 1b, we see availability internally as indicated here.
[f]There are no known training institutions to qualify persons for this job group in such a way that minority or female availability would be enhanced.
[g]Contractor training is one part of special affirmative action. To achieve these percentages of availability, we took 25% of the actual availability as indicated in number 3 above and added it to the percent already entered in number 7 above.
[h]See explanation for number 7 above.

Job Group 1b

Raw % Availability

Factors Required for Analysis	Females	Minorities Except Blacks (MEB)	Blacks	Percentage Weight Given This Factor For This Job Group	Net F	Net MEB
1. Population[a]	51.35	12.69	4.09	5%	2.56	.63
2. Unemployment force[b]	37.8	.06	.03	5%	1.89	.003
3. Requisite skills—immediate area[c]	16.3	4.7	1.5	25%	4.07	1.175
4. Requisite skills—aff. action recruiting area[d]	16.3	4.7	1.5	25%	4.07	1.175
5. Internal availability[e]	18.0	14.0	2.0	25%	4.5	3.5
6. Existence of training institutions—external[f]	16.3	4.7	1.5	5%	.8	.23
7. Contractor training[g]	20.4	5.87	1.87	5%	1.02	1.02
8. Special aff. action efforts availability[g]	20.4	5.87	1.87	5%	1.02	1.02
					19.93	8.753

Derived Availability		Present Utilization		Underutilization	
Females	19.93	Females	22	Females	No
Minorities (ex. Blacks)	8.753	Minorities (ex. Blacks)	11	Minorities (ex. Blacks)	No
Blacks	1.75	Blacks	–0–	Blacks	Yes

270

aFrom p. 1, NPDC.

bFrom p. 12, NPDC, unemployed civilian managers.

cFrom p. 2, NPDC, civilian managers.

dIncludes Denver SMSA, plus Douglas and one other suburban county. Since these counties are predominantly white, the percentages do not change upwards, to help females or minorities, and, in fact, go down slightly. Therefore, for this reason, in this entry we kept the same percentage as indicated for the Denver SMSA.

eLooking to the possible feeder job groups as interpreted most favorably to minorities and females, we see availability internally as indicated here. One of the complications is that females already hold the job titles in this job group for which we have a high percentage of females in the source pipeline.

fThere are no known training institutions to qualify persons for this job group in such a way that minority or female availability would be enhanced.

gContractor training is one part of special affirmative action. To achieve these percentages of availability, we took 25% of the actual availability as indicated in number 3 above and added it to the percent already entered in number 3 above.

hSee explanation for number 7 above.

possible way of resolving the dilemma is to submit the goals and timetables OFCCP demands, thereby obtaining AACP approval from OFCCP, and at the same time to submit a letter accompanying the AACP in which it is stated that the goals and timetables that have been set are based upon speculative availability, and that the performance of the contractor toward meeting those goals and timetables should be considered not only on the basis of the efforts of the contractor, but also on the basis of changes in society that may have changed the composition of those available for certain job groups. Generally, the OFCCP area director will accept such a letter accompanying the AACP, and it will serve as a compromise between the competing interests and a protective mechanism for the contractor in the event that goals and timetables are not met.

A sample goals-and-timetables report is shown on pages 273-276.

Affected Classes and Focus Job Groups

The OFCCP compliance manual has extensive sections giving direction to compliance offices on how they are to identify "affected classes" and "focus job groups" and what remedies they are to demand for such groups. Generally, part of the demand is back pay.

The efforts to identify affected classes and obtain back pay have been relatively recent in OFCCP's history. Executive orders prohibiting discrimination on government contracts have existed since World War II, yet it was not until the mid-1970s that OFCCP actively sought back pay for affected classes. In fact, when appearing before Congress in 1972, when Congress was considering the amendments to Title VII, OFCCP and EEOC executives made representations that led Congress to believe that OFCCP did not have authority and did not seek to obtain back pay.

Affected classes and focus job groups will generally be identified by doing adverse-impact analysis, or looking for concentrations or exclusions of minorities and/or females in certain job groups. Compliance review officers have been directed to search carefully for these in order to identify affected classes and focus job groups.

AACP DOCUMENTS AND THE FREEDOM OF INFORMATION ACT

Once documents are submitted to OFCCP, they are considered public records, available to others just by the submission of a request, under the Freedom of Information Act (FOIA).[56]

In an attempt to minimize the amount of sensitive information that can be obtained by the public—which includes competitors—government contractors

Sample Goals and Timetables

Projected Fiscal Year Goals April 1, 1979—March 31, 1980
Quality Batch Bread/Denver Region Central

	Current Employment			Anticipated Openings During P/Y				Goals Hires Promotions Transfers Projected Employment End P/Y					Available		Annual Goal		Ultimate Goal		
Job Group	Total Employees[a] (1)	Female[b,c] (2)	Minority[b] (3)	Attrition (4)	Expansion (5)	Total (6)	Anticipated Recalls (7)	Total (8)	Female[b] (9)	Minority[b] (10)	Total Employees (11)	Female[a] (12)	Minority[b] (13)	Female[a] (14)	Minority[b] (15)	Female % (16)	Minority % (17)	Female % (18)	Minority Except Blacks	Blacks	Date
1a	4	— / —	— / —	—	—	—	—	—								21%		21%[c]	5.7%	1%	1982
1b	9	2/22.2	1/11.1	2	—	2	—	2		1 Black / 11%	9	No underutilization of females or black minorities				—	—	—	—	2%	1980
4a	84	—/—	2/2.4	28	2	30	—	30	3/15%	6/15% 1/15%	86	3/3%	8/9.3% 1/1%			12%	12%	12%	20%	2%	1981
4b	10	10/100.0	—/—	2	—	2	—	2	1/10%	0/0%	10	No underutilization of females					—	—	9%	2%	1981
5	13	10/76.9	2/15.4	4	1	5	—	5	1/20%	0/0%	14						—	—	11%	—	1980
6a	14	—/—	7/50.0	4	—	4	—	4	1/7%		14	No underutilization of blacks or females				13%	13%	13%	17%	3%	1981
6b	11	—/—	1/9.1	5	—	5	—	5	1/9%	1/18% 0	11	No underutilization of any minorities				10%	10%	10%	17%	3%	1981
6c	14	—/—	2/14.3	10	—	10	—	10	2/14.2%	1/21.4% 7%	14					24%	24%	24%	20%	5%	1981

273

Sample Goals and Timetables

Projected Fiscal Year Goals April 1, 1979–March 31, 1980
Quality Batch Bread/Denver Region Central

	Current Employment			Anticipated Openings During P/Y				Goals										
								Hires Promotions Transfers Projected Employment End P/Y					Available		Annual Goal		Ultimate Goal		
Job Group	Total Employees[a] (1)	Female[b,c] (2)	Minority[b] (3)	Attrition (4)	Expansion (5)	Total (6)	Anticipated Recalls (7)	Total (8)	Female[b] (9)	Minority[b] (10)	Total Employees (11)	Female[a] (12)	Minority[b] (13)	Female[a] (14)	Minority[b] (15)	Female % (16)	Minority % (17)	Female % (18)	Minority Except Blacks	Blacks	Date
6d	29	—	8 / 27.6	20	—	20		20	5 / 17.2		29	No underutilization of minorities				25%		25%	—	—	1981
7	5	—	1 / 20.0	1	—	1		1	1 / 20%		1					25%		25%	—	5.5%	1981
8	51	13 / 25.5	14 / 27.5	40	—	40	—	40		2 / 6%	40	No underutilization of females or nonblack minorities						—	—	5%	1980

[a]Includes females of all races.
[b]Includes minorities of both sexes.
[c]Where there is a minority box split diagonally for annual goals, the upper portion is the annual goal for nonblack minorities, and the lower portion is the black annual goal.
[d]Where there are no projected vacancies in a year, then the ultimate goals apply as contingency goals, and they also apply in the event there are more vacancies than projected.
[e]Note that where boxes are split in half by a horizontal line, quantities are shown in the upper portion, percentages are shown in the lower portion.

Sample Goals and Timetables

Projected Fiscal Year Goals April 1, 1979–March 31, 1980
Quality Batch Bread/Denver Region Central

	Current Employment			Anticipated Openings During P/Y				Goals									
								Hires Promotions Transfers Projected Employment End P/Y					Available		Annual Goal		Ultimate Goal
Job Group	Total Employees[a] (1)	Female[b,c] (2)	Minority[b] (3)	Attrition (4)	Expansion (5)	Total (6)	Anticipated Recalls (7)	Total (8)	Female[b] (9)	Minority[b] (10)	Total Employees (11)	Female[a] (12)	Minority[a] (13)	Female[a] (14)	Minority[b] (15)	Female % (16)	Minority % (17)	Female % (18)	Minority Except Blacks	Blacks	Date
1a																					
1b																					
4a																					
4b																					
5																					
6a																					
6b																					
6c																					

Sample Goals and Timetables

Projected Fiscal Year Goals April 1, 1979–March 31, 1980
Quality Batch Bread/Denver Region Central

	Current Employment			Anticipated Openings During P/Y				Goals									
								Hires Promotions Transfers Projected Employment End P/Y						Available		Annual Goal		Ultimate Goal
Job Group	Total Employees[a] (1)	Female[b,c] (2)	Minority[b] (3)	Attrition (4)	Expansion (5)	Total (6)	Anticipated Recalls (7)	Total (8)	Female[b] (9)	Minority[b] (10)	Total Employees (11)	Female[a] (12)	Minority[b] (13)	Female[a] (14)	Minority[b] (15)	Female % (16)	Minority % (17)	Female % (18)	Minority Except Blacks	Blacks	Date

6d

7

8

[a] Includes females of all races.
[b] Includes minorities of both sexes.
[c] Where there is a minority box split diagonally for annual goals, the upper portion is the annual goal for nonblack minorities, and the lower portion is the black annual goal.
[d] Where there are no projected vacancies in a year, then the ultimate goals apply as contingency goals, and they also apply in the event there are more vacancies than projected.
[e] Note that where boxes are split in half by a horizontal line, quantities are shown in the upper portion, percentages are shown in the lower portion.

have adopted two mechanisms: First, they limit the data submitted to OFCCP; second, they attempt to protect the confidentiality of data submitted, by placing a protective statement such as the one below at the front of their AACP. Such a statement does not guarantee protection, but it usually ensures that the contractor will receive notification prior to the release.

> Copies of this Affirmative Action Plan and all related appendices, documents, and support data are made available on loan to the U.S. Government upon the request of said Government on the condition that the Government hold them totally confidential and not release copies to any persons whatsoever. This Affirmative Action Plan and its appendices and other supporting documents contain much confidential information which may reveal, directly or indirectly, the Company's plans for business or geographical expansion or contraction. The Company considers this Affirmative Action Plan, all portions thereof, and all supporting material to be its private and confidential property, to be on loan to the Government only under specified conditions, including non-reproduction and non-distribution, and to be exempt from disclosure under the Freedom of Information Act upon the grounds, among others, that such material constitutes (1) personnel files, the disclosure of which would constitute a clearly unwarranted invasion of personal privacy, which are exempt from disclosure under 5 U.S.C. §552(b)(6); (2) confidential, commercial or financial information, which is exempt from disclosure under 5 U.S.C. §552(b)(4); (3) investigatory records compiled for law enforcement purposes, the production of which would constitute an unwarranted invasion of personal privacy, which are exempt from disclosure under 5 U.S.C. §552(b)(7)(C); and (4) matters specifically exempted from disclosure by statute, which are exempt from disclosure under 5 U.S.C. §552(b)(3).
>
> The Company will submit further detailed documentation supporting this claim of privilege when and if necessary.
>
> The Company desires the opportunity to exercise rights available to it under the Administration Procedures Act; the Company does not believe release of this information is "authorized by law" as that term is used in the Trade Secrets Act, 18 U.S.C. Section 1905, because of a serious procedural defect noted by the U.S. Supreme Court in *Chrysler Corp.* v. *Brown,* 99 S. Ct. 1705 (1979); for these reasons the Company believes that anyone releasing such information will be subjecting himself or herself to criminal penalties, including imprisonment, and that such person would be releasing this information with full realization that such action was in violation of law. If the U.S. Government, or any agency or subdivision thereof, is considering breaching the conditions under which this Affirmative Action Plan was loaned to such Government, or is considering a request for release of this Plan under the Freedom of Information Act, request is hereby made that the Government immediately notify the Chief Executive Officer of this corporation

of any and all Freedom of Information Act requests received by the Government or any other contemplated release of this Plan by the Government which relates to information obtained by the Government from this Company. If the Chief Executive Officer is unavailable for such immediate notification, then the General Counsel, Mr. Don Boss, (212) 682-4567, should be notified. In his absence, Mr. John Goodfaith, (212) 682-4567, Corporate Director, Equal Employment Opportunity, should be notified.

The Company further requests everyone who has any contact with this Affirmative Action Plan, or its supporting appendices, documents, and other data, treat such information as totally confidential and that such information not be released to any person whatsoever.

In addition to minimizing the public access to information submitted, the contractor may find it advisable to use the FOIA affirmatively to obtain OFCCP file material. This can be done by ascertaining the identity of the appropriate FOIA officer for the agency and submitting a letter citing the FOIA and requesting the information. The letter should contain an offer to pay for the statutory costs involved.

Knowing what a complainant or witnesses or employees have said during the course of a compliance review will enable the contractor to more precisely tailor its defense. However, an FOIA request will not enable the contractor to obtain OFCCP analyses or position statements, since these will be the subject of objection by OFCCP.

ESSENTIAL ELEMENTS OF AN AFFIRMATIVE ACTION PROGRAM

There are certain basic parts of any affirmative action program for compliance with Executive Order 11246. These are "Development or Reaffirma- of EEO Policy," and "Internal and External Dissemination of Policy." There follows a commentary on these sections, a summary checklist of the points that should be covered by each of these, and a sample for each of these.

The discussion and samples relate only to Executive Order 11246, presuming that the contractor would have an entirely separate Affirmative Action Program and Reaffirmation of Policy under the Rehabilitation Act of 1973. If the contractor does expect to have a separate AAP for the Rehabilitation Act, but does not want to create a separate Reaffirmation of Policy to comply with the Rehabilitation Act, then reference to the handicapped and a commitment to nondiscrimination, affirmative action, and reasonable accommodation should be added to the Reaffirmation of Policy statement that follows.

DEVELOPMENT OR REAFFIRMATION OF EEO POLICY

This apparently simple part of an AACP is really rather detailed. Revised Order No. 4, Section 60-2.13(a) requires the "development or reaffirmation of the contractor's equal employment opportunity policy in all personnel actions," and Section 60-2.20(a) contains other rather general requirements. However, the compliance officer reviewing the affirmative action program will be looking not at Revised Order No. 4, but at Revised Order 14, of which Part B IV suggests questions for the officer to have answered to determine whether there is a "reaffirmation of EEO policy." Compliance officers have taken some or all of these questions to indicate requirements. At a minimum, most compliance officers will require:

1. That the statement of policy be dated and that it have a date on it less than one year old. This has been derived from the question, "Is the policy statement updated periodically?"

2. That the statement of policy indicate that personnel will be responsible for their performance in the EEO area. This is derived from the question, "Has management expressed any intention in writing or otherwise to take disciplinary action for failure to adhere to EEO policies and procedures?" To say in the policy statement that "performance of this responsibility shall be evaluated"* is not deemed sufficient. If you say it, compliance officers will check to see if you mean it, by examining job descriptions or reviewing employee evaluation forms to see if it is included.

Although compliance officers have not yet reached the point of establishing objective standards for rating performance in the EEO area, for purposes of follow-through in establishing an affirmative action program it may be advisable to include on the employee evaluation form used for supervisors a provision such as item 8 of the Performance Evaluation Form that is included in this book at the end of Chapter 5.

In addition to the guidance given to compliance officers by Revised Order 14, OFCCP's compliance manual contains still other requirements to be embodied in this "simple" statement. For purposes of this model affirmative action program, we will note the essential requirements of the OFCCP Manual. These are stated as follows:

> The contractor should issue a written statement that should include, but not be limited to, these elements:
> —That its commitment to equal employment opportunity for

---

*When the employer makes this statement in its model policy statement, it must have the necessary support data to be able to demonstrate that it rates its supervisors on their EEO performance.

all persons, regardless of race, color, sex, or national origin, is fundamental company policy.

—That the equal employment policy will require special affirmative action throughout the company.

—That equal employment opportunity will affect all employment practices including (but not limited to) recruiting, hiring, promotions, and training.

—That responsibility for the affirmative action program is assigned to a major company executive.

—That the company official assigned affirmative action program responsibilities should be specifically identified in the statement of policy.

—That all management personnel share in this responsibility and will be assigned specific tasks.

—That management performance on this program will be evaluated as is performance on other company goals.

—That successful performance on affirmative action goals will provide benefits to the company through fuller utilization and development of previously underutilized human resources.

Summary Checklist

1. Is there a reaffirmation of policy? 41 C.F.R. §60-2.13(a).
2. Does it mention the specific areas, as required? 41 C.F.R. §60-2.20-(a)(1).
3. Does it indicate that decisions should be based upon EEO considerations? 41 C.F.R. §60-2.20(2).
4. Does it specifically indicate the substantive areas to which the policy extends? 41 C.F.R. §60-2.20(4).
5. Does it specifically establish that only valid job requirements will be used? 41 C.F.R. §60-2.20(3).
6. Does it indicate that special affirmative action will be required? OFCCP Manual and Revised Order 14.
7. Does it assign responsibility to a major company executive and identify him? OFCCP Manual and Revised Order 14.
8. Does it indicate that all management personnel share in this responsibility and will be assigned specific tasks? OFCCP Manual.
9. Does it indicate that performance of EEO responsibilities will be evaluated as are other company goals (OFCCP Manual), and that failure to adhere to these policies will result in disciplinary action? Revised Order 14.
10. Is the policy current and dated? Revised Order 14.

The numbers in the sample below refer to items in this checklist.

Sample Development or Reaffirmation of EEO Policy

(1) This is a reaffirmation of the XYZ Company and the XYZ Industrial Products Company, a subsidiary, policy regarding equal employment opportunity in all personnel actions. (2) This policy relates to, but is not limited to,

recruiting, hiring, training, and promotion, in all job titles, without regard to race, color, religion, sex, or age. (3) All decisions regarding the personnel function should further the principle of equal employment opportunity, (4) insure that personnel actions such as compensation, benefits, transfers, layoffs, return from layoff, company sponsored training, and social and recreational programs will be administered without regard to race, color, religion, sex, or national origin, and (5) insure that promotion decisions are in accord with principles of equal employment opportunity by imposing only valid requirements for promotional opportunities.

(6) This commitment will require special affirmative action, and (7) responsibility to assure accomplishment of this commitment shall be that of John C. Goodfaith, Director of Personnel, who will report directly to the President on this matter.

(8) Performance consistent with this policy shall be expected from all management personnel, and specific tasks in furtherance of this policy will be assigned to these persons. (9) Performance of this responsibility shall be evaluated as are other company assigned duties. Failure to adhere to the company equal employment policy will result in appropriate company disciplinary action.

(10) Dated: June 1, 1980

Joseph Senior, President

INTERNAL AND EXTERNAL DISSEMINATION OF POLICY

This provision of the AACP is rather elaborate, even in Revised Order 4, 41 C.F.R. §60-2 *et seq.* Section 60-2.13(b) requires "formal internal and external dissemination of the contractor's policy." Section 60-2.21(a) indicates how that policy should be communicated internally, and Section 60-2.21(b) details methods for external communication.

The contractor should disseminate his policy internally as follows:

1. Include it in contractor's policy manual.
2. Publicize it in the company newspaper, magazine, annual report, and other media.
3. Conduct special meetings with executive, management, and supervisory personnel to explain the intent of the policy and individual responsibility for effective implementation, making clear the chief executive officer's attitude.
4. Schedule special meetings with all other employees to discuss the policy and explain individual employee responsibilities.
5. Discuss the policy thoroughly in both employee-orientation and management-training programs.

6. Meet with union officials to inform them of the policy, and request their cooperation.
7. Include nondiscrimination clauses in all union agreements and review all contractual provisions to ensure that they are nondiscriminatory.
8. Publish articles covering EEO programs, progress reports, promotions, etc., of minority and female employees in company publications.
9. Post the policy on company bulletin boards.
10. When employees are featured in product or consumer advertising, employee handbooks, or similar publications, use pictures of both minority and nonminority men and women.
11. Communicate to employees the existence of the contractors affirmative action program and make available such elements of that program as will enable employees to know of and avail themselves of its benefits.

The contractor should disseminate his policy externally as follows:

1. Inform all recruiting sources, verbally and in writing, or company policy, stipulating that these sources actively recruit and refer minorities and women for all positions listed.
2. Incorporate the equal-opportunity clause in all purchase orders, leases, contracts, etc., covered by Executive Order 11246, as amended, and its implementing regulations.
3. Notify minority and women's organizations, community agencies, community leaders, secondary schools, and colleges of company policy, preferably in writing.
4. Communicate to prospective employees the existence of the contractor's affirmative action program and make available such elements of that program as will enable prospective employees to know of and avail themselves of its benefits.
5. When employees are pictured in consumer or help-wanted advertising, show both minority and nonminority men and women.
6. Send written notification of company policy to all subcontractors, vendors, and suppliers, requesting appropriate action on their part.

When one looks to Revised Order 14, it is readily apparent how the contract compliance officers arrive at their heavy demands regarding internal and external dissemination of policy. Relative to this subject, the order says:

> Determination of good faith effort should be made which shall include but not be limited to the following:
> (a) Notification to the community organizations that the contractor has employment opportunities available and records regarding the response.
> (b) Dissemination of the contractor's EEO policy, by including it in any policy manual; by publicizing it in company or union newspapers, annual report, etc.; by conducting meetings to explain and discuss the policy; by posting of the policy; and by specific review of the policy with minority and female employees.

(c) Dissemination of the EEO policy externally by informing and discussing it with all recruitment sources; by advertising in news media, specifically including minority news media; and by notifying and discussing it with all contractors and subcontractors.

(d) Specific and constant personal (both written and oral) recruitment efforts directed at all minority and female organizations, schools with minority and female students, minority and female recruitment organizations, and training organizations, within the contractor's recruitment area.

(e) Specific efforts to encourage present minority and female employees to make referrals in the recruitment effort.

(f) The contractor must undertake every good faith effort to contract and make use of relevant recruitment and training resources available in the community and use its own resources for recruiting and training minorities and females to fill positions in job groups where underutilization exists. Data regarding promotable employees, community training facilities and company training facilities must be prepared by the company itself and related to the locality.

Finally, with respect to dissemination of policy, here are guidelines established by the OFCCP compliance manual:

Dissemination of Policy. The contractor's publication of its equal employment opportunity policy both within the plant and to the public.

(a) *Internal.* Managers and supervisors should be fully informed by:

Written communication from the Chief Executive.

Inclusion of the Affirmative Action Program and Policy in company operations manuals.

Special meetings held regularly to discuss the program, their individual responsibilities and review progress to gather input for goals and timetables.

All employees should be informed of company policy and changes through such means as:

Company EEO policy statement and Federal EEO posters placed on bulletin boards, areas near time clocks and in employment offices.

Policy inclusion in employee handbooks and Annual Reports.

Meetings with minority and female employees to request their suggestions in developing the Affirmative Action Program.

Presentation and discussion of the Program as part of employee orientation and all training programs.

Copies of the Affirmative Action Policy statement and summary of key program element provided to employees.

Union officials should be involved in developing and implementing the AAP from the start.

(b) *External.* The contractor should also provide its recruitment source with copies of its equal employment policy and any updated policy, including the appropriate media, public and private employment agencies, educational institutions, community groups, and others who have contacts with women and minority groups.

Contractors should also notify all subcontractors, vendors and suppliers of its equal employment policy and may include an equal opportunity clause in all purchase orders, contracts, leases, etc.

Summary Checklist

1. Is the EEO policy in the policy manual? 41 C.F.R. §60-2.21(a)(1).
2. Is the policy publicized? 41 C.F.R. §60-2.21(a)(2).
3. Are special meetings held to make clear the attitude of the chief executive officer and to describe individual responsibility. 41 C.F.R. §60-2.21(a)(3).
4. Are special meetings scheduled to explain the policy to all employees? 41 C.F.R. §60-2.21(a)(4).
5. Is the policy discussed in corporate orientation and management-training programs? 41 C.F.R. §60-2.21(a)(5).
6. Are union officials informed of the policy and asked to cooperate? 41 C.F.R. §60-2.21(a)(6).
7. Is the policy included in the collective-bargaining agreement? 41 C.F.R. §60-2.21(a)(7).
8. Are articles involving EEO published in company publications? 41 C.F.R. §60-2.21(a)(8).
9. Is the policy posted? 41 C.F.R. §60-2.21(a)(9).
10. In consumer advertising, are minorities and females featured? 41 C.F.R. §60-2.21(a)(10).
11. Is the program communicated to employees, and are elements of the program that are beneficial to them made available to them? 41 C.F.R. §60-2.21(a)(11).
12. Are recruiting sources informed of the policy, orally and in writing, and required to actively recruit and refer minorities and females for all positions? 41 C.F.R. §60-2.21(b)(1).
13. Is the policy incorporated in purchase orders, leases, contracts, etc., covered by Executive Order 11246? 41 C.F.R. §60-2.21(b)(2).
14. Are minority and female organizations, community agencies, community leaders, secondary schools, and colleges informed of the company policy? 41 C.F.R. §60-2.21(b)(4).
15. Are prospective employees informed of the affirmative action program and the potential benefits for them? 41 C.F.R. §60-2.21(b)(5).
16. In consumer or help-wanted advertising, are minorities and females depicted? 41 C.F.R. §60-2.21(b)(6).
17. Is written notification of the policy conveyed to subcontractors, vendors, and suppliers? 41 C.F.R. §60-2.21(b)(7).
18. Are community organizations that can refer minorities and females

informed of the company equal employment opportunity policy? Revised Order 14.

19. Is the equal employment policy reviewed specifically with female and minority-group employees? Revised Order 14.

20. Are present minority and female employees encouraged to make referrals in the recruitment effort? Revised Order 14.

21. Are managers and supervisors informed of the policy by written communication from the chief executive? OFCCP Manual.

22. Are managers and supervisors required to give input to establish goals and timetables and review progress toward meeting those goals and timetables? OFCCP Manual.

23. Are suggestions of minority and female employees solicited for purposes of developing the affirmative action program? OFCCP Manual.

24. Are union officials involved in developing and implementing the AAP from the start? OFCCP Manual.

There are many different ways to satisfy the requirements indicated on this checklist. The bracketed numbers on the left in the sample below refer to the items on the list that are intended to be satisfied. The methods indicated are only suggestive of the type of implementation that might be acceptable to OFCCP.

Sample Dissemination of Company Policy Statement

(1)   (a) The corporate EEO policy is and has been incorporated into the corporate policy manual. It is presently paragraph 502 of this manual.

(2)   (b) The corporate EEO policy is publicized in the following manners:

(15)   (i) Mr. John Goodfaith is the Director of Personnel and as such responsible for all hiring, both hourly and salaried, for the Clifton facility. During interviews with applicants for employment, he informs applicants of the corporate EEO policy.

(16)   (ii) In all job advertising placed, we include the note "An Equal Opportunity Employer."

(2,9)   (iii) The corporate EEO policy is posted on all bulletin boards, together with the EEOC/OFCCP poster.

(10, 16)   (iv) Corporate advertising, under the direction of Edward Martini, has required and will require that at least one female will appear in each television, newspaper, or other media advertisement in which persons appear, for every two persons who appear, and that at least one minority person appear for every four persons who appear.

(8)   (v) The newspaper for the corporation, *Tire and Rim,* depicts minority and female employees and advertises the accomplishments of such persons on a regular basis. Approximately the same representation as was indicated in paragraph (iv) has been

	achieved in the past and will be sought for the future.
(4,5, 15)	(vi) All new employees are given a copy of the booklet *XYZ EEO Policy and Practice* and told they must read it as part of the orientation process.
(3,4, 15)	(vii) As part of the orientation process, all new employees are orally informed of the corporate EEO policy and specifically asked if they have any questions as to what it means.
(3,4) (23)	(viii) *You and the XYZ Company Program*—Six meetings were held during the past AAP year. These were 10/1 and 12/1, 1975, and 2/1, 4/1, 6/1, and 8/1, 1979. As a result of these meetings, all employees were informed of the corporate EEO policy. Equal employment opportunity was discussed as a separate topic during these meetings. These employees were addressed by John C. Goodfaith. During these sessions, all employees, including minority and female employees, were asked for suggestions in implementation of the corporate EEO policy and the corporate AAP.
(3,4, 11)	(ix) At these sessions, described in subparagraph viii, Joseph Senior, President, personally indicated the corporate commitment to EEO and advised all the employees that John Goodfaith would be reporting directly to him concerning implementation of this policy; that all employees had a right and a duty to report possible violations of this policy to John Goodfaith; and that John Goodfaith would investigate these reports and was to have the full cooperation of all personnel for such investigations; and that John Goodfaith would advise the employee who reported the violation of the results of the investigation within 10 days; and that if either the person reporting the violation or the person found to have committed the violation was not satisfied with the fairness of the result or procedure, he, Joseph Senior, would review the complete file on the matter.

(5)   (c) The corporate EEO policy is reiterated at all management-training sessions and orientation sessions. At eight Management Awareness meetings over a two-day period, all the managers and supervisors at the Clifton facility attended. The speakers were John Goodfaith, Personnel Director; William Fair, Corporate EEO Director; and John C. Muddle, Corporate Labor Counsel. Handouts were distributed to each participant, titled, "Some Reminders on Equal Employment Opportunity."

(5)   (d) A Personnel Managers Conference was held at corporate headquarters in Akron in the past AAP year. John Goodfaith attended, representing the Clifton facility. Equal employment opportunity was addressed as a separate topic at this meeting.

(4,   (e) Every Wednesday during the AAP year, new-employee

15) orientation is conducted. All employees hired during the past week participate. During the sessions, the new employees are given a copy of the booklet "Employee's Handbook," in which the corporate EEO policy is explained.

(6,7) (f) The corporate policy of equal employment opportunity has been incorporated into the collective-bargaining agreement covering this facility, as paragraph 8, Section XII, p. 36.

(24) (g) The union representing all our production employees is the United Rubber Workers, Local 16. They have been involved and continue to be involved in developing and implementing our affirmative action program. For purposes of updating the AAP, John Goodfaith meets with William Smith, the President of Local 16, 60 days before the expiration of the AAP year to review AAP developments during the past year and assist in the formation of the program for the coming year. These parties met July 1, 1980, and thereafter for input to this affirmative action program.

(19, 20, 23) (h) Minority and female employees are consulted for purposes of establishing the affirmative action program, and their suggestions are solicited. William Black is our foreman, Maintenance Section. He meets with John Goodfaith at regular intervals, at least twice a month, to keep Mr. Goodfaith abreast of possible discontent among minority-group employees because of any failures in the implementation of the corporate EEO policy. Mr. Black has been asked to perform this function and has agreed to do so. Unless an employee specifically requests that he be identified to management, the identity of an employee who voices some complaint to Mr. Black is kept confidential. Mr. Black informs Mr. Goodfaith of problems even if there has not been a specific complaint.

Minority-group employees know that Mr. Black is available to them because we tell them so during the sessions described in paragraph (b)(ix). He is available as an alternative to Mr. John Goodfaith, for formalized complaints or as a vehicle for less formalized complaint procedures.

Through Mr. Black we receive suggestions for more effective implementation of the affirmative action program.

We have attempted a more formalized approach for gaining minority-group input to our AAP but found that the more formal procedure created friction between white and black employees and was not very beneficial to us, because the various suggestions made were often inconsistent or contradictory. They had not first been thought through before being made.

We find the present procedure more beneficial and less inclined to cause discord and polarization. All suggestions made to Mr. Black that he thinks are worthy of consideration are considered, *and* all suggestions, even if Mr. Black does not consider them worthy, are considered if the employee insists that he wants the suggestion made.

Mary French, supervisor, plexicord operations, performs the same function in the same manner as Mr. Black.

Mr. Black is black, Mrs. French is a white female.

A great deal of the success of Mr. Black and Mrs. French is attributable to the high esteem in which they are held by their co-workers and management.

(24)　　　(i) Union officials have been informed of the corporate EEO policy and agree that the corporate EEO policy be incorporated in the union collective-bargaining agreement.

(12, 14)　(j) Recruiting sources have been informed of the corporate EEO policy, orally and in writing. They have been informed that they must comply with the corporate EEO policy in forwarding candidates for employment. Copies of the letters sent to recruiting sources are included in the Affirmative Action Program.

(13)　　　(k) The corporate EEO policy and the standard 7-paragraph provision is incorporated in all purchase orders, leases, contracts, etc., of the company. A copy of a standard purchase order is attached.

(14, 18)　(l) Minority and female organizations, community agencies and community leaders, secondary schools, and colleges have been informed of the corporate EEO policy. The organizations that have been so informed are indicated on an Attachment. Notifications to these agencies are repeated each year.

(17)　　　(m) Written notification of the corporate EEO policy is given to all subcontractors, vendors, and suppliers. This is a supplemental notice, in addition to the regular notice included in the standard purchase order and contract form.

(21, 22)　(n) Managers and supervisors are informed of the corporate EEO policy in a written communication from the Chief Executive. Additionally, input from managers and supervisors in establishing goals and timetables is sought. Sixty (60) days before the end of each Affirmative Action reporting year, each department head establishes tentative goals and timetables for his department. He then forwards these tentative goals, and a breakdown of how these goals can be achieved by each unit under his jurisdiction, to the appropriate supervisor or foreman. These supervisors and foremen are asked to comment on the tentative goals and timetables established for their subsection. They are to indicate within thirty (30) days to the department head problems they feel they may encounter in achieving these goals and timetables or, alternatively, that they can achieve even higher goals in a shorter timetable. The department head then meets with these front-line supervisors and foremen and, as a result of that meeting, establishes goals and timetables for that department, and each supervisor and foreman knows exactly what that projection of goals and timetables means for his or her unit.

(6, 24)　(o) As part of the procedure for establishing goals and timetables, union officials, including shop stewards, are shown the tentative goals and timetables established for each department by the department head and asked to submit their comments on these goals and timetables prior to the time these goals and timetables are finally established by the department head.

(20)　　　(p) Present minority and female employees are contacted when we have an opening or anticipate an opening in a position for which we feel there is an underutilization. They are asked to refer someone for such a position. A list of the positions for which this type of recruiting has been conducted, with the names of the persons contacted, dates of contact, and names of the persons who did the contacting on our behalf, is an Attachment.

PROSPECTS FOR CHANGE AFFECTING OFCCP ENFORCEMENT

Through its issuance of administrative regulations, OFCCP recently established its right to require annual summaries of AAP activity from contractors. Eventually these forms will be submitted and computer scanned. Targets for compliance reviews will be identified in this manner. As a result the results of compliance activity will probably be more fruitful.

The future trend of OFCCP's administrative rule making will be the same as it has been in the past. Defensive mechanisms successfully utilized by contractors will be generally diluted, and substantive and procedural rights for claimants and the government will be increased. However, only when OFCCP has established a body of administrative law through the hearing and appeal process will it attain the credibility that it needs. The most recent proposed procedural and substantive changes put forth by OFCCP illustrate its approach to the law-making process. The procedural changes it proposed are as follows:

1. Whereas a contractor presently receives 30 days notice before it has to submit its AAP, under the proposed rules and regulations, the contractor would only have 15 days notice to submit its program. Proposed 41 C.F.R. §60-2.3.

2. Pre-award compliance reviews are presently required for contractor awards of more than $1 million unless the contractor has been reviewed and approved within the prior twelve-month period. Under the proposed modifications, if there has been a compliance review within the prior twenty-four months, then another compliance review will not be necessary. Also, whereas such reviews are presently required if the contractor has 50 or more employees, under the proposed rules and regulations, the contractor would be required to have 250 or more employees. The proposed rules and regulations would still allow OFCCP the discretion to conduct a pre-award compliance review, regardless of whether the contractor has less than 250 employees and regardless of whether there had been a compliance review in the prior twenty-four months. Proposed 41 C.F.R. §60-1.21.

3. OFCCP has proposed to abandon its position that it can deny a contract without a hearing. Previously it had lost on this issue forty-one times, while winning once. Under the procedures that OFCCP now proposes to embody in 41 C.F.R. §60-30.38, a procedure called "Preliminary Administrative Enforcement Proceeding" would be established. This would be a very expedited hearing procedure. An administrative complaint would be filed. Within 10 days after the complaint is filed, an administrative law judge would notify the parties of the time and place of the hearing. OFCCP would have submitted affidavits and other documentation with the complaint, and the respondent would have 15 days after service of the complaint to submit its affidavits and documentation

supporting its position. There would not be discovery except upon leave of the administrative law judge and for compelling reasons. The hearing would commence within 20 days of the date upon which the administrative law judge issued the notice of hearing. Thus, at the outside, there would only be 30 days from the time the administrative complaint issues until the time the hearing is supposed to commence. The decision of the administrative law judge would issue within 10 days after the conclusion of the hearing.

4. Presently, there is no provision for an expedited hearing in instances when allegations of violation of the Rehabilitation Act or the Vietnam Era Veterans Readjustment Act are made. Under the proposed rules, the expedited procedure for debarment or passover under Executive Order 11246 would also be available if there is an alleged violation of the Rehabilitation Act or the Vietnam Era Readjustment Act. Proposed 41 C.F.R. §60-1.29(e). This is significant because many contractors do not yet have AAP's for the handicapped and veterans. If this deficiency is discovered, it is possible that the government could move under 41 C.F.R. §60-30.38 for an expedited hearing to debar a contractor for this deficiency.

5. A mechanism that presently exists and is available to contractors to avoid debarment without capitulation to OFCCP would be removed. Presently the rules and regulations of OFCCP provide for the "comply and contest" procedure, 41 C.F.R. §60-1.24(c)(4). Under this procedure, if a contractor does not agree with what is demanded of it by OFCCP, the contractor can enter into a conciliation agreement agreeing to do what OFCCP demands and within 10 days thereafter repudiate the agreement and demand an administrative hearing to determine liability and damages. If the agreement calls for the payment of money, then the money need not be tendered. It is sufficient for the contractor to hold the money in escrow pending the administrative hearing. If the agreement calls for the contractor to hire and layoff by quota, the contractor need not do so until it has had a hearing and lost.

OFCCP very frequently loses track of the case after the contractor repudiates the conciliation agreement. As a result, there may never be an administrative hearing scheduled, and the contractor does not comply with the conciliation agreement, and the case "dies."

OFCCP proposes to delete this provision allowing for "comply and contest." The reason given by OFCCP is that its experience has been that most frequently the contractor does not comply with the demands of the agency prior to requesting the hearing. While that is true, that is what is allowed by the section. OFCCP has indicated in the introduction to its proposed changes that even if the "comply and contest" provision is retained, it will not provide for a hearing before an administrative law judge. If there is any hearing allowed, it will be before an OFCCP official.

Removal of the "comply and contest" provision would be a substantial loss to contractors. The fact that OFCCP desires to remove the procedure pinpoints the essential flaw in the OFCCP administrative system, namely, that OFCCP is not equipped to afford very many hearings.

6. The proposed rules and regulations would add a definition of "establishment" in the definition section, 41 C.F.R. §60-1.3, defining the term to mean "the location of a contractor's business or operations generally having some component which exercises personnel authority and responsibilities." Other sections, 41 C.F.R. §1.40 and 41 C.F.R. §60-2.2 require a contractor to have an AAP for each "establishment." Thus, a contractor could be required to have many more AAPs than it might presently have.

7. The proposed rules and regulations would allow OFCCP to aggregate contracts to reach the $50,000 contract amount plateau, which is the level at which a written AAP is required. Proposed 41 C.F.R. §60-1.40.

8. The proposed rules and regulations, 41 C.F.R. §60-1.43 would specifically authorize OFCCP to copy and remove off-site, copies of books, records, accounts and other materials, *such as computer tapes and printouts.* Presently, OFCCP usually agrees to allow the employer to keep on premises confidential payroll information and only furnish a code to the OFCCP as part of the AAP submission. When the on-site review is conducted, the code will be checked, but the compliance officer generally will not seek to take the key to the code off premises and incorporate it in the OFCCP file and, thereby, make it available to third parties under the Freedom of Information Act. Also, presently OFCCP generally does not require computer tapes to be copied and furnished to it.

9. Under the proposed rules and regulations, 41 C.F.R. §60-1.25, when a show cause notice issues, if an identified deficiency relates to a collective bargaining agreement provision, a copy of the show cause notice will be sent to the labor organizations which has a collective bargaining agreement with the contractor. Presently, this does not happen.

10. OFCCP proposes to amend the provisions of the regulations indicating what kind of contractor is to have an AAP. For example, under the proposed amendment, 41 C.F.R. §60-1.40(a), OFCCP would require any financial institution to have an AAP because it subscribes to the Federal Deposit Insurance Corporation.

11. Under the proposed procedures, 41 C.F.R. §60-1.31, reinstatement after debarment would be a very time consuming process.

12. Under existing procedures, OFCCP can defer a charge that is filed with it to EEOC and have EEOC handle it, or OFCCP can handle the charge itself. Generally, OFCCP refers charges that have individual implications to EEOC and keeps charges that have class implications. On this basis, OFCCP has effectively defended the process that is incorporated in the EEOC-OFCCP Memorandum of Understanding, whereby a charge filed with OFCCP is deemed a charge filed with EEOC. Under the proposed procedure, OFCCP could refer a charge to EEOC, yet still investigate it itself. Furthermore, in investigating one

charge that it has referred to EEOC, OFCCP could investigate other charges, even though those charges had already been referred to EEOC. Thus, the argument that OFCCP used successfully in courts to justify its memorandum of understanding with EEOC, namely, that there would be no duplication, would no longer be true.

13. Under the proposed procedures, 41 C.F.R. §60-1.25(b)(1), OFCCP would specifically set forth a provision that had hitherto appeared only in its own internal compliance manual. That provision is that there be mandatory conciliation agreements if a contractor is found not to be in compliance with the Executive Order. Additionally, the proposed rules and regulations inform the contractor "that the making of the commitments in the conciliation agreement does not preclude a future determination of noncompliance based either on a finding that the commitments are not sufficient to achieve compliance or on violations not previously revealed in a compliance review or complaint investigation." 41 C.F.R. §60-1.20(c). Up until now, in trying to convince contractors to permit this language to be incorporated in the conciliation agreement, OFCCP representatives have given oral assurances, and even side agreements in writing, that OFCCP would not come back, at some time later, and demand, for example, an additional amount of money or other relief for each woman who received under the original conciliation agreement. However, a provision of the proposed rules and regulations indicates that this may be precisely what OFCCP proposes to do, for proposed section 41 C.F.R. §60.1-25(b)(1), which discusses situations in which a show cause notice should issue, indicates that one such instance would be "where the relief obtained in a prior conciliation agreement, upon further review, is determined inadequate to correct the violation or deficiency."

The combination of these proposed rules and regulations is that a contractor that makes commitments gets no commitments or certainty from OFCCP in return.

14. Presently, both the Vietnam Era Veterans Readjustment Act, in 41 C.F.R. §60-250.26(b), and the Rehabilitation Act in 41 C.F.R. §60-741.26(b), provide that if a contractor has an internal mechanism designed to address complaints of violation of these statutes, the complaints made to the federal agencies shall first be referred to the contractor before any processing by OFCCP. The proposed regulations say that OFCCP *may* refer such complaints to the contractor, but only if the complainant gives his or her consent. Proposed 41 C.F.R. §250.23(f) and 41 C.F.R. §60-741.23(f).

15. Presently, OFCCP rules and regulations require that the AAPs for veterans and the handicapped must be made available for inspection to any employee or applicant. The proposed rules and regulations, 41 C.F.R. §60-250.5(b) and 41 C.F.R. §60-741.5(b), would also require that employees be informed of "any significant changes" in such programs.

In the substantive area of law, the proposed rules and regulations would make significant changes. These changes are as follows:

1. The comparable pay theory has been explicitly adopted by OFCCP, in proposed section 41 C.F.R. §60-20.5(a). The proposed rules and regulations indicate that wage schedules must not be related to or be based upon the sex of employees. Specifically, the regulations indicate that they are talking about more than just equal pay violations. They state that "while the most obvious cases of discrimination exist where employees of different sexes are paid different wages on jobs which require substantially equal skill, effort, and responsibility are performed under similar working conditions, compensation practices with respect to any jobs where males or females are substantially underutilized will be scrutinized closely to assure that sex has played no role in the setting of levels of pay."

2. Previously, OFCCP had required that employers unequivocally take back to work women who had been disabled by pregnancy, regardless of whether those women would have had the right to be returned to work had the disability been something other than pregnancy. Under the proposed rules and regulations, this mandatory return provision is no longer required. See 41 C.F.R. §60-20.7. Treatment of pregnancy in the same manner as other disabilities is, of course, required.

3. Sexual advances are specifically prohibited by the proposed rules and regulations, 41 C.F.R. §60-20.8.

4. The proposed rules and regulations, insofar as the Rehabilitation Act is concerned, reject the decision by the administrative hearing officer in the case of *E. E. Black*. In that case the hearing officer had determined that a person was not necessarily handicapped just because he could not successfully perform one job. Under the proposed rules and regulations, the new definition of the word "handicap" would negate such a finding. In 41 C.F.R. §60-1.3, a handicapped individual is considered to be "substantially limited," and handicapped if he or she is likely to experience difficulty in securing, retaining or advancing in employment because of a real or perceived handicap.

FOOTNOTES

[1] E.O. 11246, Section 202(1).
[2] See 41 C.F.R. §60-2 *et seq.* (Revised Order No. 4).
[3] Section 503(a).
[4] 41 C.F.R. §60-741.
[5] 38 U.S.C. Ch. 42, Sections 2012 and 2014.
[6] 42 U.S.C. §1981.
[7] 431 U.S. 324 (1977).
[8] 564 F.2d 179 (5th Cir. 1977).
[9] OFCCP compliance manual, Section 5-30.

[10] OFCCP compliance manual, Sections 5-20.2b, 5-40.1 *et seq.*
[11] 564 F.2d 663 (4th Cir. 1977).
[12] 41 C.F.R. §60-60.7(a).
[13] OFCCP compliance manual, 2-70.1 *et seq.*
[14] *Ibid.*
[15] *Op. cit.*, Section 1, Appendix 1A.
[16] *Op. cit.*, Chap. 2.
[17] 41 C.F.R. 60-1.43.
[18] *Ibid.*
[19] OFCCP compliance manual, Section 3-60 *et seq.*
[20] 41 C.F.R. 60-60.6.
[21] 41 C.F.R. 60-60.7.
[22] 41 C.F.R. 60-1.7.
[23] 41 C.F.R. 60-60.3(b).
[24] 41 C.F.R. 60-60.5.
[25] OFCCP compliance manual, Section 3-190.11 *et seq.*
[26] 41 C.F.R. 60-4.8.
[27] 41 C.F.R. 60-2.2.
[28] *Ibid.*
[29] 41 C.F.R. 60-1.20.
[30] *Ibid.*
[31] OFCCP Compliance Manual, Section 8-130.2c.
[32] See *Voutsis v. Union Carbide Corporation*, 452 F.2d 887 (2d Cir. 1971), cert. den., 406 U.S. 918 (1972).
[33] OFCCP Compliance Manual, Section 8-130.2d.
[34] 41 C.F.R. Sec. 60-40.2(b)(3).
[35] OFCCP Compliance Manual, Section 8-130.2d.
[36] *Ibid.*, Section 8-130.3.
[37] *Ibid.*, Section 8-120.
[38] *Ibid.*, Section 5-40.2.
[39] *Ibid.*, Section 5-40.3.
[40] 41 C.F.R. 60-1.24.
[41] *Ibid.*
[42] *Ibid.*
[43] 41 C.F.R. 60-2.2.
[44] Procedure provided for in 41 C.F.R. 60-1.24(c)(4).
[45] 411 F. Supp. 1220 (S.D. N.Y. 1976).
[46] Pursuant to 41 C.F.R. 60-2.2(b).
[47] OFCCP Compliance Manual, Section 5-20.4.
[48] 439 F. Supp. 487 (S.D. N.Y. 1977), 15 FEP Cases 598, 15 EPD (CCH) ¶7930.
[49] 601 F.2d 943 (7th Cir. 1979).
[50] OFCCP Compliance Manual Section 2-150.1a *et seq.*
[51] *Ibid.* Section 2-150.

[52] 41 C.F.R. 60-2.11.
[53] *Ibid.* Section 2-160.7c1.
[54] *Ibid.* Section 2-160.1d1.
[55] 11 EPD (CCH) ¶ 10,906 (N.D. Ohio 1976).
[56] 5 U.S.C. §552.

PART 4

RECORDS THE EMPLOYER MUST KEEP

Chapter 11

Documentation and Record-Keeping Systems

INTRODUCTION

This chapter describes the record-keeping requirements of the federal (*not* state or local) government relating to private employers. It identifies records that should be kept and how they should be kept—even though their retention may not be required by federal law—and records that probably should be destroyed after the period for which they must be kept has expired.

The material in this chapter is current as of the date of publication of this book. But the federal government's record-keeping requirements change frequently. For example, the EEOC record-retention requirements were to have been amended, effective November 30, 1978, to require that application forms be kept for two years. However, EEOC has indefinitely postponed its record-retention amendments. When they are finally made effective, they will appear in services such as the *Federal Register* or the *Daily Labor Report.*

Note that the federal government regulations that certain records must be retained do not mean that the employer is required to keep those records *under active consideration* for that length of time. For example, EEOC requires that applications of rejected applicants be retained for six months (and the proposed amendment, for two years) from the date of the personnel action. However, neither the existing nor the proposed regulations require the employer to keep applications under active review for either six months or two years. Thus, it is perfectly legal to institute or continue a policy of keeping applications under active review for only a stated period of time, such as 30 or 60 days. In fact, such a policy is recommended in Chapter 4 of this book.

Also, the fact that certain documents must be kept does not mean that all these documents should be made available to any investigator from any agency. For example, an investigator from EEOC who is pursuing the investigation of a race-discrimination charge is not necessarily entitled to see documents relating to sex composition, hiring practices, promotion rates, or the like. In fact, by permitting the EEOC investigator to review such documents, a personnel officer may be effecting a waiver of employer jurisdictional claims. This is discussed more fully in Chapter 9.

There is another significant aspect of record keeping that should be understood. If an employer does not ordinarily receive certain documents, the record-retention requirements do not mean that it must generate personnel activity to create these documents. For instance, nothing in the requirements mandates that an employer take applications, regardless of whether or not there is an opening, if the regular course of business for such an employer is not to take applications when there are no openings.

Additionally, nothing in the federal record-retention requirements indicates how documents are to be kept—microfilm, computer, and so on.

Finally, every employer's needs are different, and general statements about documentation and record-keeping systems may or may not be applicable to particular fact situations.

RECORDS REQUIRED TO BE KEPT

On pages 300-312 there appears a listing from the *Federal Register* of June 7, 1977, of the various records that must be kept, the time periods for which they must be kept, and the statute or regulation requiring that they be kept. Changes in these record-keeping statutes and regulations that have become effective after June 7, 1977, have been made, so the listing is current as of the time of publication.

In addition to these general record-keeping provisions, special requirements are applicable when a charge of discrimination is filed. EEOC requires that "where a charge of discrimination has been filed, or an action brought by the Attorney General, against an employer under Title VII, the respondent employer shall preserve all personnel records relevant to the charge or action until final disposition of the charge or action."[1]

There are two problems with this provision: the definitions of "relevant" and "final disposition." As we saw in Chapter 9, courts differ on what is relevant. Having the records available in the event of an EEOC investigation is a relatively minor problem, for EEOC will rarely pursue administrative action

Retention of Records

Categories of Employers or Employees Affected	Record-Retention and Posting Requirements	Retention Period
A. *Employers subject to Fair Labor Standards Act* *Authority:* Fair Labor Standards Act, 29 U.S.C. §211 and 29 C.F.R. §516	To keep employment records relating to the rate of payment (including retroactive payment of wages), length of work week, overtime compensation, name, age, sex, and occupation. *Posting:* Notices relating to the applicability of the Act must be posted in those places where they will be most likely viewed by the employees.	3 years for records containing employee information, payrolls, and certificates, agreements, notices and sales and purchase records. 2 years for basic employment and earnings records, wage-rate tables, work-time schedules, order shipping and billing records (customer bills, etc.), job evaluation, merit or seniority systems, or other matters which describe or explain the basis for payment of any wage differentials to employees of the opposite sex in the same establishment, records of deduction from or additions to pay.
B. *Employees subject to the child-labor provisions of the Fair Labor Standards Act* *Authority:* Fair Labor Standards Act, 29 U.S.C. §§203, 211, 212; 29 C.F.R. §§516, 570	(a) To maintain certificates of age. (b) To maintain written training agreements. (c) To maintain other employment records required by federal regulations. *Posting:* Notices relating to the applicability of the Act must be posted in those places where they will be most likely viewed by the employees.	(a) Until termination of employment. (b) Duration of training program. (c) 3 years.
C. *Employers subject to Age Discrimination in Employment Act of 1967* *Authority:* Age Discrimination in Employment Act of 1967, 29 U.S.C. §850	(a) To keep records of each employee containing name, address, date of birth, occupation, rate of pay and compensation earned each week. (b) When made in the regular course of business,	(a) 3 years. (b) 1 year.

(continued)

Retention of Records (Continued)

Categories of Employers or Employees Affected	Record-Retention and Posting Requirements	Retention Period
	to keep personal or employment records related to job application, promotion or discharge, job orders submitted to an employment agency or labor organization for recruitment of personnel, test papers of employer-administered aptitude or other employment tests, results of physical examinations considered in connection with personnel action, and advertisements.	
	(c) To keep any employee benefits plans; if the plan is not in writing, any memoranda explaining the plan to the employees is sufficient.	(c) Full period of plan or system and 1 year after termination.
	(d) To keep application forms for positions known to be of a temporary nature. *Posting:* Notices pertaining to the applicability of the Act must be conspicuously placed.	(d) 90 days. When an enforcement action is commenced by the U.S. Dept. of Labor, the Administrator can require an employer to retain any record relevant to such action until final disposition of that action.
D. *Employers subject to Title VII of the Civil Rights Act* *Authority:* Title VII of the Civil Rights Act, 42 U.S.C. §§ 2000e-8, 2000e-12; and 29 C.F.R. § 1602.14	To maintain personnel and employment and other records having to do with hiring, promotion, demotion, transfer, layoff or termination, rates of pay, and selection for training and apprenticeships. *Posting:* The Act requires the posting of a statement on the Title VII discrimination prohibitions and information on how to file a complaint.	6 months from date of making record or personnel action involved, whichever is later. Whenever a charge of discrimination has been filed, or an action brought by the Commission or the Attorney General, until final disposition of the charge or action, EEO-1 Report must be retained at all times and it must be made available on request by an EEOC official.

Retention of Records (Continued)

Categories of Employers or Employees Affected	Record-Retention and Posting Requirements	Retention Period
E. *Public school systems, districts, and individuals with 15 or more employees subject to Title VII* *Authority:* Title VII of the Civil Rights Act, 42 U.S.C. §2000e-8, 2000e-12; and 29 C.F.R. §1602.40	(a) To maintain records on hiring, promotion, demotion, transfer, termination (voluntary or involuntary), rates of pay or other terms of compensation of all public school employees as well as other personal and employment records. (b) To maintain information to complete Form EEO-5 as required.	(a) 2 years. (b) 3 years.
F. *Every employer, labor organization, and joint labor–management committee subject to Title VII which controls an apprenticeship program.* *Authority:* Title VII of the Civil Rights Act, 42 U.S.C. §2000e-8, 2000e-12; and 29 C.F.R. §§1602.20, 1602.21	To maintain a chronological order of names, addresses, date of application, sex, race, and other records required by EEO-2.	2 years. When a charge is commenced, all relevant documents must be retained until final disposition.
G. *Institutions of higher education employing 15 or more employees and subject to Title VII* *Authority:* 42 U.S.C. §2000e-8, 2000e-12; and 29 C.F.R. §1602.48.	To maintain all records necessary to complete EEO-6.	3 years.
H. *Employers required to report payments or agreements or arrangements under the Labor Management Reporting and Disclosure Act of 1959.* *Authority:* 29 U.S.C. §401 *et seq.*; and 29 C.F.R. §§204.3, 402.9	To maintain records providing the necessary basic information and data from which the required documents filed with the office may be verified, explained, or clarified and checked for accuracy and completeness. To be included are vouchers, worksheets, receipts, and applicable resolutions.	Not less than 5 years after filing of documents.
I. *Employers subject to*	To maintain records for	Duration of employ-

(continued)

Retention of Records (Continued)

Categories of Employers or Employees Affected	Record-Retention and Posting Requirements	Retention Period
the Occupational Safety & Health Act of 1970 *Authority:* OSHA, 29 U.S.C. §667; 29 C.F.R. §1903.5	each occupational injury and illness, including an annual summary, and also a supplemental record in detail according to OSHA Form 101. *Posting:* Post statements explaining and outlining the applicability of OSHA, as well as the Annual Summary Report for the previous year, no later than Feb. 1 of the following year until March 1.	ment plus 5 years; medical records to be kept forever.
J. *Government contractors or contractors doing work on federally financed or assisted projects:*		
1. Contractors subject to Public Contracts Act (contracts with U.S. agencies or district) *Authority:* Walsh-Healy Act, 41 U.S.C. §§15 et seq.; and 41 C.F.R. §50-501(d)	(a) To keep unexpired certificates of age of employees issued and held pursuant to the Fair Labor Standards Act.	(a) During the period of employment of such minors.
	(b) To keep employment records, including name, address, sex, occupation, date of birth of each employee under 19 years of age (if the employer has obtained a certificate of age to record the title and office issuing the certificate, the number of certificate, if any, the date of its issuance, and the name, address, and date of birth of the minor, as the same appears on the certificate of age), wage and hour records.	(b) 3 years from date of last entry.
	(c) To keep basic employment and earnings records, wage-rate tables, and work-time schedules.	(c) 2 years from date of last entry or last effective date, whichever is later.

Retention of Records (Continued)

Categories of Employers or Employees Affected	Record-Retention and Posting Requirements	Retention Period
	(d) To maintain records of radiation exposure of all employees for whom personnel monitoring is required.	(d) 5 years after date of entry.
	(e) To keep an annual summary of occupational illnesses and accidents.	(e) Not specified.
2. Contractors or subcontractors subject to Service Contract Act of 1965 *Authority:* McNamara-O'Hara Service Contract Act of 1965, 41 U.S.C. §§351, 353 5 U.S.C. §301, 29 C.F.R. §4.6(g), 1925.3, 41 C.F.R. §1-12.904-1	To maintain records indicating: (a) work classifications, wages and fringe benefits, hours worked, and (b) safety and health standards	(a) 3 years from completion of work. (b) 5 years following the end of the year to which they relate.
3. Contractors or subcontractors engaged in construction, prosecution, completion, or repair of any public building, public work, or work financed in whole or in part by loans or grants from a federal agency *Authority:* Davis Bacon Act, 40 U.S.C. §276(c), and C.F.R. §3.4, 41 C.F.R. §1-18.703-1	To maintain the payroll records detailing the name and address of each laborer and mechanic, his correct classification, rate of pay, daily and weekly number of hours worked, deductions made, and actual wages paid. *Posting:* Notices of coverage by the Davis-Bacon Act must be posted in a conspicuous place.	3 years from date of completion of contract.
4. Contractors or subcontractors subject to labor standards provisions applicable to contracts covering federally financed construction *Authority:* Davis-Bacon Act, 40 U.S.C. §276(c) and C.F.R. §5.5(a)(3)(i), 5.5(6)	(a) To keep payroll and basic records including name and address of each laborer or mechanic, correct classification, rate of pay (including rates of contributions or costs anticipated for medical or hospital care, pensions on retirement or death, compensation for injuries or illness resulting from	(a) 3 years after termination of contract.

(continued)

Retention of Records (Continued)

Categories of Employers or Employees Affected	Record-Retention and Posting Requirements	Retention Period
	occupational activity, or insurance to provide any of the foregoing; for unemployment benefits, life insurance, disability and sickness insurance, or accident insurance, for vacation and holiday pay, for defraying costs of apprenticeship programs, or for other bona fide fringe benefits), daily and weekly number of hours worked, deductions made, and actual wages paid to all laborers and mechanics.	
	(b) In the case of unfunded plans or programs for fringe benefits listed in the Davis-Bacon Act which are approved by the Department of Labor, to maintain records showing: (1) that the contractor's commitment is enforceable, (2) that it has been communicated in writing to laborers or mechanics employed by him, and (3) that it is financially responsible.	(b) 3 years after termination of contract.
5. Contractors or subcontractors subject to labor standards provisions applicable to contracts subject only to the Contract Work Hours and Safety Standards Act	To keep records relating to wages and hours.	3 years after completion of contract.
Authority: Contract Work Hours and Safety Standards Act, 40 U.S.C. §§327–330, 29 C.F.R. §5.5(e), 41 C.F.R. §1–12.303		
6. Contractors or subcontractors subject to	(a) To maintain records and documents relating to	Not specified. OFCCP expects contractors to

Retention of Records (Continued)

Categories of Employers or Employees Affected	Record-Retention and Posting Requirements	Retention Period
equal opportunity in employment regulations *Authority:* E.O. 11246, as amended 30 F.R. 12319, 41 C.F.R. §1-12.805.4	nature and use of tests, validation of tests, and test results as required. (b) To keep employment or other records as required by the Director, Office of Federal Contract Compliance, the contracting agency, or an applicant for federal assistance concerning the contract, including the development and retention of written affirmative action compliance programs to be updated annually. *Posting:* To post the "Equal Employment Opportunity is the Law" poster.	have current AACP, with support data, and AACP for past AACP year, with support data.
7. Contractors or subcontractors subject to affirmative action requirements under the Rehabilitation Act of 1973, as amended *Authority:* Rehabilitation Act of 1973, 29 U.S.C. §793, 41 C.F.R. §60-741.52	(a) To maintain pertinent books, documents, papers, and records concerning the employment and advancement in employment of the handicapped. (b) To maintain records relating to complaints and the action taken. *Posting:* Must post notices concerning affirmative action obligations under the Rehabilitation Act.	(a) Not specified. (b) 1 year.
8. Contractors or subcontractors subject to the affirmative action requirements under the Vietnam Era Veterans' Readjustment Assistance Act of 1974 *Authority:* 38 U.S.C. 2020(b)(3) and 41	(a) To maintain pertinent books, documents, papers, and records concerning the employment and advancement of disabled veterans. (b) To maintain records regarding complaints. (c) To provide reports to	(a) Not specified. (b) 1 year. (c) 1 year after final

(continued)

Retention of Records (Continued)

Categories of Employers or Employees Affected	Record-Retention and Posting Requirements	Retention Period
C.F.R. §§ 60-250.4, 60-250.52	local offices of State Employment Services regarding employment openings and hires under the mandatory listing requirement of 41 C.F.R. 60-250.4. *Posting:* Must post notices concerning the contractor's affirmative action obligations under the Act.	payment under contract.
K. *Requirements relating to limited categories of employees:* *1. Apprentices:* a. Contractors or subcontractors employing apprentices and trainees on federal and federally assisted construction *Authority:* Davis-Bacon Act, 40 U.S.C. § 276a-7 and 41 C.F.R. § 1-18.703.1	To keep records for each trade of the number of apprentices and trainees, the number of apprentices and trainees by first year of training, the number of journeymen, and the wages paid the apprentices, trainees, and journeymen.	During the performance of each contract.
b. Employers subject to Fair Labor Standards Act employing apprentices in skilled trades at wages lower than minimum wage applicable *Authority:* FLSA 29 U.S.C. § 211 and 29 C.F.R. §§ 516.5 521.8(a) and (c)	To keep records relating to wages, hours, conditions of employment, etc., as well as designation of apprentices on the payroll, and when applicable, the apprenticeship program, apprenticeship agreement, and special certificate under which an apprentice is employed.	3 years from termination of apprenticeship.
c. Employers and joint labor-management committees controlling apprenticeship programs subject to Title VII of the Civil Rights Act of 1964 *Authority:* 42 U.S.C. § 2000e-8, 2000e-12 and 29 C.F.R. §§ 1602.20, 1602.21	(a) To maintain a list in chronological order of names and addresses, sex, and minority group identification on all applicants in the apprenticeship program, and any other records relating to applicants for apprenticeship, such as completed test papers and records of interviews.	(a) 2 years or period of successful applicant's apprenticeship, whichever is later.

Retention of Records (Continued)

Categories of Employers or Employees Affected	Record-Retention and Posting Requirements	Retention Period
	(b) To maintain any other records made solely for completing Report EEO-2, or similar reports.	(b) 1 year from due date of the report. Whenever a charge of discrimination has been filed, or an action brought by the Attorney General, until final disposition of the charge.
2. *The handicapped:* Employers subject to Fair Labor Standards Act employing handicapped workers *Authority:* FLSA 29 U.S.C. §211, 29 C.F.R. §§516.5, 516.30, 524.10	To retain a copy of special certificates authorizing employment of workers whose earning capacity is impaired by physical or mental deficiencies at wages lower than the minimum wages applicable under Fair Labor Standards Act and employment record (in addition to requirements of a general nature under the FLSA).	3 years.
3. *Learners, student-learners, and student employees:* (a) Employers subject to Fair Labor Standards Act employing learners under special learner certificates *Authority:* FLSA, 29 U.S.C. §211 and 29 C.F.R. §§516.5, 516.30, 522.7	To keep payroll records of learners and occupation in which each learner is employed; any special learner certificates issued; statements obtained from learners employed under special learner's certificates of experience acquired in the industry in the 3 years prior to employment as a learner; and to maintain file of all evidence and records, including correspondence pertaining to filing or cancellation of job orders (in addition to requirements of a general nature under the FLSA).	3 years.

(continued)

Retention of Records (Continued)

Categories of Employers or Employees Affected	Record-Retention and Posting Requirements	Retention Period
(b) Employers subject to Fair Labor Standards Act employing student-learners as learners under certificate *Authority:* FLSA, 29 U.S.C. §211 and 29 C.F.R. §§516.5, 516.30, and 520.7	To maintain payroll records to student-learners, listing the occupation in which each student-learner is employed and copies of applications filed in accordance with 29 C.F.R. 520.4(a) and of any special certificates issued under which student-learners are employed (in addition to requirements of a general nature under the FLSA).	3 years.
(c) Retail or service establishments subject to Fair Labor Standards Act employing full-time students outside their school hours under special full-time student certificates *Authority:* FLSA, 29 U.S.C. §211 and 29 C.F.R. §§516.5, 516.30, 519.7, and 519.17	To maintain payroll records of full-time students employed outside their school hours in any retail or service establishments and occupations in which each full-time student is employed; statements obtained by the employer from schools attended by such students that the employee receives primarily daytime instruction at the physical location of the school in accordance with the school's accepted definition of a full-time student; records of the monthly hours of employment of full-time students at special minimum wages under a full-time student certificate and of the total hours of employment during the month of all employees in the establishment; and any special certificates issued (in addition to requirements of a general nature under the FLSA).	3 years.

Retention of Records (Continued)

Categories of Employers or Employees Affected	Record-Retention and Posting Requirements	Retention Period
4. Retail or service establishments subject to Fair Labor Standards Act employing commission employees exempt from overtime pay requirements pursuant to Section 7(i) Authority: FLSA, 29 U.S.C. §211, and 29 C.F.R. §§516.2, 516.5, 516.6, 516.28	To keep employment records relating to wages, hours, circumstances and conditions of employment, including a symbol or letter to identify each such employee; an indication that the employee's regular rate of pay in each workweek meets requirements of the exemption and basic records demonstrating this fact; copy of the agreement or understanding or summary of its terms, including the basis of compensation, applicable representative period, and the date on which the agreement or understanding was entered into; and total compensation paid to each employee in each pay period, stating separately the commission and non-commission straight-time earnings.	3 years for records containing employee information, payrolls and certificates, union agreements, and notices; 2 years for basic employment and earning records, wage-rate tables, work-time schedules, orders, shipping and billing records (customers' bills, etc.), record of deductions from or additions to pay.
5. Employers of local delivery drivers and helpers Authority: FLSA, 29 U.S.C. §211 and 29 C.F.R. §§516.5, 551.9	To keep records and computations with respect to employees for whom the overtime-pay exemption is taken.	3 years.
6. Employers subject to the provisions of the Longshoremen's and Harbor Workers' Compensation Act, as extended by the Defense Base Act, the District of Columbia Workmen's Compensation Act, the Outer Continental Shelf Lands Act, and the Nonappropriated Fund Instrumentalities Act	To keep records regarding any injury to an employee, including information on disease, other disability or death.	Not specified.

(continued)

Retention of Records (Continued)

Categories of Employers or Employees Affected	Record-Retention and Posting Requirements	Retention Period
Authority: Longshoremen's & Harbor Workers' Compensation Act, 33 U.S.C. §§901 et. seq. and 20 C.F.R. §702.11		
7. *Self-insured employers subject to Longshoremen's and Harbor Workers' Compensation Act, as extended by the District of Columbia Workmen's Compensation Act, the Defense Base Act, the Outer Continental Shelf Lands Act, and the Nonappropriated Fund Instrumentalities Act*	To make, keep, and preserve such records as the Secretary of Labor deems necessary or appropriate to carry out his responsibilities.	Not specified.
Authority: Longshoremen's and Harbor Workers' Compensation Act, 33 U.S.C. §§901 et seq. and 20 C.F.R. §702.148		
8. *Employers of maritime employees under the Longshoremen's and Harbor Workers' Compensation Act* *Authority:* (a) Longshoremen's and Harbor Workers' Compensation Act, 33 U.S.C. §§901 et seq.; and 29 C.F.R. §1918.61 (b) L.H.W.C.A., 33 U.S.C. §§901 and 29 C.F.R. §1918.93 (c) L.H.W.C.A., 33 U.S.C. §§901 et seq.; and 29 C.F.R. §§1915.10, 1916.10, 1917.10	(a) To maintain records of tests of strength of stevedoring gear. (b) To keep records of the dates, times, and locations of tests for carbon monoxide made when internal combustion engines exhaust into the hold or intermediate deck. (c) To keep records relating to tests and inspections for the existence of hazardous flammable, explosive, or toxic liquids and gases.	(a) As long as such gear is in use. (b) 30 days after the work is completed. (c) 3 months from the date of completion of the job.

against the employer for failing to have the records available. A more serious problem for the employer is having the records necessary to make its defense in the event of litigation.

Many courts, in considering the class to be certified, have permitted an employee to represent applicants, a supervisor to represent supervisory and nonsupervisory personnel, and a person at one facility to represent people at many facilities. Consequently, in theory, any one charge could put an employer on notice to retain all records on all employees indefinitely because they all may be "relevant." If the employer has destroyed records later found necessary for its defense, the courts have indicated, this predicament is not sufficient to enable the employer to have the suit dismissed. Regardless of how long a period passes between the charge under Title VII and a lawsuit under Title VII, if EEOC has not terminated its jurisdiction, the employer can be sued and is responsible for having the necessary records available to defend itself. See *Bernard* v. *Gulf Oil Co.*[2]

"Final disposition" generally means the termination of the EEOC administrative process, plus the passage of more than 90 days after the right-to-sue notice has been issued to the charging party. EEOC has told appellate courts that it automatically issues a right-to-sue notice, even if there is a finding of probable cause, if it has determined not to file a lawsuit; and one court has even ordered EEOC to undertake such action—*Zambuto* v. *American Telephone & Telegraph Co.*[3] However, despite these statements by EEOC and the order in *Zambuto*, there are literally thousands of cases for which EEOC has effectively terminated its administrative process but for which no right-to-sue notice has yet been issued. Many of these cases are more than five years old.

There is one way an employer might be able to effectively close old charge files and therefore dispose of old personnel files. First, make a Freedom of Information Act request to EEOC in Washington, D.C., asking the identity of all charges still outstanding against the company. Then, analyze this list and arrange a meeting with appropriate EEOC district-office officials. The employer can then ask that EEOC terminate its jurisdiction and issue right-to-sue notices on those cases for which the administrative process has already terminated.

MANNER AND PERIOD OF RECORD RETENTION

Applications

A description of how application records can be safely kept is incorporated in the sample directive at the end of Chapter 4. Even though that description calls for applications to be segregated by sex and kept separately for minorities and nonminorities, such a record-keeping system is legal as long as there is no adverse impact in the selection system. In fact, it is only by segregating the applications that adverse impact in the selection system can be properly assessed and prevented.

At present, applications must be kept for only one year under the ADEA and six months under Title VII. During these time periods, the necessary adverse-impact analysis computations should be calculated. However, once applications of rejected persons are no longer legally required to be kept, they should be destroyed, as should any other records relating to people who applied and were not hired.

Maintaining Sensitive EEO Information

Any record made by an employer that indicates a person's race, national origin, religion, age, or status as a handicapped person, such as the Post-Hire EEO Form referenced in Chapter 4, should *not* be kept in that person's personnel file. There should be a separate file, with access restricted to the affirmative action program coordinator, or others who might need to know such information. These records should be kept for the duration of the person's employment.

Transfer Request, Job Bidding Sheets, and Promotion Requests

As indicated in Chapter 5, personnel actions involving transfer, assignment, or promotion should be initiated by the employee, not the employer. Furthermore, there should be some kind of written document showing that a person has made such a request. This requirement should be so strictly adhered to that the employer can establish as fact in a court of law the converse—that is, if there is no such written record, there was no such request for assignment, transfer, or promotion.

These documents, which reflect employee requests and concomitantly prove the absence of a request, should be kept in the individual employees' personnel files and should not be destroyed until 300 days after the employee terminates employment; this is the filing period under Title VII for persons in most states.

These documents may never be used, but they can be invaluable. The Supreme Court indicated in *Teamsters* v. *U.S.*[4] that in order for a person to be a victim of discrimination, that person must have *personally* been denied some benefit he or she sought—that is, must have actually applied for some position or benefit and been denied it. Thus, just because an employer discriminated does not necessarily mean that each person in a certain protected group was aggrieved by that discriminatory conduct.

The employer that has complete records on requests for transfer, assignment, or promotion may be found liable in a Stage I proceeding under Title VII, yet minimize its exposure at Stage II by demonstrating that few, if any, people were actually aggrieved by the practice or policy found to be discriminatory.

Anything less than written documentation about employee requests, and anything less than a system requiring that personnel action be initiated by the employee in writing, will not suffice to accomplish the purpose intended. If the employer has a system allowing employees to initiate personnel action orally, then during a Stage II proceeding, people who stand to benefit financially may say they had sought a certain job even if they had not.

Discipline Notices

In most discipline systems, the discipline of a particular employee regarding a particular subject has no effect after a certain period of time has passed. From a practical point of view, the employer who is relying on dated disciplinary actions, even in part, as the basis for adverse action against an employee probably has a weak defense and is making it even weaker by presenting the dated material. For these reasons, it is probably advisable to sanitize all dated disciplinary notices from an employee's file after a certain period of time. Certainly no such notices that are more than three years old should remain on file.

But removing these notices from an employee's file does not mean that they should all be destroyed. Any kind of discipline system purporting to be consistent and fair should be able to demonstrate precedents for the type of discipline the employer purposes in a particular instance. Consequently, before these discipline notices are destroyed, they should be culled so that the employer has a file containing examples of the discipline administered in various situations.

Exit Interview Sheets

These documents should be maintained in the personnel file of the former employee for one year. After one year has passed without any kind of discrimination charge having been filed, it is highly unlikely that such a charge could effectively be filed at all under any of the EEO statutes or regulations, so the file is no longer necessary and should be destroyed.

FOOTNOTES

[1] 29 C.F.R. §1602.14(a).
[2] 596 F.2d 1249 (5th Cir. 1979).
[3] 544 F.2d 1333 (5th Cir. 1977).
[4] 431 U.S. 324 (1977).

Appendix A

The Uniform Guidelines on Employee Selection

Source: Federal Register, Vol. 43, No. 166 (August 25, 1978) 38290–315.

RULES AND REGULATIONS

[6570-06]

Title 29—Labor

CHAPTER XIV—EQUAL EMPLOYMENT OPPORTUNITY COMMISSION

PART 1607—UNIFORM GUIDELINES ON EMPLOYEE SELECTION PROCEDURES (1978)

Title 5—Administrative Personnel

CHAPTER I—CIVIL SERVICE COMMISSION

PART 300—EMPLOYMENT (GENERAL)

Title 28—Judicial Administration

CHAPTER I—DEPARTMENT OF JUSTICE

PART 50—STATEMENTS OF POLICY

Title 41—Public Contracts and Property Management

CHAPTER 60—OFFICE OF FEDERAL CONTRACT COMPLIANCE PROGRAMS, DEPARTMENT OF LABOR

PART 60-3—UNIFORM GUIDELINES ON EMPLOYEE SELECTION PROCEDURES (1978)

Adoption of Employee Selection Procedures

AGENCIES: Equal Employment Opportunity Commission, Civil Service Commission, Department of Justice and Department of Labor.

ACTION: Adoption of uniform guidelines on employee selection procedures as final rules by four agencies.

SUMMARY: This document sets forth the uniform guidelines on employee selection procedures adopted by the Equal Employment Opportunity Commission, Civil Service Commission, Department of Justice, and the Department of Labor. At present two different sets of guidelines exist. The guidelines are intended to establish a uniform Federal position in the area of prohibiting discrimination in employment practices on grounds of race, color, religion, sex, or national origin. Cross reference documents are published at 5 CFR 300.103(c) (Civil Service Commission), 28 CFR 50.14 (Department of Justice), 29 CFR Part 1607 (Equal Employment Opportunity Commission), and 41 CFR Part 60-3 (Department of Labor) elsewhere in this issue.

EFFECTIVE DATE: September 25, 1978.

FOR FURTHER INFORMATION CONTACT:

Doris Wooten, Associate Director, Donald J. Schwartz, Staff Psychologist, Office of Federal Contract Compliance Programs, Room C-3324, Department of Labor, 200 Constitution Avenue NW., Washington, D.C. 20210, 202-523-9426.

Peter C. Robertson, Director, Office of Policy Implementation, Equal Employment Opportunity Commission, 2401 E Street NW., Washington, D.C. 20506, 202-634-7060.

David L. Rose, Chief, Employment Section, Civil Rights Division, Department of Justice, 10th Street and Pennsylvania Avenue NW., Washington, D.C. 20530, 202-739-3831.

A. Diane Graham, Director, Federal Equal Employment Opportunity, Civil Service Commission, 1900 E Street NW., Washington, D.C. 20415, 202-632-4420.

H. Patrick Swygert, General Counsel, Civil Service Commission, 1900 E Street NW., Washington, D.C. 20415, 202-632-4632.

SUPPLEMENTARY INFORMATION:

AN OVERVIEW OF THE 1978 UNIFORM GUIDELINES ON EMPLOYEE SELECTION PROCEDURES

I. BACKGROUND

One problem that confronted the Congress which adopted the Civil Rights Act of 1964 involved the effect of written preemployment tests on equal employment opportunity. The use of these test scores frequently denied employment to minorities in many cases without evidence that the tests were related to success on the job. Yet employers wished to continue to use such tests as practical tools to assist in the selection of qualified employees. Congress sought to strike a balance which would proscribe discrimination, but otherwise permit the use of tests in the selection of employees. Thus, in title VII, Congress authorized the use of "any professionally developed ability test provided that such test, its administration or action upon the results is not designed, intended or used to discriminate * * *".[1]

At first, some employers contended that, under this section, they could use any test which had been developed by a professional so long as they did not intend to exclude minorities, even if such exclusion was the consequence of the use of the test. In 1966, the Equal Employment Opportunity Commission (EEOC) adopted guidelines to advise employers and other users what the law and good industrial psycholo-

[1] Section 703(h), 42 U.S.C. 2000e(2)(h).

RULES AND REGULATIONS

gy practice required.[2] The Department of Labor adopted the same approach in 1968 with respect to tests used by Federal contractors under Executive Order 11246 in a more detailed regulation. The Government's view was that the employer's intent was irrelevant. If tests or other practices had an adverse impact on protected groups, they were unlawful unless they could be justified. To justify a test which screened out a higher proportion of minorities, the employer would have to show that it fairly measured or predicted performance on the job. Otherwise, it would not be considered to be "professionally developed."

In succeeding years, the EEOC and the Department of Labor provided more extensive guidance which elaborated upon these principles and expanded the guidelines to emphasize all selection procedures. In 1971 in *Griggs v. Duke Power Co.*,[3] the Supreme Court announced the principle that employer practices which had an adverse impact on minorities and were not justified by business necessity constituted illegal discrimination under title VII. Congress confirmed this interpretation in the 1972 amendments to title VII. The elaboration of these principles by courts and agencies continued into the mid-1970's,[4] but differences between the EEOC and the other agencies (Justice, Labor, and Civil Service Commission) produced two different sets of guidelines by the end of 1976.

With the advent of the Carter administration in 1977, efforts were intensified to produce a unified government position. The following document represents the result of that effort. This introduction is intended to assist those not familiar with these matters to understand the basic approach of the uniform guidelines. While the guidelines are complex and technical, they are based upon the principles which have been consistently upheld by the courts, the Congress, and the agencies.

The following discussion will cite the sections of the Guidelines which embody these principles.

II. ADVERSE IMPACT

The fundamental principle underlying the guidelines is that employer policies or practices which have an adverse impact on employment opportunities of any race, sex, or ethnic group are illegal under title VII and the Executive order unless justified by business necessity.[5] A selection procedure which has no adverse impact generally does not violate title VII or the Executive order.[6] This means that an employer may usually avoid the application of the guidelines by use of procedures which have no adverse impact.[7] If adverse impact exists, it must be justified on grounds of business necessity. Normally, this means by validation which demonstrates the relation between the selection procedure and performance on the job.

The guidelines adopt a "rule of thumb" as a practical means of determining adverse impact for use in enforcement proceedings. This rule is known as the "⅘ths" or "80 percent" rule.[8] It is not a legal definition of discrimination, rather it is a practical device to keep the attention of enforcement agencies on serious discrepancies in hire or promotion rates or other employment decisions. To determine whether a selection procedure violates the "⅘ths rule", an employer compares its hiring rates for different groups.[9] But this rule of thumb cannot be applied automatically. An employer who has conducted an extensive recruiting campaign may have a larger than normal pool of applicants, and the "⅘ths rule" might unfairly expose it to enforcement proceedings.[10] On the other hand, an employer's reputation may have discouraged or "chilled" applicants of particular groups from applying because they believed application would be futile. The application of the "⅘ths" rule in that situation would allow an employer to evade scrutiny because of its own discrimination.[11]

III. IS ADVERSE IMPACT TO BE MEASURED BY THE OVERALL PROCESS?

In recent years some employers have eliminated the overall adverse impact of a selection procedure and employed sufficient numbers of minorities or women to meet this "⅘th's rule of thumb". However, they might continue use of a component which does have an adverse impact. For example, an employer might insist on a minimum passing score on a written test which is not job related and which has an adverse impact on minorities.[12] However, the employer might compensate for this adverse impact by hiring a sufficient proportion of minorities who do meet its standards, so that its overall hiring is on a par with or higher than the applicant flow. Employers have argued that as long as their "bottom line" shows no overall

---

[2] See 35 U.S.L.W. 2137 (1966).
[3] 401 U.S. 424 (1971).
[4] See, e.g., *Albemarle Paper Co.* v. *Moody*, 422 U.S. 405 (1975).
[5] *Griggs*, note 3, supra; uniform guidelines on employee selection procedures (1978), section 3A, (hereinafter cited by section number only).

[6] *Furnco* v. *Waters*, 98 S.Ct. 2943 (1978).
[7] Section 6.
[8] Section 4D.
[9] Section 16R (definition of selection rate).
[10] Section 4D (special recruiting programs).
[11] *Ibid* (user's actions have discouraged applicants).
[12] See, e.g., *Griggs* v. *Duke Power Co.*, 401 U.S. 424 (1971).

RULES AND REGULATIONS

adverse impact, there is no violation at all, regardless of the operation of a particular component of the process.

Employee representatives have argued that rights under equal employment opportunity laws are individual, and the fact that an employer has hired some minorities does not justify discrimination against other minorities. Therefore, they argue that adverse impact is to be determined by examination of each component of the selection procedure, regardless of the "bottom line." This question has not been answered definitively by the courts. There are decisions pointing in both directions.

These guidelines do not address the underlying question of law. They discuss only the exercise of prosecutorial discretion by the Government agencies themselves.[13] The agencies have decided that, generally, their resources to combat discrimination should be used against those respondents whose practices have restricted or excluded the opportunities of minorities and women. If an employer is appropriately including all groups in the workforce, it is not sensible to spend Government time and effort on such a case, when there are so many employers whose practices do have adverse effects which should be challenged. For this reason, the guidelines provide that, in considering whether to take enforcement action, the Government will take into account the general posture of the employer concerning equal employment opportunity, including its affirmative action plan and results achieved under the plan.[14] There are some circumstances where the government may intervene even though the "bottom line" has been satisfied. They include the case where a component of a selection procedure restricts promotional opportunities of minorities or women who were discriminatorily assigned to jobs, and where a component, such as a height requirement, has been declared unlawful in other situations.[15]

What of the individual who is denied the job because of a particular component in a procedure which otherwise meets the "bottom line" standard? The individual retains the right to proceed through the appropriate agencies, and into Federal court.[16]

IV. WHERE ADVERSE IMPACT EXISTS: THE BASIC OPTIONS

Once an employer has established that there is adverse impact, what steps are required by the guidelines? As previously noted, the employer can modify or eliminate the procedure which produces the adverse impact, thus taking the selection procedure from the coverage of these guidelines. If the employer does not do that, then it must justify the use of the procedure on grounds of "business necessity."[17] This normally means that it must show a clear relation between performance on the selection procedure and performance on the job. In the language of industrial psychology, the employer must validate the selection procedure. Thus the bulk of the guidelines consist of the Government's interpretation of standards for validation.

V. VALIDATION: CONSIDERATION OF ALTERNATIVES

The concept of validation as used in personnel psychology involves the establishment of the relationship between a test instrument or other selection procedure and performance on the job. Federal equal employment opportunity law has added a requirement to the process of validation. In conducting a validation study, the employer should consider available alternatives which will achieve its legitimate business purpose with lesser adverse impact.[18] The employer cannot concentrate solely on establishing the validity of the instrument or procedure which it has been using in the past.

This same principle of using the alternative with lesser adverse impact is applicable to the manner in which an employer uses a valid selection procedure.[19] The guidelines assume that there are at least three ways in which an employer can use scores on a selection procedure: (1) To screen out of consideration those who are not likely to be able to perform the job successfully; (2) to group applicants in accordance with the likelihood of their successful performance on the job, and (3) to rank applicants, selecting those with the highest scores for employment.[20]

The setting of a "cutoff score" to determine who will be screened out may have an adverse impact. If so, an employer is required to justify the initial cutoff score by reference to its need for a trustworthy and efficient work force.[21] Similarly, use of results for

---

[13] Section 4C.
[14] Section 4E.
[15] Section 4C.
[16] The processing of individual cases is excluded from the operation of the bottom line concept by the definition of "enforcement action," section 16I. Under section 4C, where adverse impact has existed, the employer must keep records of the effect of each component for 2 years after the adverse effect has dissipated.

[17] A few practices may be used without validation even if they have adverse impact. See, e.g., *McDonnell Douglas* v. *Green*, 411 U.S. 792 (1973) and section 6B.
[18] *Albermarle Paper Co.* v. *Moody*, 422 U.S. 405 (1975); *Robinson* v. *Lorillard Corp.*, 444 F. 2d 791 (4th Cir. 1971).
[19] Sections 3B; 5G.
[20] *Ibid.*
[21] See sections 3B; 5H. See also sections 14B(6) (criterion-related validity); 14C(9) (content validity); 14D(1) (construct validity).

RULES AND REGULATIONS

grouping or for rank ordering is likely to have a greater adverse effect than use of scores solely to screen out unqualified candidates. If the employer chooses to use a rank order method, the evidence of validity must be sufficient to justify that method of use.[22]

VI. TESTING FOR HIGHER LEVEL JOBS

Normally, employers test for the job for which people are hired. However, there are situations where the first job is temporary or transient, and the workers who remain are promoted to work which involves more complex activities. The guidelines restrict testing for higher level jobs to users who promote a majority of the employees who remain with them to the higher level job within a reasonable period of time.[23]

VII. HOW IS VALIDATION TO BE CONDUCTED

Validation has become highly technical and complex, and yet is constantly changing as a set of concepts in industrial psychology. What follows here is a simple introduction to a highly complex field. There are three concepts which can be used to validate a selection procedure. These concepts reflect different approaches to investigating the job relatedness of selection procedures and may be interrelated in practice. They are (1) criterion-related validity,[24] (2) content validity,[25] and (3) construct validity.[26] In criterion-related validity, a selection procedure is justified by a statistical relationship between scores on the test or other selection procedure and measures of job performance. In content validity, a selection procedure is justified by showing that it representatively samples significant parts of the job, such as a typing test for a typist. Construct validity involves identifying the psychological trait (the construct) which underlies successful performance on the job and then devising a selection procedure to measure the presence and degree of the construct. An example would be a test of "leadership ability."

The guidelines contain technical standards and documentation requirements for the application of each of the three approaches.[27] One of the problems which the guidelines attempt to meet is the "borderline" between "content validity" and "construct validity." The extreme cases are easy to understand. A secretary, for example, may have to type. Many jobs require the separation of important matters which must be handled immediately from those which can be handled routinely. For the typing function, a typing test is appropriate. It is justifiable on the basis of content validity because it is a sample of an important or critical part of the job. The second function can be viewed as involving a capability to exercise selective judgment in light of the surrounding circumstances, a mental process which is difficult to sample.

In addressing this situation, the guidelines attempt to make it practical to validate the typing test by a content strategy,[28] but do not allow the validation of a test measuring a construct such as "judgment" by a content validity strategy.

The bulk of the guidelines deals with questions such as those discussed in the above paragraphs. Not all such questions can be answered simply, nor can all problems be addressed in the single document. Once the guidelines are issued, they will have to be interpreted in light of changing factual, legal, and professional circumstances.

VIII. SIMPLIFICATION OF REPORTING AND RECORDKEEPING REQUIREMENTS

The reporting and recordkeeping provisions which appeared in the December 30 draft which was published for comment have been carefully reviewed in light of comments received and President Carter's direction to limit paperwork burdens on those regulated by Government to the minimum necessary for effective regulation. As a result of this review, two major changes have been made in the documentation requirements of the guidelines:

(1) A new section 15A(1) provides a simplified recordkeeping option for employers with fewer than 100 employees;

(2) Determinations of the adverse impact of selection procedures need not be made for groups which constitute less than 2 percent of the relevant labor force.

Also, the draft has been changed to make clear that users can assess adverse impact on an annual basis rather than on a continuing basis.

Analysis of comments. The uniform guidelines published today are based upon the proposition that the Federal Government should speak to the public and to those whom it regulates with one voice on this important subject; and that the Federal Government ought to impose upon itself obligations for equal employment opportunity which are at least as demanding as

---

[22] Sections 5G, 14B(6); 14C(9); 14D(1).
[23] Section 5I.
[24] Sections 5B, (General Standards); 14B (Technical Standards); 15B (Documentation); 16F (Definition).
[25] Sections 5B (General Standards); 14C (Technical Standards); 15C (Documentation); 16D (Definition).
[26] Sections 5B (General Standards); 14D (Technical Standards); 15D (Documentation); 16E (Definition).
[27] Technical standards are in section 14; documentation requirements are in section 15.

[28] Section 14C.

RULES AND REGULATIONS

those it seeks to impose on others. These guidelines state a uniform Federal position on this subject, and are intended to protect the rights created by title VII of the Civil Rights Act of 1964, as amended, Executive Order 11246, as amended, and other provisions of Federal law. The uniform guidelines are also intended to represent "professionally acceptable methods" of the psychological profession for demonstrating whether a selection procedure validly predicts or measures performance for a particular job. *Albemarle Paper Co. v. Moody*, 442 U.S. 405, 425. They are also intended to be consistent with the decisions of the Supreme Court and authoritative decisions of other appellate courts.

Although the development of these guidelines preceded the issuance by President Jimmy Carter of Executive Order 12044 designed to improve the regulatory process, the spirit of his Executive order was followed in their development. Initial agreement among the Federal agencies was reached early in the fall of 1977, and the months from October 1977 until today have been spent in extensive consultation with civil rights groups whose clientele are protected by these guidelines; employers, labor unions, and State and local governments whose employment practices are affected by these guidelines; State and local government antidiscrimination agencies who share with the Federal Government enforcement responsibility for discriminatory practices; and appropriate members of the general public. For example, an earlier draft of these guidelines was circulated informally for comment on October 28, 1977, pursuant to OMB Circular A-85. Many comments were received from representatives of State and local governments, psychologists, private employers, and civil rights groups. Those comments were taken into account in the draft of these guidelines which was published for comment December 30, 1977, 42 FR 66542.

More than 200 organizations and individuals submitted written comments on the December 30, 1977, draft. These comments were from representatives of private industry, public employers, labor organizations, civil rights groups, the American Psychological Association and components thereof, and many individual employers, psychologists, and personnel specialists. On March 3, 1978, notice was given of a public hearing and meeting to be held on April 10, 1978, 43 FR 9131. After preliminary review of the comments, the agencies identified four issues of particular interest, and invited testimony particularly on those issues, 43 FR 11812 (March 21, 1978). In the same notice the agencies published questions and answers on four issues of concern to the commenters. The questions and answers were designed to clarify the intent of the December 30, 1977, draft, so as to provide a sharper focus for the testimony at the hearing.

At a full day of testimony on April 10, 1978, representatives of private industry, State and local governments, labor organizations, and civil rights groups, as well as psychologists, personnel specialists, and others testified at the public hearing and meeting. The written comments, testimony, and views expressed in subsequent informal consultations have been carefully considered by the four agencies. We set forth below a summary of the comments, and the major issues raised in the comments and testimony, and attempt to explain how we have resolved those issues.

The statement submitted by the American Psychological Association (A.P.A.) stated that "these guidelines represent a major step forward and with careful interpretation can provide a sound basis for concerned professional work." Most of the A.P.A. comments were directed to clarification and interpretation of the present language of the proposal. However, the A.P.A. recommended substantive change in the construct validity section and in the definition of work behavior.

Similarly, the Division of Industrial and Organizational Psychology (division 14) of the A.P.A. described the technical standards of the guidelines as "superior" in terms of congruence with professional standards to "most previous orders and guidelines but numerous troublesome aspects remain." Division 14 had substantial concerns with a number of the provisions of the general principles of the draft.

Civil rights groups generally found the uniform guidelines far superior to the FEA guidelines, and many urged their adoption, with modifications concerning ranking and documentation. Others raised concerns about the "bottom line" concept and other provisions of the guidelines.

The Ad Hoc Group on Employee Selection Procedures representing many employers in private industry supported the concept of uniform guidelines, but had a number of problems with particular provisions, some of which are described below. The American Society for Personnel Administration (ASPA) and the International Personnel Management Association, which represents State and local governments, generally took the same position as the ad hoc group. Major industrial unions found that the draft guidelines were superior to the FEA guidelines, but they perceived them to be inferior to the EEOC guidelines. They challenged particularly the

RULES AND REGULATIONS

bottom line concept and the construct validity section.

The building trade unions urged an exclusion of apprenticeship programs from coverage of the guidelines. The American Council on Education found them inappropriate for employment decisions concerning faculty at institutions of higher education. Other particular concerns were articulated by organizations representing the handicapped, licensing and certifying agencies, and college placement offices.

General Principles

1. *Relationship between validation and elimination of adverse impact, and affirmative action.* Federal equal employment opportunity law generally does not require evidence of validity for a selection procedure if there is no adverse impact; e.g., *Griggs* v. *Duke Power Co.*, 401 U.S. 424. Therefore, a user has the choice of complying either by providing evidence of validity (or otherwise justifying use in accord with Federal law), or by eliminating the adverse impact. These options have always been present under Federal law, 29 CFR 1607.3; 41 CFR 60-3.3(a); and the Federal Executive Agency Guidelines, 41 FR 51734 (November 23, 1976). The December 30 draft guidelines, however, clarified the nature of the two options open to users.

Psychologists expressed concern that the December 30 draft of section 6A encouraged the use of invalid procedures as long as there is no adverse impact. Employers added the concern that the section might encourage the use of illegal procedures not having an adverse impact against the groups who have historically suffered discrimination (minorities, women), even if they have an adverse impact on a different group (whites, males).

Section 6A was not so intended, and we have revised it to clarify the fact that illegal acts purporting to be affirmative action are not the goal of the agencies or of the guidelines; and that any employee selection procedure must be lawful and should be as job related as possible. The delineation of examples of alternative procedures was eliminated to avoid the implication that particular procedures are either prescribed or are necessarily appropriate. The basic thrust of section 6A, that elimination of adverse impact is an alternative to validation, is retained.

The inclusion of excerpts from the 1976 Equal Employment Opportunity Coordinating Council Policy Statement on Affirmative Action in section 13B of the December 30 draft was criticized as not belonging in a set of guidelines for the validation of selection procedures. Section 13 has been revised. The general statement of policy in support of voluntary affirmative action, and the reaffirmation of the policy statement have been retained, but this statement itself is now found in the appendix to the guidelines.

2. *The "bottom line" (section 4C).* The guidelines provide that when the overall selection process does not have an adverse impact the Government will usually not examine the individual components of that process for adverse impact or evidence of validity. The concept is based upon the view that the Federal Government should not generally concern itself with individual components of a selection process, if the overall effect of that process is nonexclusionary. Many commenters criticized the ambiguity caused by the word "generally" in the December 30 draft of section 4C which provided, "the Federal enforcement agencies * * * generally will not take enforcement action based upon adverse impact of any component" of a process that does not have an overall adverse impact. Employer groups stated the position that the "bottom line" should be a rule prohibiting enforcement action by Federal agencies with respect to all or any part of a selection process where the bottom line does not show adverse impact. Civil rights and some labor union representatives expressed the opposing concerns that the concept may be too restrictive, that it may be interpreted as a matter of law, and that it might allow certain discriminatory conditions to go unremedied.

The guidelines have been revised to clarify the intent that the bottom line concept is based upon administrative and prosecutorial discretion. The Federal agencies cannot accept the recommendation that they never inquire into or take enforcement action with respect to any component procedure unless the whole process of which it is a part has an adverse impact. The Federal enforcement agencies believe that enforcement action may be warranted in unusual circumstances, such as those involving other discriminatory practices, or particular selection procedures which have no validity and have a clear adverse impact on a national basis. Other unusual circumstances may warrant a high level agency decision to proceed with enforcement actions although the "bottom line" has been satisfied. At the same time the agencies adhere to the bottom line concept of allocating resources primarily to those users whose overall selection processes have an adverse impact. See overview, above, part III.

3. *Investigation of alternative selection procedures and alternative methods of use (section 3B).* The December 30 draft included an obligation on the user, when conducting a validity

RULES AND REGULATIONS

study, to investigate alternative procedures and uses, in order to determine whether there are other procedures which are substantially equally valid, but which have less adverse impact. The American Psychological Association stated:

"We would concur with the drafters of the guidelines that it is appropriate in the determination of a selection strategy to consider carefully a variety of possible procedures and to think carefully about the question of adverse impact with respect to each of these procedures. Nevertheless, we feel it appropriate to note that a rigid enforcement of these sections, particularly for smaller employers, would impose a substantial and expensive burden on these employers."

Since a reasonable consideration of alternatives is consistent with the underlying principle of minimizing adverse impact consistent with business needs, the provision is retained.

Private employer representatives challenged earlier drafts of these guidelines as being inconsistent with the decision of the Supreme Court in *Albemarle Paper Co.* v. *Moody*, 422 U.S. 405. No such inconsistency was intended. Accordingly, the first sentence of section 3B was revised to paraphrase the opinion in the *Albemarle* decision, so as to make it clear that section 3B is in accord with the principles of the *Albemarle* decision.

Section 3B was further revised to clarify the intent of the guidelines that the obligation to investigate alternative procedures is a part of conducting a validity study, so that alternative procedures should be evaluated in light of validity studies meeting professional standards, and that section 3B does not impose an obligation to search for alternatives if the user is not required to conduct a validity study.

Just as, under section 3B of the guidelines, a user should investigate alternative selection procedures as a part of choosing and validating a procedure, so should the user investigate alternative uses of the selection device chosen to find the use most appropriate to his needs. The validity study should address the question of what method of use (screening, grouping, or rank ordering) is appropriate for a procedure based on the kind and strength of the validity evidence shown, and the degree of adverse impact of the different uses.

4. *Establishment of cutoff scores and rank ordering.* Some commenters from civil rights groups believed that the December 30 draft guidelines did not provide sufficient guidance as to when it was permissible to use a selection procedure on a ranking basis rather than on a pass-fail basis. They also objected to section 5G in terms of setting cutoff scores. Other comments noted a lack of clarity as to how the determination of a cutoff score or the use of a procedure for ranking candidates relates to adverse impact.

As we have noted, users are not required to validate procedures which do not have an adverse impact. However, if one way of using a procedure (e.g., for ranking) results in greater adverse impact than another way (e.g., pass/fail), the procedure must be validated for that use. Similarly, cutoff scores which result in adverse impact should be justified. If the use of a validated procedure for ranking results in greater adverse impact than its use as a screening device, the evidence of validity and utility must be sufficient to warrant use of the procedures as a ranking device.

A new section 5G has been added to clarify these concepts. Section 5H (formerly section 5G) addresses the choice of a cutoff score when a procedure is to be used for ranking.

5. *Scope: Requests for exemptions for certain classes of users.* Some employer groups and labor organizations (e.g., academic institutions, large public employers, apprenticeship councils) argued that they should be exempted from all or some of the provisions of these guidelines because of their special needs. The intent of Congress as expressed in Federal equal employment opportunity law is to apply the same standards to all users, public and private.

These guidelines apply the same principles and standards to all employers. On the other hand, the nature of the procedures which will actually meet those principles and standards may be different for different employers, and the guidelines recognize that fact. Accordingly, the guidelines are applicable to all employers and other users who are covered by Federal equal employment opportunity law.

Organizations of handicapped persons objected to excluding from the scope of these guidelines the enforcement of laws prohibiting discrimination on the basis of handicap, in particular the Rehabilitation Act of 1973, sections 501, 503, and 504. While this issue has not been addressed in the guidelines, nothing precludes the adoption of the principles set forth in these guidelines for other appropriate situations.

Licensing and certification boards raised the question of the applicability of the guidelines to their licensing and certification functions. The guidelines make it clear that licensing and certification are covered "to the extent" that licensing and certification may be covered by Federal equal employment opportunity law.

Voluntary certification boards, where certification is not required by law, are not users as defined in section 16 with respect to their certifying

RULES AND REGULATIONS

functions and therefore are not subject to these guidelines. If an employer relies upon such certification in making employment decisions, the employer is the user and must be prepared to justify, under Federal law, that reliance as it would any other selection procedure.

6. *The "Four-Fifths Rule of Thumb" (section 4D).* Some representatives of employers and some professionals suggest that the basic test for adverse impact should be a test of statistical significance, rather than the four-fifths rule. Some civil rights groups, on the other hand, still regard the four-fifths rule as permitting some unlawful discrimination.

The Federal agencies believe that neither of these positions is correct. The great majority of employers do not hire, promote, or assign enough employees for most jobs to warrant primary reliance upon statistical significance. Many decisions in day-to-day life are made on the basis of information which does not have the justification of a test of statistical significance. Courts have found adverse impact without a showing of statistical significance. *Griggs* v. *Duke Power Co., supra; Vulcan Society of New York* v. *CSC of N.Y.,* 490 F. 2d 387, 393 (2d Cir. 1973); *Kirkland* v. *New York St. Dept. of Corr. Serv.,* 520 F. 2d 420, 425 (2d Cir. 1975).

Accordingly, the undersigned believe that while the four-fifths rule does not define discrimination and does not apply in all cases, it is appropriate as a rule of thumb in identifying adverse impact.

Technical Standards

7. *Criterion-related validity (section 14B).* This section of the guidelines found general support among the commenters from the psychological profession and, except for the provisions concerning test fairness (sometimes mistakenly equated with differential prediction or differential validity), generated relatively little comment.

The provisions of the guidelines concerning criterion-related validity studies call for studies of fairness of selection procedures where technically feasible.

Section 14B(8). Some psychologists and employer groups objected that the concept of test fairness or unfairness has been discredited by professionals and pointed out that the term is commonly misused. We recognize that there is serious debate on the question of test fairness; however, it is accepted professionally that fairness should be examined where feasible. The A.P.A. standards for educational and psychological tests, for example, direct users to explore the question of fairness on finding a difference in group performances (section E9, pp. 43-44). Similarly the concept of test fairness is one which is closely related to the basic thrust of Federal equal employment opportunity law; and that concept was endorsed by the Supreme Court in *Albemarle Paper Co.* v. *Moody,* 422 U.S. 405.

Accordingly, we have retained in the guidelines the obligation upon users to investigate test fairness where it is technically feasible to do so.

8. *Content validity.* The Division of Industrial and Organizational Psychology of A.P.A. correctly perceived that the provisions of the draft guidelines concerning content validity, with their emphasis on observable work behaviors or work products, were "greatly concerned with minimizing the inferential leap between test and performance." That division expressed the view that the draft guidelines neglected situations where a knowledge, skill or ability is necessary to an outcome but where the work behavior cannot be replicated in a test. They recommended that the section be revised.

We believe that the emphasis on observable work behaviors or observable work products is appropriate; and that in order to show content validity, the gap between the test and performance on the job should be a small one. We recognize, however, that content validity may be appropriate to support a test which measures a knowledge, skill, or ability which is a necessary prerequisite to the performance of the job, even though the test might not be close enough to the work behavior to be considered a work sample, and the guidelines have been revised appropriately. On the other hand, tests of mental processes which are not directly observable and which may be difficult to determine on the basis of observable work behaviors or work products should not be supported by content validity.

Thus, the Principles for the Validation and Use of Personnel Selection Procedures (Division of Industrial and Organizational Psychology, American Psychological Association, 1975, p. 10), discuss the use of content validity to support tests of "specific items of knowledge, or specific job skills," but call attention to the inappropriateness of attempting to justify tests for traits or constructs on a content validity basis.

9. *Construct validity (section 14D).* Business groups and professionals expressed concern that the construct validity requirements in the December 30 draft were confusing and technically inaccurate. As section 14D indicates, construct validity is a relatively new procedure in the field of personnel selection and there is not yet substantial guidance in the professional literature as to its use in the area of employment practices. The provisions on construct

RULES AND REGULATIONS

validity have been revised to meet the concerns expressed by the A.P.A. The construct validity section as revised clarifies what is required by the Federal enforcement agencies at this stage in the development of construct validity. The guidelines leave open the possibility that different evidence of construct validity may be accepted in the future, as new methodologies develop and become incorporated in professional standards and other professional literature.

10. *Documentation (section 15).* Commenters stated that the documentation section did not conform to the technical requirements of the guidelines or was otherwise inadequate. Section 15 has been clarified and two significant changes have been made to minimize the recordkeeping burden. (See overview, part VIII.)

11. *Definitions (section 16).* The definition of work behavior in the December 30, 1977 draft was criticized by the A.P.A. and others as being too vague to provide adequate guidance to those using the guidelines who must identify work behavior as a part of any validation technique. Other comments criticized the absence or inadequacies of other definitions, expecially "adverse impact." Substantial revisions of and additions to this section were therefore made.

UNIFORM GUIDELINES ON EMPLOYEE SELECTION PROCEDURES (1978)

NOTE.—These guidelines are issued jointly by four agencies. Separate official adoptions follow the guidelines in this part IV as follows: Civil Service Commission, Department of Justice, Equal Employment Opportunity Commission, Department of Labor.

For official citation see section 18 of these guidelines.

TABLE OF CONTENTS

GENERAL PRINCIPLES

1. Statement of Purpose
   A. Need for Uniformity—Issuing Agencies
   B. Purpose of Guidelines
   C. Relation to Prior Guidelines
2. Scope
   A. Application of Guidelines
   B. Employment Decisions
   C. Selection Procedures
   D. Limitations
   E. Indian Preference Not Affected
3. Discrimination Defined: Relationship Between Use of Selection Procedures and Discrimination
   A. Procedure Having Adverse Impact Constitutes Discrimination Unless Justified
   B. Consideration of Suitable Alternative Selection Procedures
4. Information on Impact
   A. Records Concerning Impact
   B. Applicable Race, Sex and Ethnic Groups For Record Keeping
   C. Evaluation of Selection Rates. The "Bottom Line"
   D. Adverse Impact And The "Four-Fifths Rule"
   E. Consideration of User's Equal Employment Opportunity Posture
5. General Standards for Validity Studies
   A. Acceptable types of Validity Studies
   B. Criterion-Related, Content, and Construct Validity
   C. Guidelines Are Consistent with Professional Standards
   D. Need For Documentation of Validity
   E. Accuracy and Standardization
   F. Caution Against Selection on Basis of Knowledges, Skills or Abilities Learned in Brief Orientation Period
   G. Method of Use of Selection Procedures
   H. Cutoff Scores
   I. Use of Selection Procedures for Higher Level Jobs
   J. Interim Use of Selection Procedures
   K. Review of Validity Studies for Currency
6. Use of Selection Procedures Which Have Not Been Validated
   A. Use of Alternate Selection Procedures to Eliminate Adverse Impact
   B. Where Validity Studies Cannot or Need Not Be Performed
      (1) Where Informal or Unscored Procedures Are Used
      (2) Where Formal And Scored Procedures Are Used
7. Use of Other Validity Studies
   A. Validity Studies not Conducted by the User
   B. Use of Criterion-Related Validity Evidence from Other Sources
      (1) Validity Evidence
      (2) Job Similarity
      (3) Fairness Evidence
   C. Validity Evidence from Multi-Unit Study
   D. Other Significant Variables
8. Cooperative Studies
   A. Encouragement of Cooperative Studies
   B. Standards for Use of Cooperative Studies
9. No Assumption of Validity
   A. Unacceptable Substitutes for Evidence of Validity
   B. Encouragement of Professional Supervision
10. Employment Agencies and Employment Services
    A. Where Selection Procedures Are Devised by Agency
    B. Where Selection Procedures Are Devised Elsewhere
11. Disparate Treatment
12. Retesting of Applicants
13. Affirmative Action
    A. Affirmative Action Obligations
    B. Encouragement of Voluntary Affirmative Action Programs

TECHNICAL STANDARDS

14. Technical Standards for Validity Studies
    A. Validity Studies Should be Based on Review of Information about the Job
    B. Technical Standards for Criterion-Related Validity Studies
       (1) Technical Feasibility
       (2) Analysis of the Job
       (3) Criterion Measures
       (4) Representativeness of the Sample
       (5) Statistical Relationships
       (6) Operational Use of Selection Procedures
       (7) Over-Statement of Validity Findings
       (8) Fairness
          (a) Unfairness Defined
          (b) Investigation of Fairness

RULES AND REGULATIONS

    (c) General Considerations in Fairness Investigations
    (d) When Unfairness Is Shown
    (e) Technical Feasibility of Fairness Studies
    (f) Continued Use of Selection Procedures When Fairness Studies not Feasible
  C. Technical Standards for Content Validity Studies
    (1) Appropriateness of Content Validity Studies
    (2) Job Analysis for Content Validity
    (3) Development of Selection Procedure
    (4) Standards For Demonstrating Content Validity
    (5) Reliability
    (6) Prior Training or Experience
    (7) Training Success
    (8) Operational Use
    (9) Ranking Based on Content Validity Studies
  D. Technical Standards For Construct Validity Studies
    (1) Appropriateness of Construct Validity Studies
    (2) Job Analysis For Construct Validity Studies
    (3) Relationship to the Job
    (4) Use of Construct Validity Study Without New Criterion-Related Evidence
      (a) Standards for Use
      (b) Determination of Common Work Behaviors

DOCUMENTATION OF IMPACT AND VALIDITY EVIDENCE

15. Documentation of Impact and Validity Evidence
  A. Required Information
    (1) Simplified Recordkeeping for Users With Less Than 100 Employees
    (2) Information on Impact
      (a) Collection of Information on Impact
      (b) When Adverse Impact Has Been Eliminated in The Total Selection Process
      (c) When Data Insufficient to Determine Impact
    (3) Documentation of Validity Evidence
      (a) Type of Evidence
      (b) Form of Report
      (c) Completeness
  B. Criterion-Related Validity Studies
    (1) User(s), Location(s), and Date(s) of Study
    (2) Problem and Setting
    (3) Job Analysis or Review of Job Information
    (4) Job Titles and Codes
    (5) Criterion Measures
    (6) Sample Description
    (7) Description of Selection Procedure
    (8) Techniques and Results
    (9) Alternative Procedures Investigated
    (10) Uses and Applications
    (11) Source Data
    (12) Contact Person
    (13) Accuracy and Completeness
  C. Content Validity Studies
    (1) User(s), Location(s), and Date(s) of Study
    (2) Problem and Setting
    (3) Job Analysis—Content of the Job
    (4) Selection Procedure and its Content
    (5) Relationship Between Selection Procedure and the Job
    (6) Alternative Procedures Investigated
    (7) Uses and Applications
    (8) Contact Person
    (9) Accuracy and Completeness
  D. Construct Validity Studies
    (1) User(s), Location(s), and Date(s) of Study
    (2) Problem and Setting
    (3) Construct Definition
    (4) Job Analysis
    (5) Job Titles and Codes
    (6) Selection Procedure
    (7) Relationship to Job Perfromance
    (8) Alternative Procedures Investigated
    (9) Uses and Applications
    (10) Accuracy and Completeness
    (11) Source Data
    (12) Contact Person
  E. Evidence of Validity from Other Studies
    (1) Evidence from Criterion-Related Validity Studies
      (a) Job Information
      (b) Relevance of Criteria
      (c) Other Variables
      (d) Use of the Selection Procedure
      (e) Bibliography
    (2) Evidence from Content Validity Studies
    (3) Evidence from Construct Validity Studies
  F. Evidence of Validity from Cooperative Studies
  G. Selection for Higher Level Jobs
  H. Interim Use of Selection Procedures

DEFINITIONS

16. Definitions

APPENDIX

17. Policy Statement on Affirmative Action (see Section 13B)
18. Citations

GENERAL PRINCIPLES

SECTION 1. *Statement of purpose.*—A. *Need for uniformity—Issuing agencies.* The Federal government's need for a uniform set of principles on the question of the use of tests and other selection procedures has long been recognized. The Equal Employment Opportunity Commission, the Civil Service Commission, the Department of Labor, and the Department of Justice jointly have adopted these uniform guidelines to meet that need, and to apply the same principles to the Federal Government as are applied to other employers.

B. *Purpose of guidelines.* These guidelines incorporate a single set of principles which are designed to assist employers, labor organizations, employment agencies, and licensing and certification boards to comply with requirements of Federal law prohibiting employment practices which discriminate on grounds of race, color, religion, sex, and national origin. They are designed to provide a framework for determining the proper use of tests and other selection procedures. These guidelines do not require a user to conduct validity studies of selection procedures where no adverse impact results. However, all users are encouraged to use selection procedures which are valid, especially users operating under merit principles.

RULES AND REGULATIONS

C. *Relation to prior guidelines.* These guidelines are based upon and supersede previously issued guidelines on employee selection procedures. These guidelines have been built upon court decisions, the previously issued guidelines of the agencies, and the practical experience of the agencies, as well as the standards of the psychological profession. These guidelines are intended to be consistent with existing law.

SEC. 2. *Scope.*—A. *Application of guidelines.* These guidelines will be applied by the Equal Employment Opportunity Commission in the enforcement of title VII of the Civil Rights Act of 1964, as amended by the Equal Employment Opportunity Act of 1972 (hereinafter "Title VII"); by the Department of Labor, and the contract compliance agencies until the transfer of authority contemplated by the President's Reorganization Plan No. 1 of 1978, in the administration and enforcement of Executive Order 11246, as amended by Executive Order 11375 (hereinafter "Executive Order 11246"); by the Civil Service Commission and other Federal agencies subject to section 717 of Title VII; by the Civil Service Commission in exercising its responsibilities toward State and local governments under section 208(b)(1) of the Intergovernmental-Personnel Act; by the Department of Justice in exercising its responsibilities under Federal law; by the Office of Revenue Sharing of the Department of the Treasury under the State and Local Fiscal Assistance Act of 1972, as amended; and by any other Federal agency which adopts them.

B. *Employment decisions.* These guidelines apply to tests and other selection procedures which are used as a basis for any employment decision. Employment decisions include but are not limited to hiring, promotion, demotion, membership (for example, in a labor organization), referral, retention, and licensing and certification, to the extent that licensing and certification may be covered by Federal equal employment opportunity law. Other selection decisions, such as selection for training or transfer, may also be considered employment decisions if they lead to any of the decisions listed above.

C. *Selection procedures.* These guidelines apply only to selection procedures which are used as a basis for making employment decisions. For example, the use of recruiting procedures designed to attract members of a particular race, sex, or ethnic group, which were previously denied employment opportunities or which are currently underutilized, may be necessary to bring an employer into compliance with Federal law, and is frequently an essential element of any effective affirmative action program; but recruitment practices are not considered by these guidelines to be selection procedures. Similarly, these guidelines do not pertain to the question of the lawfulness of a seniority system within the meaning of section 703(h), Executive Order 11246 or other provisions of Federal law or regulation, except to the extent that such systems utilize selection procedures to determine qualifications or abilities to perform the job. Nothing in these guidelines is intended or should be interpreted as discouraging the use of a selection procedure for the purpose of determining qualifications or for the purpose of selection on the basis of relative qualifications, if the selection procedure had been validated in accord with these guidelines for each such purpose for which it is to be used.

D. *Limitations.* These guidelines apply only to persons subject to Title VII, Executive Order 11246, or other equal employment opportunity requirements of Federal law. These guidelines do not apply to responsibilities under the Age Discrimination in Employment Act of 1967, as amended, not to discriminate on the basis of age, or under sections 501, 503, and 504 of the Rehabilitation Act of 1973, not to discriminate on the basis of handicap.

E. *Indian preference not affected.* These guidelines do not restrict any obligation imposed or right granted by Federal law to users to extend a preference in employment to Indians living on or near an Indian reservation in connection with employment opportunities on or near an Indian reservation.

SEC. 3. *Discrimination defined: Relationship between use of selection procedures and discrimination.*—A. *Procedure having adverse impact constitutes discrimination unless justified.* The use of any selection procedure which has an adverse impact on the hiring, promotion, or other employment or membership opportunities of members of any race, sex, or ethnic group will be considered to be discriminatory and inconsistent with these guidelines, unless the procedure has been validated in accordance with these guidelines, or the provisions of section 6 below are satisfied.

B. *Consideration of suitable alternative selection procedures.* Where two or more selection procedures are available which serve the user's legitimate interest in efficient and trustworthy workmanship, and which are substantially equally valid for a given purpose, the user should use the procedure which has been demonstrated to have the lesser adverse impact. Accordingly, whenever a validity study is called for by these guidelines, the user should include, as a part of the validity study, an investigation of suitable

RULES AND REGULATIONS

alternative selection procedures and suitable alternative methods of using the selection procedure which have as little adverse impact as possible, to determine the appropriateness of using or validating them in accord with these guidelines. If a user has made a reasonable effort to become aware of such alternative procedures and validity has been demonstrated in accord with these guidelines, the use of the test or other selection procedure may continue until such time as it should reasonably be reviewed for currency. Whenever the user is shown an alternative selection procedure with evidence of less adverse impact and substantial evidence of validity for the same job in similar circumstances, the user should investigate it to determine the appropriateness of using or validating it in accord with these guidelines. This subsection is not intended to preclude the combination of procedures into a significantly more valid procedure, if the use of such a combination has been shown to be in compliance with the guidelines.

SEC. 4. *Information on impact.*—A. *Records concerning impact.* Each user should maintain and have available for inspection records or other information which will disclose the impact which its tests and other selection procedures have upon employment opportunities of persons by identifiable race, sex, or ethnic group as set forth in subparagraph B below in order to determine compliance with these guidelines. Where there are large numbers of applicants and procedures are administered frequently, such information may be retained on a sample basis, provided that the sample is appropriate in terms of the applicant population and adequate in size.

B. *Applicable race, sex, and ethnic groups for recordkeeping.* The records called for by this section are to be maintained by sex, and the following races and ethnic groups: Blacks (Negroes), American Indians (including Alaskan Natives), Asians (including Pacific Islanders), Hispanic (including persons of Mexican, Puerto Rican, Cuban, Central or South American, or other Spanish origin or culture regardless of race), whites (Caucasians) other than Hispanic, and totals. The race, sex, and ethnic classifications called for by this section are consistent with the Equal Employment Opportunity Standard Form 100, Employer Information Report EEO-1 series of reports. The user should adopt safeguards to insure that the records required by this paragraph are used for appropriate purposes such as determining adverse impact, or (where required) for developing and monitoring affirmative action programs, and that such records are not used improperly. See sections 4E and 17(4), below.

C. *Evaluation of selection rates. The "bottom line."* If the information called for by sections 4A and B above shows that the total selection process for a job has an adverse impact, the individual components of the selection process should be evaluated for adverse impact. If this information shows that the total selection process does not have an adverse impact, the Federal enforcement agencies, in the exercise of their administrative and prosecutorial discretion, in usual circumstances, will not expect a user to evaluate the individual components for adverse impact, or to validate such individual components, and will not take enforcement action based upon adverse impact of any component of that process, including the separate parts of a multipart selection procedure or any separate procedure that is used as an alternative method of selection. However, in the following circumstances the Federal enforcement agencies will expect a user to evaluate the individual components for adverse impact and may, where appropriate, take enforcement action with respect to the individual components: (1) where the selection procedure is a significant factor in the continuation of patterns of assignments of incumbent employees caused by prior discriminatory employment practices, (2) where the weight of court decisions or administrative interpretations hold that a specific procedure (such as height or weight requirements or no-arrest records) is not job related in the same or similar circumstances. In unusual circumstances, other than those listed in (1) and (2) above, the Federal enforcement agencies may request a user to evaluate the individual components for adverse impact and may, where appropriate, take enforcement action with respect to the individual component.

D. *Adverse impact and the "four-fifths rule."* A selection rate for any race, sex, or ethnic group which is less than four-fifths (⅘) (or eighty percent) of the rate for the group with the highest rate will generally be regarded by the Federal enforcement agencies as evidence of adverse impact, while a greater than four-fifths rate will generally not be regarded by Federal enforcement agencies as evidence of adverse impact. Smaller differences in selection rate may nevertheless constitute adverse impact, where they are significant in both statistical and practical terms or where a user's actions have discouraged applicants disproportionately on grounds of race, sex, or ethnic group. Greater differences in selection rate may not constitute adverse impact where the differences are based on small numbers and are not statistically significant, or where special recruiting or other programs cause the pool of minority or female candidates to be atypical of the normal pool of applicants from that group. Where the user's evidence concerning the impact of a selection procedure indicates adverse impact but is based upon numbers which are too small to be reliable, evidence concerning the impact of the procedure over a longer period of time and/or evidence concerning the impact which the selection procedure had when used in the same manner in similar circumstances elsewhere may be considered in determining adverse impact. Where the user has not maintained data on adverse impact as required by the documentation section of applicable guidelines, the Federal enforcement agencies may draw an inference of adverse impact of the selection process from the failure of the user to maintain such data, if the user has an underutilization of a group in the job category, as compared to the group's representation in the relevant labor market or, in the case of jobs filled from within, the applicable work force.

E. *Consideration of user's equal employment opportunity posture.* In carrying out their obligations, the Federal enforcement agencies will consider the general posture of the user with respect to equal employment opportunity for the job or group of jobs in question. Where a user has adopted an affirmative action program, the Federal enforcement agencies will consider the provisions of that program, including the goals and timetables which the user has adopted and the progress which the user has made in carrying out that program and in meeting the goals and timetables. While such affirmative action programs may in design and execution be race, color, sex, or ethnic conscious, selection procedures under such programs should be based upon the ability or relative ability to do the work.

SEC. 5. *General standards for validity studies.*—A. *Acceptable types of validity studies.* For the purposes of satisfying these guidelines, users may rely upon criterion-related validity studies, content validity studies or construct validity studies, in accordance with the standards set forth in the technical standards of these guidelines, section 14 below. New strategies for showing the validity of selection procedures will be evaluated as they become accepted by the psychological profession.

B. *Criterion-related, content, and construct validity.* Evidence of the validity of a test or other selection procedure by a criterion-related validity study should consist of empirical data demonstrating that the selection procedure is predictive of or significantly correlated with important elements of job performance. See section 14B below. Evidence of the validity of a test or other selection procedure by a content validity study should consist of data showing that the content of the selection procedure is representative of important aspects of performance on the job for which the candidates are to be evaluated. See section 14C below. Evidence of the validity of a test or other selection procedure through a construct validity study should consist of data showing that the procedure measures the degree to which candidates have identifiable characteristics which have been determined to be important in successful performance in the job for which the candidates are to be evaluated. See section 14D below.

C. *Guidelines are consistent with professional standards.* The provisions of these guidelines relating to validation of selection procedures are intended to be consistent with generally accepted professional standards for evaluating standardized tests and other selection procedures, such as those described in the Standards for Educational and Psychological Tests prepared by a joint committee of the American Psychological Association, the American Educational Research Association, and the National Council on Measurement in Education (American Psychological Association, Washington, D.C., 1974) (hereinafter "A.P.A. Standards") and standard textbooks and journals in the field of personnel selection.

D. *Need for documentation of validity.* For any selection procedure which is part of a selection process which has an adverse impact and which selection procedure has an adverse impact, each user should maintain and have available such documentation as is described in section 15 below.

E. *Accuracy and standardization.* Validity studies should be carried out under conditions which assure insofar as possible the adequacy and accuracy of the research and the report. Selection procedures should be administered and scored under standardized conditions.

F. *Caution against selection on basis of knowledges, skills, or ability learned in brief orientation period.* In general, users should avoid making employment decisions on the basis of measures of knowledges, skills, or abilities which are normally learned in a brief orientation period, and which have an adverse impact.

G. *Method of use of selection procedures.* The evidence of both the validity and utility of a selection procedure should support the method the user chooses for operational use of the procedure, if that method of use has a greater adverse impact than another method of use. Evidence which may be sufficient to support the use of a selec-

RULES AND REGULATIONS

tion procedure on a pass/fail (screening) basis may be insufficient to support the use of the same procedure on a ranking basis under these guidelines. Thus, if a user decides to use a selection procedure on a ranking basis, and that method of use has a greater adverse impact than use on an appropriate pass/fail basis (see section 5H below), the user should have sufficient evidence of validity and utility to support the use on a ranking basis. See sections 3B, 14B (5) and (6), and 14C (8) and (9).

H. *Cutoff scores.* Where cutoff scores are used, they should normally be set so as to be reasonable and consistent with normal expectations of acceptable proficiency within the work force. Where applicants are ranked on the basis of properly validated selection procedures and those applicants scoring below a higher cutoff score than appropriate in light of such expectations have little or no chance of being selected for employment, the higher cutoff score may be appropriate, but the degree of adverse impact should be considered.

I. *Use of selection procedures for higher level jobs.* If job progression structures are so established that employees will probably, within a reasonable period of time and in a majority of cases, progress to a higher level, it may be considered that the applicants are being evaluated for a job or jobs at the higher level. However, where job progression is not so nearly automatic, or the time span is such that higher level jobs or employees' potential may be expected to change in significant ways, it should be considered that applicants are being evaluated for a job at or near the entry level. A "reasonable period of time" will vary for different jobs and employment situations but will seldom be more than 5 years. Use of selection procedures to evaluate applicants for a higher level job would not be appropriate:

(1) If the majority of those remaining employed do not progress to the higher level job;

(2) If there is a reason to doubt that the higher level job will continue to require essentially similar skills during the progression period; or

(3) If the selection procedures measure knowledges, skills, or abilities required for advancement which would be expected to develop principally from the training or experience on the job.

J. *Interim use of selection procedures.* Users may continue the use of a selection procedure which is not at the moment fully supported by the required evidence of validity, provided: (1) The user has available substantial evidence of validity, and (2) the user has in progress, when technically feasible, a study which is designed to produce the additional evidence required by these guidelines within a reasonable time. If such a study is not technically feasible, see section 6B. If the study does not demonstrate validity, this provision of these guidelines for interim use shall not constitute a defense in any action, nor shall it relieve the user of any obligations arising under Federal law.

K. *Review of validity studies for currency.* Whenever validity has been shown in accord with these guidelines for the use of a particular selection procedure for a job or group of jobs, additional studies need not be performed until such time as the validity study is subject to review as provided in section 3B above. There are no absolutes in the area of determining the currency of a validity study. All circumstances concerning the study, including the validation strategy used, and changes in the relevant labor market and the job should be considered in the determination of when a validity study is outdated.

SEC. 6. *Use of selection procedures which have not been validated.*—A. *Use of alternate selection procedures to eliminate adverse impact.* A user may choose to utilize alternative selection procedures in order to eliminate adverse impact or as part of an affirmative action program. See section 13 below. Such alternative procedures should eliminate the adverse impact in the total selection process, should be lawful and should be as job related as possible.

B. *Where validity studies cannot or need not be performed.* There are circumstances in which a user cannot or need not utilize the validation techniques contemplated by these guidelines. In such circumstances, the user should utilize selection procedures which are as job related as possible and which will minimize or eliminate adverse impact, as set forth below.

(1) *Where informal or unscored procedures are used.* When an informal or unscored selection procedure which has an adverse impact is utilized, the user should eliminate the adverse impact, or modify the procedure to one which is a formal, scored or quantified measure or combination of measures and then validate the procedure in accord with these guidelines, or otherwise justify continued use of the procedure in accord with Federal law.

(2) *Where formal and scored procedures are used.* When a formal and scored selection procedure is used which has an adverse impact, the validation techniques contemplated by these guidelines usually should be followed if technically feasible. Where the user cannot or need not follow the validation techniques anticipated by these guidelines, the user should

RULES AND REGULATIONS

either modify the procedure to eliminate adverse impact or otherwise justify continued use of the procedure in accord with Federal law.

SEC. 7. *Use of other validity studies.*—A. *Validity studies not conducted by the user.* Users may, under certain circumstances, support the use of selection procedures by validity studies conducted by other users or conducted by test publishers or distributors and described in test manuals. While publishers of selection procedures have a professional obligation to provide evidence of validity which meets generally accepted professional standards (see section 5C above), users are cautioned that they are responsible for compliance with these guidelines. Accordingly, users seeking to obtain selection procedures from publishers and distributors should be careful to determine that, in the event the user becomes subject to the validity requirements of these guidelines, the necessary information to support validity has been determined and will be made available to the user.

B. *Use of criterion-related validity evidence from other sources.* Criterion-related validity studies conducted by one test user, or described in test manuals and the professional literature, will be considered acceptable for use by another user when the following requirements are met:

(1) *Validity evidence.* Evidence from the available studies meeting the standards of section 14B below clearly demonstrates that the selection procedure is valid;

(2) *Job similarity.* The incumbents in the user's job and the incumbents in the job or group of jobs on which the validity study was conducted perform substantially the same major work behaviors, as shown by appropriate job analyses both on the job or group of jobs on which the validity study was performed and on the job for which the selection procedure is to be used; and

(3) *Fairness evidence.* The studies include a study of test fairness for each race, sex, and ethnic group which constitutes a significant factor in the borrowing user's relevant labor market for the job or jobs in question. If the studies under consideration satisfy (1) and (2) above but do not contain an investigation of test fairness, and it is not technically feasible for the borrowing user to conduct an internal study of test fairness, the borrowing user may utilize the study until studies conducted elsewhere meeting the requirements of these guidelines show test unfairness, or until such time as it becomes technically feasible to conduct an internal study of test fairness and the results of that study can be acted upon. Users obtaining selection procedures from publishers should consider, as one factor in the decision to purchase a particular selection procedure, the availability of evidence concerning test fairness.

C. *Validity evidence from multiunit study.* If validity evidence from a study covering more than one unit within an organization statisfies the requirements of section 14B below, evidence of validity specific to each unit will not be required unless there are variables which are likely to affect validity significantly.

D. *Other significant variables.* If there are variables in the other studies which are likely to affect validity significantly, the user may not rely upon such studies, but will be expected either to conduct an internal validity study or to comply with section 6 above.

SEC. 8. *Cooperative studies.*—A. *Encouragement of cooperative studies.* The agencies issuing these guidelines encourage employers, labor organizations, and employment agencies to cooperate in research, development, search for lawful alternatives, and validity studies in order to achieve procedures which are consistent with these guidelines.

B. *Standards for use of cooperative studies.* If validity evidence from a cooperative study satisfies the requirements of section 14 below, evidence of validity specific to each user will not be required unless there are variables in the user's situation which are likely to affect validity significantly.

SEC. 9. *No assumption of validity.*—A. *Unacceptable substitutes for evidence of validity.* Under no circumstances will the general reputation of a test or other selection procedures, its author or its publisher, or casual reports of it's validity be accepted in lieu of evidence of validity. Specifically ruled out are: assumptions of validity based on a procedure's name or descriptive labels; all forms of promotional literature; data bearing on the frequency of a procedure's usage; testimonial statements and credentials of sellers, users, or consultants; and other nonempirical or anecdotal accounts of selection practices or selection outcomes.

B. *Encouragement of professional supervision.* Professional supervision of selection activities is encouraged but is not a substitute for documented evidence of validity. The enforcement agencies will take into account the fact that a thorough job analysis was conducted and that careful development and use of a selection procedure in accordance with professional standards enhance the probability that the selection procedure is valid for the job.

SEC. 10. *Employment agencies and employment services.*—A. *Where selection procedures are devised by agency.* An employment agency, including pri-

RULES AND REGULATIONS

vate employment agencies and State employment agencies, which agrees to a request by an employer or labor organization to device and utilize a selection procedure should follow the standards in these guidelines for determining adverse impact. If adverse impact exists the agency should comply with these guidelines. An employment agency is not relieved of its obligation herein because the user did not request such validation or has requested the use of some lesser standard of validation than is provided in these guidelines. The use of an employment agency does not relieve an employer or labor organization or other user of its responsibilities under Federal law to provide equal employment opportunity or its obligations as a user under these guidelines.

B. *Where selection procedures are devised elsewhere.* Where an employment agency or service is requested to administer a selection procedure which has been devised elsewhere and to make referrals pursuant to the results, the employment agency or service should maintain and have available evidence of the impact of the selection and referral procedures which it administers. If adverse impact results the agency or service should comply with these guidelines. If the agency or service seeks to comply with these guidelines by reliance upon validity studies or other data in the possession of the employer, it should obtain and have available such information.

SEC. 11. *Disparate treatment.* The principles of disparate or unequal treatment must be distinguished from the concepts of validation. A selection procedure—even though validated against job performance in accordance with these guidelines—cannot be imposed upon members of a race, sex, or ethnic group where other employees, applicants, or members have not been subjected to that standard. Disparate treatment occurs where members of a race, sex, or ethnic group have been denied the same employment, promotion, membership, or other employment opportunities as have been available to other employees or applicants. Those employees or applicants who have been denied equal treatment, because of prior discriminatory practices or policies, must at least be afforded the same opportunities as had existed for other employees or applicants during the period of discrimination. Thus, the persons who were in the class of persons discriminated against during the period the user followed the discriminatory practices should be allowed the opportunity to qualify under less stringent selection procedures previously followed, unless the user demonstrates that the increased standards are required by business necessity. This section does not prohibit a user who has not previously followed merit standards from adopting merit standards which are in compliance with these guidelines; nor does it preclude a user who has previously used invalid or unvalidated selection procedures from developing and using procedures which are in accord with these guidelines.

SEC. 12. *Retesting of applicants.* Users should provide a reasonable opportunity for retesting and reconsideration. Where examinations are administered periodically with public notice, such reasonable opportunity exists, unless persons who have previously been tested are precluded from retesting. The user may however take reasonable steps to preserve the security of its procedures.

SEC. 13. *Affirmative action.*—A. *Affirmative action obligations.* The use of selection procedures which have been validated pursuant to these guidelines does not relieve users of any obligations they may have to undertake affirmative action to assure equal employment opportunity. Nothing in these guidelines is intended to preclude the use of lawful selection procedures which assist in remedying the effects of prior discriminatory practices, or the achievement of affirmative action objectives.

B. *Encouragement of voluntary affirmative action programs.* These guidelines are also intended to encourage the adoption and implementation of voluntary affirmative action programs by users who have no obligation under Federal law to adopt them; but are not intended to impose any new obligations in that regard. The agencies issuing and endorsing these guidelines endorse for all private employers and reaffirm for all governmental employers the Equal Employment Opportunity Coordinating Council's "Policy Statement on Affirmative Action Programs for State and Local Government Agencies" (41 FR 38814, September 13, 1976). That policy statement is attached hereto as appendix, section 17.

TECHNICAL STANDARDS

SEC. 14. *Technical standards for validity studies.* The following minimum standards, as applicable, should be met in conducting a validity study. Nothing in these guidelines is intended to preclude the development and use of other professionally acceptable techniques with respect to validation of selection procedures. Where it is not technically feasible for a user to conduct a validity study, the user has the obligation otherwise to comply with these guidelines. See sections 6 and 7 above.

A. *Validity studies should be based on review of information about the job.* Any validity study should be

RULES AND REGULATIONS

based upon a review of information about the job for which the selection procedure is to be used. The review should include a job analysis except as provided in section 14B(3) below with respect to criterion-related validity. Any method of job analysis may be used if it provides the information required for the specific validation strategy used.

B. *Technical standards for criterion-related validity studies.*—(1) *Technical feasibility.* Users choosing to validate a selection procedure by a criterion-related validity strategy should determine whether it is technically feasible (as defined in section 16) to conduct such a study in the particular employment context. The determination of the number of persons necessary to permit the conduct of a meaningful criterion-related study should be made by the user on the basis of all relevant information concerning the selection procedure, the potential sample and the employment situation. Where appropriate, jobs with substantially the same major work behaviors may be grouped together for validity studies, in order to obtain an adequate sample. These guidelines do not require a user to hire or promote persons for the purpose of making it possible to conduct a criterion-related study.

(2) *Analysis of the job.* There should be a review of job information to determine measures of work behavior(s) or performance that are relevant to the job or group of jobs in question These measures or criteria are relevant to the extent that they represent critical or important job duties, work behaviors or work outcomes as developed from the review of job information. The possibility of bias should be considered both in selection of the criterion measures and their application. In view of the possibility of bias in subjective evaluations, supervisory rating techniques and instructions to raters should be carefully developed. All criterion measures and the methods for gathering data need to be examined for freedom from factors which would unfairly alter scores of members of any group. The relevance of criteria and their freedom from bias are of particular concern when there are significant differences in measures of job performance for different groups.

(3) *Criterion measures.* Proper safeguards should be taken to insure that scores on selection procedures do not enter into any judgments of employee adequacy that are to be used as criterion measures. Whatever criteria are used should represent important or critical work behavior(s) or work outcomes. Certain criteria may be used without a full job analysis if the user can show the importance of the criteria to the particular employment context. These criteria include but are not limited to production rate, error rate, tardiness, absenteeism, and length of service. A standardized rating of overall work performance may be used where a study of the job shows that it is an appropriate criterion. Where performance in training is used as a criterion, success in training should be properly measured and the relevance of the training should be shown either through a comparsion of the content of the training program with the critical or important work behavior(s) of the job(s), or through a demonstration of the relationship between measures of performance in training and measures of job performance. Measures of relative success in training include but are not limited to instructor evaluations, performance samples, or tests. Criterion measures consisting of paper and pencil tests will be closely reviewed for job relevance.

(4) *Representativeness of the sample.* Whether the study is predictive or concurrent, the sample subjects should insofar as feasible be representative of the candidates normally available in the relevant labor market for the job or group of jobs in question, and should insofar as feasible include the races, sexes, and ethnic groups normally available in the relevant job market. In determining the representativeness of the sample in a concurrent validity study, the user should take into account the extent to which the specific knowledges or skills which are the primary focus of the test are those which employees learn on the job.

Where samples are combined or compared, attention should be given to see that such samples are comparable in terms of the actual job they perform, the length of time on the job where time on the job is likely to affect performance, and other relevant factors likely to affect validity differences; or that these factors are included in the design of the study and their effects identified.

(5) *Statistical relationships.* The degree of relationship between selection procedure scores and criterion measures should be examined and computed, using professionally acceptable statistical procedures. Generally, a selection procedure is considered related to the criterion, for the purposes of these guidelines, when the relationship between performance on the procedure and performance on the criterion measure is statistically significant at the 0.05 level of significance, which means that it is sufficiently high as to have a probability of no more than one (1) in twenty (20) to have occurred by chance. Absence of a statistically significant relationship between a selection procedure and job performance should not necessarily discourage

RULES AND REGULATIONS

other investigations of the validity of that selection procedure.

(6) *Operational use of selection procedures.* Users should evaluate each selection procedure to assure that it is appropriate for operational use, including establishment of cutoff scores or rank ordering. Generally, if other factors reman the same, the greater the magnitude of the relationship (e.g., coorelation coefficent) between performance on a selection procedure and one or more criteria of performance on the job, and the greater the importance and number of aspects of job performance covered by the criteria, the more likely it is that the procedure will be appropriate for use. Reliance upon a selection procedure which is significantly related to a criterion measure, but which is based upon a study involving a large number of subjects and has a low correlation coefficient will be subject to close review if it has a large adverse impact. Sole reliance upon a single selection instrument which is related to only one of many job duties or aspects of job performance will also be subject to close review. The appropriateness of a selection procedure is best evaluated in each particular situation and there are no minimum correlation coefficients applicable to all employment situations. In determining whether a selection procedure is appropriate for operational use the following considerations should also be taken into account: The degree of adverse impact of the procedure, the availability of other selection procedures of greater or substantially equal validity.

(7) *Overstatement of validity findings.* Users should avoid reliance upon techniques which tend to overestimate validity findings as a result of capitalization on chance unless an appropriate safeguard is taken. Reliance upon a few selection procedures or criteria of successful job performance when many selection procedures or criteria of performance have been studied, or the use of optimal statistical weights for selection procedures computed in one sample, are techniques which tend to inflate validity estimates as a result of chance. Use of a large sample is one safeguard: cross-validation is another.

(8) *Fairness.* This section generally calls for studies of unfairness where technically feasible. The concept of fairness or unfairness of selection procedures is a developing concept. In addition, fairness studies generally require substantial numbers of employees in the job or group of jobs being studied. For these reasons, the Federal enforcement agencies recognize that the obligation to conduct studies of fairness imposed by the guidelines generally will be upon users or groups of users with a large number of persons in a a job class, or test developers; and that small users utilizing their own selection procedures will generally not be obligated to conduct such studies because it will be technically infeasible for them to do so.

(a) *Unfairness defined.* When members of one race, sex, or ethnic group characteristically obtain lower scores on a selection procedure than members of another group, and the differences in scores are not reflected in differences in a measure of job performance, use of the selection procedure may unfairly deny opportunities to members of the group that obtains the lower scores.

(b) *Investigation of fairness.* Where a selection procedure results in an adverse impact on a race, sex, or ethnic group identified in accordance with the classifications set forth in section 4 above and that group is a significant factor in the relevant labor market, the user generally should investigate the possible existence of unfairness for that group if it is technically feasible to do so. The greater the severity of the adverse impact on a group, the greater the need to investigate the possible existence of unfairness. Where the weight of evidence from other studies shows that the selection procedure predicts fairly for the group in question and for the same or similar jobs, such evidence may be relied on in connection with the selection procedure at issue.

(c) *General considerations in fairness investigations.* Users conducting a study of fairness should review the A.P.A. Standards regarding investigation of possible bias in testing. An investigation of fairness of a selection procedure depends on both evidence of validity and the manner in which the selection procedure is to be used in a particular employment context. Fairness of a selection procedure cannot necessarily be specified in advance without investigating these factors. Investigation of fairness of a selection procedure in samples where the range of scores on selection procedures or criterion measures is severely restricted for any subgroup sample (as compared to other subgroup samples) may produce misleading evidence of unfairness. That factor should accordingly be taken into account in conducting such studies and before reliance is placed on the results.

(d) *When unfairness is shown.* If unfairness is demonstrated through a showing that members of a particular group perform better or poorer on the job than their scores on the selection procedure would indicate through comparison with how members of other groups perform, the user may either revise or replace the selection instrument in accordance with these guidelines, or may continue to use the selection instrument operationally

RULES AND REGULATIONS

with appropriate revisions in its use to assure compatibility between the probability of successful job performance and the probability of being selected.

(e) *Technical feasibility of fairness studies.* In addition to the general conditions needed for technical feasibility for the conduct of a criterion-related study (see section 16, below) an investigation of fairness requires the following:

(i) An adequate sample of persons in each group available for the study to achieve findings of statistical significance. Guidelines do not require a user to hire or promote persons on the basis of group classifications for the purpose of making it possible to conduct a study of fairness; but the user has the obligation otherwise to comply with these guidelines.

(ii) The samples for each group should be comparable in terms of the actual job they perform, length of time on the job where time on the job is likely to affect performance, and other relevant factors likely to affect validity differences; or such factors should be included in the design of the study and their effects identified.

(f) *Continued use of selection procedures when fairness studies not feasible.* If a study of fairness should otherwise be performed, but is not technically feasible, a selection procedure may be used which has otherwise met the validity standards of these guidelines, unless the technical infeasibility resulted from discriminatory employment practices which are demonstrated by facts other than past failure to conform with requirements for validation of selection procedures. However, when it becomes technically feasible for the user to perform a study of fairness and such a study is otherwise called for, the user should conduct the study of fairness.

C. *Technical standards for content validity studies.*—(1) *Appropriateness of content validity studies.* Users choosing to validate a selection procedure by a content validity strategy should determine whether it is appropriate to conduct such a study in the particular employment context. A selection procedure can be supported by a content validity strategy to the extent that it is a representative sample of the content of the job. Selection procedures which purport to measure knowledges, skills, or abilities may in certain circumstances be justified by content validity, although they may not be representative samples, if the knowledge, skill, or ability measured by the selection procedure can be operationally defined as provided in section 14C(4) below, and if that knowledge, skill, or ability is a necessary prerequisite to successful job performance.

A selection procedure based upon inferences about mental processes cannot be supported solely or primarily on the basis of content validity. Thus, a content strategy is not appropriate for demonstrating the validity of selection procedures which purport to measure traits or constructs, such as intelligence, aptitude, personality, commonsense, judgment, leadership, and spatial ability. Content validity is also not an appropriate strategy when the selection procedure involves knowledges, skills, or abilities which an employee will be expected to learn on the job.

(2) *Job analysis for content validity.* There should be a job analysis which includes an analysis of the important work behavior(s) required for successful performance and their relative importance and, if the behavior results in work product(s), an analysis of the work product(s). Any job analysis should focus on the work behavior(s) and the tasks associated with them. If work behavior(s) are not observable, the job analysis should identify and analyze those aspects of the behavior(s) that can be observed and the observed work products. The work behavior(s) selected for measurement should be critical work behavior(s) and/or important work behavior(s) constituting most of the job.

(3) *Development of selection procedures.* A selection procedure designed to measure the work behavior may be developed specifically from the job and job analysis in question, or may have been previously developed by the user, or by other users or by a test publisher.

(4) *Standards for demonstrating content validity.* To demonstrate the content validity of a selection procedure, a user should show that the behavior(s) demonstrated in the selection procedure are a representative sample of the behavior(s) of the job in question or that the selection procedure provides a representative sample of the work product of the job. In the case of a selection procedure measuring a knowledge, skill, or ability, the knowledge, skill, or ability being measured should be operationally defined. In the case of a selection procedure measuring a knowledge, the knowledge being measured should be operationally defined as that body of learned information which is used in and is a necessary prerequisite for observable aspects of work behavior of the job. In the case of skills or abilities, the skill or ability being measured should be operationally defined in terms of observable aspects of work behavior of the job. For any selection procedure measuring a knowledge, skill, or ability the user should show that (a) the selection procedure measures and is a representative sample of that knowl-

RULES AND REGULATIONS

edge, skill, or ability; and (b) that knowledge, skill, or ability is used in and is a necessary prerequisite to performance of critical or important work behavior(s). In addition, to be content valid, a selection procedure measuring a skill or ability should either closely approximate an observable work behavior, or its product should closely approximate an observable work product. If a test purports to sample a work behavior or to provide a sample of a work product, the manner and setting of the selection procedure and its level and complexity should closely approximate the work situation. The closer the content and the context of the selection procedure are to work samples or work behaviors, the stronger is the basis for showing content validity. As the content of the selection procedure less resembles a work behavior, or the setting and manner of the administration of the selection procedure less resemble the work situation, or the result less resembles a work product, the less likely the selection procedure is to be content valid, and the greater the need for other evidence of validity.

(5) *Reliability.* The reliability of selection procedures justified on the basis of content validity should be a matter of concern to the user. Whenever it is feasible, appropriate statistical estimates should be made of the reliability of the selection procedure.

(6) *Prior training or experience.* A requirement for or evaluation of specific prior training or experience based on content validity, including a specification of level or amount of training or experience, should be justified on the basis of the relationship between the content of the training or experience and the content of the job for which the training or experience is to be required or evaluated. The critical consideration is the resemblance between the specific behaviors, products, knowledges, skills, or abilities in the experience or training and the specific behaviors, products, knowledges, skills, or abilities required on the job, whether or not there is close resemblance between the experience or training as a whole and the job as a whole.

(7) *Content validity of training success.* Where a measure of success in a training program is used as a selection procedure and the content of a training program is justified on the basis of content validity, the use should be justified on the relationship between the content of the training program and the content of the job.

(8) *Operational use.* A selection procedure which is supported on the basis of content validity may be used for a job if it represents a critical work behavior (i.e., a behavior which is necessary for performance of the job) or work behaviors which constitute most of the important parts of the job.

(9) *Ranking based on content validity studies.* If a user can show, by a job analysis or otherwise, that a higher score on a content valid selection procedure is likely to result in better job performance, the results may be used to rank persons who score above minimum levels. Where a selection procedure supported solely or primarily by content validity is used to rank job candidates, the selection procedure should measure those aspects of performance which differentiate among levels of job performance.

D. *Technical standards for construct validity studies.*— (1) *Appropriateness of construct validity studies.* Construct validity is a more complex strategy than either criterion-related or content validity. Construct validation is a relatively new and developing procedure in the employment field, and there is at present a lack of substantial literature extending the concept to employment practices. The user should be aware that the effort to obtain sufficient empirical support for construct validity is both an extensive and arduous effort involving a series of research studies, which include criterion related validity studies and which may include content validity studies. Users choosing to justify use of a selection procedure by this strategy should therefore take particular care to assure that the validity study meets the standards set forth below.

(2) *Job analysis for construct validity studies.* There should be a job analysis. This job analysis should show the work behavior(s) required for successful performance of the job, or the groups of jobs being studied, the critical or important work behavior(s) in the job or group of jobs being studied, and an identification of the construct(s) believed to underlie successful performance of these critical or important work behaviors in the job or jobs in question. Each construct should be named and defined, so as to distinguish it from other constructs. If a group of jobs is being studied the jobs should have in common one or more critical or important work behaviors at a comparable level of complexity.

(3) *Relationship to the job.* A selection procedure should then be identified or developed which measures the construct identified in accord with subparagraph (2) above. The user should show by empirical evidence that the selection procedure is validly related to the construct and that the construct is validly related to the performance of critical or important work behavior(s). The relationship between the construct as measured by the selection procedure and the related work behavior(s) should be supported by

RULES AND REGULATIONS

empirical evidence from one or more criterion-related studies involving the job or jobs in question which satisfy the provisions of section 14B above.

(4) *Use of construct validity study without new criterion-related evidence.*—(a) *Standards for use.* Until such time as professional literature provides more guidance on the use of construct validity in employment situations, the Federal agencies will accept a claim of construct validity without a criterion-related study which satisfies section 14B above only when the selection procedure has been used elsewhere in a situation in which a criterion-related study has been conducted and the use of a criterion-related validity study in this context meets the standards for transportability of criterion-related validity studies as set forth above in section 7. However, if a study pertains to a number of jobs having common critical or important work behaviors at a comparable level of complexity, and the evidence satisfies subparagraphs 14B (2) and (3) above for those jobs with criterion-related validity evidence for those jobs, the selection procedure may be used for all the jobs to which the study pertains. If construct validity is to be generalized to other jobs or groups of jobs not in the group studied, the Federal enforcement agencies will expect at a minimum additional empirical research evidence meeting the standards of subparagraphs section 14B (2) and (3) above for the additional jobs or groups of jobs.

(b) *Determination of common work behaviors.* In determining whether two or more jobs have one or more work behavior(s) in common, the user should compare the observed work behavior(s) in each of the jobs and should compare the observed work product(s) in each of the jobs. If neither the observed work behavior(s) in each of the jobs nor the observed work product(s) in each of the jobs are the same, the Federal enforcement agencies will presume that the work behavior(s) in each job are different. If the work behaviors are not observable, then evidence of similarity of work products and any other relevant research evidence will be considered in determining whether the work behavior(s) in the two jobs are the same.

DOCUMENTATION OF IMPACT AND VALIDITY EVIDENCE

SEC. 15. *Documentation of impact and validity evidence.*—A. *Required information.* Users of selection procedures other than those users complying with section 15A(1) below should maintain and have available for each job information on adverse impact of the selection process for that job and, where it is determined a selection process has an adverse impact, evidence of validity as set forth below.

(1) *Simplified recordkeeping for users with less than 100 employees.* In order to minimize recordkeeping burdens on employers who employ one hundred (100) or fewer employees, and other users not required to file EEO-1, et seq., reports, such users may satisfy the requirements of this section 15 if they maintain and have available records showing, for each year:

(a) The number of persons hired, promoted, and terminated for each job, by sex, and where appropriate by race and national origin;

(b) The number of applicants for hire and promotion by sex and where appropriate by race and national origin; and

(c) The selection procedures utilized (either standardized or not standardized).

These records should be maintained for each race or national origin group (see section 4 above) constituting more than two percent (2%) of the labor force in the relevant labor area. However, it is not necessary to maintain records by race and/or national origin (see § 4 above) if one race or national origin group in the relevant labor area constitutes more than ninety-eight percent (98%) of the labor force in the area. If the user has reason to believe that a selection procedure has an adverse impact, the user should maintain any available evidence of validity for that procedure (see sections 7A and 8).

(2) *Information on impact.*—(a) *Collection of information on impact.* Users of selection procedures other than those complying with section 15A(1) above should maintain and have available for each job records or other information showing whether the total selection process for that job has an adverse impact on any of the groups for which records are called for by sections 4B above. Adverse impact determinations should be made at least annually for each such group which constitutes at least 2 percent of the labor force in the relevant labor area or 2 percent of the applicable workforce. Where a total selection process for a job has an adverse impact, the user should maintain and have available records or other information showing which components have an adverse impact. Where the total selection process for a job does not have an adverse impact, information need not be maintained for individual components except in circumstances set forth in subsection 15A(2)(b) below. If the determination of adverse impact is made using a procedure other than the "four-fifths rule," as defined in the first sentence of section 4D above, a justification, consistent with section 4D above, for

337

the procedure used to determine adverse impact should be available.

(b) *When adverse impact has been eliminated in the total selection process.* Whenever the total selection process for a particular job has had an adverse impact, as defined in section 4 above, in any year, but no longer has an adverse impact, the user should maintain and have available the information on individual components of the selection process required in the preceding paragraph for the period in which there was adverse impact. In addition, the user should continue to collect such information for at least two (2) years after the adverse impact has been eliminated.

(c) *When data insufficient to determine impact.* Where there has been an insufficient number of selections to determine whether there is an adverse impact of the total selection process for a particular job, the user should continue to collect, maintain and have available the information on individual components of the selection process required in section 15(A)(2)(a) above until the information is sufficient to determine that the overall selection process does not have an adverse impact as defined in section 4 above, or until the job has changed substantially.

(3) *Documentation of validity evidence.*—(a) *Types of evidence.* Where a total selection process has an adverse impact (see section 4 above) the user should maintain and have available for each component of that process which has an adverse impact, one or more of the following types of documentation evidence:

(i) Documentation evidence showing criterion-related validity of the selection procedure (see section 15B, below).

(ii) Documentation evidence showing content validity of the selection procedure (see section 15C, below).

(iii) Documentation evidence showing construct validity of the selection procedure (see section 15D, below).

(iv) Documentation evidence from other studies showing validity of the selection procedure in the user's facility (see section 15E, below).

(v) Documentation evidence showing why a validity study cannot or need not be performed and why continued use of the procedure is consistent with Federal law.

(b) *Form of report.* This evidence should be compiled in a reasonably complete and organized manner to permit direct evaluation of the validity of the selection procedure. Previously written employer or consultant reports of validity, or reports describing validity studies completed before the issuance of these guidelines are acceptable if they are complete in regard to the documentation requirements contained in this section, or if they satisfied requirements of guidelines which were in effect when the validity study was completed. If they are not complete, the required additional documentation should be appended. If necessary information is not available the report of the validity study may still be used as documentation, but its adequacy will be evaluated in terms of compliance with the requirements of these guidelines.

(c) *Completeness.* In the event that evidence of validity is reviewed by an enforcement agency, the validation reports completed after the effective date of these guidelines are expected to contain the information set forth below. Evidence denoted by use of the word "(Essential)" is considered critical. If information denoted essential is not included, the report will be considered incomplete unless the user affirmatively demonstrates either its unavailability due to circumstances beyond the user's control or special circumstances of the user's study which make the information irrelevant. Evidence not so denoted is desirable but its absence will not be a basis for considering a report incomplete. The user should maintain and have available the information called for under the heading "Source Data" in sections 15B(11) and 15D(11). While it is a necessary part of the study, it need not be submitted with the report. All statistical results should be organized and presented in tabular or graphic form to the extent feasible.

B. *Criterion-related validity studies.* Reports of criterion-related validity for a selection procedure should include the following information:

(1) *User(s), location(s), and date(s) of study.* Dates and location(s) of the job analysis or review of job information, the date(s) and location(s) of the administration of the selection procedures and collection of criterion data, and the time between collection of data on selection procedures and criterion measures should be provided (Essential). If the study was conducted at several locations, the address of each location, including city and State, should be shown.

(2) *Problem and setting.* An explicit definition of the purpose(s) of the study and the circumstances in which the study was conducted should be provided. A description of existing selection procedures and cutoff scores, if any, should be provided.

(3) *Job anlysis or review of job information.* A description of the procedure used to analyze the job or group of jobs, or to review the job information should be provided (Essential). Where a review of job information results in criteria which may be used without a full job analysis (see section 14B(3)), the basis for the selection of

RULES AND REGULATIONS

these criteria should be reported (Essential). Where a job analysis is required a complete description of the work behavior(s) or work outcome(s), and measures of their criticality or importance should be provided (Essential). The report should describe the basis on which the behavior(s) or outcome(s) were determined to be critical or important, such as the proportion of time spent on the respective behaviors, their level of difficulty, their frequency of performance, the consequences of error, or other appropriate factors (Essential). Where two or more jobs are grouped for a validity study, the information called for in this subsection should be provided for each of the jobs, and the justification for the grouping (see section 14B(1)) should be provided (Essential).

(4) *Job titles and codes.* It is desirable to provide the user's job title(s) for the job(s) in question and the corresponding job title(s) and code(s) from U.S. Employment Service's Dictionary of Occupational Titles.

(5) *Criterion measures.* The bases for the selection of the criterion measures should be provided, together with references to the evidence considered in making the selection of criterion measures (essential). A full description of all criteria on which data were collected and means by which they were observed, recorded, evaluated, and quantified, should be provided (essential). If rating techniques are used as criterion measures, the appraisal form(s) and instructions to the rater(s) should be included as part of the validation evidence, or should be explicitly described and available (essential). All steps taken to insure that criterion measures are free from factors which would unfairly alter the scores of members of any group should be described (essential).

(6) *Sample description.* A description of how the research sample was identified and selected should be included (essential). The race, sex, and ethnic composition of the sample, including those groups set forth in section 4A above, should be described (essential). This description should include the size of each subgroup (essential). A description of how the research sample compares with the relevant labor market or work force, the method by which the relevant labor market or work force was defined, and a discussion of the likely effects on validity of differences between the sample and the relevant labor market or work force, are also desirable. Descriptions of educational levels, length of service, and age are also desirable.

(7) *Description of selection procedures.* Any measure, combination of measures, or procedure studied should be completely and explicitly described or attached (essential). If commercially available selection procedures are studied, they should be described by title, form, and publisher (essential). Reports of reliability estimates and how they were established are desirable.

(8) *Techniques and results.* Methods used in analyzing data should be described (essential). Measures of central tendency (e.g., means) and measures of dispersion (e.g., standard deviations and ranges) for all selection procedures and all criteria should be reported for each race, sex, and ethnic group which constitutes a significant factor in the relevant labor market (essential). The magnitude and direction of all relationships between selection procedures and criterion measures investigated should be reported for each relevant race, sex, and ethnic group and for the total group (essential). Where groups are too small to obtain reliable evidence of the magnitude of the relationship, need not be reported separately. Statements regarding the statistical significance of results should be made (essential). Any statistical adjustments, such as for less then perfect reliability or for restriction of score range in the selection procedure or criterion should be described and explained; and uncorrected correlation coefficients should also be shown (essential). Where the statistical technique categorizes continuous data, such as biserial correlation and the phi coefficient, the categories and the bases on which they were determined should be described and explained (essential). Studies of test fairness should be included where called for by the requirements of section 14B(8) (essential). These studies should include the rationale by which a selection procedure was determined to be fair to the group(s) in question. Where test fairness or unfairness has been demonstrated on the basis of other studies, a bibliography of the relevant studies should be included (essential). If the bibliography includes unpublished studies, copies of these studies, or adequate abstracts or summaries, should be attached (essential). Where revisions have been made in a selection procedure to assure compatability between successful job performance and the probability of being selected, the studies underlying such revisions should be included (essential). All statistical results should be organized and presented by relevant race, sex, and ethnic group (essential).

(9) *Alternative procedures investigated.* The selection procedures investigated and available evidence of their impact should be identified (essential). The scope, method, and findings of the investigation, and the conclusions reached in light of the findings, should be fully described (essential).

RULES AND REGULATIONS

(10) *Uses and applications.* The methods considered for use of the selection procedure (e.g., as a screening device with a cutoff score, for grouping or ranking, or combined with other procedures in a battery) and available evidence of their impact should be described (essential). This description should include the rationale for choosing the method for operational use, and the evidence of the validity and utility of the procedure as it is to be used (essential). The purpose for which the procedure is to be used (e.g., hiring, transfer, promotion) should be described (essential). If weights are assigned to different parts of the selection procedure, these weights and the validity of the weighted composite should be reported (essential). If the selection procedure is used with a cutoff score, the user should describe the way in which normal expectations of proficiency within the work force were determined and the way in which the cutoff score was determined (essential).

(11) *Source data.* Each user should maintain records showing all pertinent information about individual sample members and raters where they are used, in studies involving the validation of selection procedures. These records should be made available upon request of a compliance agency. In the case of individual sample members these data should include scores on the selection procedure(s), scores on criterion measures, age, sex, race, or ethnic group status, and experience on the specific job on which the validation study was conducted, and may also include such things as education, training, and prior job experience, but should not include names and social security numbers. Records should be maintained which show the ratings given to each sample member by each rater.

(12) *Contact person.* The name, mailing address, and telephone number of the person who may be contacted for further information about the validity study should be provided (essential).

(13) *Accuracy and completeness.* The report should describe the steps taken to assure the accuracy and completeness of the collection, analysis, and report of data and results.

C. *Content validity studies.* Reports of content validity for a selection procedure should include the following information:

(1) *User(s), location(s) and date(s) of study.* Dates and location(s) of the job analysis should be shown (essential).

(2) *Problem and setting.* An explicit definition of the purpose(s) of the study and the circumstances in which the study was conducted should be provided. A description of existing selection procedures and cutoff scores, if any, should be provided.

(3) *Job analysis—Content of the job.* A description of the method used to analyze the job should be provided (essential). The work behavior(s), the associated tasks, and, if the behavior results in a work product, the work products should be completely described (essential). Measures of criticality and/or importance of the work behavior(s) and the method of determining these measures should be provided (essential). Where the job analysis also identified the knowledges, skills, and abilities used in work behavior(s), an operational definition for each knowledge in terms of a body of learned information and for each skill and ability in terms of observable behaviors and outcomes, and the relationship between each knowledge, skill, or ability and each work behavior, as well as the method used to determine this relationship, should be provided (essential). The work situation should be described, including the setting in which work behavior(s) are performed, and where appropriate, the manner in which knowledges, skills, or abilities are used, and the complexity and difficulty of the knowledge, skill, or ability as used in the work behavior(s).

(4) *Selection procedure and its content.* Selection procedures, including those constructed by or for the user, specific training requirements, composites of selection procedures, and any other procedure supported by content validity, should be completely and explicitly described or attached (essential). If commercially available selection procedures are used, they should be described by title, form, and publisher (essential). The behaviors measured or sampled by the selection procedure should be explicitly described (essential). Where the selection procedure purports to measure a knowledge, skill, or ability, evidence that the selection procedure measures and is a representative sample of the knowledge, skill, or ability should be provided (essential).

(5) *Relationship between the selection procedure and the job.* The evidence demonstrating that the selection procedure is a representative work sample, a representative sample of the work behavior(s), or a representative sample of a knowledge, skill, or ability as used as a part of a work behavior and necessary for that behavior should be provided (essential). The user should identify the work behavior(s) which each item or part of the selection procedure is intended to sample or measure (essential). Where the selection procedure purports to sample a work behavior or to provide a sample of a work product, a comparison should be provided of the manner, setting, and the level of complexity of the selection procedure with those of

RULES AND REGULATIONS

the work situation (essential). If any steps were taken to reduce adverse impact on a race, sex, or ethnic group in the content of the procedure or in its administration, these steps should be described. Establishment of time limits, if any, and how these limits are related to the speed with which duties must be performed on the job, should be explained. Measures of central tend- ency (e.g., means) and measures of dispersion (e.g., standard deviations) and estimates of realibility should be reported for all selection procedures if available. Such reports should be made for relevant race, sex, and ethnic subgroups, at least on a statistically reliable sample basis.

(6) *Alternative procedures investigated.* The alternative selection procedures investigated and available evidence of their impact should be identified (essential). The scope, method, and findings of the investigation, and the conclusions reached in light of the findings, should be fully described (essential).

(7) *Uses and applications.* The methods considered for use of the selection procedure (e.g., as a screening device with a cutoff score, for grouping or ranking, or combined with other procedures in a battery) and available evidence of their impact should be described (essential). This description should include the rationale for choosing the method for operational use, and the evidence of the validity and utility of the procedure as it is to be used (essential). The purpose for which the procedure is to be used (e.g., hiring, transfer, promotion) should be described (essential). If the selection procedure is used with a cutoff score, the user should describe the way in which normal expectations of proficiency within the work force were determined and the way in which the cutoff score was determined (essential). In addition, if the selection procedure is to be used for ranking, the user should specify the evidence showing that a higher score on the selection procedure is likely to result in better job performance.

(8) *Contact person.* The name, mailing address, and telephone number of the person who may be contacted for further information about the validity study should be provided (essential).

(9) *Accuracy and completeness.* The report should describe the steps taken to assure the accuracy and completeness of the collection, analysis, and report of data and results.

D. *Construct validity studies.* Reports of construct validity for a selection procedure should include the following information:

(1) *User(s), location(s), and date(s) of study.* Date(s) and location(s) of the job analysis and the gathering of other evidence called for by these guidelines should be provided (essential).

(2) *Problem and setting.* An explicit definition of the purpose(s) of the study and the circumstances in which the study was conducted should be provided. A description of existing selection procedures and cutoff scores, if any, should be provided.

(3) *Construct definition.* A clear definition of the construct(s) which are believed to underlie successful performance of the critical or important work behavior(s) should be provided (essential). This definition should include the levels of construct performance relevant to the job(s) for which the selection procedure is to be used (essential). There should be a summary of the position of the construct in the psychological literature, or in the absence of such a position, a description of the way in which the definition and measurement of the construct was developed and the psychological theory underlying it (essential). Any quantitative data which identify or define the job constructs, such as factor analyses, should be provided (essential).

(4) *Job analysis.* A description of the method used to analyze the job should be provided (essential). A complete description of the work behavior(s) and, to the extent appropriate, work outcomes and measures of their criticality and/or importance should be provided (essential). The report should also describe the basis on which the behavior(s) or outcomes were determined to be important, such as their level of difficulty, their frequency of performance, the consequences of error or other appropriate factors (essential). Where jobs are grouped or compared for the purposes of generalizing validity evidence, the work behavior(s) and work product(s) for each of the jobs should be described, and conclusions concerning the similarity of the jobs in terms of observable work behaviors or work products should be made (essential).

(5) *Job titles and codes.* It is desirable to provide the selection procedure user's job title(s) for the job(s) in question and the corresponding job title(s) and code(s) from the United States Employment Service's dictionary of occupational titles.

(6) *Selection procedure.* The selection procedure used as a measure of the construct should be completely and explicitly described or attached (essential). If commercially available selection procedures are used, they should be identified by title, form and publisher (essential). The research evidence of the relationship between the selection procedure and the construct, such as factor structure, should be included (essential). Measures of central tendency, variability and reliability of

RULES AND REGULATIONS

the selection procedure should be provided (essential). Whenever feasible, these measures should be provided separately for each relevant race, sex and ethnic group.

(7) *Relationship to job performance.* The criterion-related study(ies) and other empirical evidence of the relationship between the construct measured by the selection procedure and the related work behavior(s) for the job or jobs in question should be provided (essential). Documentation of the criterion-related study(ies) should satisfy the provisions of section 15B above or section 15E(1) below, except for studies conducted prior to the effective date of these guidelines (essential). Where a study pertains to a group of jobs, and, on the basis of the study, validity is asserted for a job in the group, the observed work behaviors and the observed work products for each of the jobs should be described (essential). Any other evidence used in determining whether the work behavior(s) in each of the jobs is the same should be fully described (essential).

(8) *Alternative procedures investigated.* The alternative selection procedures investigated and available evidence of their impact should be identified (essential). The scope, method, and findings of the investigation, and the conclusions reached in light of the findings should be fully described (essential).

(9) *Uses and applications.* The methods considered for use of the selection procedure (e.g., as a screening device with a cutoff score, for grouping or ranking, or combined with other procedures in a battery) and available evidence of their impact should be described (essential). This description should include the rationale for choosing the method for operational use, and the evidence of the validity and utility of the procedure as it is to be used (essential). The purpose for which the procedure is to be used (e.g., hiring, transfer, promotion) should be described (essential). If weights are assigned to different parts of the selection procedure, these weights and the validity of the weighted composite should be reported (essential). If the selection procedure is used with a cutoff score, the user should describe the way in which normal expectations of proficiency within the work force were determined and the way in which the cutoff score was determined (essential).

(10) *Accuracy and completeness.* The report should describe the steps taken to assure the accuracy and completeness of the collection, analysis, and report of data and results.

(11) *Source data.* Each user should maintain records showing all pertinent information relating to its study of construct validity.

(12) *Contact person.* The name, mailing address, and telephone number of the individual who may be contacted for further information about the validity study should be provided (essential).

E. *Evidence of validity from other studies.* When validity of a selection procedure is supported by studies not done by the user, the evidence from the original study or studies should be compiled in a manner similar to that required in the appropriate section of this section 15 above. In addition, the following evidence should be supplied:

(1) *Evidence from criterion-related validity studies.*—a. *Job information.* A description of the important job behavior(s) of the user's job and the basis on which the behaviors were determined to be important should be provided (essential). A full description of the basis for determining that these important work behaviors are the same as those of the job in the original study (or studies) should be provided (essential).

b. *Relevance of criteria.* A full description of the basis on which the criteria used in the original studies are determined to be relevant for the user should be provided (essential).

c. *Other variables.* The similarity of important applicant pool or sample characteristics reported in the original studies to those of the user should be described (essential). A description of the comparison between the race, sex and ethnic composition of the user's relevant labor market and the sample in the original validity studies should be provided (essential).

d. *Use of the selection procedure.* A full description should be provided showing that the use to be made of the selection procedure is consistent with the findings of the original validity studies (essential).

e. *Bibliography.* A bibliography of reports of validity of the selection procedure for the job or jobs in question should be provided (essential). Where any of the studies included an investigation of test fairness, the results of this investigation should be provided (essential). Copies of reports published in journals that are not commonly available should be described in detail or attached (essential). Where a user is relying upon unpublished studies, a reasonable effort should be made to obtain these studies. If these unpublished studies are the sole source of validity evidence they should be described in detail or attached (essential). If these studies are not available, the name and address of the source, an adequate abstract or summary of the validity study and data, and a contact person in the source organization should be provided (essential).

RULES AND REGULATIONS

(2) *Evidence from content validity studies.* See section 14C(3) and section 15C above.

(3) *Evidence from construct validity studies.* See sections 14D(2) and 15D above.

F. *Evidence of validity from cooperative studies.* Where a selection procedure has been validated through a cooperative study, evidence that the study satisfies the requirements of sections 7, 8 and 15E should be provided (essential).

G. *Selection for higher level job.* If a selection procedure is used to evaluate candidates for jobs at a higher level than those for which they will initially be employed, the validity evidence should satisfy the documentation provisions of this section 15 for the higher level job or jobs, and in addition, the user should provide: (1) a description of the job progression structure, formal or informal; (2) the data showing how many employees progress to the higher level job and the length of time needed to make this progression; and (3) an identification of any anticipated changes in the higher level job. In addition, if the test measures a knowledge, skill or ability, the user should provide evidence that the knowledge, skill or ability is required for the higher level job and the basis for the conclusion that the knowledge, skill or ability is not expected to develop from the training or experience on the job.

H. *Interim use of selection procedures.* If a selection procedure is being used on an interim basis because the procedure is not fully supported by the required evidence of validity, the user should maintain and have available (1) substantial evidence of validity for the procedure, and (2) a report showing the date on which the study to gather the additional evidence commenced, the estimated completion date of the study, and a description of the data to be collected (essential).

Definitions

Sec. 16. *Definitions.* The following definitions shall apply throughout these guidelines:

A. *Ability.* A present competence to perform an observable behavior or a behavior which results in an observable product.

B. *Adverse impact.* A substantially different rate of selection in hiring, promotion, or other employment decision which works to the disadvantage of members of a race, sex, or ethnic group. See section 4 of these guidelines.

C. *Compliance with these guidelines.* Use of a selection procedure is in compliance with these guidelines if such use has been validated in accord with these guidelines (as defined below), or if such use does not result in adverse impact on any race, sex, or ethnic group (see section 4, above), or, in unusual circumstances, if use of the procedure is otherwise justified in accord with Federal law. See section 6B, above.

D. *Content validity.* Demonstrated by data showing that the content of a selection procedure is representative of important aspects of performance on the job. See section 5B and section 14C.

E. *Construct validity.* Demonstrated by data showing that the selection procedure measures the degree to which candidates have identifiable characteristics which have been determined to be important for successful job performance. See section 5B and section 14D.

F. *Criterion-related validity.* Demonstrated by empirical data showing that the selection procedure is predictive of or significantly correlated with important elements of work behavior. See sections 5B and 14B.

G. *Employer.* Any employer subject to the provisions of the Civil Rights Act of 1964, as amended, including State or local governments and any Federal agency subject to the provisions of section 717 of the Civil Rights Act of 1964, as amended, and any Federal contractor or subcontractor or federally assisted construction contractor or subcontactor covered by Executive Order 11246, as amended.

H. *Employment agency.* Any employment agency subject to the provisions of the Civil Rights Act of 1964, as amended.

I. *Enforcement action.* For the purposes of section 4 a proceeding by a Federal enforcement agency such as a lawsuit or an administrative proceeding leading to debarment from or withholding, suspension, or termination of Federal Government contracts or the suspension or withholding of Federal Government funds; but not a finding of reasonable cause or a conciliation process or the issuance of right to sue letters under title VII or under Executive Order 11246 where such finding, conciliation, or issuance of notice of right to sue is based upon an individual complaint.

J. *Enforcement agency.* Any agency of the executive branch of the Federal Government which adopts these guidelines for purposes of the enforcement of the equal employment opportunity laws or which has responsibility for securing compliance with them.

K. *Job analysis.* A detailed statement of work behaviors and other information relevant to the job.

L. *Job description.* A general statement of job duties and responsibilities.

M. *Knowledge.* A body of information applied directly to the performance of a function.

RULES AND REGULATIONS

N. *Labor organization.* Any labor organization subject to the provisions of the Civil Rights Act of 1964, as amended, and any committee subject thereto controlling apprenticeship or other training.

O. *Observable.* Able to be seen, heard, or otherwise perceived by a person other than the person performing the action.

P. *Race, sex, or ethnic group.* Any group of persons identifiable on the grounds of race, color, religion, sex, or national origin.

Q. *Selection procedure.* Any measure, combination of measures, or procedure used as a basis for any employment decision. Selection procedures include the full range of assessment techniques from traditional paper and pencil tests, performance tests, training programs, or probationary periods and physical, educational, and work experience requirements through informal or casual interviews and unscored application forms.

R. *Selection rate.* The proportion of applicants or candidates who are hired, promoted, or otherwise selected.

S. *Should.* The term "should" as used in these guidelines is intended to connote action which is necessary to achieve compliance with the guidelines, while recognizing that there are circumstances where alternative courses of action are open to users.

T. *Skill.* A present, observable competence to perform a learned psychomotor act.

U. *Technical feasibility.* The existence of conditions permitting the conduct of meaningful criterion-related validity studies. These conditions include: (1) An adequate sample of persons available for the study to achieve findings of statistical significance; (2) having or being able to obtain a sufficient range of scores on the selection procedure and job performance measures to produce validity results which can be expected to be representative of the results if the ranges normally expected were utilized; and (3) having or being able to devise unbiased, reliable and relevant measures of job performance or other criteria of employee adequacy. See section 14B(2). With respect to investigation of possible unfairness, the same considerations are applicable to each group for which the study is made. See section 14B(8).

V. *Unfairness of selection procedure.* A condition in which members of one race, sex, or ethnic group characteristically obtain lower scores on a selection procedure than members of another group, and the differences are not reflected in differences in measures of job performance. See section 14B(7).

W. *User.* Any employer, labor organization, employment agency, or licensing or certification board, to the extent it may be covered by Federal equal employment opportunity law, which uses a selection procedure as a basis for any employment decision. Whenever an employer, labor organization, or employment agency is required by law to restrict recruitment for any occupation to those applicants who have met licensing or certification requirements, the licensing or certifying authority to the extent it may be covered by Federal equal employment opportunity law will be considered the user with respect to those licensing or certification requirements. Whenever a State employment agency or service does no more than administer or monitor a procedure as permitted by Department of Labor regulations, and does so without making referrals or taking any other action on the basis of the results, the State employment agency will not be deemed to be a user.

X. *Validated in accord with these guidelines or properly validated.* A demonstration that one or more validity study or studies meeting the standards of these guidelines has been conducted, including investigation and, where appropriate, use of suitable alternative selection procedures as contemplated by section 3B, and has produced evidence of validity sufficient to warrant use of the procedure for the intended purpose under the standards of these guidelines.

Y. *Work behavior.* An activity performed to achieve the objectives of the job. Work behaviors involve observable (physical) components and unobservable (mental) components. A work behavior consists of the performance of one or more tasks. Knowledges, skills, and abilities are not behaviors, although they may be applied in work behaviors.

APPENDIX

17. *Policy statement on affirmative action* (see section 13B). The Equal Employment Opportunity Coordinating Council was established by act of Congress in 1972, and charged with responsibility for developing and implementing agreements and policies designed, among other things, to eliminate conflict and inconsistency among the agencies of the Federal Government responsible for administering Federal law prohibiting discrimination on grounds of race, color, sex, religion, and national origin. This statement is issued as an initial response to the requests of a number of State and local officials for clarification of the Government's policies concerning the role of affirmative action in the overall equal employment opportunity program. While the Coordinating Council's adoption of this statement expresses only the views of the signatory agencies concerning this important subject, the principles set forth below

RULES AND REGULATIONS

snould serve as policy guidance for other Federal agencies as well.

(1) Equal employment opportunity is the law of the land. In the public sector of our society this means that all persons, regardless of race, color, religion, sex, or national origin shall have equal access to positions in the public service limited only by their ability to do the job. There is ample evidence in all sectors of our society that such equal access frequently has been denied to members of certain groups because of their sex, racial, or ethnic characteristics. The remedy for such past and present discrimination is twofold.

On the one hand, vigorous enforcement of the laws against discrimination is essential. But equally, and perhaps even more important are affirmative, voluntary efforts on the part of public employers to assure that positions in the public service are genuinely and equally accessible to qualified persons, without regard to their sex, racial, or ethnic characteristics. Without such efforts equal employment opportunity is no more than a wish. The importance of voluntary affirmative action on the part of employers is underscored by title VII of the Civil Rights Act of 1964, Executive Order 11246, and related laws and regulations—all of which emphasize voluntary action to achieve equal employment opportunity.

As with most management objectives, a systematic plan based on sound organizational analysis and problem identification is crucial to the accomplishment of affirmative action objectives. For this reason, the Council urges all State and local governments to develop and implement results oriented affirmative action plans which deal with the problems so identified.

The following paragraphs are intended to assist State and local governments by illustrating the kinds of analyses and activities which may be appropriate for a public employer's voluntary affirmative action plan. This statement does not address remedies imposed after a finding of unlawful discrimination.

(2) Voluntary affirmative action to assure equal employment opportunity is appropriate at any stage of the employment process. The first step in the construction of any affirmative action plan should be an analysis of the employer's work force to determine whether precentages of sex, race, or ethnic groups in individual job classifications are substantially similar to the precentages of those groups available in the relevant job market who possess the basic job-related qualifications.

When substantial disparities are found through such analyses, each element of the overall selection process should be examined to determine which elements operate to exclude persons on the basis of sex, race, or ethnic group. Such elements include, but are not limited to, recruitment, testing, ranking certification, interview, recommendations for selection, hiring, promotion, etc. The examination of each element of the selection process should at a minimum include a determination of its validity in predicting job performance.

(3) When an employer has reason to believe that its selection procedures have the exclusionary effect described in paragraph 2 above, it should initiate affirmative steps to remedy the situation. Such steps, which in design and execution may be race, color, sex, or ethnic "conscious," include, but are not limited to, the following:

(a) The establishment of a long-term goal, and short-range, interim goals and timetables for the specific job classifications, all of which should take into account the availability of basically qualified persons in the relevant job market;

(b) A recruitment program designed to attract qualified members of the group in question;

(c) A systematic effort to organize work and redesign jobs in ways that provide opportunities for persons lacking "journeyman" level knowledge or skills to enter and, with appropriate training, to progress in a career field;

(d) Revamping selection instruments or procedures which have not yet been validated in order to reduce or eliminate exclusionary effects on particular groups in particular job classifications;

(e) The initiation of measures designed to assure that members of the affected group who are qualified to perform the job are included within the pool of persons from which the selecting official makes the selection;

(f) A systematic effort to provide career advancement training, both classroom and on-the-job, to employees locked into dead end jobs; and

(g) The establishment of a system for regularly monitoring the effectiveness of the particular affirmative action program, and procedures for making timely adjustments in this program where effectiveness is not demonstrated.

(4) The goal of any affirmative action plan should be achievement of genuine equal employment opportunity for all qualified persons. Selection under such plans should be based

RULES AND REGULATIONS

upon the ability of the applicant(s) to do the work. Such plans should not require the selection of the unqualified, or the unneeded, nor should they require the selection of persons on the basis of race, color, sex, religion, or national origin. Moreover, while the Council believes that this statement should serve to assist State and local employers, as well as Federal agencies, it recognizes that affirmative action cannot be viewed as a standardized program which must be accomplished in the same way at all times in all places.

Accordingly, the Council has not attempted to set forth here either the minimum or maximum voluntary steps that employers may take to deal with their respective situations. Rather, the Council recognizes that under applicable authorities, State and local employers have flexibility to formulate affirmative action plans that are best suited to their particular situations. In this manner, the Council believes that affirmative action programs will best serve the goal of equal employment opportunity.

Respectfully submitted,

HAROLD R. TYLER, Jr.,
Deputy Attorney General and Chairman of the Equal Employment Coordinating Council.

MICHAEL H. MOSKOW,
Under Secretary of Labor.

ETHEL BENT WALSH,
Acting Chairman, Equal Employment Opportunity Commission.

ROBERT E. HAMPTON,
Chairman, Civil Service Commission.

ARTHUR E. FLEMMING,
Chairman, Commission on Civil Rights.

Because of its equal employment opportunity responsibilities under the State and Local Government Fiscal Assistance Act of 1972 (the revenue sharing act), the Department of Treasury was invited to participate in the formulation of this policy statement; and it concurs and joins in the adoption of this policy statement.

Done this 26th day of August 1976.

RICHARD ALBRECHT,
*General Counsel,
Department of the Treasury.*

Section 18. *Citations.* The official title of these guidelines is "Uniform Guidelines on Employee Selection Procedures (1978)". The Uniform Guidelines on Employee Selection Procedures (1978) are intended to establish a uniform Federal position in the area of prohibiting discrimination in employment practices on grounds of race, color, religion, sex, or national origin. These guidelines have been adopted by the Equal Employment Opportunity Commission, the Department of Labor, the Department of Justice, and the Civil Service Commission. The official citation is:

"Section ——, Uniform Guidelines on Employee Selection Procedure (1978); 43 FR —— (August 25, 1978)."

The short form citation is:

"Section ——, U.G.E.S.P. (1978); 43 FR —— (August 25, 1978)."

When the guidelines are cited in connection with the activities of one of the issuing agencies, a specific citation to the regulations of that agency can be added at the end of the above citation. The specific additional citations are as follows:

Equal Employment Opportunity Commission
29 CFR Part 1607
Department of Labor
Office of Federal Contract Compliance Programs
41 CFR Part 60-3
Department of Justice
28 CFR 50.14
Civil Service Commission
5 CFR 300.103(c)

Normally when citing these guidelines, the section number immediately preceding the title of the guidelines will be from these guidelines series 1-18. If a section number from the codification for an individual agency is needed it can also be added at the end of the agency citation. For example, section 6A of these guidelines could be cited for EEOC as follows: "Section 6A, Uniform Guidelines on Employee Selection Procedures (1978); 43 FR ——, (August 25, 1978); 29 CFR Part 1607, section 6A."

ELEANOR HOLMES NORTON,
Chair, Equal Employment Opportunity Commission.

ALAN K. CAMPBELL,
*Chairman,
Civil Service Commission.*

RAY MARSHALL,
Secretary of Labor.

GRIFFIN B. BELL,
Attorney General.

RULES AND REGULATIONS

[6570-06]

CIVIL SERVICE COMMISSION

Title 5—Administrative Personnel

CHAPTER 1—CIVIL SERVICE COMMISSION

PART 300—EMPLOYMENT (GENERAL)

Uniform Guidelines on Employee Selection Procedures (1978)

The Uniform Guidelines on Employee Selection Procedures (1978) which are printed at the beginning of this part IV in today's FEDERAL REGISTER are adopted by the Civil Service Commission, in conjunction with the Equal Employment Opportunity Commission, Department of Justice, and the Department of Labor to establish uniformity in prohibiting discrimination in employment practices on grounds of race, color, religion, sex, or national origin. Cross reference documents are published at 29 CFR parts 1607 (Equal Employment Opportunity Commission), 28 CFR 50.14 (Department of Justice), and 41 CFR 60-3 (Department of Labor) elsewhere in this issue of the FEDERAL REGISTER.

By virtue of the authority vested in it by sections 3301, 3302, 7151, 7154, and 7301 of title 5 and section 4763(b) of title 42, United States Code, and Executive Order 10577, 3 CFR 1954-58 comp. page 218 and Executive Order 11478, 3 CFR 1959 comp. 133, and section 717 of the Civil Rights Act of 1964, as amended (42 U.S.C. 2000e-16), the Civil Service Commission amends title 5, part 300, subpart A, § 300.103(c) of the Code of Federal Regulations to read as follows:

§ 300.103 Basic requirements.

"(c) Equal employment opportunity. An employment practice shall not discriminate on the basis of race, color, religion, sex, age, national origin, partisan political affiliation, or other non-merit factor. Employee selection procedures shall meet the standards established by the "Uniform Guidelines on Employee Selection Procedures (1978), 43 FR—— (August 25, 1978)."

The Civil Service Commission rescinds the Guidelines on Employee Selection Procedures, 41 FR 51752, Federal Personnel Manual part 900, subpart F and adopts the Uniform Guidelines on Employee Selection Procedures (1978), to be issued as identical supplement appendices to supplements 271-1, Development of Qualification Standards; 271-2, Tests and Other Applicant Appraisal Procedures; 335-1, Evaluation of Employees for Promotion and Internal Placement; and 990-1 (Book III), part 900, subpart F, Administration of Standards for a Merit System of Personnel Administration of the Federal Personnel Manual in order to insure the examining, testing standards, and employment practices are not affected by discrimination on the basis of race, color, religion, sex or national origin.

Effective date: September 25, 1978.

ALAN K. CAMPBELL,
Chairman,
Civil Service Commission.

RULES AND REGULATIONS

[6570-06]

DEPARTMENT OF JUSTICE

Title 28—Judicial Administration

CHAPTER 1—DEPARTMENT OF JUSTICE

PART 50—STATEMENTS OF POLICY

Uniform Guidelines on Employee Selection Procedures (1978)

The Uniform Guidelines on Employee Selection Procedures which are provided at the beginning of this part IV in today's FEDERAL REGISTER are adopted by the Department of Justice, in conjunction with the Civil Service Commission, Equal Employment Opportunity Commission, and the Department of Labor to establish a uniform Federal position in the area of prohibiting discrimination in employment practices on grounds of race, color, religion, sex, or national origin. Cross reference documents are published at 5 CFR 300.103(c), (Civil Service Commission) 29 CFR 1607 (Equal Employment Opportunity Commission), and 41 CFR 60-3 (Department of Labor), elsewhere in this issue of the FEDERAL REGISTER.

By virtue of the authority vested in me by 28 U.S.C. 509 and 5 U.S.C. 301, Sec. 50.14 of part 50 of chapter 1 of title 28 of the Code of Federal Regulations is amended by substituting the Uniform Guidelines on Employee Selection Procedures (1978) for part I through part IV.

Effective date: September 25, 1978.

GRIFFIN B. BELL,
Attorney General.

RULES AND REGULATIONS

[6570-06]

EQUAL EMPLOYMENT OPPORTUNITY COMMISSION

Title 29—Labor

CHAPTER XIV—EQUAL EMPLOYMENT OPPORTUNITY COMMISSION

PART 1607—UNIFORM GUIDELINES ON EMPLOYEE SELECTION PROCEDURES (1978)

The Uniform Guidelines on Employee Selection Procedures which are printed at the beginning of this part IV in today's FEDERAL REGISTER are adopted by the Equal Employment Opportunity Commission, in conjunction with the Civil Service Commission, Department of Justice, and the Department of Labor to establish a uniform Federal position in the area of prohibiting discrimination in employment practices on grounds of race, color, religion, sex, or national origin. Cross reference documents are published at 5 CFR 300.103(c) (Civil Service Commission), 28 CFR 50.14 (Department of Justice) and 41 CFR 60-3 (Department of Labor), elsewhere in this issue.

By virtue of the authority vested in it by sections 713 and 709 of title VII of the Civil Rights Act of 1964 (78 Stat. 265), as amended by the Equal Employment Opportunity Act of 1972 (Pub. L. 92-261), (42 U.S.C. 2000e-12 and 2000e-8), the Equal Employment Opportunity Commission hereby revises part 1607 of chapter XIV of title 29 of the Code of Federal Regulations by rescinding the Guidelines on Employee Selection Procedures (see 35 FR 12333, August 1, 1970; and 41 FR 51984, November 24, 1976) and adopting the Uniform Guidelines on Employee Selection Procedures (1978) as a new part 1607.

Effective date: September 25, 1978.

ELEANOR HOLMES NORTON,
Chair.

TABLE OF CONTENTS

GENERAL PRINCIPLES

1607.1 Statement of Purpose
  A. Need for Uniformity—Issuing Agencies
  B. Purpose of Guidelines
  C. Relation to Prior Guidelines
1607.2 Scope
  A. Application of Guidelines
  B. Employment Decisions
  C. Selection Procedures
  D. Limitations
  E. Indian Preference Not Affected
1607.3 Discrimination Defined: Relationship Between Use of Selection Procedures and Discrimination
  A. Procedure Having Adverse Impact Constitutes Discrimination Unless Justified
  B. Consideration of Suitable Alternative Selection Procedures
1607.4 Information on Impact
  A. Records Concerning Impact
  B. Applicable Race, Sex, and Ethnic Groups for Recordkeeping
  C. Evaluation of Selection Rates. The "Bottom Line"
  D. Adverse Impact and the "Four-Fifths Rule"
  E. Consideration of User's Equal Employment Opportunity Posture
1607.5 General Standards for Validity Studies
  A. Acceptable Types of Validity Studies
  B. Criterion-Related, Content, and Construct Validity
  C. Guidelines Are Consistent With Professional Standards
  D. Need for Documentation of Validity
  E. Accuracy and Standardization
  F. Caution Against Selection on Basis of Knowledges, Skills, or Abilities Learned in Brief Orientation Period
  G. Method of Use of Selection Procedures
  H. Cutoff Scores
  I. Use of Selection Procedures for Higher Level Jobs
  J. Interim Use of Selection Procedures
  K. Review of Validity Studies for Currency
1607.6 Use of Selection Procedures Which Have Not Been Validated
  A. Use of Alternate Selection Procedures To Eliminate Adverse Impact
  B. Where Validity Studies Cannot or Need Not Be Performed
    (1) Where Informal or Unscored Procedures Are Used
    (2) Where Formal and Scored Procedures Are Used
1607.7 Use of Other Validity Studies
  A. Validity Studies Not Conducted by the User
  B. Use of Criterion-Related Validity Evidence From Other Sources
    (1) Validity Evidence
    (2) Job Similarity
    (3) Fairness Evidence
  C. Validity Evidence From Multi-Unit Study
  D. Other Significant Variables
1607.8 Cooperative Studies
  A. Encouragement of Cooperative Studies
  B. Standards for Use of Cooperative Studies
1607.9 No Assumption of Validity
  A. Unacceptable Substitutes for Evidence of Validity
  B. Encouragement of Professional Supervision
1607.10 Employment Agencies and Employment Services
  A. Where Selection Procedures Are Devised by Agency
  B. Where Selection Procedures Are Devised Elsewhere
1607.11 Disparate Treatment
1607.12 Retesting of Applicants
1607.13 Affirmative Action
  A. Affirmative Action Obligations
  B. Encouragement of Voluntary Affirmative Action Programs

TECHNICAL STANDARDS

1607.14 Technical Standards for Validity Studies
  A. Validity Studies Should Be Based on Review of Information About the Job
  B. Technical Standards for Criterion-Related Validity Studies
    (1) Technical Feasibility

RULES AND REGULATIONS

(2) Analysis of the Job
(3) Criterion Measures
(4) Representativeness of the Sample
(5) Statistical Relationships
(6) Operational Use of Selection Procedures
(7) Over-Statement of Validity Findings
(8) Fairness
  (a) Unfairness Defined
  (b) Investigation of Fairness
  (c) General Considerations in Fairness Investigations
  (d) When Unfairness is Shown
  (e) Technical Feasibility of Fairness Studies
  (f) Continued Use of Selection Procedures When Fairness Studies Not Feasible
C. Technical Standards for Content Validity Studies
(1) Appropriateness of Content Validity Studies
(2) Job Analysis for Content Validity
(3) Development of Selection Procedure
(4) Standards for Demonstrating Content Validity
(5) Reliability
(6) Prior Training or Experience
(7) Training Success
(8) Operational Use
(9) Ranking Based on Content Validity Studies
D. Technical Standards for Construct Validity Studies
(1) Appropriateness of Construct Validity Studies
(2) Job Analysis Required in Construct Validity Studies
(3) Relationship to the Job
(4) Use of Construct Validity Study Without New Criterion-Related Evidence
  (a) Standards for Use
  (b) Determination of Common Work Behaviors

DOCUMENTATION OF IMPACT AND VALIDITY EVIDENCE

1607.15 Documentation of Impact and Validity Evidence
A. Required Information
(1) Simplified Recordkeeping for Users With Less Than 100 Employees
(2) Information on Impact
  (a) Collection of Information on Impact
  (b) When Adverse Impact Has Been Eliminated in the Total Selection Process
  (c) When Data Insufficient To Determine Impact
(3) Documentation of Validity Evidence
  (a) Type of Evidence
  (b) Form of Report
  (c) Completeness
B. Criterion-Related Validity Studies
(1) User(s), Location(s), and Date(s) of Study
(2) Problem and Setting
(3) Job Analysis or Review of Job Information
(4) Job Titles and Codes
(5) Criterion Measures
(6) Sample Description
(7) Description of Selection Procedure
(8) Techniques and Results
(9) Alternative Procedures Investigated
(10) Uses and Applications
(11) Source Data
(12) Contact Person
(13) Accuracy and Completeness
C. Content Validity Studies
(1) User(s), Location(s), and Date(s) of Study
(2) Problem and Setting
(3) Job Analysis—Content of the Job
(4) Selection Procedure and Its Content
(5) Relationship Between Selection Procedure and the Job
(6) Alternative Procedures Investigated
(7) Uses and Applications
(8) Contact Person
(9) Accuracy and Completeness
D. Construct Validity Studies
(1) User(s), Location(s), and Date(s) of Study
(2) Problem and Setting
(3) Construct Definition
(4) Job Analysis
(5) Job Titles and Codes
(6) Selection Procedure
(7) Relationship to Job Performance
(8) Alternative Procedures Investigated
(9) Uses and Applications
(10) Accuracy and Completeness
(11) Source Data
(12) Contact Person
E. Evidence of Validity From Other Studies
(1) Evidence From Criterion-Related Validity Studies
  (a) Job Information
  (b) Relevance of Criteria
  (c) Other Variables
  (d) Use of the Selection Procedure
  (e) Bibliography
(2) Evidence From Content Validity Studies
(3) Evidence From Construct Validity Studies
F. Evidence of Validity From Cooperative Studies
G. Selection for Higher Level Jobs
H. Interim Use of Selection Procedures

DEFINITIONS

1607.16 Definitions

APPENDIX

1607.17 Policy Statement on Affirmative Action (see section 13B)
1607.18 Citations

RULES AND REGULATIONS

[6570–06]

DEPARTMENT OF LABOR

Title 41—Public Contracts and Property Management

CHAPTER 60—OFFICE OF FEDERAL CONTRACT COMPLIANCE PROGRAMS, DEPARTMENT OF LABOR

PART 60–3—UNIFORM GUIDELINES ON EMPLOYEE SELECTION PROCEDURES (1978)

The Uniform Guidelines on Employee Selection Procedures which are printed at the beginning of this part IV of today's FEDERAL REGISTER are adopted by the Department of Labor, in conjunction with the Civil Service Commission, Department of Justice, and the Equal Employment Opportunity Commission to establish a uniform Federal position in the area of prohibiting discrimination in employment practices on grounds of race, color, religion, sex, or national origin. Cross reference documents are published at 5 CFR 300.103(c) (Civil Service Commission), 28 CFR 50.14 (Department of Justice) and 29 CFR 1607 (Equal Employment Opportunity Commission), elsewhere in this issue of the FEDERAL REGISTER.

By virtue of the authority of sections 201, 202, 203, 203(a), 205, 206(a), 301, 303(b), and 403(b) of Executive Order 11246, as amended, 30 FR 12319; 32 FR 14303; section 60–1.2 of part 60–1 of 41 CFR chapter 60, and section 715 of the Civil Rights Act of 1964, as amended (42 U.S.C. 2000e–14), part 60–3 of chapter 60 of title 41 of the Code of Federal Regulations is revised by rescinding the Guidelines on Employee Selection Procedures (see 41 FR 51744, November 23, 1976) and adopting the Uniform Guidelines on Employee Selection Procedures (1978) as a new part 60–3.

Effective date: September 25, 1978.

RAY MARSHALL,
Secretary of Labor.

TABLE OF CONTENTS

GENERAL PRINCIPLES

60–3.1 Statement of Purpose
  A. Need for Uniformity—Issuing Agencies
  B. Purpose of Guidelines
  C. Relation to Prior Guidelines
60–3.2 Scope
  A. Application of Guidelines
  B. Employment Decisions
  C. Selection Procedures
  D. Limitations
  E. Indian Preference Not Affected
60–3.3 Discrimination Defined: Relationship Between Use of Selection Procedures and Discrimination
  A. Procedure Having Adverse Impact Constitutes Discrimination Unless Justified
  B. Consideration of Suitable Alternative Selection Procedures
60–3.4 Information on Impact
  A. Records Concerning Impact
  B. Applicable Race, Sex, and Ethnic Groups for Recordkeeping
  C. Evaluation of Selection Rates. The "Bottom Line"
  D. Adverse Impact and the "Four-Fifths Rule"
  E. Consideration of User's Equal Employment Opportunity Posture
60–3.5 General Standards for Validity Studies
  A. Acceptable Types of Validity Studies
  B. Criterion-Related, Content, and Construct Validity
  C. Guidelines Are Consistent With Professional Standards
  D. Need for Documentation of Validity
  E. Accuracy and Standardization
  F. Caution Against Selection on Basis of Knowledges, Skills, or Abilities Learned in Brief Orientation Period
  G. Method of Use of Selection Procedures
  H. Cutoff Scores
  I. Use of Selection Procedures for Higher Level Jobs
  J. Interim Use of Selection Procedures
  K. Review of Validity Studies for Currency
60–3.6 Use of Selection Procedures Which Have Not Been Validated
  A. Use of Alternate Selection Procedures To Eliminate Adverse Impact
  B. Where Validity Studies Cannot or Need Not Be Performed
    (1) Where Informal or Unscored Procedures Are Used
    (2) Where Formal and Scored Procedures Are Used
60–3.7 Use of Other Validity Studies
  A. Validity Studies Not Conducted by the User
  B. Use of Criterion-Related Validity Evidence From Other Sources
    (1) Validity Evidence
    (2) Job Similarity
    (3) Fairness Evidence
  C. Validity Evidence From Multiunit Study
  D. Other Significant Variables
60–3.8 Cooperative Studies
  A. Encouragement of Cooperative Studies
  B. Standards for Use of Cooperative Studies
60–3.9 No Assumption of Validity
  A. Unacceptable Substitutes for Evidence of Validity
  B. Encouragement of Professional Supervision
60–3.10 Employment Agencies and Employment Services
  A. Where Selection Procedures Are Devised by Agency
  B. Where Selection Procedures Are Devised Elsewhere
60–3.11 Disparate Treatment
60–3.12 Retesting of Applicants
60–3.13 Affirmative Action
  A. Affirmative Action Obligations
  B. Encouragement of Voluntary Affirmative Action Programs

TECHNICAL STANDARDS

60–3.14 Technical Standards for Validity Studies
  A. Validity Studies Should be Based on Review of Information About the Job

RULES AND REGULATIONS

B. Technical Standards for Criterion-Related Validity Studies
 (1) Technical Feasibility
 (2) Analysis of the Job
 (3) Criterion Measures
 (4) Representativeness of the Sample
 (5) Statistical Relationships
 (6) Operational Use of Selection Procedures
 (7) Over-Statement of Validity Findings
 (8) Fairness
  (a) Unfairness Defined
  (b) Investigation of Fairness
  (c) General Considerations in Fairness Investigations
  (d) When Unfairness Is Shown
  (e) Technical Feasibility of Fairness Studies
  (f) Continued Use of Selection Procedures When Fairness Studies not Feasible
C. Technical Standards for Content Validity Studies
 (1) Appropriateness of Content Validity Studies
 (2) Job Analysis for Content Validity
 (3) Development of Selection Procedure
 (4) Standards for Demonstrating Content Validity
 (5) Reliability
 (6) Prior Training or Experience
 (7) Training Success
 (8) Operational Use
 (9) Ranking Based on Content Validity Studies
D. Technical Standards for Construct Validity Studies
 (1) Appropriateness of Construct Validity Studies
 (2) Job Analysis for Construct Validity Studies
 (3) Relationship to the Job
 (4) Use of Construct Validity Study Without New Criterion-Related Evidence
  (a) Standards for Use
  (b) Determination of Common Work Behaviors

DOCUMENTATION OF IMPACT AND VALIDITY EVIDENCE

60-3.15 Documentation of Impact and Validity Evidence
 A. Required Information
  (1) Simplified Recordkeeping for Users With Less Than 100 Employees
  (2) Information on Impact
   (a) Collection of Information on Impact
   (b) When Adverse Impact Has Been Eliminated in the Total Selection Process
   (c) When Data Insufficient to Determine Impact
  (3) Documentation of Validity Evidence
   (a) Type of Evidence
   (b) Form of Report
   (c) Completeness
 B. Criterion-Related Validity Studies
  (1) User(s), Location(s), and Date(s) of Study
  (2) Problem and Setting
  (3) Job analysis or Review of Job Information
  (4) Job Titles and Codes
  (5) Criterion Measures
  (6) Sample Description
  (7) Description of Selection Procedure
  (8) Techniques and Results
  (9) Alternative Procedures Investigated
  (10) Uses and Applications
  (11) Source Data
  (12) Contact Person
  (13) Accuracy and Completeness
 C. Content Validity Studies
  (1) User(s), Location(s), and Date(s) of Study
  (2) Problem and Setting
  (3) Job Analysis—Content of the Job
  (4) Selection Procedure and Its Content
  (5) Relationship Between Selection Procedure and the Job
  (6) Alternative Procedures Investigated
  (7) Uses and Applications
  (8) Contact Person
  (9) Accuracy and Completeness
 D. Construct Validity Studies
  (1) User(s), Location(s), and Date(s) of Study
  (2) Problem and Setting
  (3) Construct Definition
  (4) Job Analysis
  (5) Job Titles and Codes
  (6) Selection Procedure
  (7) Relationship to Job Performance
  (8) Alternative Procedures Investigated
  (9) Uses and Applications
  (10) Accuracy and Completeness
  (11) Source Data
  (12) Contact Person
 E. Evidence of Validity From Other Studies
  (1) Evidence From Criterion-Related Validity Studies
   (a) Job Information
   (b) Relevance of Criteria
   (c) Other Variables
   (d) Use of the Selection Procedure
   (e) Bibliography
  (2) Evidence From Content Validity Studies
  (3) Evidence From Construct Validity Studies
 F. Evidence of Validity From Cooperative Studies
 G. Selection for Higher Level Jobs
 H. Interim Use of Selection Procedures

DEFINITIONS

60-3.16 Definitions

APPENDIX

60-3.17 Policy Statement on Affirmative Action (see section 13B)
60-3.18 Citations

[FR Doc. 78-23997 Filed 8-22-78; 4:48 pm]

Appendix B

Summary of Tests, by Test Name or Treatment by Courts and EEOC

Case or Decision

1. Former rule of OFCCP, describes 80% rule in detail, and description is still appropriate; relates to all selection standards

2. EEOC Decision 71-1504 (Test invalid despite high minority hiring), CCH EEOC Decisions (1973) ¶6223

3. EEOC Decision 71-1563 (Preference for incumbent office and clerical employees is race bias), CCH EEOC Decisions (1973) ¶6236

4. EEOC Decision 71-1552 (Eight hours work limit imposed on females), CCH EEOC Decisions (1973) ¶6234

5. EEOC Decisions 71-2344, CCH EEOC Decisions (1973) ¶6257

Test(s) Involved

Testing and Selection Order, 41 C.F.R. 60-3 (1977)

High school diploma, paper-and-pencil test

High school diploma, paper-and-pencil test for clericals

State protective law relied upon to detriment, by employer

Wonderlic, Bennett Mechanical Comprehension Test

Case or Decision	Test(s) Involved
6. EEOC Decision 71-1683 (Good grammar rule for computer programmers is racially biased), CCH EEOC Decisions (1973) ¶ 6262	Programmer Aptitude Test (PAT), Wonderlic
7. Arbitration Decision and Award (Day & Zimmerman, Inc. and Int'l Chemical Workers, Local 526), 60 LA (BNA) 495 (1972)	Qualification and aptitude test for quality-control trainee—eliminated unilaterally by employer because it could not be validated and had disparate effect on minorities; action found to have violated collective-bargaining agreement
8. EEOC Decision 71-2040 (Testing of female employees before transfer is unlawful sex bias), CCH EEOC Decisions (1973) ¶ 6275	Pre-employment test
9. EEOC Decision 71-2237 (Running ad "Some College Test Required" was unlawful bias), CCH EEOC Decisions (1973) ¶ 6276	Respondent's personnel test
10. EEOC Decision 71-2682 (Gambling arrest was not valid basis for denying job to Negro applicant), CCH EEOC Decisions (1973) ¶ 6288	Wonderlic
11. EEOC Decision 72-0265 (Racial bias results from union referral preference based on experience), CCH EEOC Decisions (1973) ¶ 6291	"Aptitude" tests
12. EEOC Decision 72-0066 (Newspaper biased in assigning jobs to females), CCH EEOC Decisions (1973) ¶ 6296	Wonderlic
13. EEOC Decision 72-0284 (Bias against females uncovered in charge by male), CCH EEOC Decisions (1973) ¶ 6304	Otis test
14. EEOC Decision 72-0455 (Pre-employment coding of job applicants indicated racial discrimination), CCH EEOC Decisions (1973) ¶ 6306	Arithmetic test

Case or Decision	Test(s) Involved
15. EEOC Decision 72-0427 (Rejection of Negro applicant for poor credit record was racial bias), CCH EEOC Decisions (1973) ¶ 6312	SRA verbal aptitude
16. EEOC Decision 72-0591 (Recruiter evaluation standards were biased in favor of males and whites), CCH EEOC Decisions (1973) ¶ 6314	High school diploma, some college preferred
17. EEOC Decision 72-0687 (Job refusal properly based on GATB), CCH EEOC Decisions (1973) ¶ 6323	GATB
18. EEOC Decision 72-0691 (Some GATB employment tests were racially biased), CCH EEOC Decisions (1973) ¶ 6327	GATB
19. EEOC Decision 72-0703 (Testing, recruiting, hiring policies show racial bias), CCH EEOC Decisions (1973) ¶ 6328	Wonderlic, Bennett, Minn. Clerical Test
20. EEOC Decision 72-0708 (Job tests validated for each minority group), CCH EEOC Decisions (1973) ¶ 6329	Tool Planner Test
21. EEOC Decision 73-0499 (Employer's testing, high school education requirement, and job assignment practices showed racial bias), 2 Empl. Prac. Guide (CCH) ¶ 6402 (1973)	APT performance test
22. EEOC Decision 74-13 (Failure to hire Negro applicant was bias; testing and nepotism practices were improper), 2 Empl. Prac. Guide (CCH) ¶ 6403 (1973)	Clerical aptitude test
23. EEOC Decision 74-33 (Test validation procedure was racially biased; suspension for refusal to take biased test was improper reprisal), 2 Empl. Prac. Guide (CCH) ¶ 6406 (1973)	Test validation procedure

Case or Decision	Test(s) Involved
24. EEOC Decision No. 73-0479, 2 Empl. Prac. Guide (CCH) ¶ 6381 (1973)	Use of supervisors' personal recommendations, lack of written policies on promotion procedure, vague selection standards
25. EEOC Decision No. 72-1885, 2 Empl. Prac. Guide ¶ 6385 (1972)	Use of subjective evaluations by foremen, without review by other company officials
26. EEOC Decision No. 73-0520, 2 Empl. Prac. Guide ¶ 6389 (1973)	Mandatory fixed leave period for maternity
27. *Culpepper* v. *Reynolds Metals Co.*, 442 F.2d 1078 (5th Cir. 1971)*	Reliance on dated test results
28. *United States* v. *Virginia Elec. & Power Co.*, 327 F. Supp. 1034 (E.D. Va. 1971)	GATB
United States v. *Virginia Elec. & Power Co.*, 4 EPD ¶ 7502 (Consent Decree) (E.D. Va. 1971)	
29. *Colbert* v. *H-K Corp.*, 444 F.2d 1381 (5th Cir. 1971)	Otis, 16 Personality Factor Test
Colbert v. *H-K Corp.*, 4 EPD 7779 (N.D. Ga. 1971) (decision reconsidered)	
30. *Chance* v. *Board of Examiners*, 330 F. Supp. 203 (S.D. N.Y. 1971), aff'd, 458 F.2d 1167 (2d Cir. 1972)	Board of Examiners Tests
31. *United States* v. *Georgia Power Co.*, 3 EPD ¶ 8318 (N.D. Ga. 1971), aff'd in part, vacated in part and remanded, 474 F.2d 906 (5th Cir. 1973)	Bennett, Personal Test for Industry (PTI)
United States v. *Georgia Power Co.*, 7 EPD ¶ 9167 (N.D. Ga. 1974) (Consent Decree)	PTI Numerical, Short Employment Test (SET)
32. *United States* v. *Jacksonville Terminal Co.*, 451 F.2d 418 (5th Cir. 1900), cert. denied, 406 U.S. 906 (1972)	Supervisor-devised test

*Many of the court decisions were the subject of further proceedings. Subsequent history can be found in the case index at the end of this book, or in official reporter services.

Case or Decision	Test(s) Involved
33. *United States* v. *Chesapeake & Ohio Ry.*, 3 EPD 8331 (E.D. Va. 1971), *vacated in part and remanded* 471 F.2d 582 (4th Cir. 1972), *cert. denied*, 411 U.S. 939 (1973)	EQ Form B
34. *Carter* v. *Gallagher*, 452 F.2d 315 (8th Cir. 1971), *cert. denied*, 406 U.S. 950 (1972)	Fire dept. written exam
35. *Castro* v. *Beecher*, 334 F. Supp. 930 (D. Mass. 1971) *aff'd in part, rev'd in part*, 459 F.2d 725 (1st Cir. 1972)	Swim test, 1972 civil-service exam
36. *Allen* v. *City of Mobile*, 331 F. Supp. 1134 (S.D. Ala. 1971), *aff'd*, 466 F.2d 122 (5th Cir. 1972), *cert. denied*, 412 U.S. 909 (1973)	Subjective service ratings of police officers
37. *United States* v. *Central Motor Lines, Inc.*, 338 F. Supp. 532 (W.D. N.C. 1971)	Road tests
38. *Western Addition Community Organization* v. *Alioto*, 330 F. Supp. 536 (N.D. Cal. 1971) *Western Addition Community Organization* v. *Alioto*, 340 F. Supp. 1351 (N.D. Cal. 1972) (preliminary injunction) *Western Addition Community Organization* v. *Alioto*, 5 EPD ¶ 7970 (N.D. Cal. 1972) (supp. order) *Western Addition Community Organization* v. *Alioto*, 360 F. Supp. 733 (N.D. Cal. 1973) (decision) *Western Addition Community Organization* v. *Alioto*, 7 EPD ¶ 9320 (N.D. Cal. 1973) (supp. order) *appeal dismissed* 514 F.2d 542 (9th Cir.), *cert. denied*, 423 U.S. 1014 (1975)	Fireman's H-2 civil-service exam
39. *NAACP* v. *Allen*, 340 F. Supp. 703 (M.D. Ala. 1972), *aff'd*, 493 F.2d 614 (5th Cir. 1974)	Oral interview, state trooper's test

Case or Decision	Test(s) Involved
40. *United States* v. *Household Finance Corp.*, 4 EPD 7680 (N.D. Ill. 1972) (Consent Decree)	Kuder Preference Test, Wonderlic
41. *Cooper* v. *Allen,* 4 EPD 7695 (N.D. Ga. 1971) *aff'd in part, rev'd in part* 467 F.2d 836 (5th Cir. 1972) *decision on remand* 8 EPD ¶9476 (N.D. Ga. 1973), *aff'd* 493 F.2d 765 (5th Cir. 1974)	Otis-Lennon Mental Ability Test, Form J
42. *Douglas* v. *Hampton,* 338 F. Supp. 18 (D.D.C. 1972) *aff'd in part, rev'd in part* 512 F.2d 976 (D.C. Cir. 1975)	FSEE
43. *Buckner* v. *Goodyear Tire & Rubber Co.,* 339 F. Supp. 1108 (N.D. Ala. 1972), *aff'd per curiam,* 476 F.2d 1287 (5th Cir. 1973)	California Test Bureau, math test, Otis test, Bennett, Education Minn. Paper Board Test
44. *Baker* v. *Columbus Municipal Separate School Dist.,* 462 F.2d 1112 (5th Cir. 1972)	NTE (National Teacher's Exam)
45. *Davis* v. *Washington* (D.D.C.), 348 F. Supp. 15 (D.D.C. 1972), *dismissed on merits* 352 F. Supp. 187 (D.D.C. 1972), *rev'd* 512 F.2d 956 (D.C. Cir. 1975), *rev'd,* 426 U.S. 229 (1976)	Multiple-choice judgment supervisor test
46. *Mitchell* v. *International Distributors, Inc.,* 5 EPD ¶7946 (W.D. Tenn. 1972)	Line mechanic test
47. *Griggs* v. *Duke Power Co.,* 5 EPD 8017 (M.D. N.C. 1972) (issuing order reversed on issues appealed), *ff,* 515 F.2d 86 (4th Cir. 1973)	Personnel/aptitude tests, diploma requirement
48. *Jackson* v. *Poston et al.,* 40 App. Div. 2d 19, 337 N.Y.S.2d 108 (3d Dep't 1972)	State civil-service exam
49. *Hester* v. *Southern Ry.,* 349 F. Supp. 812 (N.D. Ga. 1972), *rev'd in part, modified in part and re-*	Science Research Assn. verbal test (SRA), nonverbal typing test, J.P. Cleaver Institute self-description test

Case or Decision	Test(s) Involved
manded, 497 F.2d 1374 (5th Cir. 1974)	
50. *Johnson* v. *Goodyear Tire & Rubber, Co.,* 349 F. Supp. 3 (S.D. Tex. 1972), *modified,* 491 F.2d 1364 (5th Cir. 1973) *Johnson* v. *Goodyear Tire & Rubber, Co.,* 6 EPD 8832 (S.D. Tex. 1972) (Consent Decree)	Education, non-EEOC-validated paper-and-pencil tests
51. *Fowler* v. *Schwarzwalder,* 351 F. Supp. 721 (D. Minn. 1972)	St. Paul civil-service exam (firemen)
52. *Sims* v. *Sheet Metal Workers, Local 65,* 353 F. Supp. 22 (N.D. Ohio 1972), *aff'd in part, remanded in part,* 489 F.2d 1023 (6th Cir. 1973)	Journeymen, Flanagan aptitude and industrial tests
53. *United States* v. *Local 212, Electrical Workers,* 472 F.2d 634 (6th Cir. 1973)	Minority training program
54. *Vulcan Society of N.Y. City Fire Dept.* v. *Civil Service Comm., City of N.Y.,* 353 F. Supp. 1092 (S.D. N.Y. 1972), *decision on merits,* 360 F. Supp. 1265 (S.D. N.Y. 1972), *aff'd in part, rev'd in part,* 490 F.2d 387 (2d Cir. 1973)	Police promotion tests
55. *Russell* v. *American Tobacco Co.,* 374 F. Supp. 286 (M.D. N.C. 1973), *aff'd in part and modified in part,* 528 F.2d 357 (4th Cir. 1975), *cert. denied,* 425 U.S. 935 (1976)	Screen tests for craft positions
56. *Sontag* v. *Bronstein,* 33 N.Y.2d 197, 351 N.Y.S.2d 389 (1973)	Audio-visual aide tech. test
57. *Meadows* v. *Ford Motor Co.,* 62 FRD 98 (W.D. Ky. 1973), *aff'd in part as modified and remanded in part,* 510 F.2d 939 (6th Cir. 1975), *cert. denied sub nom. United Automobile Aerospace & Agricultural Implement Workers, Local 862* v. *Ford Motor Co.,* 425 U.S. 998 (1976)	Weight requirement

Case or Decision	Test(s) Involved
58. *Moody* v. *Albemarle Paper Co.*, 474 F.2d 134 (4th Cir. 1973), *rev'd and remanded*, 422 U.S. 407 (1973)	Preemployment tests
59. *United States* v. *Bricklayers Local #1*, 5 EPD ¶ 8480 (W.D. Tenn. 1972-73), *aff'd as modified sub nom. United States* v. *Masonry Contractors Ass'n of Memphis, Inc.*, 497 F.2d 871 (6th Cir. 1974)	GATB
60. *Commonwealth of Penn.* v. *O'Neill*, 348 F. Supp. 1084 (E.D. Pa. 1972), *aff'd in part, vacated and remanded in part*, 473 Fed. 1029 (3d Cir. 1973) See also *Commonwealth of Penn.* v. *O'Neill*, 431 F. Supp. 700 (E.D. Pa. 1977)	Written tests for promotion in police dept.
61. *Bridgeport Guardians, Inc.* v. *Bridgeport Civil Service Comm.*, 354 F. Supp. 778 (D. Conn.), *aff'd in part, rev'd in part and remanded*, 482 F.2d 1333 (2d Cir.), *on remand* 8 EPD (CCH) ¶ 9508 (D. Conn. 1973), *aff'd* 497 F.2d 1113 (2d Cir. 1975), *cert. denied* 421 U.S. 991 (1974)	Patrolmen's test
62. *United States* v. *Nansemond County School Board*, 351 F. Supp. 196 (E.D. Va. 1972), *rev'd and remanded*, 492 F.2d 919 (4th Cir. 1974), *on remand sub nom. United States* v. *School Board of City of Suffolk*, 418 F. Supp. 639 (E.D. Va. 1976)	NTE
63. *Stevenson* v. *International Paper Co.*, 352 F. Supp. 230 (S.D. Ala. 1972), *rev'd in part and vacated in part and remanded*, 516 F.2d 103 (5th Cir. 1975)	Wonderlic, Bennett, Minn. Paper Board Test-45

Case or Decision	Test(s) Involved
64. *United States* v. *N.L. Industries, Inc.*, 479 F.2d 354 (8th Cir.), *reh. denied* 5 EPD ¶ 8628 (1973)	Makeshift tests
65. *Banks* v. *Seaboard Coast Line RR Co.*, 5 EPD ¶ 8577 (N.D. Ga. 1972), *decision on merits*, 360 F. Supp. 1372 (N.D. Ga. 1973)	Assn. of American RR Car Inspectors exam
66. *Brito* v. *Zia Co.*, 6 EPD ¶ 8742 (D.N.M. 1972), *aff'd* 478 F.2d 1200 (10th Cir. 1973)	General intelligence test
67. *Harper* v. *Mayor of Baltimore*, 359 F. Supp. 1187 (D. Md.), *modified and aff'd* 486 F.2d 1134 (4th Cir. 1973)	Firefighter test
68. *Woods* v. *North American Rockwell Corp.*, 6 EPD 8792 (D. Okla. 1971), *aff'd* 480 F.2d 644 (10th Cir. 1973)	Departmental promotion test
69. *Rios* v. *Local 638, Enterprise Assn. of Steamfitters*, 979 (S.D. N.Y. 1973), *remanded for modification and aff'd* 501 F.2d 622 (2d Cir. 1974)	Differential Aptitude, Form M, SCAT 2A
70. *Feinerman* v. *Jones*, 6 EPD ¶ 8731 (M.D. Pa. 1973)	State civil-service exam
71. *Crockett* v. *Virginia Folding Box Co.*, 6 EPD ¶ 8773 (E.D. Va. 1973)	Aptitude tests
72. *Patmon* v. *Van Dorn*, 6 EPD ¶ 8779 (N.D. Ohio 1973), *aff'd* 498 F.2d 544 (6th Cir. 1974)	Electrician test
73. *United States* v. *Chesterfield County School District* (D.S.C. 1972), *aff'd in part, rev'd in part*, 484 F.2d 70 (4th Cir. 1973)	NTE
74. *Smith* v. *City of East Cleveland*, 363 F. Supp. 1131 (N.D. Ohio 1973), *rev'd in part, aff'd in part*, 520 F.2d 492 (6th Cir. 1975)	Army General Classification Test (AGCT)

Case or Decision	Test(s) Involved
75. *Button* v. *Rockefeller*, 76 Misc. 2d 701, 351 N.Y.S.2d 488 (App. T. Albany Co. 1973)	Written physical-agility exam
76. *Wilson-Sinclair Co.* v. *Griggs*, 7 EPD ¶9083 (La. Dist. Ct. 1972), *aff'd* 211 WW 2d 133 (La. Sup. Ct. 1973)	Bennett, Wonderlic, Wilson-Sinclair arith. test
77. *Henderson* v. *First National Bank*, 360 F. Supp. 531 (M.D. Ala. 1973)	Bennett-Gelink, SET
78. *Gay* v. *Wheeler*, 363 F. Supp. 764 (S.D. Tex. 1973)	NTE
79. *Stamps* v. *Detroit Edison Co.*, 365 F. Supp. 87 (E.D. Mich. 1973), *rev'd sub nom. EEOC* v. *Detroit Edison Co.*, 515 F.2d 301 (6th Cir. 1975), *vacated and remanded*, 431 U.S. 951 (1977) *on remand* 17 EPD ¶8583 (E.D. Mich. 1978)	Mech. placement test, clerical placement test, appren. lineman, appren. draftsman, customer servicemen, substation oper., appren. cable splicing, meter reader, power plant, Henry Ford Comm. College Proficiency Test
80. *Watkins* v. *Scott Paper Co.*, 6 EPD 8912 (S.D. Ala. 1973) *aff'd in part, rev'd in part, vacated in part*, 530 F.2d 1159 (5th Cir.), *cert. denied* 429 U.S. 861 (1976)	Bennett, Perceptual Speed, Purdue Nonlanguage
81. *Young* v. *Edgcomb Steel Co.*, 363 F. Supp. 961 (M.D. N.C. 1973), *aff'd in part, rev'd in part*, 499 F.2d 97 (5th Cir. 1974)	Wonderlic (Forms A, B, 1, 2)
82. *United States* v. *Inspiration Consolidated Copper Co.*, 6 EPD 8918 (D. Ariz. 1973)	SRA Verbal Test
83. *Laffey* v. *Northwest Airlines, Inc.*, 366 F. Supp. 763 (D.D.C. 1973) *modified* 567 F.2d 429 (D.C. Cir. 1976), *cert. denied*. U.S. (1978)	Self-description inventory test
84. *Officers for Justice* v. *Civil Service Comm., S.F.*, 371 F. Supp. 1328 (N.D. Cal. 1973)	Admission, promotion exams
85. *Guardians Assn.* v. *Civil Service Comm.*, 490 F.2d 400 (2d Cir. 1973)	Entry-level, promotional exams

Case or Decision	Test(s) Involved
86. *Wilson* v. *Woodward Iron Co.*, 362 F. Supp. 886 (N.D. Ala. 1973)	Oral test
87. *King* v. *Civil Serv. Comm'n,* 6 EPD ¶ 8999 (S.D. N.Y. 1973), *dismissed,* 382 F. Supp. 1128 (S.D. N.Y. 1974)	Exam #2084
88. *Pennsylvania* v. *Sebastian,* 6 EPD ¶ 9038 (W.D. Pa. 1973)	Police tests
89. *United States* v. *Lee Way Motor Freight, Inc.,* 7 EPD ¶ 9066 (W.D. Okla. 1973)	Road tests
90. *Richardson* v. *Civil Service Comm'n,* 387 F. Supp. 1267 (S.D. N.Y. 1973)	Narcotic rehabilitation counselor's exam
91. *Pennsylvania* v. *Glickman,* 370 F. Supp. 724 (W.D. Pa. 1974)	Firefighters' test
92. *Walston* v. *Nansemond County School,* 492 F.2d 919 (4th Cir. 1974) *United States* v. *School Bd.,* 418 F. Supp. 639 (E.D. Va. 1976), *aff'd in part, rev'd in part and remanded sub nom. Walston* v. *School Bd.,* 566 F.2d 1201 (4th Cir. 1977)	NTE
93. *Boston Chapter, NAACP, Inc.* v. *Beecher,* 371 F. Supp. 507 (D. Mass.), *aff'd* 504 F.2d 1017 (1st Cir. 1974), *cert. denied,* 421 U.S. 910 (1975)	Entrance exam for firemen
94. *Wade* v. *Mississippi Cooperative Extension Serv.,* 372 F. Supp. 126 (N.D. Miss. 1974), *aff'd in part, rev'd in part and remanded,* 528 F.2d 508 (5th Cir. 1976) *Wade* v. *Mississippi Cooperative Extension Serv.,* 424 F. Supp. 1242 (N.D. Miss. 1976)	Degree, years of experience, testing for technical knowledge, subjective interview and evaluation criteria
95. *Afro Am. Patrolmen's League* v. *Duck,* 366 F. Supp. 1095 (N.D. Ohio 1973), *aff'd in part, remanded in part,* 503 F.2d 294 (6th Cir. 1974)	Civil-service promotion exam

Case or Decision	Test(s) Involved
96. *Kirkland* v. *New York State Dep't of Correctional Services*, 374 F. Supp. 1361 (S.D. N.Y. 1974), *aff'd in part, rev'd in part*, 520 F.2d 420 (2d Cir. 1975), *cert. denied*, 429 U.S. 823 (1976)	CSC Exam #34-444
97. *Salton* v. *Western Elec. Co.*, 7 EPD 9327 (D. Colo. 1972)	Dexterity tests
98. *Coffey* v. *Braddy*, 372 F. Supp. 116 (M.D. Fla. 1971)	Firemen's exam
99. *Shield Club* v. *Cleveland*, EPD ¶9606 (N.D. Ohio 1974)	1972 sergeant's promotional exam
100. *Pennsylvania* v. *Rizzo* 8 EPD ¶9681 (E.D. Pa. 1974) *aff'd.* 530 F.2d 501 (3d Cir.), *cert. denied*, 426 U.S. 921 (1976)	Firefighters' test
101. *Stallworth* v. *Monsanto Co.*, 8 EPD ¶9695 (N.D. Fla. 1974) *Stallworth* v. *Monsanto Co.*, 558 F.2d 257 (5th Cir. 1977)	Wonderlic, Bennett
102. *Nance* v. *Union Carbide Corp., Consumer Prods. Div.*, 397 F. Supp. 436 (W.D. N.C. 1975), *modified*, 540 F.2d 718 (4th Cir. 1976), *cert. denied*, 431 U.S. 953 (1977)	Light/heavy job classifications
103. *Arnold* v. *Ballard*, 390 F. Supp. 723 (N.D. Ohio 1975), *aff'd*, 12 EPD ¶11,000 (6th Cir.), *vacated and remanded*, 12 EPD 11,224 (6th Cir. 1976)	Public Personnel Association policeman tests
104. *Rogers* v. *International Paper Co.*, 510 F.2d 1340 (8th Cir.), *vacated and remanded*, 423 U.S. 809 (1975)	Wonderlic
105. *Smith* v. *St. Louis-San Francisco Ry.*, 397 F. Supp. 580 (N.D. Ala. 1975)	General clerical test, Wonderlic
106. *Bailey* v. *DeBard*, 10 EPD ¶10,389 (S.D. Ind. 1975)	Otis Gamma Form C, SRA Adaptability Test

Case or Decision	Test(s) Involved
107. *Adams* v. *Texas & Pac. Motor Transport Co.*, 408 F. Supp. 156 (E.D. La. 1975)	Driving test
108. *Privette* v. *Union Carbide Corp.*, 10 EPD ¶ 10,413 (W.D. N.C. 1975)	Bennett Mechanical, Modified Alpha
109. *Mele* v. *United States Department of Justice*, 395 F. Supp. 592 (D.N.J. 1975)	Unvalidated employment test
110. *EEOC* v. *Local 638, Sheet Metal Workers' International Association*, 401 F. Supp. 467 (S.D. N.Y. 1975), *modified and, as modified, aff'd,* 532 F.2d 821 (2d Cir. 1976)	Written and practical exam
111. *Tyler* v. *Vickery*, 517 F.2d 1089 (5th Cir. 1975), *cert. denied,* 426 U.S. 940 (1976).	State bar examination
112. *League of United Latin American Citizens* v. *City of Santa Ana*, 410 F. Supp. 873 (C.D. Cal. 1976)	California Short Form Test of Mental Maturity; Fire Aptitude Test Form 45; SRA Pictorial Reasoning Test
113. *Jones* v. *New York City Human Resources Administration*, 391 F. Supp. 1064 (S.D.N.Y. 1975), *aff'd* 528 F.2d 696 (2d Cir.), *cert. denied,* 429 U.S. 825 (1976)	Civil-service examinations
114. *United States* v. *City of Chicago*, 411 F. Supp. 218 (N.D. Ill. 1976), *aff'd in part, rev'd in part, and remanded,* 549 F.2d 417 (7th Cir.), *cert. denied, sub nom. Arado* v. *United States,* 434 U.S. 875 (1977)	State civil-service written exam (patrolman, sergeant, lieutenant)
115. *Pennsylvania* v. *Flaherty*, 404 F. Supp. 1022 (N.D. Pa. 1975)	State civil-service examination (based on International Personnel Management Association's police officer exam)
116. *Davis* v. *County of Los Angeles*, 566 F.2d 1334 (9th Cir. 1977), *vac'd and rem'd,* 99 S.Ct 1379 (1979).	Verbal aptitude test

Case or Decision	Test(s) Involved
117. *Richardson* v. *McFadden*, 540 F.2d 744 (4th Cir. 1976), *on rehearing, aff'd*, 563 F.2d 1130 (4th Cir. 1977), *cert. denied* 98 S.Ct. 1606 (1978)	State bar examination
118. *Morrow* v. *Dillard*, 412 F. Supp. 494 (S.D. Miss. 1976)	Written examination, proficiency examination (based on tests marketed by International Personnel Management Association)
119. *NAACP, Ensley Branch* v. *Seibels*, 13 EPD ¶ 11,504 (N.D. Ala. 1977)	International Personnel Management Association tests; policemen test 10-C; fireman test 20-B
120. *Guardians Association of New York City Police Department, Inc.* v. *Civil Service Commission*, 431 F. Supp. 526 (S.D. N.Y.), *vacated and remanded*, 562 F.2d 38 (2d Cir. 1977)	Written examination
121. *Firefighters Institute for Racial Equality* v. *City of St. Louis*, 12 EPD ¶ 11,071 (E.D. Mo. 1976), *aff'd in part, rev'd in part*, 549 F.2d (8th Cir. 1977), *cert. denied sub nom. Banta* v. *United States*, 98 S.Ct. 60 (1977).	Written examination (firefighter, captain, battalion chief)
122. *Jackson* v. *Nassau County Civil Service Comm.*, 424 F. Supp. 1162 (E.D. N.Y. 1976)	State civil-service examination
123. *Blake* v. *City of Los Angeles*, 435 F. Supp. 55 (C.D. Cal. 1977)	Physical-ability test
124. *Washington* v. *Shell Research & Development Co.*, 14 EPD ¶ 7821 (S.D. Tex. 1977)	Validation of janitor's test not required because no adverse impact
125. *United States* v. *State of North Carolina*, 425 F. Supp. 579 (E.D. N.C. 1977), *rev'd* 17 EPD ¶ 8629 (4th Cir. 1978)	NTE
126. *Richardson* v. *Pennsylvania Dept. of Health*, 561 F.2d 489 (3d Cir. 1977)	State civil-service examination
127. *Woodard* v. *Virginia Board of*	State bar examination

Case or Decision	Test(s) Involved
Bar Examiners, 420 F. Supp. 211 (E.D. Va. 1976)	
128. *Fisher* v. *Proctor & Gamble Mfg. Co.,* 14 EPD ¶ 7662 (N.D. Tex. 1977)	Written aptitude test
129. *James* v. *Stockholm Valves & Fittings Co.,* 559 F.2d 310 (5th Cir. 1977), *cert. denied,* 98 S.Ct. 767 (1978)	Bennett, Wonderlic
130. *United States* v. *South Carolina,* 445 F. Supp. 1094 (D.S.C. 1977), *aff'd,* 98 S.Ct. 756 (1978)	NTE
131. *Friend* v. *Leidinger,* 446 F. Supp. 361 (E.D. Va. 1977)	Firefighters B-1(m) test (International Personnel Management Association); written and oral promotion test
132. *Lewis* v. *Bethlehem Steel Corp.,* 440 F. Supp. 949 (D. Md. 1977), *aff'd in part, rev'd in part,* 17 EPD 8597 (1978)	Electrical helpers test
133. *Dickerson* v. *U.S. Steel Corp.,* 17 EPD ¶ 8528 (E.D. Pa.), *aff'd in part, rev'd in part,* 17 EPD ¶ 8597 (1978)	Bennett Mechanical, RMPFB, Wonderlic, Personnel, DAT-NA
134. *Scott* v. *Van Scoy,* 17 EPD 8563 (D. Neb. 1978)	Written promotional exam
135. *Alvarez-Ugarte* v. *City of New York,* 391 F. Supp. 1223 (S.D. N.Y. 1975)	Civil-service examination
136. *Bannerman* v. *Department of Youth Authority,* 436 F. Supp. 1273 (N.D. Cal. 1977)	State personnel board written examination
137. *Ivey* v. *Western Electric Co.,* 16 EPD ¶ 8297 (N.D. Ga. 1977)	Electronic tests
138. *Dendy* v. *Washington Hospital Center,* 17 EPD ¶ 8438 (D.C. Cir. 1978)	Written examination

Case Index

Aaron v. Davis, 424 F. Supp. 1238, 14 FEP Cases 362, 13 EPD (CCH) ¶11,484 (E.D. Ark. 1976)

Abrams v. Johnson, 534 F.2d 1226, 12 FEP Cases 1293, 11 EPD (CCH) ¶10,871 (6th Cir. 1976)

Allen v. Lovejoy, 553 F.2d 522, 14 FEP Cases 1194, 14 EPD (CCH) ¶7509 (6th Cir. 1977)

American Cyanamid Co. v. Roundebush, 411 F.Supp. 1220, 12 FEP Cases 1147, 12 EPD (CCH) ¶11,006 (S.D.N.Y. 1976)

Arritt v. Grisell, 567 F.2d 1267, 17 FEP Cases 753, 15 EPD (CCH) ¶8012 (4th Cir. 1977)

Barnes v. Costle, 561 F.2d 983, 15 FEP Cases 345, 14 EPD (CCH) ¶7755 (D.C. Civ. 1977)

Barnett v. W. T. Grant Co., 396 F. Supp. 327, 7 FEP Cases 434 (W.D. N.C. 1974), *aff'd in relevant part and rev'd in part,* 518 F.2d 543, 10 FEP Cases 1057, 9 EPD (CCH) ¶10,199 (4th Cir. 1975)

Batyko v. Pennsylvania Liquor Control Board, 450 F. Supp. 32, 17 FEP Cases 856 (W.D. Pa. 1978)

Baxter v. Savannah Sugar Refining Corp., 495 F.2d 437, 8 FEP Cases 84, 8 EPD (CCH) ¶9579 (5th Cir. 1974), *cert. den.,* 419 U.S. 1033, 8 FEP Cases 1142, 8 EPD (CCH) 9789 (1975)

Case Index   369

Bernard v. *Gulf Oil Co.*, 596 F.2d 1249, 20 EPD (CCH) ¶30,001, 19 FEP Cases 1682 (5th Cir. 1979)
Billingsley v. *Service Technology Corp.*, 6 EPD (CCH) ¶8879 (S.D. Tex. 1973)
Blizard v. *Fielding,* 17 FEP Cases 146 (D. Mass. 1977)
Board of Trustees of Keene State College v. *Sweeney,* 95 S.Ct. 295, 18 FEP Cases 520, 18 EPD (CCH) ¶8673 (1978)
Bowe v. *Colgate-Palmolive Co.,* 416 F.2d 711, 2 FCP Cases 121, 2 EPD (CCH) ¶10,090 (7th Cir. 1969)
Brennan v. *Paragon Employment Agency, Inc.,* 356 F. Supp. 286, 5 FEP Cases 915, 5 EPD (CCH) ¶8614 (S.D. N.Y. 1973), *aff'd mem.,* 489 F.2d 752, 7 FEP Cases 1258, 8 EPD (CCH) ¶9529 (2d Cir. 1974)
Brennan v. *Reynolds & Co.,* 367 F. Supp. 440, 7 EPD (CCH) ¶9219, 7 FEP Cases 369, (N.D. Ill. 1973)
Brito v. *Zia Co.,* 478 F.2d 1200, 5 FEP Cases 1207, 5 EPD (CCH) ¶8626 (10th Cir. 1973)
Burns v. *Rohr Corp.,* 346 F. Supp. 994, 4 FEP Cases 939, 4 EPD (CCH) ¶7924 (S.D. Cal. 1972)
Cariddi v. *Kansas City Chiefs Football Club, Inc.,* 568 F.2d 87, 16 FEP Cases 462, 15 EPD (CCH) ¶8014 (8th Cir. 1977)
Carmi v. *St. Louis School District,* 20 FEP Cases 162 (E.D. Mo. 1979)
Carroll v. *Talman Federal Savings & Loan Association,* 20 FEP Cases 764 (7th Cir. 1979), reversing 448 F. Supp. 79, 17 FEP Cases 215, 17 EPD (CCH) ¶8579 (N.D. Ill. 1978), *cert. denied,* 22 EPD (CCH) ¶30,672
Castro v. *Beecher,* 459 F.2d 725, 4 FEP Cases 700, 4 EPD (CCH) ¶7783 (1st Cir. 1972)
Cates v. *TWA,* 561 F.2d 1064, 15 FEP Cases 329, 14 EPD (CCH) ¶7792 (2d Cir. 1977)
Chicago, Milwaukee, St. Paul & Pacific R.R. Co. v. *Department of Industry, Labor & Human Relations,* 62 Wis.2d 392, 215 N.W.2d 443, 8 FEP Cases 937, 7 EPD (CCH) ¶9200 (1974)
Chrapliwy v. *Uniroyal, Inc.,* 458 F.Supp. 252, 15 FEP Cases 795, 14 EPD (CCH) ¶7708 (N.D. Ind. 1977)
Chrysler Corp. v. *Brown,* 99 S.Ct. 1705, 19 FEP Cases 475, 19 EPD (CCH) ¶9121 (1979)
Chrysler Outboard Corp. v. *DILAR,* 14 FEP Cases 344, 13 EPD (CCH) ¶11,526 (Wis. 1976)
Circle K Corp. v. *EEOC,* 501 F.2d 1052, 8 FEP Cases 758, 8 EPD (CCH) ¶9599 (10th Cir. 1972)
City of Wisconsin Rapids v. *Wisconsin Department of Industry,* Labor & Human Relations, 15 EPD (CCH) ¶7846 (Cir. Ct. Wis. 1977)
Clark v. *Milwaukee Road,* 12 FEP Cases 1103 (Wash. 1975)
Coates v. *National Cash Register,* 433 F. Supp. 655, 15 FEP Cases 222, 15 EPD (CCH) ¶7830 (E.D. Va. 1977)

Coleman v. *Darden,* 15 FEP Cases 272, 13 EPD (CCH) ¶ 11,502 (D. Col. 1977), *aff'd,* 595 F.2d 533, 19 FEP Cases 137, 19 EPD (CCH) ¶ 8980, (10th Cir. 1979), *cert. denied,* 21 EPD ¶ 30,316, 21 FEP Cases 96

Commercial Envelope Mfg. Corp. v. *Dunlop,* 10 EPD (CCH) ¶ 10,252 (S.D. N.Y. 1975)

Condit v. *United Air Lines, Inc.,* 558 F.2d 1176, 15 FEP Cases 676, 14 EPD (CCH) ¶ 7752 (4th Cir. 1977), *cert. den.,* 435 U.S. 934, 17 FEP Cases 87, 16 EPD (CCH) ¶ 8181 (1978)

Connecticut General Life Insurance Co. v. *DILHR (Department of Industry, Labor & Human Relations)* 86 Wis.2d 393, 273 N.W.2d 206, 18 FEP Cases 1447, 18 EPD (CCH) ¶ 8880 (1979)

Coopersmith v. *Rouderbush,* 517 F.2d 818, 11 FEP Cases 247, 10 EPD (CCH) ¶ 10,354 (D.C. Cir. 1975)

Counts v. *U.S. Postal Service,* 17 FEP Cases 1161, 18 EPD (CCH) ¶ 8788 (N.D. Fla. 1978)

Cox v. *Delta Air Lines, Inc.,* 14 FEP Cases 1767 (S.D. Fla. 1976), 14 EPD (CCH) ¶ 7600, *aff'd,* 553 F.2d 99 (5th Cir. 1977), 14 EPD (CCH) ¶ 7601

Crockett v. *Green,* 388 F. Supp. 912, 10 FEP Cases 165, 9 EPD (CCH) ¶ 10,029 (E.D. Wis. 1975), *aff'd,* 534 F.2d 715, 12 FEP Cases 1078, 11 EPD (CCH) ¶ 10,781 (7th Cir. 1976)

Croker v. *Boeing Co.,* 437 F. Supp. 1138, 15 FEP Cases 165, 16 EPD (CCH) ¶ 8185 (E.D. Pa. 1977)

Crosslin v. *Mountain States Tel. & Tel. Co.,* 422 F.2d 1028, 2 FEP Cases 480, 2 EPD (CCH) ¶ 10,185 (9th Cir. 1970), vacated, 400 U.S. 1004, 3 FEP Cases 70, 3 EPD (CCH) ¶ 8083 (1971)

Crown Zellerbach Corp. v. *Raymond Marshall,* 441 F. Supp. 1110, 15 FEP Cases 1628, 15 EPD (CCH) ¶ 7898 (E.D. La. 1977)

Crown Zellerbach Corp. v. *Wirtz,* 281 F. Supp. 337, 1 FEP Cases 274, 1 EPD (CCH) ¶ 9846 (D. D.C. 1968)

Danielson v. *Board of Higher Education,* 358 F. Supp. 22, 4 FEP Cases 885, 4 EPD (CCH) ¶ 7773 (S.D. N.Y. 1972)

Danner v. *Phillips Petroleum Co.,* 447 F.2d 159, 3 FEP Cases 858, 3 EPD (CCH) ¶ 8319 (5th Cir. 1971)

Davis v. *Bucher,* 451 F. Supp. 791, 17 FEP Cases 918, 17 EPD (CCH) ¶ 8437 (E.D. Pa. 1978)

Davis v. *County of Los Angeles,* 566 F.2d 1334, 15 FEP Cases 396, 15 EPD (CCH) ¶ 8046 (9th Cir. 1977)

deLaurier v. *San Diego School District,* 588 F.2d 674, 18 FEP Cases 1148, 18 EPD (CCH) ¶ 8695 (9th Cir. 1978)

DeVolld v. *Bailar,* 568 F.2d 1162, 16 FEP Cases 999, 16 EPD (CCH) ¶ 8150 (5th Cir. 1978)

Diaz v. *Pan American World Airways, Inc.,* 442 F.2d 385, 3 FEP Cases 337, 3 EPD (CCH) ¶ 8166 (5th Cir.), *cert. den.,* 404 U.S. 950, 3 FEP Cases 1218, 4 EPD (CCH) ¶ 7560 (1971)

Case Index

Dickerson v. *U.S. Steel Corp.*, 439 F. Supp. 55, 15 FEP Cases 752, 15 EPD (CCH) ¶7823 (E.D. Pa. 1977), *rev'd on other grounds,* 582 F.2d 827, 17 FEP Cases 1393, 17 EPD (CCH) ¶8597 (3d Cir. 1978); decision cited in text, 17 EPD (CCH) ¶8528 (E.D. Pa. 1978)

Dobbins v. *Local 212, IBEW,* 292 F. Supp. 413, 1 FEP Cases 387, 1 EPD (CCH) ¶9912 (S.D. Ohio 1968)

Donahue v. *Shoe Corporation of America,* 337 F. Supp. 1357, 4 FEP Cases 393, 4 EPD (CCH) ¶7743 (C.D. Cal. 1972)

Donnell v. *General Motors Corp.*, 576 F.2d 1292, 17 FEP Cases 712, 16 EPD (CCH) ¶8315 (8th Cir. 1978)

Dothard v. *Rawlinson,* 433 U.S. 321, 15 FEP Cases 10, 14 EPD (CCH) ¶7632 (1977)

Dozier v. *Chupka,* 395 F. Supp. 836, 11 FEP Cases 1331 (S.D. Ohio 1975)

DuBois v. *Packard Bell Corp.,* 470 F.2d 973, 5 FEP Cases 265, 5 EPD (CCH) ¶8083 (10th Cir. 1972)

Duran v. *City of Tampa,* 430 F. Supp. 75, 17 FEP Cases 914, 14 EPD (CCH) ¶7799 (M.D. Fla. 1977)

East Texas Motor Freight Systems, Inc. v. *Rodriguez,* 431 U.S. 395 (1977), 14 FEP Cases 1505, 14 EPD (CCH) ¶7578

EEOC v. *Anchor-Continental, Inc.,* 74 F.R.D. 523, 17 FEP Cases 90 (D. S.C. 1977)

EEOC v. *Bailey Co., Inc.,* 563 F.2d 439, 15 FEP Cases 972, 15 EPD ¶7840 (6th Cir. 1977), *cert. den., sub nom. Bailey Co. Inc.* v. *EEOC,* 435 U.S. 915, 16 FEP Cases 1093, 18 EPD (CCH) ¶8148) (1978)

EEOC v. *Bell Helicopter Co.,* 426 F. Supp. 785, 14 FEP Cases 658 (N.D. Tex. 1976), *aff'd* (5th Cir. 1980)

EEOC v. *Blue Bell Boots, Inc.,* 418 F.2d 355, 2 FEP Cases 228, 2 EPD (CCH) ¶10,115 (6th Cir. 1969)

EEOC v. *Colby College,* 589 F.2d 1139, 18 FEP Cases 1125, 18 EPD (CCH) ¶8737 (1st Cir. 1978)

EEOC v. *E. I. du Pont de Nemours & Co.*, 445 F. Supp. 223, 16 FEP Cases 881, 16 EPD (CCH) ¶8146 (D. Del. 1978)

EEOC v. *Hickey Mitchell Co.,* 376 F. Supp. 117, 7 FEP Cases 134, 6 EPD (CCH) ¶8962 (E.D. Mo. 1973), *aff'd,* 507 F.2d 944, 8 FEP Cases 1281, 8 EPD (CCH) ¶9834 (8th Cir. 1974)

EEOC v. *Mississippi Baptist Hospital,* 12 FEP Cases 411, 11 EPD (CCH) ¶10,822 (S.D. Miss. 1976)

EEOC v. *Moore Group,* 416 F. Supp. 1002, 12 FEP Cases 868, 11 EPD (CCH) ¶10,886 (N.D. Ga. 1976)

EEOC v. *National Academy of Sciences,* 12 FEP Cases 1690, 12 EPD (CCH) ¶11,010 (D. D.C. 1976)

EEOC v. *National Electric Co. Benefit Fund,* 12 FEP Cases 1006, 11 EPD (CCH) ¶10,801 (D.C. Cir. 1976)

EEOC v. *North Hills Passavant Hospital,* 466 F. Supp. 783, 19 FEP Cases 211,

19 EPD (CCH) ¶9037 (W.D. Pa. 1979)
EEOC v. *Occidental Life Ins. Co.,* 535 F.2d 533, 12 FEP Cases 1300, 11 EPD (CCH) ¶10,954 (9th Cir. 1976), *aff'd,* 432 U.S. 355, 14 FEP Cases 1718, 14 EPD (CCH) ¶7619 (1977).
EEOC v. *Packard Elec. Div., General Motors Corp.,* 569 F.2d 315, 17 FEP Cases 9, 16, EPD (CCH) ¶8155 (5th Cir. 1978)
EEOC v. *Quick-Shop Markets, Inc.,* 526 F.2d 802, 11 FEP Cases 871, 10 EPD (CCH) ¶10,519 (8th Cir. 1975)
EEOC v. *U.S. Fidelity & Guaranty Co.,* 420 F. Supp. 244 (D. Md. 1975), 13 FEP Cases 990, 10 EPD (CCH) ¶10,549 *aff'd,* 13 FEP Cases 1005 (4th Cir. 1976), 12 EPD (CCH) ¶11,017, *cert. den.,* 429 U.S. 1023, 12 EPD (CCH) ¶11,280 (1976)
EEOC v. *University of New Mexico,* 504 F.2d 1296, FEP Cases 1037, 8 EPD (CCH) ¶9758 (10th Cir. 1974)
EEOC Dec. No. AL68-1-155E (May 19, 1969)
EEOC Dec. No. 75-031, 16 FEP Cases, 1813 (1974)
EEOC Dec. No. YBI 9C-144, 2 FEP Cases 308 (1969)
EEOC Dec. No. 68-8-257E, and EEOC Dec. No. 68-9-329E (July 8, 1969), 2 FEP Cases 79
EEOC Dec. No. 71-2444
EEOC Dec. No. 71-332, 2 FEP Cases 1016 (Sept. 28, 1976)
EEOC Dec. No. 71446, 2 FEP Cases 1127 (1970)
EEOC Dec. No. 72-0427 (Aug. 31, 1971), 4 FEP Cases 304
EEOC Dec. No. 72-0947
EEOC Dec. No. 72-1176 (Feb. 28, 1972), 5 FEP Cases 960
EEOC Dec. No. F4-02 (July 10, 1973), 6 FEP Cases 830
English v. *Seaboard Coast R.R. Co.,* 12 FEP Cases 75, 10 EPD (CCH) ¶10,476 (S.D. Ga. 1975)
Espinoza v. *Farah Manufacturing Co.,* 414 U.S. 85, 6 FEP Cases 933, 5 EPD (CCH) ¶8944 (1973)
Evans v. *Oscar Mayer & Co.,* U.S. 99 S.Ct. 2066, 60 L. Ed. 2d 609, 19 FEP Cases 1167, 19 EPD (CCH) ¶9216 (1979)
Fagan v. *National Cash Register Co.,* 481 F.2d 1115, 5 FEP Cases 1335, 6 EPD (CCH) ¶8700 (D.C. Cir. 1973)
Fekete v. *U.S. Steel Corp.,* 353 F. Supp. 1177, 5 FEP Cases 639, 5 EPD (CCH) ¶8569 (W.D. Pa. 1973)
Fernandez v. *Avco Corp.,* 14 FEP Cases 1004 (D. Conn. 1977)
Ficlin v. *Sabatini,* 14 FEP Cases 1128 (E.D. Pa. 1977)
Fix v. *Swinerton & Walberg Co.,* 320 F. Supp. 58, 3 FEP Cases 9, 3 EPD (CCH) ¶8082 (D. Col. 1970)
Flight Attendants v. *Ozark Air Lines, Inc.,* 19 FEP Cases 1087 (N.D. Ill. 1979)
Fountain v. *Safeway Stores, Inc.,* 555 F.2d 753, 15 FEP Cases 96, 14 EPD (CCH) ¶664 (9th Cir. 1977)

Francis v. *AT&T, Long Lines Dept.,* 55 F.R.D. 202, 4 FEP Cases 777, 4 EPD (CCH) ¶7811 (D. D.C. 1972)

Fraser Shipyard Inc. v. *DILAR,* 13 FEP Cases 1809, 13 EPD (CCH) ¶11,515 (Wis. 1976)

Friend v. *Leidinger,* 588 F.2d 61, 18 FEP Cases 1052, 18 EPD ¶8704 (4th Cir. 1978)

Garber v. *Saxon Business Products,* 552 F.2d 1032, 15 FEP Cases 344, 14 EPD (CCH) ¶7587 (4th Cir. 1977)

General Electric Company v. *FEPC,* 15 FEP Cases 1486 (Ill. App. Ct. 1976)

Georgia Power Co. v. *EEOC,* 295 F. Supp. 950, 1 FEP Cases 351, 1 EPD (CCH) ¶9903 (N.D. Ga. 1968), *aff'd,* 412 F.2d 462, 1 FEP Cases 787, 2 EPD (CCH) ¶10,019 (5th Cir. 1969)

Gerdom v. *Continental Airlines, Inc.,* 13 FEP Cases 1205, 13 EPD (CCH) ¶11,320 (C.D. Cal. 1976)

Gill v. *Union Carbide Corp.,* 368 F. Supp. 364, 7 FEP Cases 571, 5 EPD (CCH) ¶9265 (E.D. Tenn. 1973)

Gillin v. *Federal Paper Board Co.,* 479 F.2d 97, 5 FEP Cases 1094, 5 EPD (CCH) ¶8163 (2d Cir. 1973)

Goodman v. *Schlesinger,* 584 F.2d 1325, 18 FEP Cases 191, 18 EPD (CCH) ¶8659 (4th Cir. 1978)

Graniteville Co. (Sibley Division) v. *EEOC,* 438 F.2d 32, 3 FEP Cases 155, 3 EPD (CCH) ¶8109 (4th Cir. 1971)

Green v. *Missouri Pacific R.R.,* 523 F.2d 1290, 10 FEP Cases 1409, 10 EPD (CCH) ¶10,314 (8th Cir. 1974)

Gregory v. *Litton Systems, Inc.,* 472 F.2d 631, 5 FEP Cases 267, 5 EPD (CCH) ¶8089 (9th Cir. 1972)

Griggs v. *Duke Power Co.,* 401 U.S. 424, 3 FEP Cases 175, 3 EPD (CCH) ¶8137 (1971)

Gurmankin v. *Costanzo,* 556 F.2d 184, 14 FEP Cases 1359, 14 EPD (CCH) ¶7519 (3rd Cir. 1977)

Haire v. *Calloway,* 572 F.2d 632, 17 FEP Cases 252, 17 EPD (CCH) ¶8187 (8th Cir. 1978)

Hardison v. *Trans World Airlines, Inc.,* 432 U.S. 63, 67 S.Ct. 2264, 53 L.Ed. 2d 113, 14 FEP Cases 1697, 14 EPD (CCH) ¶7620 (1977)

Harper v. *General Grocer Co.,* 451 F. Supp. 513, 18 FEP Cases 1356, (E.D. Mo. 1978), *aff'd in relevant part, rev'd in part,* 590 F.2d 713, 18 FEP Cases 1359, 18 EPD (CCH) ¶8776 (8th Cir. 1979)

Harper v. *Trans World Airlines, Inc.,* 525 F.2d 409, 11 FEP Cases 1074, 10 EPD (CCH) ¶10,498 (8th Cir. 1975)

Hays v. *Potlach Forests, Inc.,* 465 F.2d 1081, 4 FEP Cases 1037, 4 EPD (CCH) ¶7928 (8th Cir. 1972)

Hazelwood School District v. *United States,* 433 U.S. 299, 15 FEP Cases 1, 14 EPD (CCH) ¶7633 (1977)

Hester v. *Southern Railway Co.,* 497 F.2d 1374, 8 FEP Cases 646, 8 EPD (CCH) ¶9582 (5th Cir. 1974)

Hodgson v. *Approved Personnel Services, Inc.,* 539 F.2d 760, 11 FEP Cases 688, 10 EPD (CCH) ¶10,472 (4th Cir. 1975)

Hodgson v. *Career Counsellors International, Inc.,* 5 FEP Cases 129, 5 EPD (CCH) ¶7983 (N.D. Ill. 1972)

Hodgson v. *First Federal Savings & Loan Assn.,* 455 F.2d 818 4 EPD (CCH) ¶7629, 4 FEP Cases 269 (5th Cir. 1972)

Hodgson v. *Greyhound Lines, Inc.,* 499 F.2d 859, 7 FEP Cases 817, 7 EPD (CCH) ¶9286 (7th Cir. 1974), *cert. den.* 419 U.S. 1122, 9 FEP Cases 58, 9 EPD (CCH) ¶9882 (1975)

Holland v. *Boeing Co.,* 12 FEP Cases 975, 11 EPD (CCH) ¶10,861 (Wash. 1976)

Huckeby v. *Frozen Food Express,* 427 F. Supp. 967, 14 FEP Cases 1501, 14 EPD (CCH) ¶7695 (N.D. Tex. 1977)

Illinois Tool Works v. *Marshall,* 17 FEP Cases 520, 17 EPD (CCH) ¶8460 (N.D. Ill. 1978) *aff'd in part and rev'd in part,* 20 EPD (CCH) ¶30,134 (7th Cir. 1979)

In re Consolidated Pretrial Proceedings in the Airline cases, 582 F.2d 1142, 17 FEP Cases 1513, 17 EPD ¶8586 (7th Cir. 1978)

In re National Airlines, Inc., 434 F. Supp. 249, 14 FEP Cases 1807 (S.D. Fla. 1977)

Inda v. *United Airlines, Inc.,* 405 F. Supp. 426, 11 EPD (CCH) 10,933 (C.D. Cal. 1975)

International Brotherhood of Teamsters v. *United States,* 431 U.S. 324, 97 S.Ct. 1843, 52 L.Ed. 2d 396 (1977), 14 FEP Cases 1514, 14 EPD (CCH) ¶7579

James v. *Stockham Valves & Fittings Co.,* 559 F.2d 310, 15 FEP Cases 827, 15 EPD (CCH) 7842 (5th Cir. 1977), *cert. denied,* 434 U.S. 1034, 16 FEP Cases 501, 15 EPD (CCH) ¶8019 (1978)

Jersey Central Power & Light Co. v. *Electrical Workers (IBEW),* 508 F.2d 687, 9 FEP Cases 117, 9 EPD (CCH) ¶9923 (3d Cir. 1975), *vacated and remanded sub nom. EEOC* v. *Jersey Central Power & Light Co.,* 425 U.S. 987, 12 FEP Cases 1335, 11 EPD (CCH) ¶10,925, *cert. den. Jersey Central Power & Light Co.* v. *EEOC,* 425 U.S. 998, 12 FEP Cases 1335 (1976)

Johnson v. *City of New York,* Case No. GCD-36562-75 (N.Y.S. Div. on Human Rights)

Johnson v. *Georgia Highway Express Co.,* 417 F.2d 1122, 2 FEP Cases 231, 2 EPD (CCH) ¶10,119 (5th Cir. 1969)

Jones v. *Klassen,* 389 F. Supp. 408 (E.D. Mo. 1974), 11 FEP Cases 767, *aff'd. sub nom Haire* v. *Calloway* 526 F. 2d 246 (8th Cir. 1975), 11 FEP Cases 769, *vacated and rem'd on other g'ds,* 537 F.2d 318 (8th Cir. 1976), 13 FEP Cases 1182

Joslin Dry Goods Co. v. *EEOC,* 483 F. 2d 178, 6 FEP Cases 293, 6 EPD (CCH) ¶8774 (10th Cir. 1973)

Case Index

Junesson v. *Kisco Co.,* 542 F.2d 1008, 13 FEP Cases 977, 12 EPD (CCH) ¶11,222 (8th Cir. 1976)

Laffey v. *Northwest Airlines, Inc.,* 366 F. Supp. 763 (D.D.C. 1973), *modif. on other gds,* 567 F. 2d 429 (D.C. Cir. 1976), *cert. denied,* 434 U.S. 1086 (1978)

Lanigan v. *Bartlett and Company Grain,* 466 F. Supp. 1388 (W.D. Mo. 1979), 20 EPD (CCH) ¶30,006

Latino v. *Rainbo Bakers, Inc.,* 358 F. Supp. 870, 5 FEP Cases 917, 5 EPD (CCH) ¶8597 (D. Col. 1973)

Laugesen v. *Anaconda Co.,* 510 F.2d 313, 10 FEP Cases 567, 9 EPD (CCH) ¶9870, (6th Cir. 1975)

League of United Latin American Citizens v. *City of Santa Ana,* 410, F. Supp. 873, 12 FEP Cases 651, 11 EPD (CCH) ¶10,818 (C.D. Cal. 1976)

Leechburg Area School District v. *Pennsylvania Human Relations Commission,* 19 Pa. Commonwealth Ct. 614, 16 FEP Cases 1333, 11 EPD (CCH) ¶10,719 (1975).

Kaiser Aluminum & Chemicals Corp. v. *Weber,* 99 S.Ct. 2721 (1979), 20 EPD (CCH) ¶30026.

Lester v. *Ellis Trucking Co.,* 10 FEP Cases 1036 (W.D. Tenn. 1975)

Lewis v. *Ford Motor Co.,* 17 FEP Cases 933, 17 EPD (CCH) ¶8453 (E.D. Mich. 1978)

Lewis v. *Tobacco Workers Int'l Union,* 577 F.2d 1135, 17 FEP Cases 622, 16 EPD (CCH) ¶8310 (4th Cir. 1978)

Lewis v. *Western Airlines, Inc.,* 379 F. Supp. 684, 8 FEP Cases 373, 8 EPD (CCH) ¶9609 (N.D. Cal. 1974)

Local 104, Sheet Metal Workers v. *EEOC,* 303 F. Supp. 528, 2 FEP Cases 93, 1 EPD ¶9955 (N.D. Cal. 1969), *aff'd in part, rev'd in part,* 439 F.2d 237, 3 FEP Cases 218, 3 EPD ¶8134 (9th Cir. 1971)

Loeb v. *Textron, Inc.,* 600 F.2d 1003, 20 EPD ¶30,028, 20 FEP Cases 29, (1st Cir. 1979)

Loper v. *American Airlines, Inc.,* 582 F.2d 956, 18 FEP Cases 1131, 18 EPD ¶8668 (5th Cir. 1978)

McBride v. *Delta Airlines,* 551 F.2d 113, 14 FEP Cases 1137, 13 EPD (CCH) ¶11,566 (6th Cir. 1977), *cert. den.* 434 U.S. 927, 15 FEP Cases 1618, 15 EPD (CCH) ¶9897 (1977)

McDonald v. *Santa Fe Trail Transportation Co.,* 513 F.2d 90, 9 EPD (CCH) ¶10,161 (5th Cir. 1975), *rev'd,* 423 U.S. 923, 12 EPD (CCH) ¶10,997 (1976)

McDonnell Douglas Corp. v. *Green,* 411 U.S. 792, 5 FEP Cases 965, 5 EPD (CCH) ¶8607 (1973)

McNutt v. *Hills,* 426 F. Supp. 990, 15 FEP Cases 1370, 14 EPD (CCH) ¶7535 (D. D.C. 1977)

Magruder v. *Selling Areas Blanketing Inc.,* 439 F. Supp. 1155, 16 EPD (CCH) ¶8143 (N.D. Ill. 1977)

Maloof v. *City Commission on Human Rights,* 38 N.Y.2d 329, 342 N.E.2d 563, 379 N.Y.S.2d 788, 11 EPD (CCH) ¶10,749 (1975)

Manhart v. *City of Los Angeles, Department of Water & Power,* 435 U.S. 702, 16 EPD (CCH) ¶8250, 17 FEP Cases 395 (1978)

Marshall v. *Board of Education of Salt Lake City,* 15 FEP Cases 368, 15 EPD (CCH) ¶8056 (D. Utah 1977)

Martin v. *Dann,* 10 FEP Cases 944, 9 EPD (CCH) ¶10,128 (D. D.C. 1975)

Martinez v. *Bethlehem Steel Corp.,* 17 FEP Cases 113 (E.D. Pa. 1978)

Mastie v. *Great Lakes Steel Corp.,* 424 F. Supp. 1299, 14 FEP Cases 952, 14 (CCH) ¶7707 (E.D. Mich. 1976)

Meadows v. *Ford Motor Co.,* 510 F.2d 939, 11 FEP Cases, 1047, 9 EPD (CCH) ¶9907 (6th Cir. 1975), *cert. den. sub nom. Automobile Workers Local 862* v. *Ford Motor Co.,* 425 U.S. 998, 12 FEP Cases 1335, 12 EPD (CCH) ¶10,925 (1976)

Mejia v. *N.Y. Sheraton Hotel,* 459 F. Supp. 375, 18 FEP Cases 602, 18 EPD (CCH) ¶8701 (S.D. N.Y. 1979)

Merriweather v. *American Cast Iron Pipe Co.,* 362 F. Supp. 670, 6 FEP Cases 1242, 6 EPD (CCH) ¶8966 (N.D. Ala. 1973)

Mistretta v. *Sandia Corp.,* 15 FEP Cases 1690, 15 EPD (CCH) ¶7902 (D. N.M. 1977)

Monsanto Co. v. *EEOC,* 2 FEP Cases 50 (N.D. Fla. 1969)

Montgomery Ward & Co. v. *Bureau of Labor,* 280 Ore. 163, 570 P.2d 76, 14 FEP Cases 1091, 15 EPD (CCH) ¶7990 (1977)

Moore v. *Sears, Roebuck & Co.,* 19 FEP Cases 246 (N.D. Ga. 1979)

Moore v. *Sunbeam Corp.,* 459 F.2d 811, 4 FEP Cases 454, 4 EPD (CCH) ¶7722 (7th Cir. 1972)

Moses v. *Falstaff Brewing Corp.,* 550 F.2d 1113, 14 FEP Cases 813, 13 EPD (CCH) ¶11,564 (8th Cir. 1977)

Motorola, Inc. v. *EEOC,* 460 F.2d 1245, 4 FEP Cases 755, 4 EPD (CCH) ¶7834 (9th Cir. 1972)

Motorola, Inc. v. *EEOC,* 5 FEP Cases 1379, 6 EPD (CCH) ¶787 (D. Ariz. 1973)

Nance v. *Union Carbide Corp.,* 397 F. Supp. 436, 13 FEP Cases 211, 9 EPD ¶10,114 (W.D. N.C. 1975)

National Organization for Women, Inc. v. *Minnesota Mining and Manufacturing Co.,* 14 FEP Cases 829, 9 EPD ¶10,231 (D. Minn. 1976)

New Orleans Public Service, Inc. v. *Brown,* 507 F.2d 160, 9 FEP Cases 134, 9 EPD ¶9928 (5th Cir. 1975)

New York City Transit Authority v. *Beazer,* 99 S.Ct. 1355, 19 EPD (CCH) ¶9027 (1979)

New York State Div. of Human Rights, on the complaint of Bonita Bilicki v. *Thomas J. Lipton, Inc.,* 67 AD2d 1029 (3rd Dept. 1979), 413 N.Y.S.2d 233.

New York State Div. Human Rights on the complaints of Clark and Jones v. *City of New York,* Case Nos. GCD-39208-75 and GCDs-34885-74
Officers for Justice v. *Civil Service Commission,* 395 F. Supp. 378, 11 FEP Cases 815, 11 EPD ¶10,618 (N.D. Cal. 1975)
Olson v. *Rembrandt Printing Co.,* 511 F.2d 1228, 10 FEP Cases 27, 9 EPD ¶9941 (8th Cir. 1975)
Pan American World Airways, Inc. v. *Marshall,* 439 F. Supp. 487, 15 FEP Cases 1607, 15 EPD ¶7930 (S.D. N.Y. 1977)
Parliament House Motor Hotel v. *EEOC,* 444 F.2d 1335, 3 FEP Cases 663, 3 EPD ¶8277 (5th Cir. 1971)
Patterson v. *American Tobacco Co.,* 425 F. Supp. 713, 8 FEP Cases 778, 8 EPD ¶9722 (E.D. Va. 1974), *aff'd in relevant part,* 535 F.2d 257, 11 EPD ¶10,728 (4th Cir.,), *cert. denied,* 429 U.S. 920, 13 EPD ¶11,282 (1976)
Payne v. *Travenol Laboratories, Inc.,* 565 F.2d 895, 17 FEP Cases 186, 17 EPD ¶8383 (5th Cir.), *cert. denied,* 99 S.Ct. 118, 17 FEP Cases 186, 17 EPD ¶8604A (1978)
Pettway v. *American Cast Iron Pipe Co.,* 494 F.2d 211, 7 FEP Cases 1115, 7 EPD ¶9291 (5th Cir. 1974)
Phillips v. *Martin Marietta Corp.,* 400 U.S. 542, 3 FEP Cases 40, 3 EPD ¶8088 (1971)
Price v. *Maryland Casualty Co.,* 561 F.2d 609, 16 FEP Cases 84, 15 EPD ¶7890 (5th Cir. 1977)
Providence Journal Co. v. *Mason,* 116 R.I. 614, 359 A.2d 682, 13 FEP Cases 385, 12 EPD ¶11,080 (1976)
Ramsey v. *Hopkins,* 320 F. Supp. 477, 3 FEP Cases 87, 3 EPD ¶8112 (N.D. Ala. 1970), *remanded* 447 F.2d 128, 3 FEP Cases 857, 3 EPD ¶8322 (5th Cir. 1971)
Randolph v. *United States Elevator Corp.,* 19 FEP Cases 368 (S.D. Fla. 1978)
Reynolds Metals Co. v. *Rumsfeld,* 564 F.2d 663, 15 FEP Cases 1185, 15 EPD (CCH) ¶7878 (4th Cir. 1977)
Rhoades v. *The Book Press,* 18 FEP Cases 494 (D. Vt. 1978)
Richardson v. *Hotel Corp. of America,* 332 F. Supp. 519, 3 FEP Cases 1031, 4 EPD ¶7666 (E.D. La. 1971)
Roberts v. *General Mills, Inc.,* 337 F. Supp. 1055, 3 FEP Cases 1080, 4 EPD ¶7681 (N.D. Ohio 1971)
Robinson v. *Union Carbide Corp.,* 538 F.2d 652, 13 FEP Cases 645, 12 EPD ¶11,179 (5th Cir. 1976), *mod. on other grounds,* 544 F.2d 1258 (5th Cir. 1977), *cert. denied,* 434 U.S. 822, 15 FEP Cases 1184, 15 EPD ¶7856 (1977)
Rodriguez v. *Taylor,* 428 F. Supp. 1118, 14 FEP Cases 605, 13 EPD ¶11,362 (E.D. Pa. 1976), *aff'd in part,* 569 F.2d 1231, 16 FEP Cases 533, 15 EPD ¶8029 (3d Cir. 1977), *cert. denied,* 436 U.S. 913, 17 FEP Cases 699, 16 EPD ¶8291 (1978)

Rogers v. *EEOC,* 454 F.2d 234, 4 FEP Cases 92, 4 EPD ¶ 7597 (5th Cir. 1971), *cert. denied,* 406 U.S. 957, 4 FEP Cases 771, 4 EPD ¶ 7838 (1972)

Rogers v. *EEOC,* 551 F.2d 456, 14 FEP Cases 625, 13 EPD ¶ 11,549 (D.C. Cir. 1977)

Roller v. *City of San Mateo,* 572 F.2d 1311, 18 FEP Cases 1144, 15 EPD ¶ 8062 (9th Cir. 1977)

Roman v. *ESB, Inc.,* 550 F.2d 1343, 13 EPD (CCH) ¶ 11,285, 14 FEP Cases 235 (4th Cir. 1976)

Rosen v. *Public Service Gas & Electric Co.,* 477 F.2d 90, 5 FEP Cases 709, 5 EPD ¶ 8499 (3d Cir. 1973)

Rosenfeld v. *Southern Pacific Co.,* 444 F.2d 1219, 3 FEP Cases 604, 3 EPD ¶ 8247 (9th Cir. 1971)

Rowe v. *General Motors Corp.,* 457 F.2d 348, 2 FEP Cases 445, 4 EPD ¶ 7689 (5th Cir. 1972)

Sanchez v. *Standard Brands, Inc.,* 431 F.2d 455, 2 FEP Cases 788, 2 EPD ¶ 10,252 (5th Cir. 1970), *reh'g en banc den,* same citations

Saucedo v. *Brothers Well Service, Inc.,* 464 F. Supp. 919, 19 FEP Cases 91, 19 EPD ¶ 9135 (S.D. Tex. 1979)

Schultz v. *Hickok Mfg. Co., Inc.,* 358 F. Supp. 1208 (N.D. Ga. 1973)

Sheetmetal Workers, Local 104 v. *EEOC,* 303 F. Supp. 528 (N.D. Cal. 1969)

Smith v. *Borough of Wilkinsburg,* 15 FEP Cases 365 (E.D. Pa. 1977)

Smith v. *City of East Cleveland,* 520 F.2d 492, 10 FEP Cases 1380, 10 EPD ¶ 10,263 (6th Cir. 1975), *cert. denied sub nom., Smith* v. *Troyan,* 426 U.S. 934, 12 FEP Cases 1560, 12 EPD ¶ 11,032 (1976)

Smith v. *Fletcher,* 393 F. Supp. 1366, 15 FEP Cases 1081, 10 EPD ¶ 10,329 (S.D. Tex. 1975)

Smith v. *Mutual Benefit Life Insurance Co.,* 13 FEP Cases 252, 11 EPD ¶ 10,876 (D. N.J. 1976)

Smith v. *Olin Chemical Corp.,* 555 F.2d 1283, 15 FEP Cases 290, 14 EPD ¶ 7702 (5th Cir. 1977)

Southeastern Community College v. *Davis,* 99 S.Ct. 236 (1979)

Sprogis v. *United Airlines, Inc.,* 444 F.2d 1194, 3 FEP Cases 621, 3 EPD ¶ 8239 (7th Cir. 1971), *cert. denied* 405 U.S. 991 (1972)

Spurlock v. *United Airlines, Inc.,* 475 F.2d 216, 5 FEP Cases 17, 5 EPD ¶ 7996 (10th Cir. 1972)

Stallworth v. *Monsanto Co.,* 13 FEP Cases 825, 8 EPD ¶ 9695 (N.D. Fla. 1974)

State Division of Human Rights v. *Averill Park Central School District,* 59 A.D.2d 449, 399 N.Y.S.2d 926, 17 EPD ¶ 8449 (3d Dept. 1977)

State Division of Human Rights v. *County of Monroe,* 64 A.D.2d 811, 407 N.Y.S.2d 281, 19 EPD ¶ 8954 (4th Dept. 1978)

Stevenson v. *International Paper Co.,* 516 F.2d 103, 10 FEP Cases 1386, 10 EPD ¶ 10,320 (5th Cir. 1975)

Stewart v. *General Motors Corp.,* 542 F.2d 445, 13 FEP Cases 1035, 12 EPD

¶11,260 (7th Cir. 1976), *cert. denied* 433 U.S. 919, 15 FEP Cases 31, 14 EPD ¶7636 (1977)

Strain v. *Philpott,* 4 FEP Cases 825, 4 EPD ¶7521 (M.D. Ala. 1971)

Stringfellow v. *Monsanto Co.,* 370 F. Supp. 1175 (W.D. Ark. 1970)

Stroud v. *Delta Airlines, Inc.,* 544 F.2d 892, 14 FEP Cases 206, 13 EPD ¶11,302 (5th Cir.), *cert. denied* 434 U.S. 844, 15 FEP Cases 1184, 15 EPD ¶7856 (1977)

Sundstrand Corp. v. *Marshall,* 15 FEP Cases 432, 17 EPD ¶8609 (N.D. Ill. 1978)

Taylor v. *Safeway Stores, Inc.,* 524 F.2d 263, 11 FEP Cases 449, 10 EPD ¶10,410 (10th Cir. 1975)

Teamsters v. *United States,* 431 U.S. 324, 97 S. Ct. 1843, 14 FEP Cases 1514, 14 EPD ¶7579 (1977)

Thomas v. *Parker,* 19 FEP Cases 49, 19 EPD ¶8983 (D. D.C. 1979)

Timken Co. v. *Marshall,* 11 EPD (CCH) ¶10,906 (N.D. Ohio 1976)

Timken Co. v. *Vaughan,* 413 F. Supp. 1183, 12 FEP Cases 1140, 11 EPD ¶10,906 (N.D. Ohio 1976)

Tomkins v. *Public Service Electric & Gas Co.,* 568 F.2d 1044, 16 FEP Cases 22, 15 EPD ¶7954 (3d Cir. 1977)

Townsend v. *Nassau County Medical Center,* 558 F.2d 117, 15 FEP Cases 237, 14 EPD ¶7673 (2d Cir. 1977), *cert denied* 434 U.S. 1015, 16 FEP Cases 501, 15 EPD ¶8018 (1978)

Trans World Airlines, Inc. v. *Hardison,* 432 U.S. 63, 14 FEP Cases 1697, 14 EPD ¶7620 (1977)

Trivett v. *Tri-State Container Corp.,* 368 F. Supp. 137, 7 FEP Cases 1292, 7 EPD ¶9318 (E.D. Tenn. 1973)

Tuck v. *McGraw-Hill, Inc.,* 421 F. Supp. 39, 13 FEP Cases 778, 13 EPD ¶11,367 (S.D. N.Y. 1976)

United Airlines, Inc. v. *Evans,* 431 U.S. 553, 14 FEP Cases 1510, 14 EPD ¶7577 (1977)

United Airlines, Inc. v. *McMann,* 434 U.S. 192, 16 FEP Cases 146, 15 EPD ¶7971 (1977)

United Handicapped Ltd. v. *Andre,* 558 F.2d 413 (8th Cir. 1977)

United States v. *City of Los Angeles,* 15 FEP Cases 229, 14 EPD ¶7785 (C.D. Cal. 1977)

United States v. *East Texas Motor Freight,* 564 F.2d 179, 17 FEP Cases 163, 15 EPD ¶7961 (5th Cir. 1977)

United States v. *Georgia Power Co.,* 474 F.2d 906, 5 FEP Cases 583, 5 EPD ¶8460 (5th Cir. 1973)

United States v. *Lee Way Motor Freight, Inc.,* 7 FEP Cases 710, 7 EPD ¶9066 (W.D. Okla. 1973)

United States v. *Local 3, Operating Engineers,* 4 FEP Cases 1088, 4 EPD ¶7944 (N.D. Cal. 1972)

United States v. *New Orleans Public Service, Inc.,* 553 F.2d 459, 14 FEP Cases

1730, 14 EPD ¶7602 (5th Cir. 1977), *vacated and remanded,* 436 U.S. 942, 17 FEP Cases 897, 15 EPD ¶8315A (1978)

United States Steel Corp. v. *United States,* 6 EPD (CCH) ¶8980 (W.D.Pa.1973), *aff'd* 353 F.2d 545 (3rd Cir. 1973)

University of California Board of Regents v. *Bakke,* 438 U.S. 265, 17 FEP Cases 1000, 17 EPD ¶8402 (1978)

Usery v. *Tamiami Trail Tours, Inc.,* 531 F.2d 224, 12 FEP Cases 1233, 11 EPD ¶10,916 (5th Cir. 1976)

Vogler v. *McCarty, Inc.,* 294 F. Supp. 368, 1 FEP Cases 197, 1 EPD ¶9791 (E.D. La. 1968), *aff'd sub nom. Local 53, International Association of Heat and Frost Insulation* v. *Vogler,* 407 F.2d 1047, 1 FEP Cases 577, 1 EPD ¶9952 (5th Cir. 1969)

Voyles v. *Ralph K. Davies Medical Center,* 403 F. Supp. 456, 11 FEP Cases 1199, 11 EPD ¶10,716 (N.D. Cal. 1975)

Waters v. *Furnco Construction Corp.,* 98 S. Ct. 2943 (1978), 17 EPD (CCH) ¶8401

Watkins v. *Scott Paper Co.,* 530 F.2d 1159, 12 FEP Cases 1191, 11 EPD ¶10,880 (5th Cir.), *cert. denied* 429 U.S. 861 13 FEP Cases 963, 12 EPD ¶11,207 (1976)

Wells v. *Meyer's Bakery,* 561 F.2d 1268, 15 FEP Cases 930, 15 EPD ¶7867 (8th Cir. 1977)

Westinghouse Electric Co. v. *State Division of Human Rights,* 63 A.D.2d 170, 406 N.Y.S.2d 912, 18 FEP Cases 1423, 18 EPD 8868 (3rd Dept. 1978), *aff'd* N.Y.2d (1980)

Wetzel v. *Liberty Mutual Insurance Co.,* 508 F.2d 239, 9 FEP Cases 211, 9 EPD #9931 (3d Cir. 1975), *cert. denied* 421 U.S. 1011, 9 FEP Cases 211, 9 EPD ¶10,176 (1975)

Whitaker v. *City University of New York,* 461 F. Supp. 99, 18 FEP Cases 906, 18 EPO ¶8693 (E.D. N.Y. 1978)

White v. *Bailar,* 14 FEP Cases 383 (E.D. Mo. 1976)

Willingham v. *Macon Telegraph Publishing Co.,* 507 F.2d 1084, 9 FEP Cases 189, 9 EPD ¶9957 (5th Cir. 1975)

Wilson v. *Sharon Steel Corp.,* 442 F. Supp. 231, 19 FEP Cases 336, 16 EPD ¶8219 (W.D. Pa. 1979)

Wilson v. *Woodward Iron Co.,* 362 F. Supp. 886, 6 EPD ¶8972 (N.D. Ala. 1973)

W. R. Grace & Co. v. *Local 759, Rubber Workers,* 565 F.2d 913, 16 FEP Cases 507, 15 EPD ¶8020 (5th Cir. 1978)

Yukas v. *Libbey-Owens Ford Co.,* 562 F.2d 496, 17 FEP Cases 891, 15 EPD (CCH) ¶7861 (7th Cir. 1977)

Zambuto v. *American Telephone & Telegraph Co.,* 544 F.2d 1333, 14 FEP Cases 259, 13 EPD (CCH) ¶11,385 (5th Cir. 1977)

Exec Order 11246

Case Index

Exec. Orders 11246, §209(1)(6)
§208(b)
§202(1)
(Revised Order No. 4) §60.2.13(a)
§60.2.20(a)
§60.2.20 (2)
(4)
(3)
Exec. Order 11246
Revised Order No. 4
§60-2.13(b)	11-32
§60-2.21(a)	11-32
§60-2.21(b)	11-32
§60.2.21(A) (1-11)	11-36
§60.2.21(B) (1-2,4-5)	11-36
§60.2.21(B) (6-7)	11-37

Revised Order No. 14
Exec. Order 11821
OFCCP Compl. Man.,
§8-200, 8-300	11-14
§8-300, 8-400	11-14
§8-300	11-6
§8-300	11-7
Chap. 5	11-8
§6-500	11-9
§7-200	11-9
§7-101	11-12
§3-501(b)(1)	11-19
§3-501(b)	11-20

OFCCP Compl. Man., §3-504(a) 11-37
Title VII, §503(a)
Title VII, §703(h)
Title VII, §705(g)
Title VII, §710
6 U.S.C. §552(b)(3,4,6,7(c))   11-69
5 U.S.C., §552 et seq.
29 U.S.C. §623
38 U.S.C. Ch. 42, §2012, 2014
42 U.S.C. §1481
29 C.F.R. §521.2, 521.3
29 C.F.R. §860.102(e)
29 C.F.R. §860.103(h)
29 C.F.R. §860.120 (g)   7-2

§1601.14	10-32
§1601.15(b)	10-31
§1601.16	10-19
§1601.19(e), 20	10-13
§1601.20	10-5, 10-13
§1601.21(d)	10-33
§1601.25	10-37
§1601.26(b)	10-16
§1601.28, 28(b)	10-37
§1601.28(b)(2)	10-36
41 C.F.R. §60-1.20	11-14
§60-60.3	11-15
§60-1.24	11-15
§60-2.2	11-13, 11-15
§60-2.2(b)	11-16, 11-17
§60-1.24(c)(4)	11-17
§60-2.11	11-22
41 C.F.R. §60-4.8	11-13
§60-2 et seq.	11-1
§60-741	11-1
§60-60.6, 60.7	11-9
§60-1.43	11-7, 11-10
§60-60.3(b)	11-11
§60-1.32	11-11
§60-60.5	11-11
§60-1.7	11-12

41 C.F.R. §1610.18
    §1610.4

Department of Labor, Wage and Human Administration Opinion, July 31, 1968, FEPM §401 at 5208, *Discriminatory Layoffs*

Index

AACP, 246, 247, 248, 250, 251, 258, 261, 272, 277, 279, 281, 307
Aaron v. *Davis,* 48
Abrams v. *Johnson,* 103
Accent issue, 50, 51
Administrative Procedures Act, 202, 277
Advancement potential, 132
Adverse impact, 4-6, 25-29
  bottom-line, 27, 30, 32
  discharge, 143-147
  promotions, transfers, and assignments, 108-118
    applicant/hire ratio, 109-110
    bidding system, 115-116
    evaluation system, 113
    future prospects in assessing, 116-118
    self-identification, 110-116
    seniority system, 114
  in selection procedures, 25-32, 67-77
    applicant pool and hire rates, comparison of, 71-72
    campus recruiting, 47
    educational requirements, 54, 55
    80 percent rule, 68, 72
    example of, 73-76
    recruiting, 69-71
    standard-deviation analysis, 68, 72
Affected classes, 250, 272
Affirmative action program, 13-15, 18, 19, 24, 26-27, 139

Affirmative action program *(Cont'd.)*.
  affected classes and focus job groups, 272
  essential elements of, 278
  Freedom of Information Act and, 272, 277-278
  goals and timetables, 268, 272-276
  internal and external dissemination of policy, 281-288
  job grouping, 260-263
  utilization analysis, 263-271
Affirmative Action Program Guidelines (BNA), 244
Age discrimination:
  discharge, 130-133
  promotions, transfers, and assignments, 100-103
    appearance, 102-103
    insurance benefits, 103
    physical-fitness requirements, 102
    preferential consideration, 101
    promotion potential, 100, 101
    time left to retirement, 100
  reductions in force, 130-133, 145-147
  retirement plans, 152-153
  selection procedures, 46-50
Age Discrimination in Employment Acts of 1967 and 1972 (ADEA), 7, 15-17, 24, 46, 47, 50, 130-133, 147, 151, 173, 176, 183, 301-302, 314
  Amendments of 1978, 151-153

Alaskan natives, 25
Alcoholism, 18, 19, 65, 142
Aliens, 10
Allen v. Lovejoy, 62-63, 140
Alternative selection procedures, 31
American Cyanamid Co. v. Roudebush, 258
American Indians, 10, 25
American Telephone & Telegraph Company (AT&T), 108
Annuity plans, 160
Apache Floor Company, 13
Apparent availability, 99, 104
Appearance standards, 50, 57, 60, 102-103, 139
Applicant flow, 68, 69, 71, 72
Applicant/hire ratio, 109-110
Application forms, 77-86
Apprenticeship, 4, 57
Aptitude, 37, 39, 77
Arizona Civil Rights Commission, 182-183
Armstrong Corporation, 13
Arrest-record standard, 51
Arritt v. Grisell, 48
Asians, 25
Assessment centers, 108
Assignments, *see* Promotions, transfers, and assignments
Asthma, 141
Availability pools, 28, 67-68

Bantering, 153-155
Barnes v. Costle, 161
Barnett v. W. T. Grant Co., 57
BARS (Behaviorally Anchored Rating Scale), 120
Batyko v. Pennsylvania Liquor Control Board, 140
Baxter v. Savannah Sugar Refining Corp., 104
Bernard v. Gulf Oil Co., 313
Best-achieving group, 4
Bidding system, 100, 115-116
Billingsley v. Service Technology Corp., 131
Blacks, 25-28
  arrest-record standard, 51
  conviction information, 51-52
  credit references, 52-53
  discipline, 136-137
  educational requirements, 54-56
  medical standards, 57-58
  suburbs, migration to, 137
Blindness, 64
Blizard v. Fielding, 105
Board of Trustees of Keene State College v. Sweeney, 172, 174
Bona fide occupational qualification (BFOQ), 4, 5, 6, 46
Bona fide seniority system, 133-135, 147
Bondability, 79
Bottom-line adverse impact, 27, 30, 32
Bowe v. Colgate-Palmolive Company, 138
Brennan v. Paragon Employment Agency, Inc., 47
Brennan v. Reynolds & Co., 131

Brito v. Zia Co., 155
Bryan v. California Brewers Association, 131
Buddy system, 116
Burdens of proof, 171-172, 175
Bureau of National Affairs (BNA), 21, 177, 244
Burns v. Rohr Corp., 160
Business necessity, 4-6, 45n, 46, 54, 58

C.F.R., 248, 249, 251, 256, 258, 280, 281, 284, 289, 290-293
Campus recruiting, 47
Cariddi v. Kansas City Chiefs Football Club, Inc., 154, 161
Carmi v. St. Louis School District, 67, 143
Carroll v. Talman Federal Savings & Loan Association, 60
Castro v. Beecher, 54
Cates v. TWA, 185
Central Americans, 25
Certiorari, writ of, 55
Chicago, Milwaukee, St. Paul, & Pacific RR Co. v. State of Wisconsin, The Department of Industry, Labor, and Human Relations (DILHR), 141
Child-rearing, 156, 158
Chrapliwy v. Uniroyal, Inc., 138
Chrysler Corp. v. Brown, 277
Chrysler Outboard Corp. v. DILAR, 66
Circle K Corp. v. EEOC, 192
City of Wisconsin Rapids v. Wisconsin Department of Industry, Labor, and Human Relations, 141
Civil Rights Act of 1866, 7, 114, 244
Civil Rights Act of 1964, Title VII of, 9-12, 16, 47, 51-54, 57, 59, 131, 133, 135, 147, 176
  comparable pay theory, 117
  coverage of, 10
  maternity, 156-160
  procedural mechanism of, 10-12
  promotions, transfers, and assignments, 109, 114, 117
  race discrimination, 9-12, 154-156, 172, 173
  record keeping, 300, 302, 303, 308, 313, 314
  sex discrimination, 9-12, 138-141
  significance of, 9
  Uniform Guidelines and, 24-26
  See also EEOC charge and investigation; OFCCP compliance review or complaint investigation
Civil Service Commission, 24
Claims, *see* EEOC charge and investigation; Individual claims; OFCCP compliance review or complaint investigation
Clark v. Milwaukee Road, 66
Class action, 16
Coates v. National Cash Register, 131
Code of Federal Regulations, 177
Coleman v. Darden, 64
Collective-bargaining agreements, 106, 133-135, 145, 147, 166

Index   385

College-degree requirements, 54-55, 78
Commerce Clearing House, Inc. (CCH), 21, 177
Commission decision, 201-202
"Commission's Decision Precedents" (CDPs), 11, 202
Communist party, 10
Comparable pay theory, 117-118, 293
Complaint investigation, 246-247, 257
Comply and contest, 258, 290
Compulsory retirement, 17, 152
Conciliation agreement, 253-257
Conciliation attempt (EEOC), 203-205
Concurrent validation study, 35
Condit v. *United Air Lines, Inc.*, 63, 158
Connecticut General Life Insurance Co. v. *Department of Industry, Labor, and Human Relations* (DILAR), 67, 142
Constructive seniority, 134
Construct validity, 30, 41-42
Content validity, 30, 32, 37-41
"Continued effects" theory, 196
Continuing violations, 184-185
Contract compliance, 12-15
Contract Work Hours and Safety Standards Act, 306
Conviction information, 51-52, 78
Coopersmith v. *Rouderbush*, 59-60
Counts v. *U.S. Postal Service*, 64
Cova v. *Coca-Cola Bottling Co. of St. Louis, Inc.*, 131
Cox v. *Delta Air Lines*, 61
Credit references, 52-53
Criterion validity, 30, 33-37
Crockett v. *Green*, 57
Croker v. *Boeing Co.*, 133
Crosslin v. *Mountain States Tel. & Tel. Co.*, 182
Cubans, 25

Daily Labor Report, 299
Danielson v. *Board of Higher Education*, 158
Danner v. *Phillips Petroleum Company*, 138
Davis Bacon Act, 305-306, 308
Davis v. *Bucher*, 64
Davis v. *County of Los Angeles*, 58
Deafness, 142-143
Decision B170536, 13
Decision No. 71-2444, 57
Declaratory Judgment, 135
Defense Base Act, 311, 312
Defense procedures, individual claims and, 171-175
Deferral of EEOC charge, 182-183
Deficiency letter, 252
Defined-benefit plans, 152
Defined-contribution plan, 153
deLaurier v. *San Diego School District*, 160
Desk audit, 249
De Volld v. *Bailar*, 52, 173
Dickerson v. *U.S. Steel Corp.*, 26, 136
Disabled, *see* Handicapped and disabled

Disabled veterans, 20-21, 47
See also Handicapped and disabled
Discharge, 129
  adverse impact, 143-147
  age standards, 130-133
  forms, 147-149
  handicapped and disabled, 141-143
  sex standards, 139-141
Discipline, race and national-origin standards and, 136-137, 138
Discipline notices, 315
Dishonorable discharge, 52
District of Columbia Workmen's Compensation Act, 311, 312
Dobbins v. *Local 212, IBEW*, 56
Donnell v. *General Motors Corp.*, 54, 55
Dothard v. *Rawlingson*, 61
Dozier v. *Chupka*, 52, 54
Dress code, *see* Appearance standards
Drug abuse, 18, 64-65
DuBois v. *Packard Bell Corp.*, 184
Duran v. *City of Tampa*, 64

Early retirement, 146-147
Eastern Airlines, 108
East Texas Motor Freight Systems, Inc. v. *Rodriguez*, 129
Educational requirements, 54-56, 78, 129
EEOC v. *Anchor-Continental, Inc.*, 192
EEOC v. *Bailey Co., Inc.*, 190, 193
EEOC v. *Blue Bell Boots, Inc.*, 194
EEOC v. *C&D Sportswear Corp.*, 181
EEOC charge and investigation, 176-242
  action to be taken on receipt of charge, 181-186
  commission decision, 201-202
  computer tapes, access to, 199
  conciliation attempt, 203-205
  deferral of, 182-183
  documents, access to, 199-200
  exhibits, 208-240
  expansion of investigation, 193-195
  joinder of necessary parties, 185
  legitimate scope of investigation, 192
  litigation review, 206
  nature of, 189-192
  negotiated settlement (no-fault conference), 180, 186-189
  no-cause determination, 188, 203
  private interviews with respondent's employee, 197-199
  receipt of charge or notice of charge, 180-181
  respondent's position statement, 200-201
  standing of, 181-182
  stating a claim, 185
  summary chart of process, 177-179
  timeliness of, 183-185
  time period of investigation, 196
EEOC v. *Colby College*, 160
EEOC Compliance Manual, 198, 199, 207
EEOC v. *E. I. du Pont de Nemours & Co.*, 55

EEOC v. *Mississippi Baptist Hospital*, 189
EEOC v. *National Academy of Sciences*, 53, 54
EEOC v. *National Electric Co. Benefit Fund*, 199
EEOC v. *North Hills Passavant Hospital*, 137
EEOC v. *Occidental Life Ins. Co.*, 189, 190, 193, 196
EEOC v. *Packard Elec. Div., General Motors Corp.*, 193
EEOC v. *Quick-Shop Markets, Inc.*, 193
EEOC v. *U.S. Fidelity & Guaranty Co.*, 193
EEOC v. *United Virginia Bank*, 175
EEOC v. *University of New Mexico*, 193
EEOC v. *Westinghouse Electric Corp.*, 181
Effeminacy, 63
80 percent rule, 68, 72
Employee Retirement Income Security Act (ERISA), 152
Employment Practices Guide (Commerce Clearing House), 177
Employment Standards Administration, 245
Employment Training Administration, 255, 256
English v. *Seaboard Coast R.R. Co.*, 106
Epilepsy, 19, 64
Equal Pay Act of 1963, 7, 17-18, 24, 160, 176
Espinoza v. *Farah Manufacturing Co.*, 51
Evaluation system, 104-105, 113
Evans v. *Oscar Mayer & Co.*, 183
Executive Order 11246, 8, 9, 12-15, 19, 21, 24, 69, 72, 86, 114, 118, 133, 139, 243-246, 248, 250-253, 258, 260, 267, 278, 282, 284, 290, 292
Executive Order 11375, 12
Exit conference, 252
Exit interview, 147-149
Experience requirements, 56-57, 59-60

Fagan v. *National Cash Register Co.*, 60
Failure to perform, 129
Fair Employment Practice Manual (Bureau of National Affairs), 177
Fair Labor Standards Act of 1938, 17, 250, 301, 304, 308, 309-311
Fairness, 37, 76-77
Federal Aviation Administration (FAA), 63, 102
Federal Deposit Insurance Corporation (FDIC), 291
Federal Register, 299, 300
Federal Reports Act, 247, 251
Federal Rules of Civil Procedure, 199, 200
Fekete v. *U.S. Steel Corp.*, 154
Fernandez v. *Avco Corp.*, 129
Ficlin v. *Sabatini*, 138
Field Operations Handbook (Department of Labor), 49, 50, 130
Final disposition, 300, 313
Financial-status information, 52-53
Fix v. *Swinerton & Walberg Co.*, 193
Flight Attendants v. *Ozark Air Lines*, 61

Focus job groups, 272
Forms:
 application, 77-86
 discharge, 147-149
 performance-assessment, 118-127
 post-hire EEO, 86-90
Fountain v. *Safeway Stores, Inc.*, 60
Francis v. *AT&T, Long Lines Dept.*, 155, 174
Fraser Shipyard, Inc., v. *DILAR*, 67
Freedom of Information Act (FOIA), 49, 176, 197, 207, 254, 272, 277, 278, 291, 313
Friend v. *Leidinger*, 105, 136

Garber v. *Saxon Business Products*, 161
Garnishment information, 52
Gate cards, 70-71
General Electric Company v. *FEPC*, 140
General Services Administration (GSA), 259
Georgia Power Co. v. *EEOC*, 192, 196, 199
Gerdom v. *Continental Airlines, Inc.*, 60-61
Gill v. *Union Carbide Corporation*, 101, 102, 119, 132
Gillin v. *Federal Paper Board Co.*, 105, 106, 131, 172, 173
Goals and timetables, 268, 272-276
Government contractors, 12-15, 69, 143, 144
 Rehabilitation Act and, 18-20
 Vietnam Era Veteran's Readjustment Act and, 20-21
 See also OFCCP compliance review or complaint investigation
Graham, Diane, 258
Grandfather clauses, 58
Graniteville Co. (Sibley Division) v. *EEOC*, 192
Green v. *Missouri Pacific Railroad*, 51
Gregory v. *Litton Systems, Inc.*, 51
Grievance procedure, 166-171
Griggs v. *Duke Power Co.*, 54, 58, 175
Grooming standards, 50, 57, 60, 102-103, 139
Gurmankin v. *Costanzo*, 64

Haire v. *Calloway*, 103
Handicapped and disabled, 7, 62, 169
 definition of, 19
 discharge, 141-143
 promotions, transfers, and assignments, 107-108
 selection procedures, 63-67
  alcoholism, 65
  application forms, 78
  blindness, 64
  drug abuse, 64-65
  epilepsy, 64
  obesity, 65
Harper v. *General Grocer Company*, 138
Harper v. *TransWorld Airlines, Inc.*, 63
Hays v. *Porlatch Forests, Inc.*, 160

Index

Hazelwood School District v. *United States,* 68
Health, Education and Welfare (HEW), Department of, 18
Health insurance, 157-159
Height standards, 27, 58, 60-82
Hester v. *Southern Railway Co.,* 38, 76, 104, 111
High school diploma requirement, 54, 55-56, 78, 129
Hiring, *see* Selection procedures
Hispanics, 25-28, 50-51, 58, 86
Hodgson v. *Approved Personnel Services, Inc.,* 46-47
Hodgson v. *Career Counsellors International Inc.,* 47
Hodgson v. *First Federal Savings & Loan Assn.,* 132
Hodgson v. *Greyhound Lines, Inc.,* 48, 102
Holland v. *Boeing Co.,* 67
Huckeby v. *Frozen Food Express,* 106

Illinois Tool Works v. *F. Ray Marshall,* 260
Inda v. *United Airlines, Inc.,* 62
Individual claims, 165-175
 defense procedures, 171-175
 prevention procedures, 165-171
  internal investigation, handling, 169-170
  open-door systems, 167
  personnel office, use of, 167-169
  posting systems, 166-167
In re Consolidated Pretrial Proceedings in the Airline cases, 63
In re National Airlines, Inc., 158
Insubordination, 129
Intelligence, 37, 39, 77
Internal grievance procedure, 166-171
Internal investigation, 186
Interview, 27, 32
Interviewing, *see* Selection procedures
Italian-Americans, 154

James v. *Stockham Valves & Fitting Co.,* 54, 104
Jersey Central Power & Light Company v. *Electrical Workers (IBEW), Local 327,* 135
Job analysis, 30-31
 for content validity, 40
 for criterion validity, 34-35
Job bidding sheets, 314-315
Job descriptions, 116, 139
Job grouping, 260-263
Job pools, 28
Job posting system, 100, 104, 105
Job previews, 106-107
Job qualification, upgrading, 29
Johnson v. *Georgia Highway Express Co.,* 195
Joking, 153-155
Jones v. *Klassen,* 158

387

Joslin Dry Goods Co. v. *EEOC,* 193, 194, 195
Justice, Department of, 7, 8, 12, 19, 20, 24, 56, 245

Kaiser Aluminum & Chemical Corp. v. *Weber,* 72
Kyrizai v. *Western Electric Co.,* 154

Labor, Department of, 3, 9, 12-20, 39, 46, 50, 53, 66, 101-103, 130, 133, 152-153, 259, 302, 306
Labor Management Recruiting and Disclosure Act of 1959, 303
Labor-Management Relations Act, 8
Laches, 180-181, 205
Laffey v. *Northwest Airlines, Inc.,* 60
Language proficiency standard, 51
Lanigan v. *Bartlett and Company Grain,* 60
Late-night entertaining, 106
Latino v. *Rainbo Bakers, Inc.,* 193
Laugesen v. *Anaconda Co.,* 131
Layoffs, 145
 race and national-origin standards, 133-136
 sex standards, 138
 See also Discharge; Reduction-in-force
League of United Latin American Citizens v. *City of Santa Ana,* 54, 58
Leechburg Area School District v. *Pennsylvania Human Relations Commission,* 157
Letter of commitment, 256
Letter of substantial issue of law or fact, 259
Lewis v. *Ford Motor Co.,* 140
Lewis v. *Tobacco Workers International Union,* 69, 107
Lewis v. *Western Airlines, Inc.,* 52
Litigation potential, 11
Litigation review, 206
Loeb v. *Textron, Inc.,* 173
Longshoremen's and Harbor Workers' Compensation Act, 311, 312
Lunch period, sex discrimination and, 160

McBride v. *Delta Airlines,* 137
McDonald v. *Santa Fe Trail Transportation Co.,* 46, 72, 139
McDonnell Douglas Corp. v. *Green,* 172
McNamara-O'Hara Service Contract Act of 1965, 305
McNutt v. *Hills,* 107
Manhart v. *City of Los Angeles, Department of Water & Power,* 160
Marital status rules, 62-63, 140, 156-160
Marshall v. *Board of Education of Salt Lake City,* 100, 101
Martin v. *Dann,* 158
Martinez v. *Bethlehem Steel Corp.,* 129
Mastie v. *Great Lakes Steel Corp.,* 118, 119, 130-132

Maternity, 63, 140, 141, 156-160
Mayor's Executive Order, 8
Meadows v. *Ford Motor Co.*, 61
Medicaid, 153
Medical expenses, 157-159
Medical standards, 57-58
Medicare, 153
Mejia v. *New York Sheraton Hotel*, 51
Mental impairments, 18, 19
Merit system, 17
Methadone maintenance, 64-65
Mexican-Americans, 25, 136-137
Migration to suburbs, 137
Military discharge, 52, 78
Miller v. *Bank of America*, 161
Minimum job requirements, 27, 32
Mistretta v. *Sandia Corp.*, 47, 48
Monsanto Company v. *EEOC*, 199
Montgomery Ward & Co. v. *Bureau of Labor*, 66
Moore v. *Sears, Roebuck & Co.*, 131
Moore v. *Sunbeam Corp.*, 184
Moses v. *Falstaff Brewing Corp.*, 131
Motorola, Inc. v. *EEOC*, 182, 199

Nance v. *Union Carbide Corp., Consumer Products Division*, 107
National Labor Relations Act, 200
National Labor Relations Board, 192, 200
National Organization for Women, Inc., (NOW), St. Paul Chapter v. *Minnesota Mining and Mfg. Co.*, 185
National-origin discrimination, *see* Race discrimination
Negotiated settlement, 180, 186-189
Nepotism rules, 58, 63, 79
New Orleans Public Service, Inc. v. *Brown*, 199
New York City Commission on Human Rights, 8
New York City Transit Authority v. *Beazer*, 64-65
New York State Division of Human Rights, 8, 62, 142
N.Y.S. Div. of Human Rights v. *City of New York*, 62
N.Y.S. Div. of Human Rights v. *Thomas J. Lipton, Inc.*, 62
New York Times, 108
No-cause determination, 188, 203
No-fault conference, 11, 180, 186-189
Non-appropriated Fund Instrumentalities Act, 311, 312
No-probable cause determination, 201
No-reasonable cause determination, 188, 191

Obesity, 19, 62, 65
Occupational Safety & Health Act of 1970, 304
OFCCP (Office of Federal Contract Compliance Programs), 3, 8, 12, 13, 21, 25, 108, 118, 138, 191
  comparable pay theory, 118, 293

OFCCP *(Cont'd.)*.
  Executive Order 11246 and, 243-246, 248, 250-253, 258, 260, 267, 278, 282, 284, 290, 292
  handicapped and, 65-67
  job posting, 104
  pregnancy and, 159
  private clubs and, 156
  Rehabilitation Act and, 18, 19, 143, 169, 243-244, 246-248, 292, 293
  Vietnam Era Veterans' Readjustment Act, 244, 246-248, 253, 292
OFCCP *Compliance Manual*, 249, 254, 259, 260, 279, 280, 285
OFCCP compliance review or complaint investigation, 243-295
  administrative structure of, 245
  affected classes and focus job groups, 272
  complaint investigation, 246-247, 257
  comply and contest, 258, 290
  goals and timetables, 268, 272-276
  internal and external dissemination of policy, 281-288
  job grouping, 260-263
  letter of substantial issue of law or fact, 259
  pre-award compliance review, 246, 257
  prospects for changing, 289-293
  regular compliance review, 247-257
    conciliation agreement, 253-257
    deficiency letter, 252
    desk audit, 249
    information from contractor, 247-248
    on-site review, 249-250, 291
    private interviews, 251-252
    records needed, 251, 291
    show-cause letter, 252, 291
    time period, 250
  relevant hiring area, 265
  types of reviews, 245-247
  utilization analysis, 263-271
OFCCP v. *E. E. Black, Ltd.*, 18, 66, 293
Office of Economic Opportunity (OEO), 3
Office of Federal Contract Compliance Programs, *see* OFCCP; OFCCP compliance review or complaint investigation
Office of Management and Budget (OMB), 21, 53, 247
Officers for Justice v. *Civil Service Commission*, 61
Olson v. *Rembrandt Printing Co.*, 184
On-site review, 14, 249-250, 291
Open-door systems, 167
Oral interview, 105
Orientals, 58
Outer Continental Shelf Lands Act, 311, 312
Overtime, 78, 160

Pacific Islanders, 25
Page v. *Bolger*, 103
Pan American World Airways, Inc. v. *F. Ray Marshall et al.*, 259
Paper-and-pencil tests, 58, 353-367

Index   **389**

Parliament House Motor Hotel v. EEOC, 193
"Pass over" procedure, 14
Patterson v. American Tobacco Co., 105
Payne v. Travenol Laboratories, Inc., 55
Performance-assessment forms, 118-127, 132
Personality, 37, 39, 77
Personnel office, grievances and, 167-169
Pettway v. American Cast Iron Pipe Co., 59
Phillips v. Martin Marietta Corp., 59
Physical-fitness requirements, 48, 102
Piece-of-the-job tests, 37
Position statement of respondent, 200-201
Post-hire EEO Form, 86-90, 314
Posting systems, 166-167
Pre-award compliance review, 246, 257
Predictive validation study, 35
Preferential consideration, 101
Pregnancy, 63, 140, 141, 156-160
Preliminary Administrative Enforcement Proceeding, 289-290
Prentice-Hall, Inc., 21
Preselection, 103
Presentation memo, 206
Prevention procedures, individual claims and, 165-171
  internal investigation, handling, 169-170
  open-door systems, 167
  personnel office, use of, 167-169
  posting systems, 166-167
Price v. Maryland Casualty Co., 131, 173
Prima facie case, 103, 108, 112, 113, 135-138, 171-172, 175
Prior record of unsatisfactory performance, 105
Prior training, 41
Private clubs, 156
Private interviews with contractor's employees, 251-252
Progressive discipline system, 144
Promotions, transfers, and assignments, 4, 99-128
  adverse impact, 108-118
    applicant/hire ratio, 109-110
    bidding system, 115-116
    evaluation system, 113
    future prospects in assessing, 116-118
    self-identification, 110-116
    seniority system, 114
  age standards, 100-103
    appearance, 102-103
    insurance benefits, 103
    physical-fitness requirements, 102
    preferential consideration, 101
    promotion potential, 100, 101
    time left to retirement, 100
  apparent availability, 99, 104
  handicapped and disabled, 107-108
  performance-assessment form, 118-127, 132
  race and national-origin standards, 103-105
    evaluation system, 104-105
    job posting, 104, 105

Promotions, transfers and assignments (Cont'd.).
  requests, 314-315
  sex standards, 105-107
    job previews, 106-107
    late-night entertaining, 106
    restrictive bidding, 107
    training, 106
Protected group, defined, 4
Providence Journal Co. v. Mason, 66
Psychology Today, 108
Public Contracts Act, 304
Puerto Ricans, 25

Quota system, 69, 147

Race discrimination:
  adverse impact, 25-28
  discipline, 136-137, 138
  layoffs, 133-136
  promotions, transfers, and assignments, 103-105
    evaluation system, 104-105
    job posting, 104, 105
  selection procedures, 50-58
    appearance and grooming standards, 50, 57
    application forms, 78
    arrest-record inquiries, 51
    conviction information, 51-52
    credit references, 52-53
    educational requirements, 54-56
    experience requirements, 56-57
    height and weight requirements, 58
    language proficiency standard, 51
    medical standards, 57-58
    military discharge, 52
    nepotism rules, 58
    paper-and-pencil tests, 58
  Title VII and, 9-12, 154-156, 172, 173
  verbal harassment, 153-155
  See also EEOC charge and investigation; Individual claims; OFCCP compliance review or complaint investigation
Ramsey v. Hopkins, 57
Randolph v. U.S. Elevator Corp., 135
Ranking system, 31
Reasonable accommodation, doctrine of, 67
Reasonable-cause determination, 188, 192, 201
Rebuttal statement, 207
Recent experience requirement, 59-60
Record keeping, 26, 29-30, 144-145, 174, 186, 251, 291, 297-315
Recruiting, see Selection procedures
Reduction-in-force (RIF), 101, 102, 129-133, 144-147
Reference checks, 52-53
Regular compliance review, 247-257
  conciliation agreement, 253-257
  deficiency letter, 252
  desk audit, 249
  information from contractor, 247-248

Regular compliance review *(Cont'd.)*
  on-site review, 249-250, 291
  private interviews, 251-252
  records needed, 251, 291
  show-cause letter, 252, 291
  time period, 250
Rehabilitation Act of 1973, 7, 8, 18-20, 24, 63-65, 67, 78, 87, 141-143, 169, 243-244, 246-248, 253, 278, 290, 293, 307
Relevant hiring area, 265
Religious discrimination:
  Executive Order 11246 and, 12, 13
  Title VII and, 9-12
Rest, sex discrimination and, 160
Restrictive bidding, 107
Retesting, 31
Retirement, 17, 144, 146-147, 152
Retirement plans, 4, 17, 152-153, 160
Retroactive seniority, 6
Reverse discrimination, 72
Review of application, 32
Revised Order 4, 28, 69, 279, 281
Revised Order 14, 279-282, 285
Reynolds Metals Co. v. *Rumsfeld,* 246
Rhoades v. *The Book Press,* 131
Richardson v. *Hotel Corporation of America,* 52
Right-to-sue notice, 11-12, 202, 203, 205, 207
Robinson v. *Union Carbide Corp.,* 105
Rodriguez v. *Taylor,* 48
Rogers v. *EEOC,* 156, 193
Roller v. *City of San Mateo,* 157
Roman v. *ESB, Inc.,* 131
Rosen v. *Public Service Gas & Electric Co.,* 160
Rosenfeld v. *Southern Pacific Company,* 160
Rowe v. *General Motors Corp.,* 104, 105

Samples, representativeness of, 35-36
Sanchez v. *Standard Brands, Inc.,* 192, 193, 203
Saucedo v. *Brothers Well Service, Inc.,* 136
Schultz v. *Hickock Mfg. Co., Inc.,* 132
Segregated housing, 156
Selection procedures, 3-6, 45-98
  adverse impact, 25-32, 67-77
    applicant pool and hire rates, comparison of, 71-72
    campus recruiting, 47
    educational requirements, 54, 55
    80 percent rule, 68, 72
    example of, 73-76
    recruiting, 69-71
    standard-deviation analysis, 68, 72
  age standards, 46-50
  fairness in, 76-77
  forms, 77-90
    application, 77-86
    post-hire EEO, 86-90
  of handicapped and disabled, 63-67
    alcoholism, 65

Selection procedures *(Cont'd.)*
  application forms, 78
  blindness, 64
  drug abuse, 64-65
  epilepsy, 64
  obesity, 65
  post-hire EEO form, 86-87
  race and national-origin standards, 50-58
    appearance and grooming standards, 50, 57
    application forms, 78
    arrest-record inquiries, 51
    conviction information, 51-52
    credit references, 52-53
    educational requirements, 54-56
    experience requirements, 56-57
    height and weight requirements, 58
    language proficiency standard, 51
    medical standards, 57-58
    military discharge, 52
    nepotism rules, 58
    paper-and-pencil tests, 58
  sex standards, 58-63
    appearance and grooming standards, 60
    height and weight requirements, 60-62
    marital status rules, 62-63
    nepotism rules, 63
    recent experience requirement, 59-60
  Uniform Guidelines and, 24-32
  validation techniques, 30-42
    concurrent, 35
    construct validity, 30, 41-42
    content validity, 30, 32, 37-41
    criterion validity, 30, 33-37
    predictive, 35
Self-identification systems, 100, 110-116
Seniority system, 6, 17, 25, 114, 133-135, 145, 147
Sex change, 140
Sex discrimination:
  adverse impact, 25-28
  BFOQ defense, 5
  comparable pay theory, 117-118, 293
  discharge, 139-141
  Equal Pay Act and, 7, 17-18, 24, 160, 176
  layoffs, 138
  pregnancy, 63, 140, 141, 156-160
  promotions, transfers, and assignments, 105-107
    job previews, 106-107
    late-night entertaining, 106
    restrictive bidding, 107
    training, 106
  retirement plans, 160
  selection procedures, 58-63
    appearance and grooming standards, 60
    height and weight requirements, 60-62
    marital status rules, 62-63
    nepotism rules, 63
    recent experience requirement, 59-60
  sexual harassment, 141, 161
  Title VII and, 9-12, 138-141
  working hours, overtime, rest, and lunch period, 160

Index 391

Sex discrimination *(Cont'd.)*
 See also EEOC charge and investigation;
   Individual claims; OFCCP compliance
   review or complaint investigation
Sexual harassment, 141, 161
Sexual preference, 63, 140
Sheetmetal Workers Local 104 v. *EEOC*, 199
Shift work, availability for, 78
Show-cause letter, 14-15, 252, 291
Sickness-and-accident plan, 153
Signature blank on application form, 79
Sixth Count data, 71
Skill test, 27
Smith v. *Borough of Wilkinsburg*, 62
Smith v. *City of East Cleveland*, 62
Smith v. *Fletcher*, 107
Smith v. *Liberty Benefit Life Insurance Co.*, 63
Smith v. *Mutual Benefit Life Insurance Co.*, 63
Smith v. *Olin Chemical Corp.*, 57
Social Security, 3
South Americans, 25
Southeastern Community College v. *Davis*, 67, 142, 143
Sprogis v. *United Airlines, Inc.*, 62, 140
Spurlock v. *United Airlines, Inc.*, 54
SRA verbal test, 38
Stallworth v. *Monsanto Co.*, 54
Standard industrial code (SIC), 12
Standing of EEOC charge, 181-182
State Division of Human Rights v. *Averill Park Central School District*, 67, 142
State Division of Human Rights v. *County of Monroe*, 66
State Employment Service, 256, 308
State of New York Human Rights Commission Guidelines, 77
State workmen's compensation statutes, 132
Statistical relationships, 36
Statistical sampling, 26
Statute of limitations, 16
Stevenson v. *International Paper Co.*, 54
Stewart v. *General Motors Corp.*, 104, 111
Strain v. *Philpott*, 105
Stringfellow v. *Monsanto Co.*, 132
Stroud v. *Delta Air Lines, Inc.*, 62, 140

Tardiness, 129, 144
Taylor v. *Safeway Stores, Inc.*, 57
Teamsters v. *United States*, 69, 114, 133, 134, 196, 244, 314
Technical feasibility of criterion validity, 34
Termination, *see* Discharge
Testing, *see* Selection procedures
Tests, 58, 108, 353-367
 See also Selection procedures
Theft, 144
Thomas v. *Parker*, 136
Thomasville Furniture Co., 13
Thurow, Lester, 3

Time left to retirement, 100
Timeliness of EEOC charge, 183-185
Timken Company v. *Marshall*, 265
Title VII, *see* Civil Rights Act of 1964, Title VII of
Tomkins v. *Public Service Electric & Gas Co.*, 161
Townsend v. *Nassau County Medical Center*, 55, 112
Trade Secrets Act, 277
Training programs, 4, 77, 106
Transaction-analysis approach, 49-50, 130
Transfers, *see* Promotions, transfers, and assignments
Trivett v. *Tri-State Container Corp.*, 138
Tuck v. *McGraw-Hill*, 63

University of California at Los Angeles (UCLA), 51
Underutilization analysis, 263
Undue hardship, 21
Uniform Guidelines on Employee Selection Procedures of 1978, 5, 24-32, 50, 72, 75
 sampling and, 26
 selection procedures, 24-32
 text, 316-352
 Title VII and, 24-26
 user responsibilities, 29-32
 validation techniques, 30-42
  concurrent, 35
  construct validity, 30, 41-42
  content validity, 30, 32, 37-41
  criterion validity, 30, 33-37
  predictive, 35
Unions, experience requirements and, 56-57
United Airlines, Inc. v. *Evans*, 110, 134, 185, 196
United Airlines, Inc. v. *McMann*, 17
United Handicapped Fed. v. *Andre*, 141
United States v. *East Texas Motor Freight, Inc.*, 133, 244
United States v. *Georgia Power Co.*, 54
United States v. *Leeway Motor Freight, Inc.*, 57, 155
United States v. *Operating Engineers, Local 3*, 56
United States Postal Service, 64
United States Steel Corp. v. *U.S.*, 193, 194, 195
Usery v. *Tamiami Trail Tours, Inc.*, 48, 102
Utilization analysis, 263-271

Vacancies, posting of job, 104
Validation techniques, 4, 5, 30-42, 108
 concurrent, 35
 construct validity, 30, 41-42
 content validity, 30, 32, 37-41
 criterion validity, 30, 33-37
 predictive, 35
Verbal harassment, 153-155
Veterans, 20-21, 47
 See also Handicapped and disabled

Veterans Administration, 20
Vietnam Era Veterans' Readjustment Assistance Act of 1974, 20–21, 244, 246–248, 253, 290, 292, 307
Vogler v. *McCarty, Inc.*, 58
Voyles v. *Ralph K. Davis Medical Center*, 140

W. R. Grace & Co. v. *Rubber Workers, Local 759*, 189
Walsh-Healy Act, 304
Watkins v. *Scott Paper Co.*, 54
Weekend work, 78
Weight standards, 27, 58, 60–61
Wells v. *Meyer's Bakery*, 104, 105
Westinghouse Electric Co. v. *State Division of Human Rights*, 66
Wetzel v. *Liberty Mutual Insurance Co.*, 110
White v. *Bailar*, 140
Willingham v. *Macon Telegraph Publishing Co.*, 57
Wilson v. *Sharon Steel Corp.*, 171
Wilson v. *Woodward Iron Company*, 38, 57
Word-of-mouth recruiting, 116
Working hours, sex discrimination and, 160
Written job descriptions, 116

Yukas v. *Libbey-Owens-Ford Co.*, 63, 175

Zambuto v. *American Telephone & Telegraph Co.*, 313

M